Reconstructing the Confucian Dao

SUNY series in Chinese Philosophy and Culture
──
Roger T. Ames, editor

Reconstructing the CONFUCIAN DAO

Zhu Xi's Appropriation of Zhou Dunyi

JOSEPH A. ADLER

STATE UNIVERSITY OF NEW YORK PRESS

Published by
STATE UNIVERSITY OF NEW YORK PRESS, ALBANY

© 2014 State University of New York

All rights reserved

Printed in the United States of America

No part of this book may be used or reproduced in any manner whatsoever without written permission. No part of this book may be stored in a retrieval system or transmitted in any form or by any means including electronic, electrostatic, magnetic tape, mechanical, photocopying, recording, or otherwise without the prior permission in writing of the publisher.

For information, contact State University of New York Press, Albany, NY
www.sunypress.edu

Production and book design, Laurie Searl
Marketing, Michael Campochiaro

Library of Congress Cataloging-in-Publication Data

Adler, Joseph Alan.
 Reconstructing the Confucian Dao : Zhu Xi's appropriation of Zhou Dunyi / Joseph A. Adler.
        pages cm. — (SUNY series in Chinese philosophy and culture)
 Includes bibliographical references and index.
 ISBN 978-1-4384-5157-2 (hardcover : alk. paper)
 ISBN 978-1-4384-5156-5 (pbk. : alk. paper)
 1. Zhou, Dunyi, 1017–1073.
2. Neo-Confucianism.   3. Zhu, Xi, 1130–1200.   I. Title.

B128.C44A63 2014
181'.112—dc23   2013025545

10 9 8 7 6 5 4 3 2 1

For Ruth and Anna

Contents

ix   Acknowledgments

PART I

  3   Introduction

15   Chapter 1: Zhu Xi, Zhou Dunyi, and the Confucian *dao*

37   Chapter 2: Zhou Dunyi's Role in the *daotong*

77   Chapter 3: The Interpenetration of Activity and Stillness

111   Chapter 4: *Taiji* as "Supreme Polarity"

137   Conclusions

PART II: Translations of Zhou Dunyi's Major Works and Zhu Xi's Commentaries, with Further Discussions by Zhu Xi and His Students

147   Introduction

151   Chapter 5: The Supreme Polarity Diagram (*Taijitu* 太極圖)

- 167 Chapter 6: Discussion of the Supreme Polarity Diagram (*Taijitu shuo* 太極圖說)

- 203 Chapter 7: Penetrating the Scripture of Change (*Tongshu* 通書)

- 299 Chapter 8: Zhu Xi's Postfaces and Notes

- 309 Bibliography

- 323 Index

Acknowledgments

I remember the precise moment when I began to look into Zhu Xi's appropriation of Zhou Dunyi. It was in Taipei, in February 1990, and I was sitting in a bare office at National Taiwan University with my hands poised over the keyboard of an old (even at the time) "IBM-compatible" PC. I had not yet decided which of two options to pursue under my Language and Research fellowship at the Inter-University Program in Chinese Language Studies: to revise my dissertation for publication, or to look further into Zhu Xi's use of Zhou Dunyi's texts, a topic that I had touched on in the dissertation. Finding the latter more intriguing, I began translating Zhu's commentary on Zhou's *Tongshu*. The work continued sporadically over the intervening two decades, as other writing projects pushed it to the back burner. I am extremely grateful to the Inter-University Program and the Academia Sinica Committee on Scientific and Scholarly Cooperation with the U.S.A. for providing that fellowship. In 1994 I received a grant from the Pacific Cultural Foundation to continue work on the translation (Part II of this book), and in 2008 I received a Scholar Grant from the Chiang Ching-kuo Foundation to support the writing of Part I. For both, and for my 2008–09 sabbatical leave from Kenyon College, I am extremely grateful.

I also wish to express my heartfelt thanks to those who provided feedback at various stages of this project: the late Professor Yang Youwei of Taipei, who helped me with the earliest stages of the translation; Kidder Smith Jr. and the participants in the New England Symposium on Chinese Thought at Bowdoin College for their comments in 1992 on my first attempt to make sense of Zhu Xi's appropriation of Zhou Dunyi (ultimately a dead end); Philip J. Ivanhoe, for his detailed written comments in 1999 on the paper I read at the Association for Asian Studies annual meeting in Washington, D.C. (the first statement of this book's argument); Hoyt Tillman for organizing that panel at the AAS and Robert Gimello for his comments as discussant; Daniel Gardner for his supportive comments and his several examples of excellent studies and translations of Zhu Xi; Conrad Schirokauer for his penetrating comments on the whole manuscript, Steve Angle for inviting me to participate in the Neo-Confucianism and Global Philosophy Conference at Wesleyan University in 2006; my Kenyon colleague Yang Xiao for invaluable help on a number of translation problems; Kirill Thompson for reading the entire first draft of Part I and providing excellent and detailed feedback; and Tu Weiming for first challenging me to work on Zhu Xi way back in 1979. Finally, I would like to thank Laurie Searl at SUNY Press for her excellent work on this project.

Part I

Introduction

The story of the early development of "Neo-Confucianism"—the revival of Confucianism in Song 宋 dynasty China (960–1279), after eight hundred years during which Buddhism and Daoism had dominated the religious landscape—has taken pretty much a standard form ever since the late twelfth century.[1] It begins with Zhou Dunyi 周敦頤 (1017–1073), who contributed three major items to the tradition: the *Taiji* Diagram (*Taijitu* 太極圖); a "Discussion of the *Taiji* Diagram" (*Taijitu shuo* 太極圖說, usually translated as "Explanation"); and a longer text called (in very loose translation) *Penetrating the Scripture of Change* (*Tongshu* 通書).[2] The "Discussion" is said to provide

---

1. Some of the most familiar histories in English are Fung Yu-lan, *A History of Chinese Philosophy*; Carsun Chang, *The Development of Neo-Confucian Thought*; and Wing-tsit Chan, *A Source Book in Chinese Philosophy*.

2. The *Scripture of Change* is the *Yijing* 易經, sometimes called the *Classic* or *Book of Changes*. I use "Scripture" because this text, like the rest of the so-called "Five Classics" (*wujing* 五經), were considered sacred texts by Confucians. Referring to them as "Classics" preserves the bias of nineteenth-century Protestant missionaries and translators who were unwilling to consider anything other than Christianity as a real religion. The "Five Classics" were therefore put in the same category as the classic literature of ancient Greece and Rome. Note also that *jing* was the word chosen to translate *sūtra* from Sanskrit.

Zhou's texts are translated in Part II of this book. The diagram, the explanation, and the most important sections of the *Tongshu* can also be found in de Bary and Bloom, eds., *Sources of Chinese Tradition,* 2nd ed., vol. 1, 669–78 (my translations).

the cosmological basis of Neo-Confucian philosophy—cosmology in terms of *qi* 氣 (the "psycho-physical stuff" of which all things are composed), which has two modes of activity, *yin* 陰 (dark, moist, sinking, condensing) and *yang* 陽 (light, dry, rising, expanding).

The story continues with Zhou acting as tutor to his two nephews, Cheng Hao 程顥 (1032–1085) and Cheng Yi 程頤 (1033–1107), for about a year when they were teenagers. The Cheng brothers then grow up to form the nucleus of a group of Confucian thinkers in the city of Luoyang, in north-central China (Henan province). The Chengs and their many disciples come to be known as the Luo 洛 school—usually referred to in Western scholarship as the Cheng school. They become quite influential in philosophical circles and are actively involved in government, especially as part of the conservative opposition to the reformist prime minister, Wang Anshi 王安石 (1021–1086).

About twenty years after Cheng Yi dies, comes a catastrophe. The capital, Kaifeng, is captured by the Jurchen, a nomadic ethnic group from the northeast. The emperor is abducted. The remaining court flees to the south and establishes a new Song capital in Lin'an (modern Hangzhou), but the northern half of their former domain is now ruled by the Jurchen. (The dynastic era is thenceforth divided into two parts, the Northern Song [960–1127] and Southern Song, which was finally conquered by the Mongols in 1279.) Some of the Chengs' disciples also move south and spread their teachings there. Zhu Xi 朱熹 (1130–1200), born three years after the loss of the north, studies with some third-generation Cheng disciples and eventually, after seriously flirting with Buddhism, becomes committed to their school of thought and spreads their teachings prolifically. He becomes even more influential than the Cheng brothers, and his teachings eventually dominate those of his competitors. He combines the ideas of the Chengs and their associates with his own, creating a new synthesis called *Daoxue* 道學 (Learning of the Way)—also called the "school of principle" (*lixue* 理學) or (preferably) the Cheng-Zhu school. While never without serious competition, this school dominates the later history of Chinese thought right up to the twentieth century, becoming in many people's minds synonymous with "Neo-Confucianism."

This "standard" history is recognized by scholars today as at best a partial view of the development of Confucian thought and practice in the Song dynasty, which was much more varied than the simplified story allows. At worst it is a reductionistic identification of "Neo-Confucianism" with the Cheng-Zhu school alone—perhaps admitting the Lu-Wang school as a counterpoint.³ It is no longer sufficient to limit the story to the Northern Song masters Zhou Dunyi, the Cheng brothers, Zhang Zai 張載 (1020–1077), Shao Yong 邵雍 (1012–1077),⁴ Zhu Xi, and Lu Jiuyuan 陸九淵 (commonly known as Lu Xiangshan 陸象山) in the Southern Song (1127–1279); and Wang Yangming 王陽明 in the Ming dynasty (1368–1644). We now know how important Zhu Xi's correspondence with Zhang Shi 張栻 (1133–1180) was to the development of his thought; we know more about Zhu's friend and sometime collaborator Lü Zuqian 呂祖謙 (1137–1181), and his rivals Chen Liang 陳亮 (1143–1194), Lu Jiuyuan, and Lu's brothers.⁵

We also know, although it is not widely acknowledged, that the placement of Zhou Dunyi at the head of the lineage of Song "sages" was entirely the invention of Zhu Xi.⁶ We also know how problematic that choice was for Zhu: Zhou Dunyi was widely regarded as having strong Daoist leanings, and Zhu Xi was vehemently opposed to Daoism, at least after the 1150s. Zhou's *Taiji* Diagram, in fact, almost certainly was given to him by his Daoist friends, and this was well known in Zhu Xi's time (although he denied it). The key terms in the "Discussion" of the diagram, written by Zhou himself, were largely or exclusively Daoist terms (*taiji* and *wuji*). And some of Zhu's colleagues—notably the Lu brothers—objected strongly to Zhu's elevation of Zhou to the position of first Confucian sage of the Song because of his Daoist connections. This dispute produced a rather bitter split between Zhu Xi and Lu Jiuyuan, who had previously been good friends.

All this raises the obvious question: Why did Zhu Xi declare Zhou Dunyi to be the first true Confucian sage since Mencius (Mengzi 孟子, 4th century BCE)? He could easily have followed the consensus of his colleagues that Cheng Hao had rediscovered the Confucian *dao,* as his younger brother, Cheng Yi, had first suggested. After all, the philosophy of the Cheng brothers was the core upon which Zhu Xi built his synthesis. It was they who made

---

3. The Lu-Wang school is named after Lu Jiuyuan/Xiangshan and Wang Shouren/Yangming. On the problematic nature of the term *Neo-Confucianism* see below.

4. Shao Yong's dates are usually given as 1011–1077, but Alan Berkowitz has shown that he was actually born on January 21, 1012 (Berkowitz, "On Shao Yong's Dates").

5. See especially Hoyt Cleveland Tillman, *Confucian Discourse and Chu Hsi's Ascendancy.*

6. See my discussion of Zhou in de Bary and Bloom, eds., *Sources of Chinese Tradition,* 2nd ed., vol. 1, 669–71.

the concept of *li* (principle, pattern, order) central to what became the Cheng-Zhu school of Confucian thought.

The prevailing answer to this question is that it was Zhou Dunyi's concept of *taiji* 太極 (usually translated as "Supreme Ultimate") that enabled Zhu Xi to systematically link together the cosmological discourse centered on *qi* 氣 with the metaphysical discourse of the Cheng brothers, centered on *li* 理.[7] This is therefore a philosophical solution to our problem. But *taiji* was also found in the *Yijing* 易經 (Scripture of Change)—one of the Confucian "Five Classics (Scriptures)"—in one of the appendices attributed to Confucius himself![8] In fact, this is the first occurrence of the term in extant Chinese literature, and its usage there closely parallels Zhou Dunyi's usage of the term.[9] So Zhu could easily have based his philosophical usage of *taiji* on that text, thereby avoiding the unpleasantness of Zhou Dunyi's Daoist connections.

I have taken a different approach to the problem, looking not only at Zhu Xi's philosophical system but also at his personal religious practice. We actually know quite a bit about this, because one of the well-known episodes in Zhu's life was a "spiritual crisis" he experienced during his late thirties, which is well documented. What has not been remarked by any scholars, to my knowledge, is that immediately after resolving this crisis he turned to work on Zhou Dunyi's writings, and his campaign to place Zhou at the head of the Cheng-Zhu lineage began at that time. This alone could, of course, be coincidence. But the possibility of coincidence is greatly diminished by the fact that the particular solution he found for his spiritual crisis—what I call the "interpenetration of mental activity and stillness"—is also found prominently in both of Zhou Dunyi's major texts, the *Taijitu shuo* and the *Tongshu*. And Zhu Xi foregrounds this idea whenever he discusses *taiji* (see chapter 4).

Demonstrating how Zhu Xi's religious *praxis* conditioned his philosophical system throws new light on both his methodology of self-cultivation and the linchpin of his philosophy, the concept of *taiji*. In particular, it means that *taiji* should not be translated as "Supreme Ultimate" but as "Supreme Polarity" (chapter 4). Since Zhu equated *taiji* with the central concept of *li*, and since Zhu exerted enormous influence on the past eight hundred years of Chinese thought—including both his followers and his critics—the significance of this reinterpretation should not be underestimated.

---

7. See, for example, Wing-tsit Chan, "Chu Hsi's Completion of Neo-Confucianism," 116.

8. *Yijing, Xici* 繫辭 A.11.5 (Zhu, *Zhouyi benyi* 3:14b).

9. See chapter 2.

Deconstructing the traditional story of the Northern Song revival, a story wholly constructed by Zhu Xi, reminds us of the variety of ways in which a religious-philosophical tradition can redefine itself. First, the Song revival and reconstruction of Confucianism has long been understood as a response to the challenge of Buddhism, which was extremely popular among Song literati, and to the failure of the activist political reforms attempted during the Northern Song: a case of adaptation to a changing cultural environment. Second, the eventual dominance of the Cheng-Zhu school is undoubtedly due to the enormously prolific work and strong personality (as Hoyt Tillman has shown) of Zhu Xi, and by his choices of what to include and what to exclude: an example of what we might call a "great man" theory of intellectual history. What I hope to demonstrate is that the particular shape taken by the Cheng-Zhu school, including its ideas, its practices, and its textual canon, owes much to Zhu Xi's personal religious practice. Although this book is not a "psychohistory," one may be reminded of the influence of Martin Luther's interior life on his thought and career,[10] or Paul's experience on the road to Damascus. Religious and philosophical traditions evolve not simply according to the internal logic of their components or in response to historical events. Traditions are expressions of the entire ever-changing fabric of human life and culture. Traditions pass down through history the imprints, as it were, of all (in theory) the eras, events, and people they have influenced and been influenced by. As Robert Bellah puts it, "In an important sense, all culture is one: human beings today owe something to every culture that has gone before us," and "nothing is ever lost."[11]

In the case of the Cheng-Zhu tradition of Confucianism, we will see that its canonical texts, its historical self-understanding, its ideas, and its practices concretely embody the imprint of an interior struggle Zhu Xi experienced in the late 1160s.

Previous scholars have analyzed the development of Zhu's understanding of *taiji* in the context of his spiritual crisis in the late 1160s. Tomoeda Ryūtaro, for example, argued in 1969 that Zhu's solution to the "*weifa-yifa*" problem strongly influenced his mature conception of *taiji*.[12] *Weifa* 未發 (unexpressed) and *yifa* 已發 (expressed) refer to the still and active phases of mind, and their

---

10. Erik Erikson, *Young Man Luther*, which influenced Tu Weiming's *Neo-Confucian Thought in Action: Wang Yang-ming's Youth* (1472–1509).

11. Bellah, *Religion in Human Evolution*, 225, 267.

12. Tomoeda, *Shushi no shisō keisei*, 146–61.

relationship was the problem that Zhu had to work out, both in philosophical and practical terms. But Tomoeda deals with it strictly as a philosophical problem, and does not relate Zhu's solution—the interpenetration of activity and stillness—to the same idea found in Zhou Dunyi's *Taijitu shuo* and *Tongshu*; nor does he relate it to Zhu's nomination of Zhou as the first sage of the Song. The same is true of Mou Zongsan, Tang Junyi, Qian Mu, Chen Lai, and Julia Ching.[13]

It should already be clear that I am treating Confucianism as a religious tradition. As this is a matter still being debated in some circles, a brief discussion of the issue is in order.[14] If we are to make use of definitions of religion—and even that assumption is questioned—we should follow two guidelines. First, a general definition must be culture-neutral. It is still not unusual to find statements to the effect that "while Confucianism may contain religious dimensions, it is not a religion *in the Western* (or *usual*) *sense of the word.*" This, obviously, will not do. We cannot assume Western religion to be the model of what a religion must look like. Second, we should admit the possibility that multiple definitions—each illuminating a particular aspect of religion—might be required. This is because religion is a multidimensional set of phenomena; to reduce it to a single essence may be, ironically, to lose its essence.

Some scholars, in fact, have said that there is no such thing as religion per se. Wilfrid Cantwell Smith, in 1963, made the seemingly audacious claim that "[n]either religion in general nor any one of the religions . . . is in itself an intelligible entity, a valid object of inquiry or of concern either for the scholar or for the man of faith."[15] Jonathan Z. Smith, in a similar vein, claimed in 1982 that "religion is solely the creation of the scholar's study" and "has no independent existence apart from the academy."[16] The argument of the two

---

13. Mou, *Xinti yu xingti*, 1:321–404; Tang, *Zhongguo zhexue yuanlun: Taolun pian*, 419–38, 471–78, 509–13; Qian, *Zhuzi xin xue'an*, 1:263–82, 2:123–82, 3:49–81; Chen, *Zhu Xi zhexue yanjiu*, 2–48; and Ching, *The Religious Thought of Zhu Xi*, 3–53, 235–41. Ching did see Zhu Xi as primarily a religious philosopher, and devotes the first two chapters of her book to his concept of *taiji*, but she does not make the connections I am making.

14. For earlier thoughts on this subject and further references, see Adler, "Varieties of Spiritual Experience," "Confucianism as Religion / Religious Tradition / Neither," and "Divination and Sacrifice in Song Neo-Confucianism."

15. Wilfrid Cantwell Smith, *The Meaning and End of Religion*, 12.

16. Jonathan Z. Smith, *Imagining Religion*, xi.

Smiths is that "religion" as a general category is merely a construct arising from the particular social and historical circumstances of the modern West, and with the possible exception of Islam, the various religions until modern times were never named as such and never conceptualized as distinguishable entities. In Buddhist terminology, neither religion in general nor any specific religion has any "own-being" (*svabhāva*) or self-nature (*zixing* 自性), and so all statements about religion or religions are statements about nothing. But it is important to note that referring to religion in general does *not* necessarily imply that such a thing exists apart from specific actors, institutions, or traditions. What we are trying to define is the characteristics or qualities that distinguish some actors, institutions, and traditions as "religious" from others that are not religious. We can ask that question meaningfully without falling into the trap of reification.

With these considerations in mind, I would suggest that Frederick Streng's definition of religion is especially suitable to Chinese religions. Streng wrote, in 1985, that religion is "a means to ultimate transformation," where "ultimate" can be understood in whatever terms are appropriate to the tradition.[17] This is, therefore, a formal, culture-neutral definition. In the case of Confucianism, the goal of sagehood is the endpoint of that transformation, and Heaven (*tian*) symbolizes the ultimacy that makes it religious. Heaven is the unconditioned source of moral value and symbolizes the creative power that constitutes all that exists. As Cheng Yi put it, "The mind of Heaven and Earth is to produce things."[18] That creative power is manifested in human beings, and only in human beings, as "moral power" or "virtue" (*de* 德), the power to create ourselves as fully human (i.e., humane) beings, to create a humane society, and to bring to fruition the moral potential that is inherent in the cosmos.

---

17. Frederick Streng, *Understanding Religious Life,* 3rd ed. (1985), 2. I have suggested that Streng's definition should be expanded: religion is a means of ultimate transformation and/or *ultimate orientation* (Adler, "Varieties of Spiritual Experience"). This is to take account of forms of religious practice, such as praying for mundane benefits, that cannot reasonably be considered a process of ultimate transformation. By "ultimate orientation" I mean orientation in terms of sacred space and sacred time or communicating with sacred beings, as in Mircea Eliade's theory (e.g. Eliade, *The Sacred and the Profane*). The implicit assumption of much "popular" religious practice is that by standing in proper relation with the sacred one maximizes one's well-being and good fortune.

18. This is in Cheng Yi's commentary on hexagram 24 (Fu, Return) of the *Yijing*; see Smith, Bol, Adler, and Wyatt, *Sung Dynasty Uses of the I Ching,* 247.

This is the process of transformation, or self-transformation, by which human beings become sages (*shengren* 聖人), or fully humane (*ren* 仁). Sagehood is a religious goal: the sage transcends his given conditions and transforms others and society itself through his moral power.[19] The word *sheng* itself has clear religious connotations. For example, it is part of the Chinese name for the Judeo-Christian Bible (*sheng jing* 聖經, or Holy Scriptures), and the same word translated in a Confucian context as "sage" (*shengren*) is used as the Chinese translation of "saint." So by Streng's definition—one that focuses on what we might call the "spirituality" of the Confucian tradition—it is not difficult to justify referring to Confucianism as a religious tradition.

"Spirituality" is of course another term fraught with difficulty. I understand spirituality to refer to an aspect of religion, not something distinct from religion. Specifically, spirituality refers to those dimensions of religion involving the individual person considered apart from his or her social context and action. So, for example, it refers to the emotional/experiential dimension of one's religious life rather than to the public, performative, or social (although these might very well have inner, experiential aspects). Or it refers to personal beliefs and values rather than to official or orthodox doctrines. In the case of Confucian spirituality, what it *cannot* entail is a distinction between spirit or mind and body, because the category of *qi* covers the entire spectrum from matter to energy to spirit.[20]

"Transcendence" also requires discussion. David Hall and Roger Ames have argued that transcendence in a philosophical sense, defined as a relationship in which B depends on A but A does not depend on B, is not found in the characteristic Chinese concept of order, which they call "aesthetic order." Aesthetic order emerges from the dynamic pattern of contingent events; it is not imposed on things by a transcendent principle or lawgiver.[21] Other scholars, however, have tried to preserve the notion of transcendence in Chinese or Confucian thought by suggesting that this is a form of transcendence that is simultaneously immanent.[22] Heaven, as noted above, is the unconditioned source of value, yet is also manifest in human

---

19. See Rodney L. Taylor, *The Cultivation of Sagehood as a Religious Goal in Neo-Confucianism,* and idem., *The Religious Dimensions of Confucianism.*

20. See my "Varieties of Spiritual Experience: *Shen* in Neo-Confucian Discourse."

21. Hall and Ames, *Thinking Through Confucius,* 11–25, 131–38.

22. E.g., Liu Shu-hsien, "The Confucian Approach to the Problem of Transcendence and Immanence."

nature, or what Zhu Xi called the "mind of *dao*" (*daoxin* 道心). The sage has transcended the ordinary human condition: the *Yijing,* Zhou Dunyi, and Zhu Xi all describe the sage as a "spiritual" or god-like being.[23] Thus, the sage may have "powers and abilities far beyond those of mortal men," such as the ability to foresee with "spiritual clarity" (*shenming* 神明) the results of present actions without resorting to divination.[24] But he is not a Superman—he is Everyman, because what he has perfected is the moral nature inherent in every human being. This may be considered one of the central paradoxes of Confucian thought, or indeed the defining feature of Confucian religiosity. It is nicely captured in Herbert Fingarette's phrase, "the secular as sacred."[25] The human nature that is common to us all, and that makes us what we are, is also that which makes us more than we are. The capacity for transcendence—i.e., becoming a sage—is immanent.

I have put the term "Neo-Confucianism" in quotation marks thus far because it is a problematic term deserving of some discussion—as is the term *"Confucianism"* itself, but for different reasons. Neither term was used in premodern China. The name *Confucius* was invented by Jesuit missionaries in the sixteenth century, based on the very rarely used Chinese name Kongfuzi, a variant of "Kongzi" (Master Kong), the most common way of referring to Kong Qiu (551–479 BCE), especially after his death. His followers were called *ru* 儒, a word whose semantic range and intent varied throughout the Warring States period (475–221 BCE). It originally meant "weak" or "pliable," perhaps referring to the dispossessed members of either the defeated Shang people or to the "collateral members of the Zhou royal family who had been disinherited after the breakdown of the feudal order in 770 BC[E]."[26] By the end of the period, though, the meaning had more or less settled on something like "scholars" or "literati" or "classicists," and had come to refer specifically to the followers of Master Kong. Although Mencius referred to that tradition as the "Way of the sages" (*shengrenzhi dao* 聖人之道), the primary names for the tradition since the late Warring States period have

---

23. *Yijing, Xici* A.11.2; Zhou, *Tongshu* 4; Zhu, *Zhouyi benyi,* 3:13b.
24. See Adler, "Divination and Sacrifice in Song Neo-Confucianism."
25. Fingarette, *Confucius: The Secular as Sacred.*
26. Michael Nylan, *The Five "Confucian" Classics,* 23. For a discussion of other possible meanings of the term and an argument that we should use the term *Ru* instead of "Confucian," see Mark Csikszentmihalyi, *Material Virtue: Ethics and the Body in Early China,* 17–18.

been *Rujia* 儒家 (the *ru* school) and *Rujiao* 儒教 (the teaching of the *ru*).[27] So the indigenous names for the tradition never incorporated the name of the reputed founder—consistent with his overly modest claim that he was a "transmitter, not a creator."[28]

"Neo-Confucianism," also a Western term, is more problematic than "Confucianism," largely because of the dominance of the Cheng-Zhu school. As mentioned above, it is often used in the narrowest of senses to refer strictly to that school, ignoring the Lu-Wang school as well as the "conventional Confucians" who are not identified with either the Cheng-Zhu or Lu-Wang schools. Even if its usage is broadened to include all of these, it omits post–Han dynasty Confucians, such as Fu Xuan 傅玄 (217–278),[29] who are considered neither "classical" Confucians (up to 221 BCE), nor Han Confucians (206 BCE-220 CE), nor Neo-Confucians.[30]

Many of the Song Confucians themselves used the term *daoxue* 道學 (Learning of the Way) to refer to their tradition. Hoyt Tillman has aptly called them the "*daoxue* fellowship," and has convincingly shown that *daoxue* originally included much more than the Cheng-Zhu school.[31] Because of the eventual "ascendancy" of this school and its continuing influence up through the twentieth century, both "*daoxue*" and "Neo-Confucianism" came to refer primarily, if not exclusively, to it alone. While this book is in fact strictly about the Cheng-Zhu school, I will generally avoid "Neo-Confucianism," and where it does occur it will be in the broadest sense, from the Song dynasty onward. As for "Confucius," and likewise "Mencius," I have no objection to using these common appellations even though they are of Western origin.

Throughout this book I have noted precise dates wherever possible. In part this is because my argument draws attention to the chronology of Zhu Xi's spiritual crisis and his most concentrated period of work on Zhou Dunyi. Awareness of dates, as well as geographical locations, contributes to a fuller understanding of Zhu Xi's life, which is the context in which I wish to set his appropriation of Zhou Dunyi. For Zhu's chronology I have relied

---

27. Nylan, op. cit., 2, 23–26, 32–33, 36–37, 364–66. See also the discussion by Xinzhong Yao in the introduction to his *RoutledgeCurzon Encyclopedia of Confucianism*, 1–4.

28. *Analects* 7:1.

29. Jordan D. Paper, *The Fu-Tzu: A Post-Han Confucian Text*.

30. See Thomas A. Wilson, *Genealogy of the Way: The Construction and Uses of the Confucian Tradition in Late Imperial China*, 16–20.

31. Tillman, *Confucian Discourse and Chu Hsi's Ascendancy*.

exclusively on the most recent "*nianpu*" 年譜 (yearly chronicle) of his life: Shu Jingnan, *Zhu Xi nianpu changbian* 朱熹年譜長編 (Zhu Xi's chronological record, extended edition) (2 volumes, 2001). Shu, a well-respected scholar, compiled this book from scratch, as it were, instead of relying on previous biographies, such as Wang Mouhong's 王懋竑 *Zhuzi nianpu* of 1706. While the dating of some specific letters and events may still be open to some debate, those questions are not critical to my argument.[32]

Chapter 1 introduces the competing visions of the *dao* (Way) that were contested during the Song. The *dao* was as significant to Confucians as it was to Daoists, although they understood it differently. Confucius is reported to have said, "If the Way prevailed under Heaven I would not be trying to change things" (*Analects* 18:6). Restoring the Way of the ancient sage-kings who had founded the Zhou dynasty (1045–256 BCE)—primarily their benevolent rulership, which he believed would have a transformative effect on the rest of society—was Confucius's self-appointed mission in life. At roughly the same time a more transcendental concept of *dao* was developing, which would later be recorded in the words of a mythic sage called Laozi (Old Master) and would become the central concept in Daoist thought and religion.[33] The chief difference between the Confucian and Daoist concepts of *dao* was that for Confucians it was the ideal social-ethical-political order, while for Daoists it was the natural order and, in the *Laozi* at least, a transcendental source of all being. In that sense these two versions of the *dao* played complementary roles throughout the history of Chinese thought. A third *dao* came to China from India with Buddhism, beginning in the first century CE. At first this simply referred to the Eightfold Path (*dao* literally means path or road) of Buddhist practice. But later Chinese Buddhist texts (such as the *Platform Sutra*) sometimes used the term in the Daoist sense of the ultimate reality, a usage that also strongly influenced Confucian thought. As we shall see in chapter 1, we can understand the early development of Song Confucianism as an attempt to assert the superiority of the Confucian vision of the *dao* over the other two forms.

---

32. I have also consulted Chen Lai's 1989 chronology of Zhu Xi's letters, *Zhuzi shuxin biannian kaozheng* (Critical examination of the dating of Zhu Xi's letters).

33. The *Laozi* text, also called the *Daodejing* (Scripture of the Way and its power), and a more philosophical text called the *Zhuangzi* (Master Zhuang), attributed to Zhuang Zhou of the fourth century BCE, became the core of the Classical Daoist school of thought. The Daoist religion did not begin to develop until the second century CE, from rather different roots than these two classics, although it incorporated them.

Chapter 2 examines Zhu Xi's concept of *daotong* 道統, or the "succession of the Way," that is, the lineage of sages who transmitted the true Confucian *dao*. This was a concept dating back to Mencius, although *daotong* was a new term in the Song. As mentioned earlier, Zhu Xi changed the accepted line of transmission by inserting Zhou Dunyi before the Cheng brothers, for reasons that have never been adequately explained. Chapter 3 provides the core of the argument for solving this puzzle by connecting his choice of Zhou Dunyi with the solution to his spiritual crisis in the 1160s. Chapter 4 argues that by translating *taiji* 太極 as "Supreme Polarity" instead of "Supreme Ultimate" we can make better sense of this mysterious term and its equation with *li* 理 (principle/pattern/order), the central term in Cheng-Zhu thought. Part II of this book includes my translations of Zhou Dunyi's most important works, Zhu Xi's published commentaries on them, and selections from Zhu's conversations with his students about them.

Zhu Xi's appropriation of Zhou Dunyi has not been completely ignored in Asian and Western scholarship, but for the most part it has been treated as a philosophical topic: how Zhu used Zhou's ideas in creating his selective synthesis of Song Confucian thought. By placing it in the context of Zhu Xi's life story and religious practice we will find not only a fuller picture but new interpretations of some of Zhu's most important ideas.

Chapter One

Zhu Xi, Zhou Dunyi, and the Confucian *dao*

The world into which Zhu Xi was born, as he came to understand it, was in crisis. In 1127, three years before his birth, the capital of Song China, Kaifeng, had been overrun by Jurchen forces from the northeast,[1] and both Emperor Qinzong 欽宗 (r. 1126–1127) and the recently abdicated Emperor Huizong 徽宗 (r. 1101–1126) had been abducted. The Song court had fled south and had reestablished itself at the "temporary" capital of Lin'an (modern Hangzhou). The Jurchen, under their Jin dynasty, ruled the northern half of China until 1234, when they in turn were conquered by the Mongols, who proceeded to conquer the rest of China in 1279. So Zhu Xi lived his entire life (1130–1200) with almost half of his homeland under foreign rule, facing the very real threat of a complete loss. These circumstances deeply affected his worldview: China, he felt, needed to reassert itself both militarily and culturally. His father, Zhu Song 朱松 (1097–1143), had been part of the faction that had opposed the appeasement policy followed by Chief Councilor Qin Gui 秦檜 (1090–1155), arguing for more aggressive military action against the Jin,[2] and in his earlier career Zhu Xi had argued along the same lines. But

---

1. The Jurchen (Nuzhen 女真 in Chinese) were the ancestors of the Manchus, who later would overthrow the Ming 明 dynasty (1368–1644) and establish the last imperial Chinese dynasty, the Qing 情 (1644–1911).

2. Chan, "Chu Hsi," in Franke, *Sung Biographies,* vol.1:282. For Zhu Xi's official biography see Tuo, *Song shi,* 188:12751–770.

as he matured he came to direct his efforts primarily toward the moral and cultural "self-strengthening" (to use a nineteenth-century term) that he felt was necessary for Song China to regain its rightful place in the world.[3]

In *Analects* 18:6, Confucius is quoted as saying, "If the Way prevailed in the world (*tianxia you dao* 天下有道) I would not be trying to change things."[4] This was also how Zhu Xi conceptualized his own situation. The Way (*dao* 道) as he understood it was the underlying moral order of the cosmos and norm of human behavior, both on the individual and social/political levels.[5] The problem was that, although the Way was somehow immanent in the world, it was not "prevailing," or being put into effect; social institutions, rites, and the conduct of human relations were no longer aligned with the "Way of Heaven" (*tian dao* 天道). The loss of the North to the Jurchen was ample evidence of this, and a large part of the responsibility for the catastrophe, according to Zhu, had come from within: in particular, the divisive factional politics of the Northern Song period. Wang Anshi 王安石 (1021–1086), as prime minister, had instituted ambitious institutional reforms (the "New Laws"), which were overturned by his successor Sima Guang 司馬光 (1019–1086), and then reinstated by Cai Jing 蔡京 (1047–1126) shortly before the Jurchen conquest.[6] Wang's reforms were ostensibly based on his reading of one of the ancient ritual texts, the *Zhou li* 周禮 (Rituals of Zhou), which was part

---

3. See Tillman, *Utilitarian Confucianism*, 169–80, and Qian, *Zhuzi xin xue'an*, 5: 75–84. Zhu Xi was by no means alone in seeing the occupation of the North as an unmitigated catastrophe. For some, it was not only a political and cultural disaster but a threat to the cosmological vision of China as the Middle Kingdom (*Zhongguo* 中國) occupying the center of the "civilized" world. According to Chen Liang (1143–1194), Jurchen control of the Chinese heartland gave them access to the more vital *qi* of the central plains, so the longer they held their position the stronger they would become, while the Chinese would become progressively weaker. See Tillman, "Proto-Nationalism in Twelfth-Century China?" 417–21, and *Utilitarian Confucianism*, ch. 6.

4. This is undoubtedly a very late addition to the *Analects*, possibly two hundred years after Confucius's death in 479 BCE (see Brooks and Brooks, *The Original Analects*, 173–75, where the passage is dated to 262 BCE). Song Confucians, however, considered it to be the authentic words of the sage.

5. Zhang Dainian summarizes the range of meanings of the word *dao* in *Key Concepts in Chinese Philosophy*, 11–26.

6. See Liu, *Reform in Sung China*, and Levine, *Divided by a Common Language*. On the opposition to Wang Anshi by Zhu Xi and his predecessors in the Cheng school see de Bary and Bloom, *Sources of Chinese Tradition*, 609–28.

of the Confucian canon. This kind of reform was therefore well within the parameters of what Confucians in the Song regarded as proper application of the Confucian Way. Yet Wang was strongly opposed by a group of Confucian scholar-officials centered on Sima Guang, the Cheng brothers, and their associates—a group later called the Yuanyou (元祐) party, after the name of the reign period (1086–1093) during which Sima Guang was in power. Their opposition was based not so much on the policies themselves, most of which were quite reasonable and progressive, but on the forceful manner in which they were instituted. The Yuanyou party felt rudely excluded from the decision-making process and their written works were put under a ban during the reform period.[7] Even aside from the animus this engendered in the later followers of the Cheng school in the Southern Song (including, of course, Zhu Xi), it seemed evident to them in hindsight that this rough and tumble internal political conflict was a distraction from the real and imminent danger posed by the Jurchen.

COMPETING VISIONS OF THE *DAO*

Zhu Xi concluded from this unfortunate recent history that one pole of the Confucian project—the perfection of society through good government—had been emphasized during the Northern Song at the expense of the other pole—the perfection of the self through moral cultivation. Because of the extraordinary influence that Zhu Xi exerted in the last couple decades of the twelfth century, this "inward turn" came to characterize late Southern Song Confucianism.[8] But the external threat posed by the Jurchen was only part of the crisis he perceived. The other part, and a contributor to the weakness that had led to the fall of the North, was the internal threat of Buddhism, especially the Chan 禪 (Zen) school of Mahayana Buddhism.

Song Confucian objections to Buddhism, although often based on caricatures of Buddhist thought, had both ethical and metaphysical grounds. While some were attracted by the Buddhist notion of self-perfection based on inherent Buddha-nature, with its obvious parallels to Mencian thought, many Song Confucians were repelled by Buddhism's alleged socioethical failings. Confucianism, of course, had always strongly supported full, active

---

7. See Schirokauer, "Neo-Confucians Under Attack."
8. See Liu, *China Turning Inward*. For Zhu Xi's influence see Tillman, *Confucian Discourse and Chu Hsi's Ascendancy*.

engagement with the world, especially in the family and in government. Scholars such as Cheng Yi, therefore, repeatedly accused the Buddhists of selfishness in leaving behind social and familial relationships. Even though their teachings may be "lofty and profound," Cheng said, they are essentially wrong because one simply cannot deny one's relationships even if one flees from them.[9] According to this view, Buddhism was a debilitating influence on Chinese culture because it undermined the traditional social-mindedness of the Chinese spirit and the Confucian sense of responsibility to work for the betterment of society, primarily through government. By encouraging men and women to live in monasteries, Buddhism did serious harm to the single most important institution in Chinese society—the family—and contravened the most fundamental Confucian value: filial respect (xiao 孝) for elders. Confucius had said (quite prominently in the second passage of the Analects) that filial respect was the "root" of the Way.[10] Hence the seriousness of this issue for committed Confucians.

On the metaphysical questions, Zhu Xi said that the major difference between Buddhism and Confucianism could be seen in their different interpretations of the first line of the Zhongyong (Centrality and Commonality), "What Heaven imparts to man is called human nature."[11] Buddhists, he said, understand "human nature" (xing 性) as "empty awareness," while Confucians interpret it as "concrete principle."[12] The Confucian interpretation meant, for

---

9. Chan, Source Book, 555, 564. This was also the theme of Han Yu's critique of Buddhism (ibid., 454–56). For a short history of anti-Buddhist polemic through the Tang, see Abramson, Ethnic Identity in Tang China, ch. 3 ("Buddhism as a Foreign Religion").

10. Analects 1:2 in full: "Master You said, 'A young person who is filial and respectful of his elders rarely becomes the kind of person who is inclined to defy his superiors, and there has never been a case of one who is disinclined to defy his superiors stirring up rebellion. The gentleman [junzi] applies himself to the roots. Once the roots are firmly established, the Way will grow. Might we not say that filial piety and respect for elders constitute the root of Goodness [ren, or humanity]?'" (trans. Slingerland, Confucius: Analects). Note the connection with the larger social order.

11. Chan, Source Book, 98.

12. Ibid., 616, 647–48. The Mahayana Buddhist concept that all things are "empty of own-being" is really equivalent to saying that they are interdependent with all things. This is quite different from saying that things do not exist or are void of all content. The Confucians never engaged with this important point, although they were most likely aware of it, as most of them had studied Buddhism seriously for a time before "returning" to the Confucian Way. Their philosophical arguments against Buddhism tended to caricature it, whether deliberately or not.

Zhu Xi, that even when the mind is "vacuous" or unoccupied and peaceful it is "full" of moral principle, since every thing (including the mind) has a principle/pattern/order (*li* 理), and the *li* of the mind is the moral nature. "Principle" in Mahayana Buddhist theory refers to the principle that all elements of existence (*dharma*s / *fa* 法) are "empty" (*śunya* / *kong* 空) of "own-being" (*svabhāva* / *zixing* 自性); that is, they have no self-existent, knowable nature. Principle for Confucians has definite, intelligible, and ultimately moral content. And self-actualization, or the process of becoming a sage, requires knowledge and fulfillment of the "five-fold nature"—the nature characterized by the "five constant virtues"—not the realization of an "empty" Buddha-nature. As Mencius had said, "He who fully develops his mind knows his nature; knowing his nature he knows Heaven. To preserve the mind and nourish the nature is the way to serve Heaven" (*Mencius* 7A1). Thus, while Buddhism was attractive (especially to literati) because of its highly sophisticated theories of mind, ignorance, and human suffering, these very theories denied the ultimate truth of the cognitive categories and socioethical values and institutions that were so central to the Confucian worldview.

The Confucian Way that was at stake here was not simply one way among others, like a martial art or a skilled technique.[13] It was the one true Way, a universal set of *principles* (not specific rules)[14] that governed the natural world and constituted the guidelines for a flourishing life and flourishing society. For the Song Confucians it was the Way of the Sages who had first intuited it and had recorded its various dimensions in the Scriptures (or "Classics"). This was the Way that the Cheng-Zhu Confucians appropriated as the name for their particular path: the Learning of the Way (*daoxue* 道學).[15]

---

13. E.g., the "Way of tea" (*cha dao* 茶道), or the Japanese art of *kendō* 劍道 (Way of the sword).

14. For a good discussion of this distinction between principle and rule see Liu Shu-hsien, "A Philosophical Analysis of the Confucian Approach to Ethics," 421–25.

15. "*Daoxue*" had been used by the Cheng brothers and by Zhang Zai (their father's cousin) in the eleventh century, and was widely used by Zhu Xi and his followers in the twelfth. Over the course of the twelfth century, mainly through Zhu Xi's influence, it gradually narrowed in scope until it came to refer specifically to the Cheng-Zhu school, as defined by Zhu Xi. See Hoyt Tillman, *Confucian Discourse,* where he aptly refers to this group as the *daoxue* "fellowship." See Graham, *Two Chinese Philosophers,* 178, n. 4, for uses of the term by the Chengs, Zhang Zai, and Chengs' student, Yang Shi.

Zhu Xi's lifelong mission was to assist the literati (*shi* 士) of his time to learn and practice this Confucian *dao*, which would help revitalize the moral and cultural fiber of Chinese civilization. For Zhu this meant defining the Confucian *dao* as the tradition created by the ancient sages and transmitted by Confucius and Mencius, and distinguishing it clearly from both the Daoist *dao*—which he understood as the teachings of the Daoist classic *Laozi* 老子 and the cultivation practices of the Daoist religion—and the Buddhist *dao*, or "Eightfold Path." Of these two, Chan Buddhism was the chief rival for the affections of Song literati.

Until about the 1990s, the conventional wisdom concerning the history of Chan Buddhism in China was that its "Golden Age" was the Tang 唐 dynasty (618–906), when Huineng 惠能 (638–713), an illiterate monastic kitchen helper, became the Sixth Patriarch and a series of charismatic successors developed the iconoclastic teachings and practices that we associate today with Zen, especially as practiced in Japan.[16] During the Song, according to this view, Chan Buddhism began a long period of decline: no new teachings or schools were developed and a gradual process of syncretism with Pure Land Buddhism began, resulting in the virtual disappearance of Chan as a distinct school of Buddhism in China.[17] The major story of the Song period (again according to this conventional view) was the rise of "Neo-Confucianism," which displaced Buddhism as the most vital and innovative Chinese religio-philosophical tradition.

This story no longer reflects the consensus of academic opinion. To put it succinctly, the Huineng story has been shown to be a complete fabrication, and scholars today agree that Chan developed its characteristic teachings and practices in the Song dynasty, not the Tang.[18] It was during the Song that the three major genres of Chan literature were developed: discourse

---

16. The Huineng story comes from the seminal Chan/Zen text, *The Platform Sutra of the Sixth Patriarch* (Yampolsky 1967). The fact that Japanese Zen Buddhism was one of the earliest Buddhist schools to become well known in the West—basically by historical accident—has strongly skewed our view of Chinese Chan.

17. See Wu, *The Golden Age of Zen,* and Ch'en, *Buddhism in China.*

18. For the Huineng story see McRae, *Seeing Through Zen*; and Jorgensen, *Inventing Hui-neng, the Sixth Patriarch.* For more on Chan in the Song see Gregory and Getz, *Buddhism in the Sung*; Hershock, *Chan Buddhism*; and Schlütter, *How Zen Became Zen.* It should be noted that the syncretism with Pure Land Buddhism did in fact occur, and that Buddhism in Ming-Qing China was not characterized by the institutionally distinct schools that developed in Japan since the Kamakura period (1185–1333).

records (*yulu* 語錄), "lamp" records (*denglu* 燈錄), and *gongan* (*kōan* 公案) collections.[19] It was in these works that the view of the "mind to mind transmission" of the Buddha's wordless teaching and the colorful stories of the Tang dynasty masters, which today we associate with Chan/Zen Buddhism, were developed. Chan Buddhism thrived institutionally during the Song with considerable government support, especially for the large public monasteries, almost all of which were designated as Chan.[20] Buddhist monks and Confucian literati moved in the same social circles,[21] and virtually all of the major Song Confucian thinkers took Buddhism quite seriously, either before turning strictly to Confucianism or as a continuing contributor to their views of the Way.[22]

While Chan Buddhism was the major competitor to Song Confucianism, Daoism was also a thriving alternative.[23] One of the two major Daoist sects of today, the Quanzhen 全真 (Complete Perfection) tradition, began in the Song, as did several other sects. Two emperors of the Northern Song, Zhenzong (r. 998–1023) and Huizong (r. 1101–1126), actively supported Daoism.[24] "Inner alchemy," other forms of Daoist meditation, and other forms of self-cultivation were widespread. The Daoist focus on the human body as the locus of spiritual practice contributed significantly to traditional Chinese medicine, which was beginning to be systematized and professionalized during the Song.[25] It was

---

19. Discourse records are collections of "encounter dialogues" of individual Chan teachers, along the lines of the *Analects* (*Lunyu* 論語) of Confucius. "Lamp" records are collections of encounter dialogues of multiple teachers in a tradition, illustrating the mind-to-mind transmission of the Buddha's "lamp" of enlightenment, such as the *Jingde chuandeng lu* 景德傳燈錄, or *Transmission of the Lamp of the Jingde Era* (the reign period, 1004–07, when the book was compiled). *Gong'an* collections contain short encounter dialogues of various teachers that are thought to be especially useful as teaching devices.

20. See Foulk, "Myth, Ritual, and Monastic Practice in Sung Ch'an Buddhism."

21. See Gimello, "Learning, Letters, and Liberation in Sung Ch'an."

22. Two important examples of the second variety were Zhang Jiucheng 張九成 (1092–1159) and Yang Shi 楊時 (1053–1135), the student of the Cheng brothers who brought their teachings to the south. On Zhang see Ari Borrell, "Ko-wu or Kung-an?"; on Yang see Jameson, *South-Returning Wings*.

23. See Kohn, *Daoism Handbook*, chs. 15–19; Davis, *Society and the Supernatural in Song China*; Hymes, *Way and Byway*; and Kohn, *Daoism and Chinese Culture*, chs. 7–9.

24. Hymes, *Way and Byway*, 27.

25. See Needham and Lu, *Science and Civilisation in China*, vol. 6, part 6, 95–113.

widely accepted that Daoist practices of nourishing the essence (*jing* 精), breath (*qi* 氣), and spirit (*shen* 神), although long and arduous, could lead to extension of the normal lifespan or preservation of the body after death.[26]

Both Buddhism and Daoism claimed special access to the *dao*: Chan through its unbroken line of "patriarchs" or ancestors (*zu* 祖) going right back to the Buddha; Daoism through its claim that the human body was a microcosm of the *dao,* embodying (in potential form that must be activated by cultivation practices) all the spiritual powers that animate the universe. The universalistic meanings of the word *dao* were first expressed in the *Laozi* or *Daodejing* 道德經. This scripture of classical Daoism, compiled in the third century BCE from earlier sources, spoke of the *dao* as the Way of nature, the spontaneous patterns of cyclical growth that characterize the natural world, which human beings should emulate if they wish to enhance their lives and rulers should emulate to enable their states to flourish. The roughly contemporaneous *Analects* of Confucius, by contrast, does not develop the trans-human dimensions of the Way. In the *Analects* the Way is the ideal sociopolitical order, the Way of good government and the Way of life to be followed by a morally noble person (*junzi* 君子).[27] When Buddhism entered China in the first century CE, it came with its own "Path" or Way, the Eightfold Path of right wisdom, morality, and meditative practice.[28] This too originally lacked a cosmic dimension. But the broader Daoist meaning of *dao* eventually influenced both the Confucian and Buddhist meanings in China. While the term never had the prominence in Buddhist literature that it came to have in Song Confucianism,[29] in the latter it came to be nearly synonymous with *li,* the natural/moral order.

---

26. Even as strong an opponent of Daoism as Zhu Xi accepted these claims; see Hu Guang, *Xingli daquan shu,* 28:15b.

27. As mentioned earlier, the *Analects* began to be compiled shortly after the Master's death in 479 BCE, a process that continued for one or two hundred years. Given that the earlier, oral sources of the *Laozi* must have circulated long before they were written down, the two texts can be considered roughly contemporaneous, although the earlier parts of the *Analects* predate the first known written form of the *Laozi.*

28. Right views and intention are considered wisdom (*prajñā*); right speech, action, and livelihood are morality (*sīla*); right effort, mindfulness, and concentration are meditative practice (*samādhi*).

29. We do see trans-human implications in the seminal Chan text, the *Platform Sutra of the Sixth Patriarch*: "Tao [*dao*] must be something that circulates freely; why should he impede it? If the mind does not abide in things the Tao circulates freely; if the

THE CONFUCIAN *DAO*

The idea of a line of Confucian sages who transmitted the *dao* goes back to Mencius (fourth century BCE), who spoke of the "Way of the sages" (*shengrenzhi dao* 聖人之道) beginning with the mythic sage-kings Yao 堯 and Shun 舜:

> After the death of Yao and Shun, the way of the Sages declined, and tyrants arose one after another. They pulled down houses in order to make ponds, and the people had nowhere for repose. They turned fields into parks, depriving the people of their livelihood. Moreover, heresies and violence arose. With the multiplication of parks, ponds and lakes, arrived birds and beasts. By the time of the tyrant Zhou [the evil last king of the Shang],[30] the Empire was again in great disorder. The Duke of Zhou helped King Wu to punish Zhou. . . .
>
> > Lofty indeed were the plans of King Wen [founder of the Zhou dynasty]!
> > Great indeed were the achievements of King Wu!
> > Bless us and enlighten us, your descendants,
> > So that we may act correctly and not fall into error.
>
> When the world declined and the Way fell into obscurity, heresies and violence again arose. There were instances of regicides and parricides. Confucius was apprehensive and composed the *Spring and Autumn Annals*. . . . No sage kings have appeared since then. Feudal lords do as they please; people lacking in official position are uninhibited in the expression of their views, and the words of Yang Zhu and Mo Di fill the empire.[31]

---

mind abides in things, it becomes entangled" (trans. Yampolsky, *The Platform Sutra*, 136). However, most Buddhist usage of the term, including in the *Platform Sutra*, is in the sense of "the Buddha Way," which mainly implies the Way of thought and practice.

30. The names of the tyrant Zhou and the Duke of Zhou are different, unrelated homonyms.

31. *Mencius* 3B.9, trans. D. C. Lau. The quoted verse is from the *Shujing*. Yang Zhu was considered a "hedonist," and Mo Di, or Mozi (Master Mo), argued for "universal love," or love without distinctions, which Confucians considered wrong because one should love one's relatives more than others.

> From Yao and Shu to Tang [founder of the Shang dynasty] it was over five hundred years. Men like Yu and Gao Yao knew Yao and Shun personally, while those like Tang knew them only by reputation. From Tang to King Wen [founder of the Zhou dynasty] it was over five hundred years. Men like Yi Yin and Lai Zhu knew Tang personally, while those like King Wen knew him only by reputation. From King Wen to Confucius it was over five hundred years. Men such as Taigong Wang and Sanyi Sheng knew King Wen personally, while those like Confucius knew him only by reputation. From Confucius to the present it is over a hundred years. In time we are so near to the age of the sage while in place we are so close to his home, yet if there is no one who has anything of the sage, well then, there is no one who has anything of the sage.[32]

Mencius clearly emphasizes here the discontinuity or interruptions in the propagation of the Way. But he also implies that even over a span of five hundred years it is possible for the rare, "prophetic" individual to "repossess" the Way.[33] This became the standard structure of Confucian accounts of their Way in later periods. The fact that the Confucian transmission of the Way was discontinuous is, of course, an important difference from the continuous lineage of teachers claimed by the Chan school of Buddhism, and posed a serious problem for Zhu Xi, as we shall see.

In the Tang dynasty (618–906), Han Yu 韓愈 (768–824)—considered one of the precursors of the "Neo-Confucian" revival of the Song—specifically

---

32. *Mencius* 7B.38, trans. D. C. Lau, replacing Wade-Giles with *pinyin* romanization. For the other names in this passage, see Lau's "Glossary of Personal and Place Names."

33. The words in quotation marks are those of Wm. Theodore de Bary, in *Neo-Confucian Orthodoxy and the Learning of the Mind-and-Heart,* where he defines "prophetic" as "an extraordinary access to and revelation of truth not vouchsafed to everyone, which by some process of inner inspiration or solitary perception affords an insight beyond what is received in scripture, and by appeal to some higher order of truth gives new meaning, significance, and urgency to certain cultural values or scriptural texts. Confucian tradition does not customarily speak of such a revelation as 'supernatural,' but it has an unpredictable, wondrous quality manifesting the divine creativity of Heaven" (9–10). de Bary develops the idea further in *The Trouble with Confucianism,* ch. 1. Although a reluctance to import terminology from alien traditions is a good general principle, it should not rule it out completely—if (and only if) we limit its usage to our analysis and refrain from injecting it into the texts themselves. In this case I believe it sheds useful light on the Confucian tradition, and I shall return to it later.

identified Daoism and Buddhism as the major opponents of the Confucian Way. Both had been flourishing for about five hundred years by his time, while the teachings of Yang Zhu and Mo Di had faded into relative obscurity. In his "Inquiry into the Way" (*Yuan dao* 原道), Han Yu said that the succession had ceased altogether after the death of Mencius:

> What Way is this? It is what I call the Way, not what the Daoists and Buddhists have called the Way. Yao passed it on to Shun, Shun to Yu, Yu to Tang, Tang to King Wen, King Wu, and the Duke of Zhou; then these passed it on to Confucius, who passed it on to Mencius. But after the death of Mencius it was not passed on.[34]

Han Yu may been the first to describe the Confucian *dao* as a universal, cosmic Way.[35] In addition to his spirited defense of the Confucian Way, he was known for his elegantly simple prose style. He was the originator of the *guwen* 古文 ("literature of antiquity") movement: an attempt to return to the simpler prose style of the Zhou dynasty and to avoid the flowery, overly structured styles that had become popular since the Han dynasty. This movement was continued by the Song Confucians, and is another reason why Han Yu was held in high esteem by them. Early in the Song, Shi Jie 石介 (1005–1045)[36] wrote an essay, "Revering Han [Yu]," in which he ranked Han higher than Mencius. But he made another innovation that is particularly relevant to our study of Zhou Dunyi and Zhu Xi:

> The Dao began with Fuxi and was brought to completion by Confucius. The Dao had already been realized, and yet sages were not produced. Thus, in the 2,000 or so years since Confucius, no sages have been born. Men like Mencius, Yang Xiong, Wang Tong, and Han Yu transmitted [the Way of] Confucius and revered him

---

34. Han Yu, *Yuan dao* 原道 (On the origin of the Way), in de Bary and Bloom, *Sources of Chinese Tradition,* 573; and in *Han Yu wen,* 1–7. King Wu, the son of King Wen, was the king under whom the Zhou conquered the Shang in 1045 BCE. When King Wu died, his son was too young to rule, so King Wu's brother, the Duke of Zhou, acted as regent until the young King Cheng came of age. The doctrine of the Mandate of Heaven is traditionally attributed to the Duke of Zhou. See also Hartman, *Han Yü.*

35. Bol, *"This Culture of Ours,"* 127.

36. For Shi Jie see Huang and Quan, *Song Yuan xue'an,* 2:33a–42a.

as a teacher. But their knowledge was [only] sufficient for them to become worthies (*xian*). After Confucius the Dao was repeatedly neglected and blocked up. It was discussed by Mencius and greatly clarified by [Han Yu]. . . .

Alas! Fuxi, Shennong, Huangdi, Shaohao, Zhuanxu, Gaoxin, Yao of Tang, Shun of Yu, Yu, Tang, [kings] Wen and Wu, the Duke of Zhou, and Confucius—of these fourteen sages Confucius was the most perfected sage. Alas! Mencius, Xunzi, Yang Xiong, Wang Tong, Han Yu—of these five worthies, [Han Yu] was the most perfected worthy.[37]

Here, in addition to his relative denigration of Mencius (a point that most later Confucians rejected), Shi Jie introduces the category of "worthy" (*xian* 賢), one step below "sage" (*sheng* 聖). This too became a standard Confucian category, reflected for example in the ranking of figures in Confucian temples. But Shi Jie's most striking innovation was to push back the origin of the Way beyond Yao, Shun, and Yu 禹 to the primordial sages Fuxi 伏羲, Shennong 神農, and Huangdi 黃帝. Zhu Xi followed this pattern, giving special weight to Fuxi, for reasons that will be developed presently.

While the identities of the sages who transmitted the Way varied, the basic structure remained: a discontinuous transmission from ancient times to the present, punctuated by "heroic" or "prophetic" individuals, who either reestablished benevolent government after periods of tyranny (e.g., the end of the Shang) or disunity (the Warring States period), or recovered the teachings of the prior sages (e.g., Confucius and Mencius). This discontinuity stood in stark contrast to the continuity of transmission claimed by the Chan Buddhists. After Han Yu, the Confucian Way was understood as the ultimate source of moral values, which periodically required the appearance of an extraordinary individual—a sage—to apprehend it anew and resume its transmission. The theory developed by the Song Confucians to explain how their sagely Way was in fact accessible in the present, despite the gaps in its transmission, combined the models used by the Buddhists and the Daoists. They, like the

---

37. Translated by Neskar, *The Cult of Worthies,* 340–41, with Wade-Giles replaced by *pinyin* romanization. Fuxi was the inventor of hunting and fishing, and the creator of the hexagrams and divination system of the *Yijing*. Huangdi (the Yellow Emperor) was the inventor of government; Shennong (the Divine Farmer) the inventor of agriculture. All of these are mythic culture-heroes. Shaohao, Zhuanxu, Gaoxin were Huangdi's son, grandson, and great-grandson.

Chan Buddhists, claimed to have a line of ancestors/patriarchs, which they called sages. And like the Daoists, they claimed that the human body/mind/heart was where the *dao* was to be found.

THE CHENG BROTHERS

Zhu Xi's most important predecessor in the Northern Song was Cheng Yi, the younger of the two Cheng brothers. The Chengs were born and spent most of their lives in Luoyang, near the Yellow River in Henan province. Cheng Hao, the elder brother (by one year), had the more distinguished political career. His reputation was that of a kind, warmhearted man, while his brother came to be known as more of a hardheaded moralist. When Cheng Hao died at the age of fifty-three, his brother composed a eulogy in which he spoke of the restoration of the Confucian *dao* in the Song:

> After the demise of the Duke of Zhou, the Way of the sages was not carried on, and after the death of Mencius the teaching of the sages was not transmitted. When the Way was not carried on there was no good government for a hundred generations, and when the teaching was not transmitted, there were not true scholars for a thousand years. Even without good government, scholars could explain the way of good government for the edification of men and transmission to later generations, but without true [Confucian] scholars the world fell into darkness and people lost their way, human desires ran amok, and heavenly principles were extinguished. The Master [Cheng Hao] was born 1,400 years after Mencius and was able to recover the untransmitted teachings that survived in the classics, resolving to enlighten the people with this Way.[38]

And in his brief biography of Cheng Hao, Cheng Yi says:

---

38. *Er Cheng ji*, 640, translated by de Bary, *Neo-Confucian Orthodoxy*, 3–4 (de Bary inadvertantly omits the word *untransmitted*). Cheng Yi outlived his brother by twenty-two years. Note also the two different kinds of discontinuity outlined by Cheng Yi: the Way was *practiced* during the reigns of Kings Wen and Wu and the Duke of Zhou, after which it fell into disuse. The Way was *taught* by Confucius, his disciples, and Mencius, although it was not currently being put into practice. The second kind of disruption was worse than the first.

In his pursuit of learning, when he was fifteen or sixteen, the Master heard Zhou Maoshu 周茂叔 of Runan 汝南 [Zhou Dunyi] discuss the Way. He gave up forthwith the endeavor to prepare for civil service examinations and enthusiastically made up his mind to seek the Way. As he did not know the essentials, he drifted among the different schools and went in and out of the Daoist and Buddhist schools for almost ten years. Then he returned to seek the Way in the Six Classics, and found it there. . . . He said that, after Mencius, the Learning of the Sage was no longer transmitted, and he took it as his own responsibility to restore the cultural tradition.[39]

These two pieces by Cheng Yi were well known by the Chengs' many disciples, both during the remainder of the Northern Song and in the Southern Song. The eulogy clearly identifies Cheng Hao as the first to revive the Confucian Way since Mencius. The biography introduces a slight ambiguity, in that he "heard Zhou [Dunyi] discuss the Way" before he "returned to seek the Way in the Six Classics, and found it there." But in the end the meaning is the same in both pieces, because after studying with Zhou—along with Cheng Yi, incidentally—Cheng Hao "drifted among the different schools and went in and out of the Daoist and Buddhist schools for almost ten years." So despite having heard Zhou discuss the Way, he failed to get it himself for a long time, and when he did get it, it was from the classics. So it cannot be said, according to this account, that Zhou Dunyi transmitted the Way to Cheng Hao. At best one could say that Zhou inspired Cheng to seek the Way, but when he did so he eventually got it himself. This interpretation does give Zhou a significant role in the transmission of the Way, but it is clearly not the role of an independent "repossessor" of the Way.[40]

This was the prevailing view among the followers of the Chengs in the early Southern Song. No one since Mencius had fully understood and transmitted the Confucian Way until Cheng Hao, the elder of the two brothers. After much confusion and dalliance with Buddhism and Daoism, he had "returned" to the Confucian classics, apprehended the Way on his

---

39. *Er Cheng ji* 2:638, translated by de Bary, ibid., 4.

40. The term "getting it" sounds a bit like English slang, but in fact it is an accurate translation of *de* 得, which is often used in this context. For example, Zhu Xi later argued that one should engage in learning to "get it for oneself" (*zide* 自得), meaning that the purpose of learning is to become a sage, not to gain a career.

own from the classics, and with his brother taught it to their disciples. Zhou Dunyi's role was decidedly secondary.

The Chengs and their students came to be known as the Luo school, after the Luo River that flows into the Yellow River near their hometown Luoyang, in Henan province (north-central China).[41] The Chengs were also associated with Shao Yong, who was their colorful and somewhat reclusive friend and also lived in Luoyang; Zhang Zai (1020–1077), who was their father's cousin; and of course Zhou Dunyi, who was briefly their teacher when they were teenagers.[42] One of the Chengs' students, Yang Shi 楊時 (1053–1135), later moved south to Zhu Xi's home province of Fujian on the southeast coast, bringing the teachings of the Chengs with him.[43] One of Yang's students, Luo Congyan 羅從彥 (1072–1135), became the teacher of Zhu Xi's father, Zhu Song. And another of Luo's students, Li Tong 李侗 (1093–1163), became Zhu Xi's teacher. So Zhu Xi was a fourth-generation disciple of the Cheng brothers. Yang Shi, Luo Congyan, and Li Tong later became known as the Daonan 道南 school, because it derived from Yang Shi, who had brought the *dao* south (*nan*).

Meanwhile, another branch of the Cheng school developed in Hunan province (in the interior, west of Fujian). Zhu Xi's relationship with this Hunan 湖南 school (also called the Hu-Xiang 湖湘 school)[44] is a crucial part of the puzzle we are attempting to solve, and will be developed further in chapter 3. The founder of the Hunan school, Hu Anguo 胡安國 (1074–1138), had a nephew, Hu Xian 胡憲 (1082–1162), who was one of three men asked by Zhu Song to be Zhu Xi's teacher after his father's death when Zhu Xi was thirteen (well before he went to study with Li Tong). More significantly, Hu Anguo's son, Hu Hong 胡宏 (1106–1161)—who had also been a student of Yang Shi and is sometimes considered the founder of the Hunan school—became an important figure for Zhu Xi, although they never

---

41. They were also called the Yi-Luo 伊洛 school, adding the name of the Yi River (Yichuan, which was also Cheng Yi's honorary name) that flows into the Luo near Luoyang. The Chengs themselves were usually referred to as the Chengs of Henan.

42. Zhou Dunyi is sometimes identified as the "Lian school" 濂學 after the stream along which he built his retirement home; Zhang Zai and his disciples are sometimes referred to as the "Guan school" 關學 after his home area of Guanzhong (the area of Chang'an, or modern Xi'an).

43. See Jameson, *South-Returning Wings*.

44. Xiang 湘, the name of a river in the province, is an alternate name for Hunan.

met personally. Zhu Xi was a severe critic of Hu Hong, yet Hu Hong's student, Zhang Shi 張栻 (1133–1180), became Zhu Xi's very close friend and a crucial collaborator with Zhu on the elevation of Zhou Dunyi to the position of first sage of the Song.

ZHOU DUNYI

Although Zhou Dunyi's family had originally come from Henan province, he was born in Hunan and spent most of his life in the south. His father died when he was about fourteen, and he was adopted by his maternal uncle, Zheng Xiang 鄭向, through whom he received his first government position. He never received the *jinshi* 進士 degree, the highest level of the civil service examination system. He spent his official career in a series of mid-level government positions in Hunan, Jiangxi, Guangxi, and Sichuan.[45] In 1046 the Cheng brothers, in their mid-teens, came to study with him for a year or two, because their father had met Zhou and had been highly impressed by him. But Zhou never achieved any position of prominence during his lifetime, either as a private teacher or as a government official. Except for one or two people with whom Zhou is said to have discussed the Way, he is not known to have had any other students besides the Cheng brothers.[46] As mentioned in the Introduction, he is best known for his "*Taiji* Diagram" (*Taijitu*), the short "Discussion of the *Taiji* Diagram" (*Taijitu shuo*), and the *Tongshu* (Penetrating the *Scripture of Change*). He also developed a lasting reputation as a humane, kind-hearted man who exemplified the Confucian notion of being "authentic" (*cheng* 誠): expressing in thought and behavior one's moral nature (*dexing* 德性). Huang Tingjian (1045–1105) said of him:

> Maoshu [Zhou's "style" or professional name] is a man of lofty character, fresh and vigorous as a breeze in sunlight, or the bright

---

45. Chan, "Chou Tun-i," in Franke, *Sung Biographies* 1:277–81, where Yingdao (present-day Dao) county is mistakenly identified as being in Henan (277)—one of many typographical errors in this book. Zhou's birthplace was Chongling village, Yingdao county, Daozhou prefecture; about fifty miles south-southeast of present-day Yongzhou city in Hunan. For a more detailed account of Zhou's life see Liang, *Zhou Dunyi pingzhuan*.

46. See Huang and Quan, *Song Yuan xue'an* 11:1a. According to Zhu Xi's student, Wei Liaoweng (1178–1237), Zhang Zongfan, from Sichuan, "received instruction" and praise from Zhou (Wei Liaoweng, "Hezhou jian Lianxi xiansheng citang ji"; see also Huang and Quan, *Song-Yuan xue'an,* 12:25a), but faded into obscurity.

moon. An avid reader, his elegant thoughts forest the valleys and he is ever unflappable and forthright. Modest in striving for renown yet ardent in seeking [self-realization], he is indifferent to worldly success yet steadfast in friendship.[47]

A popular story about Zhou was that he refrained from cutting the grass around his house because he didn't want to suppress the spirit of life.[48] Such an attitude could be understood in terms of the evolving Confucian reverence for life, as expressed by Cheng Yi ("The mind of Heaven and earth is to give birth to things") and Zhang Zai ("Heaven is my father and Earth is my mother, and even such a small creature as I finds an intimate place in their midst").[49] But it also might have been related to his understanding of Buddhism; Zhou, like many Song Confucians, associated freely with Buddhist literati, such as Shou Ya 壽崖.[50] And after the three works mentioned above, his next best-known piece of writing was a poem, "On the Loving the Lotus" (*Ai lian shuo* 愛蓮說)—the lotus flower being first and foremost a Buddhist symbol.[51]

According to A. C. Graham, "Zhou Dunyi was not known as a philosopher in the eleventh century," and "the works of Zhou Dunyi were little known in the eleventh century."[52] There are no extant contemporary documents, including the extensive writings and recorded conversations of the Cheng brothers, that claim any kind of special role for Zhou Dunyi. Li Xinchuan's 李心傳 (1166–1243) *Daoming lu* 道命錄 (Record of the Fate of the Way)—a collection of official documents concerning the *daoxue* school from 1083 to 1224—begins with Sima Guang's recommendation of Cheng Yi for an

---

47. Quoted by Qian Mu, *Zhuzi xin xue'an*, 1:17. Translated by Kirill Ole Thompson in *An Overview of Zhu Xi's Learning*, by Qian Mu (unpublished).

48. Related by one of the Cheng brothers in *Henan Chengshi yishu*, 3 (*Er Cheng ji*, 60).

49. Cheng Yi was elaborating on *Yijing*, *Xici* B.1.11 ("The great virtue of Heaven and earth is life"; *Zhouyi benyi* 3:18a). Zhang's statement is the first line of his "Western Inscription" (Chan, *Source Book*, 497).

50. See Part II, "Introduction" to the Supreme Polarity Diagram.

51. In Buddhist iconography, Buddhas are often depicted sitting on lotus thrones, and one of the most influential Mahayana scriptures is the *Lotus Sūtra*. The lotus also symbolizes the Mahayana conception of enlightenment, as the purity of the flower (the enlightened mind) rises from the muck at the bottom of the pond (ordinary life with its suffering and mental defilements, or *kleśa*).

52. Graham, *Two Chinese Philosophers*, 156, 166.

appointment as imperial tutor.[53] The same text contains a memorial written by Hu Anguo in 1137 (ten years after the fall of the north) requesting posthumous honors for the first generation of *daoxue* scholars—Shao Yong, Zhang Zai, and the two Chengs—but not for Zhou.[54] The earliest document in the *Daoming lu* mentioning Zhou Dunyi is dated 1211, when Zhu Xi's influence was already well established.[55] Li Yuangang 李元綱, in his 1170 diagram *Daozhuan zhengtong* 傳道正統 (Legitimate succession of the transmission of the Way), lists the Cheng brothers (equally) as the successors to Mencius.[56] And Hu Hong (1106–1161), in his preface to Zhou's *Tongshu*, says that "the followers of the Learning of the Way all say [in roughly the mid-twelfth century] that it was Cheng Hao who continued Mencius' untransmitted learning."[57]

It was probably Hu Hong who first claimed that Zhou Dunyi had "continued Mencius' untransmitted learning."[58] Here is Hu Hong's undated preface to the *Tongshu*:

Preface to Master Zhou's *Tongshu*
(*Zhouzi Tongshu xu* 周子通書序) by Hu Hong[59]

The *Tongshu*, in forty sections, was written by Master Zhou. Master Zhou, whose name was Dunyi 敦頤 and style name Maoshu 茂叔,

---

53. Li, *Daoming lu*, 1:1a–2a. On this text see Hartman, "Bibliographic Notes." On Li Xinchuan see Chaffee, "Sung Biographies"; Chafee, "The Historian as Critic"; Wang and Ching, "Li Hsing-ch'üan."

54. Ibid., 3:10b. Hu Anguo says explicitly that the Cheng brothers revived Mencius's Way in his epitaph for Yang Shi (reproduced in Zhu Xi's *Yi-Luo yuan-yuan lu*, 10:1048). But see chapter 2 at note 71, where he seems to give the credit to Zhou Dunyi.

55. Ibid., 8:6b–10a ("Memorial on education, Zhu Xi's Four Books and acolyte status [in the Confucian temple] for Zhou Dunyi, Shao Yong, the Cheng brothers, and Zhang Zai," by Li Daochuan [Li Xinchuan's brother]).

56. The diagram is found in Li Yuangang (fl. 1170s), *Shengmen shiye tu* (Diagrams of the accomplishments of the sages).

57. *Hu Hong ji*, 161.

58. There is contradictory evidence on whether Hu Hong's father, Hu Anguo, shared this view (see above, note 54, and chapter 2, note 71). But the bulk of the evidence suggests that Hu Anguo went along with the prevailing view that Cheng Hao had independently revived the Way.

59. *Hu Hong ji*, 160–62 (also in Zhou *Lianxi ji*, 7:1b–2b, with a few significant textual variants that seem to be errors). I am grateful to my colleague Yang Xiao for his help with this translation.

was from Chongling 舂陵.⁶⁰ Speculating on where his Learning of the Way (*daoxue* 道學) came from, some say that the transmission of the Taiji Diagram came from Mu Xiu, that [Mu] Xiu received [it and] the Xiantian 先天 (Prior to Heaven, or *A Priori*) Diagram from Chong Fang 种放, and that [Chong] Fang received [both] from Chen Tuan 陳摶 (d. 989). But is he [Chen Tuan] then the only teacher [source] of Zhou's learning? He is not the ultimate one. Mr. Xiyi 希夷 [Chen Tuan] had concerns for the world, but when he died he was associating with only five recluses.⁶¹ In comparison to the Sage's [Confucius's] indifference [to living in retirement from society],⁶² it seems that he [Chen Tuan] did not measure up to him.⁶³

Teacher Cheng Mingdao used to say to his disciples, "In the past, when I received learning from Master Zhou, he told me to seek for what Zhongni [Confucius] and Master Yan [Yan Hui 顏回] enjoyed (*yue* 樂)."⁶⁴ And Teacher Mingdao himself looked back to how Master Zhou "sang of the wind and moon."⁶⁵ The followers of the Learning of the Way all say that Cheng Hao continued Mencius' untransmitted learning. So how could Master Zhou have been limited to the learning of Chong [Fang] and Mu [Xiu]? If we examine antiquity, Confucius taught the Way of the Three Kings and established the methods by which the hundred kings could manage the world. Meng Ke (Mencius) rejected Yang [Zhu] 楊朱 and Mo

---

60. See above, note 45.

61. "Recluses" is a loose rendering of *feng ge he diao* 鳳歌荷蓧 (phoenix song, shoulder basket), which seems to be an allusion to *Analects* 18:5 and 18:7, two stories of recluses who meet Confucius.

62. Alluding to *Analects* 18:8.

63. I.e., Chen Tuan was too extreme in his preference for a reclusive life.

64. *Analects* 6:3: "There was one [disciple] named Yan Hui who loved (*hao* 好) learning" and 6:11: "What a worthy man was Yan Hui! Living in a narrow alley, subsisting on a basket of grain and gourdful of water—other people could not have born such hardship, yet it never spoiled Hui's joy (*yue* 樂)" (trans. Slingerland, *Confucius: Analects,* 53, 56). What Yan Hui loved or enjoyed, according to Cheng Yi, was "learning to attain the Way of the sage" ("Essay on what Master Yan loved to learn" [*Er Cheng ji* 8:1a; trans. Chan, *Source Book,* 547–50]).

65. *Yin feng nong yue* 吟風弄月. In *Henan Chengshi yishu* 3 (*Er Cheng ji,* 59) the phrase is not attributed to either brother specifically. It became a standard characterization of Zhou Dunyi.

[Di] 墨翟, and further clarified Confucius' beneficence, so that the myriad generations would not be cut off [from the Way]. Indeed it is said that Mencius' achievement was no less than Yu's. More recently, Master Zhou revealed his [Mencius's] untransmitted learning to the elder and younger Chengs, returning at once to the brilliance of the myriad ancients. Like the sun hanging in the sky, he benefitted a hundred generations. Like water spreading over the earth, his merit was like that of Confucius and Mencius. People see the brevity of his writings (*shu* 書) but do not understand the greatness of his Way. They see the quality of his writing (*wen* 文) but do not understand the essence of his ideas. They see the simplicity of his words but do not understand the extent of their flavor.

How can I be up to understanding him? I have been taking this to heart for years. I will try one or two statements so that like-minded [comrades] may benefit from my attempts. [Master Zhou] worried about people who are concerned with having deliberate plans, healthy bodies and prosperous families, and enjoying worldly favors. Thus he said: "Be intent on having Yi Yin's intention [to learning the Way]."[66] He also worried about those who exhaust themselves on sensory knowledge, not wanting to wait for [positions of] value and selling themselves short.[67] Thus he said: "Learn what Yan Hui learned."[68] People who are truly able to establish Yi Yin's intention and to cultivate Yan Hui's learning will only then understand the extreme greatness contained in the words of the *Tongshu,* and the inexhaustibility of the sagely enterprise.

Thus what this single-scroll book begins to show people is to model themselves after the various excellent masters, and to flow out [extend one's virtue] to the world along with the *Yi* (Changes), *Shi* (Odes), *Shu* (Documents), *Chunqiu* (Spring and Autumn), [*Lun*] *yu* (Analects), and *Meng*[*zi*] (Mencius). Therefore tell [others] about it and store it. When you meet "good *literati*" in the world who want to "ascend to discuss" prior worthies and read their books, pass it on to them.[69]

---

66. *Tongshu,* section 10c.
67. Alluding to *Analects* 9:3.
68. *Tongshu,* section 10c.
69. Quoting *Mencius* 5B.8.

Hu Hong's estimation of Zhou Dunyi was probably, in some way, influenced by the fact that Zhou, like Hu, lived most of his life in Hunan. Hu's argument for Zhou had minimal influence until it was picked up by Zhu Xi later in the twelfth century. But there is one other record of Zhou being considered the reviver of Mencius's Way before Zhu Xi's campaign: a text written probably in the early 1160s (around the time of Hu Hong's death) by students of Zhang Jiucheng (1092–1159), called *Zhuru mingdao ji* 諸儒鳴道集 (Record of various Confucians propagating the Way).[70] This text, the first known Neo-Confucian anthology, begins with Zhou's *Tongshu*, but does not include his *Taijitu shuo*. Zhang Jiucheng, like Hu Hong, had been a student of Yang Shi, so Yang seems to be a crucial link in this story.

Zhu Xi first read the writings of Zhou Dunyi in 1152, at the age of twenty-two, but he later says he didn't understand them at that time.[71] Zhu at that time was seriously studying both Chan Buddhism and Daoism, including the Daoist practical arts of immortality.[72] He had begun studying with the Chan monk Daoqian 道謙 six years earlier.[73] Daoqian was a student of the most famous Chan teacher of the Song, Dahui Zonggao 大慧宗杲 (1089–1163). Three years after Daoqian's death in 1152, Zhu paid a visit to Dahui, who referred to him as "Layman Zhu."[74] This suggests that Dahui considered Zhu a serious student of Chan. And the fact that Zhu first read Zhou Dunyi during this period, when he was also studying Daoist texts, suggests that Zhu may have considered Zhou to be at least a Daoist-influenced writer. This would be entirely consistent with Zhou's reputation at the time. Zhu Zhen 朱震 (1072–1138) had proposed two decades earlier that Zhou had received the *Taiji* Diagram from Mu Xiu 穆修 (979–1032), who had received it from Chong Fang 种放 (956–1015), who in turn had received it from the famous Daoist priest Chen Tuan 陳搏 (d. 989). This claim was well known in Zhu Xi's circles, and Zhu makes a weak attempt to refute it in his 1179 postface to Zhou's *Taijitu shuo* and *Tongshu*.[75] Lu Jiuyuan repeated it in his first letter

---

70. Hoyt Cleveland Tillman discusses this text in *Confucian Discourse and Chu Hsi's Ascendancy*, 29, 117–18.
71. See Zhu's Preface to the *Tongshu*, translated in Part II.
72. Shu Jingnan, *Zhuzi Nianpu changbian*, 153.
73. Ibid., 104.
74. Ibid., 188.
75. *Wenji* 3652 (translated in Part II). His refutation consists merely in referring to Hu Hong's claim that the teaching of Chen Tuan and his followers was not at Zhou's level.

to Zhu Xi (1188), focusing on the fact that the term *wuji* was first used by Laozi. In his letter in response to Lu, Zhu Xi merely says that Zhou used the term in a different sense than Laozi, and he doesn't even mention Zhu Zhen's claim that the *Taijitu* was given to Zhou by Daoists.[76]

In 1153, Zhu began visiting and corresponding with Li Tong, developing a close master-disciple relationship that lasted until Li's death. Li did not like Buddhism and turned Zhu Xi's interest back to Confucianism. In particular, Li taught Zhou Dunyi's idea of "emphasizing stillness" (*zhu jing* 主靜, in the *Taijitu shuo*) and the practice of "quiet-sitting" (*jing zuo* 靜坐), a Confucian form of meditation that both of the Cheng brothers had taught.[77] This emphasis on stillness/quietude (*jing*) became the hallmark of the Daonan school. So in 1160, Zhu read Zhou Dunyi's writings again and began discussing them with Li.[78] In 1163, the same year that Li Tong died and two years after Hu Hong died, Zhu met Zhang Shi of the Hunan school (Hu Hong's student), and they became fast friends. It is very likely that Zhu Xi received Hu Hong's preface to the *Tongshu* (translated above) from Zhang Shi. This, in combination with Li Tong's use of Zhou's ideas, may have planted the seed of Zhu Xi's eventual reevaluation of Zhou Dunyi. The key to that reevaluation was the "spiritual crisis" that Zhu Xi experienced and resolved in the late 1160s, which is the topic of chapter 3. First we will examine the evidence for the reevaluation itself.

---

76. *Wenji* 1566–70.

77. Qian Mu, *Zhuzi xin xue'an*, 1:106. This will be discussed in greater detail in chapter 3.

78. *Nianpu*, 251.

Chapter Two

Zhou Dunyi's Role in the *daotong*

In 1169, immediately after the resolution of his spiritual crisis (to be discussed in chapter 3), Zhu Xi re-edited and published the texts of Zhou's *Taijitu shuo* (Discussion of the *Taiji* Diagram) and *Tongshu* (Penetrating the Scripture of Change), without commentaries.[1] In his postface he makes it clear that the Chengs followed Zhou, not vice versa:

> The profundity of the Master's learning is embodied in the *Taiji* Diagram, and the words of the *Tongshu* manifest the comprehensiveness of this Diagram. The sayings of the Cheng brothers on the nature and endowment all follow his theories.[2]

Probably at this same time he began writing a commentary on the *Taijitu shuo*, because he completed a draft in the spring of 1170.[3] No one at this time had written commentaries on Zhou's major works, the *Taijitu shuo* or the *Tongshu*.[4] He sent the draft to Zhang Shi and his other close colleague,

---

1. *Nianpu*, 412. Zhu had earlier (1166) edited and published Zhou's *Tongshu*, without a commentary, but in the 1169 edition he made changes to the order and titles of chapters.
2. "*Zhouzi Taiji Tongshu houxu*," in *Wenji* 75:3628; translated in Part II.
3. *Nianpu*, 426.
4. Qian Mu, *Zhuzi xin xue'an*, 1:24.

Lü Zuqian 呂祖謙 (1137–1181), for feedback. Oddly though, he would not publish this commentary until 1188. He explains that decision only partially, saying that originally he had been reluctant to share it because Zhou was criticized by many scholars. Perhaps he also knew that his unconventional interpretation of *li* (equating it with *taiji*) would not be received well because of the latter term's Daoist associations (see chapter 3). But by 1188 his dispute with Lu Jiuyuan on that very topic (see below) was in full swing, so he published the commentary at that time.[5]

Three years later, in 1173, Zhu wrote "An appreciation of portraits of the Six Masters [of the Northern Song]," the first of whom was Zhou Dunyi. He writes:

> The *dao* was [seemingly] lost for a thousand years, and the sages' distant words were hidden. Without having prior awareness, how could it have been revealed to us? The *Tongshu* would not have been fully expressed and the Diagram not fully conceived.[6]

In that same year he completed his influential history of the *daoxue* school, *Yi-Luo yuan-yuan lu* 伊洛淵源錄 (Sources of the Yi-Luo school), which likewise begins with a chapter on Zhou Dunyi.[7]

In 1177, Zhu wrote his most thorough discussion of Zhou's place in the "fate of the Way" or "succession of the Way" (*daotong*). This was a period in which he and Zhang Shi were active in building and writing commemorations for shrines honoring Zhou Dunyi and the Cheng brothers.[8] The text is the "Record of the reconstruction of Zhou Dunyi's library/study (*shutang* 書堂) in Jiangzhou." Jiangzhou (near present-day Jiujiang, in Jiangxi province) was the site of Zhou Dunyi's retirement home near Mount Lu. At the time of the reconstruction of Zhou's study Zhu Xi could not be present, but four years later he would make a pilgrimage there. The 1177 text reads as follows:

---

5. See his "Postface to Commentaries on the *Taiji* [*tu shuo*] and *Ximing* [Zhang Zai's 'Western Inscription']," *Wenji* 82:3880, translated in Part II.

6. *Wenji* 85:4001. The other five masters are Cheng Hao, Cheng Yi, Shao Yong, Zhang Zai, and Sima Guang, in that order.

7. In *Zhuzi quanshu*, 12:923–1113. Zhu separated out his biographical account of Zhou Dunyi in the *Yi Luo yuan-yuan lu,* presumably for circulation, in 1179 (*Wenji* 98:4558).

8. See Neskar, *The Cult of Worthies,* 225–42.

Record of the reconstruction of Zhou Dunyi's study in Jiangzhou
(*Jiangzhou chongjian Lianxi xiansheng shutang ji* 江州重建濂溪先生書堂記)

The Way has never been lost from the world. It is only that its being entrusted to man [to carry out] has sometimes been interrupted and sometimes been continuous. Thus in its practice in the world there have been periods of clarity and periods of obscurity. This is all the result of the Decree of Heaven (*tianming*); it is not something that the power of human wisdom is capable of achieving.

Of the variety of individual things produced and supported by the two [modes of] *qi* [i.e., *yin* and *yang*] and the Five Phases, in their mixed and confused rising and falling and coming and going throughout Heaven above and earth below, nothing lacks a definite pattern/order/principle (*li*). The greatest of these are the human nature [consisting] of humanity, rightness, propriety and wisdom,[9] and the human relations of master and servant, father and son, brothers, husband and wife, and friends.[10]

This being the case, the cyclical flow [of the *dao*] includes everything without exception.[11] So how can we think that the [alternation of] order and disorder from ancient times to the present is [evidence for] the existence and perishing [of the *dao*]?[12] In the circulation of *qi* there are inequalities [in terms] of homogeneity and heterogeneity, discontinuity and unity, so in the human endowment there are differences [in terms] of purity and turbidity, dullness and clarity. Therefore, how the *dao* is entrusted to man and carried out in the world is only due to what Heaven confers and humans receive. It is certainly not due to the clever and presumptuous individual's ability to speculate and conjecture. [For example] the River Chart (*Hetu* 河圖) came out [of the Yellow River] and the Eight Trigrams were drawn; the Luo Writing (*Luoshu* 洛書) appeared and

---

9. The "four constant virtues" in *Mencius* 2A.6 and 6A.6.

10. The "five human relations" in *Mencius* 3A.4 and *Zhongyong* 20.

11. That is, the *dao* is the dynamic flow of cosmic order (*li*), which is immanent throughout the natural and social worlds.

12. That is, although social and political order can break down, it is nevertheless the case that things happen for reasons. Thus, the presence of disorder in society does not mean that the natural and moral order (*li*) has ceased to exist.

the Nine Regions were arranged.¹³ Confucius, in reference to the flourishing and decline of "this culture" (*siwen* 斯文),¹⁴ never failed to attribute it to Heaven. It is clear that the Sage did not deceive us in regard to this.

As for Master [Zhou] Lianxi, if he did not receive the propagation of this *dao* conferred by Heaven, how did he continue it so easily after such a long interruption, and bring it to light so abruptly after such extreme darkness?

With the decline of the Zhou and the death of Mencius, the propagation of this *dao* was not continued; even less so from the Qin through the Han, Jin, Sui and Tang, until our Song. Then the Sage-ancestor [Taizu, founding father of the Song] received the Mandate. The Five Planets were in conjunction in Kui, marking a turning point in culture.¹⁵ Only then did the heterogeneous *qi* homogenize and

---

13. Paraphrasing *Yijing, Xici* (Appended remarks) A.11.8 (Zhu, *Zhouyi benyi* 3:15a). The River Chart was a numerological diagram that appeared to the mythical sage Fuxi on the back of a dragon horse coming out of the Yellow River, and was used by him in his creation of the hexagrams and divination system of the *Zhou Yi* (or *Yijing*, Scripture of Change). The Luo Writing was a similar drawing that appeared to the mythical Yu the Great (founder of the Xia dynasty) on the shell of a spirit-tortoise as he was controlling the flooding of the Yellow River, and figured into his laying out of the Nine Regions of ancient China. See Zhu, *Introduction to the Study of the Classic of Change*, 1–14. Both diagrams had been associated with the *Yijing* ever since the Han dynasty.

Zhu Xi's point here is that Fuxi and Yu were able to do what they did only because they happened to be exposed to the River Chart and Luo Writing. Similarly, the chance allotment of *qi* in each person's physical endowment determines "how the *dao* is entrusted to man and carried out in the world." Factors such as these, occurring either by chance or for unknowable yet completely natural reasons—i.e., factors beyond human control—are typically attributed to Heaven.

In other contexts, Zhu places more emphasis on another myth about Fuxi's creations of the *Yi*, according to which Fuxi intuits the *yin-yang* patterns from an exhaustive examination of heaven and earth. This is also found in the *Yijing* (*Xici* B.2.1, in Zhu, *Zhouyi benyi* 3:18a). Zhu regards this as a mythic paradigm of the "investigation of things."

14. See *Analects* 9:5: "If Heaven intended this culture to perish, it would not have given it to those of us who live after King Wen's death" (trans. Slingerland, *Confucius: Analects*, 87).

15. Kui, or "Straddler" in Edward H. Schafer's translation (*Pacing the Void*, 76), one of the twenty-eight "lunar lodges" (*xiu* 宿), was associated with Wenchang 文昌, the god of literature and civil service examinations (Williams, *Chinese Symbolism and Art Motifs*, 213–14).

the divided [*qi*] coalesce; a clear and bright endowment was received in its entirety by one man, and the Master [Zhou Dunyi] appeared. Without following a teacher (*shifu* 師傅), he silently registered the substance of the Way, constructed the Diagram and attached a text to it,[16] to give an ultimate foundation to the essentials.

At that time, the Chengs were among those who saw and knew him, and they subsequently expanded and clarified his teaching. They caused the subtlety of Heavenly principle, the manifest human relations, the multitude of phenomenal things, and the mystery of ghosts and spirits all to be fully joined together into one [system]. Thus the tradition of the Duke of Zhou, Confucius, and Mencius was brilliantly illuminated again in that era, and determined literati were able to study and respectfully practice [the Way], without losing its correctness, like those who appeared before the Three Dynasties [Xia, Shang and Zhou]. Ah! Such grandeur! Were it not for what Heaven conferred [on Zhou], how could we participate in this?

The Master was from the Zhou 周 family. His taboo name was Dunyi 敦頤,[17] his style name was Maoshu 茂叔; his family was from Chongling 舂陵.[18] He retired to the foot of Mount Lu 盧, naming the river there after one from his old village, Lianxi 濂溪 (Lian Stream). He took that as his honorific name and built his study on its bank. His grave is now ten *li* 里 south, in Jiujiang 九江 district, and has been overgrown for years.

. . . I have been fortunate to have heard the teachings of the Chengs, and consequently read the Master's writings and saw how he was as a man. . . . I have inquired into how the Master received the Way from Heaven and transmitted it to others, in order to likewise transmit the events of his life, to enable later gentlemen to contemplate, examine, and promote it.[19]

---

16. The "Discussion of the Supreme Polarity Diagram," translated below in Part II.

17. He changed his given name, Dunshi 敦實, to Dunyi in 1063 to avoid the personal name of the new emperor, Zhao Zongshi (Emperor Yingzong), even though Zhao Zongshi had changed his name to Zhao Shu in 1062.

18. In Hunan province. See chapter 1, note 45.

19. *Wenji* 78:3739–41. I have omitted two short sections in which Zhu Xi discusses the local officials responsible for the rebuilding of the study. The text is dated the seventh day of the second (lunar) month of 1177.

We see very clearly here Zhu Xi's concern with access to the *dao* across the long span of time since Mencius; with what Wm. Theodore de Bary has called "the struggle to repossess the Way" in the face of its apparent discontinuity.[20] Zhu discusses this problem in terms of three points: (1) the metaphysical status of the Confucian *dao* when it is not being put into practice; (2) the mechanism by which a sage can appear without benefit of a direct "mouth to ear" transmission from previous sages; and (3) the claim that it was Zhou Dunyi who first revived it after the 1400-year-long hiatus since Mencius. The first point concerns the larger context of the Song Confucian revival vis-à-vis the main rival for the affections of Song literati—Chan Buddhism—which we have already discussed. Given the vitality of Buddhism (and Daoism to a lesser extent) during the Song, it is not surprising that the question of access to the true *dao* was on Zhu Xi's mind. How could Song Confucians claim to have special access to their *dao* while simultaneously admitting that it had not been transmitted since Mencius? As he puts it, "Were it not for what Heaven conferred [on Zhou], how could we participate in this?" It was a crucial question, especially in view of the Chan claim to an unbroken line of mind-to-mind transmission from the Buddha, through Bodhidharma (the twenty-eighth Indian and first Chinese patriarch), right down to the present-day lineage-holders, all of whom could trace their master-disciple lineages directly to Huineng, the Sixth Patriarch.

The argument that the Confucian *dao* was directly accessible by sages such as Mencius and Zhou Dunyi, who could then transmit it to others, was a crucial strategy of legitimation for Song Confucians in the face of the strong competition from Chan Buddhism for the hearts and minds of literati. Ultimately, according to Zhu, this was the result of Heaven's decree, which is to say that it was natural and beyond human control. He makes this claim *six times* in the above text.

But what exactly does it mean to say it is "due to Heaven?" This question has an important bearing on what it means to be a Confucian sage. In one respect there seems to be an element of chance, in terms of Zhou Dunyi having been born when the five planets were in conjunction in a section of the heavens associated with the god of literature and examinations—the business of *ru* (scholars). It is also significant that Zhu stresses that "what Heaven confers and humans receive . . . is certainly not due to the clever and presumptuous individual's ability to speculate and conjecture"—seemingly

---

20. de Bary, *Neo-Confucian Orthodoxy*, 6.

minimizing the uniqueness of the sage. In a similar passage in the preface to his *Yixue qimeng* 易學啟蒙 (Introduction to the study of the *Yijing*), he says of the creation of the hexagram divination system by the primordial sage Fuxi,

> How could this have been achieved by the Sage's cogitation and wise deliberation? [I.e., it was not.] It was simply the naturalness of the particular phases of *qi*, formed into the patterns and images seen in the [River] Chart and [Luo] Writing, that exposed this to his mind, and he lent his hand to it.[21]

Here too we might be tempted to say that it is simply a matter of chance. But later in the *Yixue qimeng* he says of the Chart and Text, "They both originate from the intention (*yi* 意) of Heaven."[22] And in the piece translated above he says, "[N]othing lacks a definite *li*," which is to say that everything happens for a reason. Therefore, the attribution of these circumstances to Heaven does not simply relegate it all to chance. A better way to understand it is in terms of David Hall's and Roger Ames's concept of "aesthetic order." This is the idea that meaning in Chinese thought emerges from the shifting patterns of exigent circumstances; meaning is not imposed on those circumstances by correspondence with a transcendent principle.[23] In this case, the shifting patterns of *qi* in the cosmos produced the "one man" (a term normally used by the emperor in reference to himself) who had the "psycho-physical nature" (*qizhizhi xing* 氣質之性) to enable him to intuit the Way directly.

We are dealing here with the slippery conception of Heaven (*tian* 天) in Confucian thought. Heaven seems to have a will or a mind (Cheng Yi had spoken of "the mind of Heaven and Earth to produce things"),[24] but that seeming intentionality is revealed in *natural* processes. In other words, natural, nonintentional processes result in events that seemed to be intentional—as in the modern understanding of biological evolution, which is *directional* but not *directed*. The classical "Mandate of Heaven" (*tianming* 天命) similarly

---

21. Zhu Xi, *Yixue qimeng*, 1203.

22. Ibid., 1210.

23. Hall and Ames, *Thinking Through Confucius*, 11–25, 131–38.

24. This is from Cheng Yi's commentary on hexagram 24 (Fu, Return) of the *Yijing* (*Er Cheng ji*, 819; Smith, Bol, Adler, and Wyatt, *Sung Dynasty Uses of the I Ching*, 247). Cheng Yi also said, "The Way spontaneously produces all things" (*Er Cheng ji*, 149; Chan, *Source Book*, 553).

straddled this line between intentional and nonintentional action. Most people probably understood it as the willful choice of Heaven—conceived as an at least partly personalistic deity—to remove the authority to rule from one family and confer it on another, like the Biblical God choosing a person to be his prophet.[25] As early as the classical Confucian philosopher Xunzi (third century BCE), though, some understood Heaven to be simply the natural world (surely Xunzi was not the only person to do so). Although Zhu Xi likewise leaned toward the naturalistic side of the spectrum,[26] he still retains a sense of transcendence in his conception of Heaven. His view of the appearance of sages such as Fuxi and Zhou Dunyi is, I think it is fair to say, a Neo-Confucian analogue of *revelation*.

The "heavenly" origin or basis of Zhou's sagely mind allowed Zhu Xi to anchor *daoxue* in a source of transcendent moral authority entirely independent of the political sphere, with its corrupt personal motives, its factional strife, and its increasing scarcity of government positions for the growing class of successful examination candidates. This was an alternative, especially for literati without positions in government, to the moral authority of the Mandate of Heaven, which flowed through the emperor.[27] It was part of a trend among Song literati (well documented in recent literature) to shift their frames of reference away from the central government toward more local concerns.[28]

Zhu Xi's answer to the question of the metaphysical status of the Way during periods when it is not being practiced or taught is that it still resides in human nature (*xing*), and in fact is immanent in the *li* that orders the

---

25. See de Bary's discussion of the prophetic nature of "repossessing the Way" in his *The Trouble with Confucianism*, and my review of the book in *Journal of Chinese Religions*, no. 21 (1993): 137–42, where I discuss the "prophetic" issue.

26. He also interprets "ghosts and spirits" (*gui-shen* 鬼神) as natural manifestations of *qi*: "*Gui* and *shen* are nothing more than the growth and dispersion of *yin* and *yang*. . . . That which alternately contracts and expands is *qi*. Within Heaven-and-earth there is nothing that is not *qi*. Human *qi* and the *qi* of Heaven-and-earth are constantly interacting, with no interruption" (quoted in Hu Guang, *Xingli daquan shu*, 28:2a, 2b, 609). See my discussion of this in Adler, "Varieties of Spiritual Experience: *Shen* in Neo-Confucian Discourse," 122–28.

27. The dynamics of this process have been described by Peter Bol and Patricia Ebrey, among others. Bol has argued that the followers of *daoxue* were concerned to establish direct access to the Way as a basis for values rooted in Heaven-and-earth, independent of the cultural tradition (Bol, "Cheng Yi and the Cultural Tradition"). Ebrey has shown how Sung Confucians developed new guidelines for ancestral rites appropriate to literati without office (Ebrey, *Confucianism and Family Rituals*, ch. 3).

28. See, for example, Hymes, *Statesmen and Gentlemen,* and Neskar, *The Cult of Worthies.*

universe. But the human moral nature is obscured by the impure physical natures (*qizhizhi xing*) with which people are endowed at birth. In other contexts Zhu refers to these two aspects of human nature as the "moral mind" (*daoxin* 道心), which is its *li*, and the "human mind" (*renxin* 人心), which is the *qi* that is ordered by the *li*. The variations in physical endowments are due to factors beyond human control—i.e., they are due to Heaven—such as the quality of *qi* surrounding one's birth and the positions of the five planets. Thus, the same factors that determine the extreme difficulty—and the possibility—of individuals being able to see and put into practice their own moral nature accounts for both the extreme scarcity of sages in history and the possibility of their appearance.[29] Zhou Dunyi was fortunate enough to have been born with an extremely fine constitution of *qi,* which enabled him to see the Way directly. That is, he did not find it in the classics, as in Cheng Yi's account of Cheng Hao. Nor did he get it from the previous sage, Mencius. Zhou Dunyi in this respect was like Fuxi, the very first sage, who had intuited the Way directly from the patterns in heaven and earth.[30]

As already mentioned, Shi Jie had been the first to push the origins of the Way back beyond Yao, Shun, and Yu to the primordial sages Fuxi, Shennong, and Huangdi—to the very origins of Chinese civilization. Fuxi, in particular, was a sage par excellence for Zhu Xi. With his spiritual intelligence (*shenming* 神明) he had intuited the moral principles inherent in the natural world, and on that basis had constructed the oracular system of the hexagrams that formed the core of the *Yijing,* the first and most profound of the Confucian scriptures. Thus, according to Zhu Xi, Fuxi's creation of the *Yi* was the first cultural manifestation of the Confucian *dao*; it symbolized the continuity of the natural order (*tianli* 天裡) and the moral order (*daoli* 道理)—the linkage of cosmology and ethics—which has been a fundamental assumption of the Confucian worldview since its beginnings.[31]

---

29. Cheng Yi had first made this connection, and had also said that the *dao* can never expire (*Henan Chengshi yishu* 17, in *Er Cheng ji,* 176).

30. See Neskar, *The Cult of Worthies,* 382–92.

31. The linkage of cosmology and ethics is implicit in the doctrine of the Mandate of Heaven (*tianming*), which is found in the *Scripture of Odes* (*Shijing*) and the *Scripture of Documents* (*Shujing*) and is attributed to the Duke of Zhou. The Mandate of Heaven is the idea that Heaven confers the authority of dynastic rule on a particular family based on its virtue or moral power (*de*), and removes that mandate when the dynasty's virtue dissipates. Since Heaven (*tian*) had both naturalistic and personalistic characteristics, but with more emphasis on the former, this implies that nature has a moral dimension, as it responds to human virtue. For more on Fuxi and the *Yijing*, see Smith et al., *Sung Dynasty Uses of the I Ching,* 175–77, 222–23.

Fuxi, being the first sage, could only have perceived the *dao* on his own. His ability was natural and spontaneous (*ziran* 自然), which is to say that it was "given by Heaven." The same was true of Zhou Dunyi:

> Only the Master's Learning of the Way was profoundly excellent; he received its transmission from Heaven. He succeeded Confucius and Master Yan [Hui], and in turn enlightened (*qi* 啟) the Chengs. He enabled students of that generation to perceive a thousand generations of past sages and worthies, as if hearing their voices and seeing their faces [like Chan students with their masters]. Giving and receiving in a direct line, ordering all affairs, handing down the eternal without failing to be correct, his merit was extremely abundant. Since Mencius there have been none [like him].[32]

Like Fuxi, Zhou Dunyi perceived the Way directly; he "rose up from beneath [the weight of] a hundred generations, . . . apprehended it [the Way] with his mind alone,"[33] and actualized the trans-temporal continuity of the Way. Both had intuited the Way on their own, without benefit of prior teachers. In other words, even though there had been an earlier transmission before Zhou Dunyi, it had stopped with Mencius, fourteen hundred years earlier—a much longer gap than those identified by Mencius or Shi Jie. As Cheng Yi had said in his eulogy for Cheng Hao, "[A]fter the death of Mencius the teaching of the sages was not transmitted."[34] And Zhou's retrieval of the Way did not come from books—he saw the Way directly, just as Fuxi had. Perhaps this is one of the reasons why both Fuxi and Zhou Dunyi are closely associated with diagrams (*tu* 圖): their ideas were so subtle as to transcend the capacity of words to express them.[35]

---

32. *"Feng'an Lianxi xiansheng ciwen"* (Commemoration of the shrine to Master Lianxi at Feng'an, 1179), *Wenji* 86:4038. See also *Nianpu*, 623.

33. *"Yuanzhou zhouxue san xiansheng ciji"* (Commemoration of the shrine to the Three Masters at the Yuanzhou prefectural school, 1178), translated more fully below; *Wenji* 78:3743. Cf. Qian, *Zhuzi xin xue'an*, 3:56.

34. *Er Cheng ji* 2:640 (see chapter 1 above).

35. In addition to creating the Eight Trigrams, Fuxi is also associated with the "Prior Heaven" (or "Prior-to-Heaven" or "A Priori") sequence of the trigrams and hexagrams, in which the diagrams are ordered in a binary number sequence. The Cheng brothers' friend, Shao Yong built his entire philosophy on the a priori order of such binary operations. See, for example, Birdwhistell, *Transition to Neo-Confucianism*.

In 1181, Zhu Xi, along with a group of disciples and friends (including one Buddhist monk), made a pilgrimage to Zhou Dunyi's retirement home on Mount Lu (Jiangxi province), where the library he had commemorated in 1177 had been reconstructed. Afterward he wrote a poem:

Going north I crossed the Stone Pond Bridge,
Going west I visited Lianxi's home.
Of stately trees, not one remains,
The empty halls, only four walls.
I reverently gaze at the virtuous face [Zhou's portrait].
On my knees I make offerings by the blue cold stream.
How fortunate to have had this man!
He once again opened the Undifferentiated [*hundun* 混沌].³⁶

The last line is an allusion to Fuxi, who first created order from chaos by initiating the Confucian *dao*. This connection between Zhou Dunyi and Fuxi was later repeated by Zhu Xi's disciples.³⁷ As Neskar puts it, "Zhou Dunyi has become, like Fuxi, an inspired creator of a new civilization and cultural order. The link between Zhou Dunyi and Fuxi in effect endows the culture that Zhou created and the Way he revived with the authority of the highest of antiquity and the first creation of civilization in China's history."³⁸ She also points out that Zhu Xi's claim that Zhou got the Way directly from Heaven, not from any texts, "obviated any need to seek the historical origins of Zhou's learning."³⁹ This is significant in light of Zhu's arguments with Lu Jiuyuan ten years later about the possible Daoist origins of Zhou's *Taijitu* (Supreme Polarity Diagram).

Although Zhu Xi did not find much guidance for moral cultivation in Shao Yong's writings, he made considerable use of Shao's cosmological and numerological ideas, e.g., in his *Yixue qimeng* (Introduction to the Study of the *Yi*). For more on *tu* see the Introduction to the *Taiji* Diagram below.

36. *Wenji* 7:492, translated by Neskar, *The Cult of Worthies*, 388–89.

37. E.g., Chen Chun (1159–1223), in his essay "The Source of Teachers and Friends" (*shi you yuanyuan*), translated by Chan, *Neo-Confucian Terms Explained*, 178–82, partly quoted below.

38. Neskar, *The Cult of Worthies*, 391.

39. Ibid., 383.

By establishing Fuxi as the first Confucian sage, Zhu Xi was making the implicit claim that the Confucian *dao* was coeval with Chinese civilization itself. In other words, Confucianism—not Buddhism, not Daoism—was China's most authentic *dao*. By establishing Zhou Dunyi in a parallel position as the first sage of the Song, Zhu Xi was claiming that the teacher of the Cheng brothers had revived this same *dao*. Therefore, it was the Cheng school—not Chen Liang's "utilitarian" approach to the Way, not Lu Jiuyuan's "idealistic" approach—that deserved the allegiance of literati and official support from the government.

Zhu Xi's version of the full lineage of Confucian sages, from the earliest times through the Song, was as follows:[40]

- Fuxi (traditionally dated to the twenty-seventh century BCE), the inventor of the hexagrams of the *Zhouyi* 周易 or *Yijing* (Scripture of Change), as well as nets for hunting and fishing;

- Shennong (twenty-sixth century BCE), the Divine Farmer, inventor of agriculture;

- Huangdi (twenty-fifth century BCE), the Yellow Emperor, inventor of government;

- Yao, Shun, and Yu (twentieth century BCE), mythic sage-kings, the last being the founder of the Xia dynasty;

- King Tang 湯 (eighteenth century BCE), founder of the Shang dynasty;

- Kings Wen 文 and Wu 武 and the Duke of Zhou 周公 (twelfth century BCE), first rulers of the Zhou dynasty;

- Confucius (Kongzi 孔子, 551–479 BCE);

- Yanzi 顏子 (Yan Hui 顏回, 521?–481? BCE) Confucius's favorite disciple, admired especially by both Zhou Dunyi and Cheng Yi;

- Zengzi 曾子 (Zeng Shen/Can 曾參, 505?–435? BCE), Confucius's senior disciple; reputed author of the *Daxue* 大學 (Great Learning);[41]

---

40. Chan, "Chu Hsi's Completion," 121–22.

41. Zeng Shen and You Ruo are the only two of Confucius's disciples who are referred to in the *Lunyu* as "Master." This may mean that the earliest stratum of the *Lunyu* was compiled by their students. See Dawson, *The Analects*, 83.

- Zisi 子思 (Kong Ji 孔伋, 483?–402? BCE), Confucius's grandson, possibly Zengzi's disciple and possibly Mencius's teacher; reputed author of the *Zhongyong* 中庸 (Centrality and Commonality);[42]
- Mencius (Mengzi 孟子, fourth century BCE);
- Zhou Dunyi;
- Cheng Hao and Cheng Yi;
- Zhu Xi himself (by implication; his students made the explicit claim after his death).[43]

Mencius had called the earlier part of this lineage the "Way of the sages" (*shengrenzhi dao*). Zhu Xi used a different term, *daotong* 道統, or "succession of the Way."[44] It appears most prominently in the 1189 preface to his commentary on the *Zhongyong*, which we will examine more closely later. The term had originally been used in reference to Song Emperor Gaozong (r. 1127–1163) as the successor to the Way of the sages.[45] Zhu Xi first used it in 1179 and in 1181, both times in reference to Zhou Dunyi. In 1179 he said:

> Master Lianxi was concerned about transmitting the succession of the way (*chuan daotong* 傳道統) of the mind/heart of the Duke of Zhou, and was the first of the age to realize it.[46]

---

42. The traditional attribution of the *Zhongyong* to Confucius's grandson is widely rejected by modern scholars. See, e.g., Plaks, *Ta Hsüeh and Chung Yung*, 118–22.

43. E.g., Huang Gan, Chen Chun, and Zhen Dexiu. See Chan, *New Studies*, 325–27.

44. It is tempting to translate it as "transmission of the Way," but then one would be left with the problem how to translate *"daotongzhi chuan"* 道統之傳 where *chuan* means "handing down" or transmission. In fact the modern vernacular word for tradition is *chuantong* 傳統.

45. Until recently it was thought that Zhu Xi had coined the term *daotong*. But Cho-ying Li and Charles Hartman discovered an 1155 inscription by the "appeasement" Chief Councilor Qin Gui in which he used the term in reference to the Emperor Gaozong (r. 1127–1163) as the successor to the Way of the sages, not private individuals such as the Chengs. See Li and Hartman, "A Newly Discovered Inscription by Qin Gui: Its Implications for the History of Song *Daoxue*." This discovery throws new light upon Zhu Xi's use of the term: it is much more of a direct challenge to imperial authority than previously thought. See above, note 27. "*Daotong*" alludes to the older expression *zhengtong*, "legitimate [dynastic] succession," which has a less explicitly moral connotation (see Bol, "*This Culture of Ours*," 369 n. 124).

46. *Wenji* 99:4582. See also Chu Ping-tzu, "*Ping Yu Yingshi xiansheng de Zhu Xi de lishi shijie: Songdai shidafu zhengzhi wenhua de yanjiu*," 295.

His second use of *daotong* was his 1181 account of his pilgrimage to Zhou's retirement home (mentioned above), where he says:

> In the eighth year of Chunxi [1181], a *xinchou* 辛丑 year, on the sixth day of the fourth month (summer), the later scholars Zhu Xi [etc., naming eleven others], reverently prayed before Master Lianxi's study. Only the Master received Heaven's gift and continued the succession of the Way (*daotong*), in order to connect the beginnings and ends and to help us later men.[47]

Tong 統 clearly implies continuity or connection. By using this term Zhu Xi was making an implicit claim that, despite the evident historical *dis*continuities in the propagation of the Way, there was in fact some basis for his claim to have access to the Way of the ancient sages.

Between 1169 and 1196, when the ban on the *daoxue* school began, Zhu Xi wrote, by my count, twenty-two pieces about Zhou Dunyi—not including discussions of Zhou in letters. In sixteen of them Zhu either explicitly affirms or implies that Zhou was the first sage of the Song. Seven of them were commemorations of local shrines to Zhou himself or to Zhou and the Cheng brothers (the Three Masters). The complete list is as follows, with an asterisk indicating an item in which Zhu clearly says or implies that it was Zhou Dunyi who first recovered the *dao*:

1. ★1169: "Postface to Master Zhou's *Taiji* and *Tongshu*" (*Zhouzi Taiji Tongshu houxu* 周子太極通書後序)[48]
2. ★1173: "Final notes to commentary on *Taijitu shuo*" (*Taijitushuo jie houji* 太極圖說解後記)[49]
3. ★1173: "Master Lianxi" (*Lianxi xiansheng* 濂溪先生): first part of "Appreciation of the portraits of the Six Masters" (*Liu xiansheng huaxiang zan* 六先生畫像贊)[50]

---

47. "*Shu Lianxi guangfeng jiyue ting*" (On Lianxi's pavilion of the light breeze and clear moon), in *Wenji* 84:3984. Also in *Zhou Lianxi ji* 9, along with accounts by five of Zhu's traveling companions.

48. *Wenji* 75:3628–30; *Nianpu*, 412.

49. *Zhuzi quanshu*, vol. 13:79; *Zhou Lianxi ji*, 1:38a–39a; *Nianpu*, 487; translated below, 196–97. Preceding this postface is an undated section called "Discussions" (*lun*) or "Appended arguments" (*fubian*); translated below, 198-200.

50. *Wenji* 85:4001–4002; *Nianpu*, 501.

4. ★1173: "Master Lianxi's deeds" (*Lianxi xiansheng shizhuang* 濂溪先生事狀): first section of Zhu's *Yi Luo yuan-yuan lu* 伊洛淵源錄 (his history of the Cheng school)[51]

5. 1176: "Three poems on Mr. Zhou's stream garden" (*Ti Zhoushi xiyuan sanshou* 題周氏溪園三首)[52]

6. ★1177: "Record of the reconstruction of Zhou Dunyi's study hall in Jiangzhou" (*Jiangzhou chongjian Lianxi xiansheng shutang ji* 江州重建濂溪先生書堂記)[53]

7. ★1178: "Essay commemorating the shrine to the Three Masters at the Yuanzhou prefectural school" (*Yuanzhou zhouxue san xiansheng ciwen* 袁州州學三先生祠記)[54]

8. 1179: "Postface to Master Zhou's *Tongshu* printed in Wuyuan county, Huizhou" (*Shu Huizhou Wuyuan xian Zhouzi Tongshu banben hou* 書徽州婺源縣周子通書板本後)[55]

9. ★1179: "Essay commemorating the shrine to Master Lianxi at Feng'an" (*Feng'an Lianxi xiansheng ciwen* 奉安濂溪先生祠文)[56]

10. ★1179: "Postface to revised *Taiji* [*tushuo*] and *Tongshu*" (*Zaiding Taiji Tongshu houxu* 再定太極通書後序)[57]

11. 1179: "Postface to Master Zhou's 'Loving the Lotus'" (*Shu Lianxi xiansheng "Ailianshuo" hou* 書濂溪先生愛蓮說後)[58]

---

51. *Yiluo yuan-yuan lu*, in *Zhuzi quanshu*, vol. 12:923. In this case it is the placement of the section on Zhou, not the text itself, that indicates his precedence over the Chengs. The section is also found in *Wenji* 98:4558, entitled "Actual record of Master Lianxi's deeds" (*Lianxi xiansheng shi shiji*).

52. *Wenji* 6:414; *Nianpu*, 555.

53. *Wenji* 78:3739–41; *Nianpu*, 580.

54. *Wenji* 78:3743–44; *Nianpu*, 609.

55. *Wenji* 81:3840; *Nianpu*, 612. This was a postface to an edition of the *Tongshu* published by someone else. Although I have not awarded this piece an asterisk, it does include the line, "Since this book [the *Tongshu*] brings to light (*faming*) the tradition of sagely learning, scholars cannot fail to read it."

56. *Wenji* 86:4038; *Nianpu*, 623.

57. *Wenji* 76:3652–54; *Nianpu*, 628.

58. *Wenji* 81:3844; *Nianpu*, 635.

12. 1179: "Postface to Master Zhou's 'Rhapsody on Dullness'" (*Shu Lianxi xiansheng "Zhuofu" hou* 書濂溪先生拙賦後)⁵⁹

13. ★1179: "Record of the shrine to Master Lianxi at the Longxing prefectural school" (*Longxing fuxue Lianxi xiansheng ciji* 隆興府學濂溪先生祠記)⁶⁰

14. ★1181: "On Lianxi's pavilion of the light breeze and clear moon" (*Shu Lianxi guangfeng jiyue ting* 書濂溪光風霽月亭)⁶¹

15. ★1181: "Essay commemorating the shrine to the Three Masters at the Wuyuan county school at Huizhou" (*Huizhou Wuyuan xianxue san xiansheng ciwen* 徽州婺源縣學三先生祠記)⁶²

16. ★1183: "Record of the shrine to Master Lianxi at the Shaozhou [Guangxi] prefectural school" (*Shaozhou zhouxue Lianxi xiansheng ciji* 韶州州學濂溪先生祠記)⁶³

17. ★1187: "Postface [or Preface] to Master Zhou's *Tongshu*" (*Zhouzi Tongshu houji* 周子通書後記)⁶⁴

18. 1188: "Postface to Commentaries on [Zhou Dunyi's] *Taiji[tu shuo]* and [Zhang Zai's] *Ximing*" (*Ti Taiji Ximing jie hou* 題太極西銘解後)⁶⁵

---

59. *Wenji* 81:3845; *Nianpu*, 635.
60. *Wenji* 78:3747–49; *Nianpu*, 641.
61. *Wenji* 84:3984–85; *Nianpu*, 698, 701.
62. *Wenji* 79: 3760–61; *Nianpu*, 708. In this piece the relevant statement is quoted by Zhu, with obvious approval, from the letter of invitation to write the essay that he received from Zhou Hou, the official who built the shrine. Zhou Hou says, "Only the learning of Master Lianxi [reveals] the nature of Heaven, [makes] the self authentic, and connects with the tradition of the former sages" (3760).
63. *Wenji* 79: 3768–70; *Nianpu*, 770.
64. *Wenji* 81:3856; *Nianpu*, 871. In *Wenji* 81 and in *Zhou Dunyi ji* (Beijing: Zhonghua shuju, 1990) this is called a postface, but in *Zhou Lianxi ji* (ch. 5) and *Zhuzi quanshu* (v. 13) it is the preface to the *Tongshu* (similarly below in Part II).
65. *Wenji* 82:3880; *Nianpu*, 886. Zhu had written these commentaries in the early 1170s. See above p. 38, and Tillman, *Confucian Discourse*, 209.

19. 1188: "Notes on [Zhou] Lianxi's biography" (*Ji Lianxi zhuan* 記濂溪傳)[66]

20. ★1193: "Record of the shrine to Master Lianxi at the Shaozhou [Hunan] prefectural school" (*Shaozhou zhouxue Lianxi xiansheng ciji* 韶州州學濂溪先生祠記)[67]

21. ★1194: "Essay in homage to the reconstructed shrine to the Three Masters at Daozhou" (*Ye xiu Daozhou san xiansheng ciwen* 謁修道州三先生祠文)[68]

22. ★1194: "Report to the Former Sage at [the completion of] the Cangzhou [Zhulin] retreat" (*Cangzhou jingshe gao xiansheng wen* 滄州精舍告先聖文)[69]

Mention should also be made of the *Jinsilu* 近思錄 ("Reflections on Things at Hand"), the compilation of sayings by Zhou Dunyi, Zhang Zai, and the Cheng brothers that Zhu Xi and Lü Zuqian compiled in 1175 for use as an introduction to the first generation of *daoxue* thinkers. The first item in it, in the chapter called "The substance of the *dao*," is Zhou Dunyi's *Taijitu shuo*.[70]

Zhu Xi was not alone in writing such shrine commemorations. The earliest ones were written by members of the Hu family. As early as 1159, Hu Quan 胡銓, a relative of Hu Anguo and Hu Hong, wrote a commemoration for the shrine to Zhou Dunyi at Daozhou, his birthplace, that had been

---

66. *Wenji* 71: 3410; *Nianpu*, 910. This is a response to the official biography of Zhou Dunyi written by Hong Mai (1123–1202). Hong had inserted two words into the first sentence of Zhou's *Taijitu shuo*, making it read "From *wuji* comes *taiji*." Zhu objected to this because it implied a temporal sequence, making them two different things, contrary to his interpretation that *wuji* simply indicates the undifferentiation of *taiji* (to be discussed in chapter 4).

67. *Wenji* 80: 3803–04; *Nianpu*, 1098.

68. *Wenji* 86: 4049; *Nianpu*, 1133.

69. *Wenji* 86: 4050–51; *Nianpu*, 1199. According to Wing-tsit Chan, the name of this retreat (or "study") was changed from Zhulin to Cangzhou sometime after Zhu Xi's death and before the compilation of the *Wenji* in 1532 (*New Studies* 340–43). For a translation of this prayer see Tillman, "Zhu Xi's Prayers to Confucius," 503–504.

70. This, however, does not necessarily imply that Zhou was the first to recover the *dao*. For the *Jinsilu* see *Zhuzi quanshu*, vol. 13, and many other editions (English translation by Wing-tsit Chan, *Reflections on Things at Hand*).

built in 1135 (also commemorated by both Zhu Xi and Zhang Shi). In it he quotes Hu Anguo, who said, "When I read the recorded conversations of [the Chengs of] Henan, I saw that the source of the Chengs' [learning] was Zhou Lianxi."[71]

The seventh item listed above ("Essay commemorating the shrine to the Three Masters at the Yuanzhou prefectural school," 1178) is a good example of Zhu Xi's shrine commemorations. The person who built the shrine, identified here as "his honor Zhang of Guanghan," is Zhang Shou 張守, the brother of Zhang Shi (who also wrote a commemoration for this occasion).[72]

> When his honor Zhang of Guanghan, Prefect of Yichun [city, in Yuanzhou, Jiangxi], renovated the district school, he established a shrine to the Three Masters, [Zhou] Lianxi and [the two Chengs of] Henan, in the eastern wing of the lecture hall. So he sent me a letter asking me to commemorate it.
>
> Since the death of Mencius of Zou, the Way of the Sages had not been transmitted; what was commonly called the learning of the scholars (*ru*) was limited to the practice of punctuating essays and was mixed up with the sayings of Laozi and the Buddhists. The means by which to cultivate the self and to rule (*zhi*) others[73] accordingly appeared as the forced action of individual wisdom; it was superficial and removed, and did not emphasize [self-] mastery. This prevented gentlemen's virtues from being as great as in the Three Dynasties [Xia, Shang, Zhou], and the people's customs from being as healthy as in the Three Dynasties. It was like this for more than a thousand years.
>
> Master Zhou Lianxi rose up from beneath [the weight of] a hundred generations and was the first to deeply explore the profundity of the sages and worthies. He effortlessly contemplated the source of creation and apprehended it with his mind alone. He set up the image [the *Taiji* Diagram] and wrote the text [*Tongshu*], disclosing hidden secrets. Although his words were brief, the subtlety of the

---

71. Neskar, *The Cult of Worthies,* 222. Hu Anguo seems to have been inconsistent on this point. See chapter 1, note 54.

72. Ibid., 229.

73. "Cultivating the self" and "ruling others" refer to the two poles of Confucian practice mentioned earlier: perfecting the self and perfecting society.

innate endowment of Heaven and humanity and the essentials of cultivating the self and ruling others were completely presented.

When the two Chengs from Henan met him and received his transmission, his learning was spread throughout the world. When scholars discussed his theories they were finally able to dismiss the superficiality of common learning and the confusions of heterodoxy. His ideas about cultivating the self and ruling others eventually stood out and were no longer confused by the individual benefit and harm of common customs;[74] [scholar-officials] generously determined to make the relations between rulers and people like those of Yao and Shun.

So the Three Masters' contributions to that era were not small. But when those who discuss them fail to examine their learning and seize on the differences in clarity and obscurity or past and present,[75] no one understands them completely and some criticize them. As for those who only know them cursorily, they "neglect what is near but seek the distant" or "stay low but search for what is high."[76] They understand neither fully investigating principle in affairs nor seeking the solution in the reality of cultivating the self and ruling others. Alas! This must be the reason why his honor Zhang created this shrine and wrote to me.[77]

Other examples of the shrine commemoration genre include Wang Ge 汪格, the prefect of Shaozhou, where Zhou Dunyi had served as sub-prefect

---

74. I.e., they rejected what today we would call careerism (learning for the sake of passing the civil service examinations and gaining a government position), and turned back to learning for the purpose of becoming a sage.

75. I.e., rejecting the Northern Song masters either because of the difficulty of some of their writings (especially the *Taijitu shuo*) or because they are too recent, lacking the authority of the earlier sages.

76. The first phrase, *she jin qiu yuan* 舍近求遠, is an idiom based on *Mencius* 4A.11, "The Way lies at hand but it is sought afar off" (trans. D. C. Lau, *Mencius*). A variant, *she jin mou yuan* 舍近謀遠, is found in *Hou Han shu*, ch. 18. The second phrase, *chu xia kui gaoi* 處下窺高, is probably based on *Mencius* 4A.1, "For height one must start from a mound or hill; for depth one must start from a valley or marsh" (my trans.).

77. "Yuanzhou zhouxue san xiansheng ciji" (Commemoration of the shrine to the Three Masters at the Yuanzhou prefectural school), *Wenji* 78:3743–44.

in 1067, who built a shrine to Zhou at the prefectural school in 1179.[78] In his commemorative essay Wang says:

> For more than 1,000 years after the death of Mencius, the learning of the sages had not been illumined. The master [Zhou] alone obtained it in his mind-and-heart. He set up the *Diagram* and wrote [the *Tongshu*], clarifying the mysteries. The two masters Cheng of Henan personally transmitted his teachings, and later scholars were able to share in knowing this Way.[79]

Zhang Shi and others in the Hunan school were also writing such pieces. Here, for example, is Zhang Shi's preface to the *Taijitu shuo*:

Preface to Master Zhou's Explanation of the Taiji Diagram (*Zhouzi taijitujie xu* 周子太極圖解序),[80] by Zhang Shi

> The two Cheng brothers' tradition of the Learning of the Way (*daoxue*) appeared with Master Zhou Lianxi in the mystery of the *Taiji Diagram*, which he apprehended himself and handed down to them. The brevity of its words and the subtlety of its meanings had not existed since Mencius. The discussions in the *Tongshu* basically bring to light its intentions. For example, [the *Tongshu*'s] first section says:
>
>> Being authentic is the foundation of the sage. "Great indeed is the originating [power] of Qian! The myriad things rely on it for their beginnings."[81] It is the source of being authentic. "The way of Qian transforms and each receives

---

78. This shrine was for Zhou Dunyi and Zhang Jiucheng, a student of the Cheng brothers, because both had served as local officials there. Zhu Xi's commemoration in 1193 was for a different shrine at the same school, for Zhou Dunyi alone.
79. Translated by Neskar, *The Cult of Worthies*, 232.
80. *Zhang Shi quanji*, supplement, 1180–81.
81. *Yijing*, *Tuan* commentary on hexagram 1 (Qian 乾, symbolizing Heaven). See Zhu Xi, *Zhouyi benyi* (The Original Meaning of the *Scripture of Change*), 1:3a.

its correct nature and endowment." In this way authenticity is established.[82]

In saying that the foundation of the sage is the source of being authentic, this profoundly clarifies the source of the myriad things and displays the sage's essential profundity. This is precisely what the *Yi* calls "secret" (*mi* 密) and the *Zhongyong* calls "without sound or smell."[83] "The way of Qian transforms and each receives its correct nature and endowment" is the appearance of the flowing forth of the original substance; hence it says, "In this way authenticity is established." The [*Tongshu* also] says:

> The Five Phases are *yin* and *yang*; [*yin* and *yang* are] the Supreme Polarity. The Four Seasons revolve; the myriad things end and begin [again]. How undifferentiated! How extensive! And how endless![84]

The tradition of the Learning of the Way (*daoxue*) is really in this. While I am dull, not bright, together with my friend [Zhu Xi] I acknowledge and raise this point.

Zhang also wrote a commentary on the *Taijitu shuo*,[85] a postface to the *Tongshu*,[86] and commemorations of five shrines to Zhou

---

82. Ibid. See Part II for the *Tongshu*.

83. "Secret" is a reference to *Yijing, Xici* A.11.2: "The Sage uses them [the spiritual powers of the milfoil and hexagrams] to purify his mind and retire into secrecy" (*Zhouyi benyi* 3:13b). "Without sound and smell" is from *Zhongyong* 33, quoted from *Shijing* ode 235: "The operations of Heaven have neither sound nor smell" (trans. Chan, *Source Book,* 113). Zhu Xi uses this sentence in his interpretation of the first line of Zhou Dunyi's *Taijitu shuo* (*wuji er taiji*).

84. *Tongshu* 16.

85. Su Xuansheng, *"Zhang Shi taiji jieyi"* (Zhang Shi's explanation of the meaning of *taiji*), in Chen Lai, ed., *Zaoqi daoxue huayu de xingcheng yu yanbian,* 517. I am relying on Tillman and Soffel, "Zhang Shi's Philosophical Perspectives" (136), for the name Su Xuansheng, as no authors are listed in Chen's book. For the preface and postface to this commentary see *Zhang Shi quanji,* supplement: 1180–81.

86. *Zhang Shi quanji,* 33:1007–1008.

Dunyi.⁸⁷ In the postface to his commentary on the *Taijitu* he deals with the question why the term *taiji* does not appear in the writings or recorded conversations of the Cheng brothers. He says:

> I respond by saying that while the two Cheng masters did not encounter this diagram, nevertheless their theories were definitely based on it. If you examine this closely it should be self-evident. If students are authentically able to conduct their affairs with reverent composure and truly exert continuous effort, then in the incipient juncture (*ji* 幾) between activity and stillness they will deeply experience the extent of its [the diagram's] profound subtlety, and the mystery of this diagram will silently register in their breast. Otherwise, even if they debate in detail it will not be advantageous. Alas, the Teacher's statements about the "penetrating [quality] of authenticity" and the "recovery of authenticity" [*Tongshu* 1] are perfect indeed!⁸⁸

"The incipient juncture between activity and stillness" refers to the point at which a mental stimulus has been received but a response has not yet begun. In the terminology of the *Zhongyong*, this is the moment between

---

87. 1. *"Daozhou zhongjin Lianxi Zhou xiansheng citang ji"* (Record of the rebuilding of the sacrificial hall for Zhou Lianxi in Daozhou) (*Zhang Shi quanji* 10:698–99);

2. *"Yongzhou zhouxue Zhou xiansheng citang ji"* (Record of the sacrificial hall for Zhou Lianxi at the Yongzhou prefectural school) (ibid., 10:703–704);

3. *"Lianxi Zhou xiansheng citang ji"* (Record of the sacrificial hall for Zhou Lianxi [at Shaozhou]) (ibid., 10:704–706);

4. *"Nankang jun xinli Lianxi ci ji"* (Record of the reestablishment of sacrifices to [Zhou] Lianxi at the Nankang military [school?]) (ibid.,10:706–707); and

5. *"San xiansheng ci ji"* (Record of sacrifice to the Three Teachers) (ibid., 10:707–708).

In all of these Zhang confirms that the Cheng brothers' learning came from Zhou Dunyi. Two other appreciations of Zhou Dunyi, in which this claim does not appear (but is not contradicted), are:

6. *"Ba Lianxi xiansheng tie"* (Colophon to [two] rubbings of Teacher Lianxi) (ibid., 34:1019); and

7. *"Lianxi xiansheng"* (Master Lianxi): first part of *"Sanzi huaxiang zan"* (Appreciation of the portraits of the Three Masters) (ibid., 36:1050).

88. *Zhang Shi quanji*, supplement: 1181.

zhong 中 (centrality) and *he* 和 (harmony), or the unexpressed (*weifa* 未發) and expressed (*yifa* 已發) phases of mind. *Ji* 幾 (incipience) is a key term in Zhou Dunyi's *Tongshu* (sections 3, 4, 9) and in the *Xici* 繫辭 appendix to the *Yijing* 易經 (A.10 and B.5). Zhang Shi's reference here to the problem of the activity/stillness of the mind supports my thesis (developed in the next chapter) that this was the context in which Zhang and Zhu Xi found Zhou Dunyi's texts useful, and indeed crucial.[89]

So there was a concerted campaign, begun by the Hunan school and continued by Zhu Xi and Zhang Shi, to elevate Zhou Dunyi to the position of first sage of the Song, contrary to the prevailing opinion at the time.[90] Five days before Zhu Xi died, he discoursed on the *Taiji* Diagram from his deathbed to a group of students.[91]

By the time of Zhu Xi's death in 1200, the reevaluation of Zhou Dunyi had begun to prevail. The earliest "history" of the *daoxue* movement, written by Li Xinchuan 李心傳 in 1202, is pessimistically entitled "The rise and fall of *daoxue*" because at that time the writings of the Cheng-Zhu school were still officially under the ban that had begun in 1196.[92] It begins:

> In the Xining 熙寧 and Yuanfeng 元豐 reign periods [1068–1085], the two Chengs of Henan began to propagate *daoxue* throughout the empire. In their youth they had studied with Zhou Maoshu 周茂叔 [Zhou Dunyi] of Runan 汝南, and their later students all considered him their founder [literally ancestor, *zu* 祖, or "patriarch"].[93]

Zhu Xi's students and later followers continued this interpretation. The most prominent in the first two generations were Huang Gan 黃幹 (1152–

---

89. For more on "incipience" see Smith, Bol, Adler, and Wyatt, *Sung Dynasty Uses of the I Ching*, 190–99; and Adler, "Response and Responsibility: Chou Tun-i and Neo-Confucian Resources for Environmental Ethics."

90. Many of these pieces are collected in *juan* 11–12 of Zhang Boxing's *Zhou Lianxi ji*.

91. According to Cai Shen, the son of Cai Yuanding (*Nianpu* 2:1412). Qian Mu says that this occurred on the day before Zhu died (*Zhuzi xin xue'an*, 1:25).

92. The ban was effectively lifted in 1202, the same year this text was written, but was not officially revoked until 1212.

93. "Daoxue xingfa," in Li, *Jianyan yilai chaoye zaji jiaji*, 6:137. Runan is the county in Henan where Zhou's family originally came from, although he was born in Yingdao county, Daozhou prefecture, Hunan. *Zu* (ancestor) is the same word used by the Chan Buddhists for their "patriarchs" of the "mind-to-mind transmission" (see chapter 1).

1221), his son-in-law and designated successor; Chen Chun 陳淳 (1159–1223); and Zhen Dexiu 真德秀 (1178–1235). Huang Gan wrote:

> The Way originates in Heaven, is embodied in the human mind/heart, is displayed in events and things, and is conveyed in ancient records. The ability to clarify and practice it exists in humans. . . .[94]
>
> When it came to Master Zhou, he regarded authenticity as the foundation and desires as a warning, and that was the tradition Master Zhou continued from Confucius and Mencius. When it came to the two Chengs, they said, "Self-cultivation requires seriousness; the pursuit of learning depends on the extension of knowledge."[95] This is the tradition that the two Chengs continued from Master Zhou.[96]

Chen Chun wrote:

> From a very obscure beginning, Fuxi created the system of Change [the *Zhouyi* hexagram divination system] and thus opened up the universe from chaos. . . . Confucius was unable to obtain a position to spread his doctrines. He therefore collected the standard teachings of the sages to produce the Six Classics and became the teacher of ten thousand generations. His teachings were transmitted by [Yan] Hui, [Zeng] Can, [Kong] Ji [i.e., Zisi], and [Meng] Ke [i.e., Mencius]. Throughout the ages, for several thousand years there was no other tradition. But the transmission was lost after Ke (Mencius), and the world plunged into vulgar learning. For more than a thousand and four hundred years, the world was in a slumber and lived a befuddled life without realizing it. With the rise of our Song dynasty, enlightened and sagely (rulers) succeeded one another. For a long time, there has been peace. The truly original *qi* gathered here once more. Master Lianxi (Zhou Dunyi) and the two Masters Cheng (Cheng Hao and Cheng Yi) of Henan, with their outstanding gift of being the first

---

94. In Hu, *Xingli daquan shu,* 38:3b.

95. *Henan Chengshi Yishu* (in *Er Cheng ji*), 18:188.

96. Translated by Chan, *New Studies,* 326; from Huang Gan's "General Treatise on the Transmission of the Tradition of the Way of the Sages and Worthies," *Mianzhai ji* 3:17a–20b. For a similar excerpt from Huang Gan's biography of Zhu Xi, see Chan, "Chu Hsi and Yüan Neo-Confucianism," 202.

to know the first to understand, appeared one after the other. Lianxi did not receive instruction from any teacher but got it himself from Heaven. He raised the main points and provided the key. His wonderful teachings are embodied in the Diagram of the Great Ultimate (*Taiji*). The forty chapters in his *Tongshu* (Penetrating the *Book of Changes*) further developed what the Diagram left incomplete. These works formed a perfect whole with the system of Change of Fuxi in the past and revived the discontinued heritage of Confucius and Mencius in the future. As has been said, he once more opened up the universe from chaos. The two Chengs personally received the basic doctrines from him and went on to make them great and glorious.[97]

Zhen Dexiu wrote:

> After the Warring States and the Qin dynasty, the teaching and practice of the Way were disrupted and dispersed, and there was no way to unify them. Dong Zhongshu 董仲舒 [c. 179–104 BCE] and Han Yu carried on through the Han and Tang, but they were not always able to penetrate to the true source of the substance and function of the Way; so they could do no more than perpetuate the Way in their own time and could not undertake the full responsibility for transmitting the Way to later ages.
>
> With Heaven's inaugurating of the sagely rule [of the Song], letters and government flourished together in peace, and from the Tianxi and Mingdao eras [1017–1033][98] to the age of revival [the Southern Song], great scholars appeared to proclaim this culture[99] and take personal responsibility for it. Thus the Way of Confucius and Mencius[100] was rediscovered by Master Zhou [Dunyi], the Way of Master Zhou was further clarified by the two Cheng brothers, and the Way of the Chengs was brilliantly expounded by Master Zhu. In his view the transmissions from Zengzi, Zisi, and Mencius fitted together like the pieces of a tally. Man could not have achieved this

---

97. Translated by Chan, *Neo-Confucian Terms Explained*, 179–80.

98. Zhou Dunyi was born in the Tianxi era (1017–1021) and Cheng Hao in the Mingdao era (1032–1033).

99. de Bary has "this Way" here. "This culture" is an allusion to *Analects* 9:5.

100. de Bary omits Mencius.

without the aid of Heaven. Likewise with the learning of the Four Masters, how could they have offered such novel views and put forward new interpretations, such as their predecessors had not been able to arrive at, were it not simply due to Heaven?[101]

The campaign to canonize Zhou Dunyi's and Zhu Xi's version of *daoxue* culminated during the reign of Emperor Lizong 理宗 (r. 1225–1264), whose posthumous name accurately suggests his support for the Cheng-Zhu school (Li is the same *li*, or "principle," that was its fundamental concept). In 1227, Lizong ennobled Zhu Xi as "Great Master and Trusted Duke of State,"[102] and in 1241 he installed the five leading figures of the *daoxue* school in the Confucian temple, thus officially canonizing the school and its texts:

> We believe that the Dao of Confucius was not received by anyone after Mencius. Only in our own dynasty, with the authentic insight, concrete practice, and profound search into the Sage's domain by Zhou Dunyi, Zhang Zai, Cheng Hao, and Cheng Yi did the learning that was terminated long ago finally have a point of convergence. After this revival, Zhu Xi's subtle thought and brilliant analysis harmonized form and content, thoroughly illuminating the *Great Learning, Analects, Mencius,* and *Doctrine of the Mean* [*Zhongyong*] from beginning to end and greatly manifesting the Dao of Confucius in the world.[103]

And finally, Zhu Xi's version of the Confucian *dao* achieved "orthodoxy" during the Yuan 元 (Mongol) dynasty (1279–1368) when it became the basis of the civil service examination system in 1313 and was incorporated into the official history of the Song (*Song shi* 宋史) in 1345.[104]

---

101. Zhen Dexiu, *"Nanxiong zhouxue si xiansheng citang ji"* (Record of the memorial hall to the Four Masters at the Nanxiong provincial school); the Four Masters are Zhou Dunyi, the Cheng brothers, and Zhu Xi. Translated by de Bary, *Neo-Confucian Orthodoxy and the Learning of the Mind-and-Heart*, 10, with Wade-Giles changed to *pinyin* romanization. A slightly modified version is found in Hu, *Xingli daquan shu* (38:10b), a Ming dynasty classified compilation of Sung and Yuan writings of the Cheng-Zhu school.

102. Wilson, *Genealogy of the Way*, 42.

103. Ibid., 43.

104. See Tuo Tuo, *Song shi,* ch. 427.

Before we move to the historical problems presented by Zhou Dunyi's role in Zhu Xi's construction of the *daotong*, we should discuss two rather glaring exceptions in Zhu's published writings: the prefaces to his commentaries on the *Daxue* (Great Learning) and *Zhongyong* (Centrality and Commonality). As is well known, Zhu combined these two short texts—originally chapters in the *Liji* 禮記 (Record of ritual), one of the Five "Classics" (Scriptures)—with the *Analects* (*Lunyu* 論語) and *Mencius* (*Mengzi* 孟子) to create the "Four Books."[105] This compilation was designed to serve as the basic introductory text of higher education in Zhu Xi's system, and did so after 1313. Zhu's commentaries on the Four Books are considered by some to be the culmination of his mature thought; they were first published in 1190 and he made the final emendation to his *Daxue* commentary three days before he died.[106] And in both prefaces he appears to attribute the recovery of the Way in the Song to the Cheng brothers, not to Zhou Dunyi. Toward the end of the *Daxue* preface he says:

> No doubt, among the three thousand disciples of Confucius, none failed to hear his teachings, but it was only Zengzi who got the essential message and wrote this commentary[107] to expound its meaning. Then, with the death of Mencius, the transmission vanished. This work survived, but few understood it. Thereafter came the vulgar Confucian scholarship [of later times], stressing memorization and literary composition, which took double the exertion of the elementary education but was of no real use, and the quietistic and nihilistic teachings of the deviant doctrines [Buddhism and Daoism], which were loftier even than the higher learning (*Great Learning*) but lacked solid substance....
>
> Yet Heaven's cycle goes on turning, and nothing goes forth without returning [for a new start]. The virtuous power of the Song Dynasty rose up, and both government and education shone with great luster, whereupon the two Cheng masters of Henan appeared and connected up with the tradition from Mencius [that had been

---

105. See Gardner, *Chu Hsi and the Ta-hsueh,* and *The Four Books.*
106. *Nianpu,* 1415; Chan, *New Studies,* 148.
107. Zhu Xi, following Cheng Yi, believed that the first section of the *Daxue* is the words of Confucius as transmitted by Zengzi, and that the rest is commentary by Zengzi. The evidence for any connection of Zengzi to the text is very weak. See Plaks, *Ta Hsueh and Chung Yung,* 118.

broken off]. The first truly to recognize and believe in this work, they expounded it to the world and further rearranged the fragmented text so as to bring out its essential message. With that, the method whereby the ancients taught men through the *Great Learning* with the guidance of the classic text of the Sage [Confucius] and the commentary of the Worthy [Zengzi], was once again made brilliantly clear to the world.[108]

And in first paragraph of the *Zhongyong* preface he says:

> Why was the *Mean* written? Master Zisi wrote it because he was worried lest the transmission of the Learning of the Way (*daoxue*) be lost. When the divine sages of highest antiquity had succeeded to the work of Heaven and established the Supreme Norm [of governance], the transmission of the Succession to the Way (*daotong*) had its inception. As may be discovered from the classics, "hold fast the Mean"[109] is what Yao transmitted to Shun. That "the human mind is precarious" and "the mind of the Way is barely perceptible," that one should be discriminating [with regard to the human mind], be one [with the mind of the Way], and should "hold fast the Mean" is what Shun transmitted to Yu.[110]

In the *Zhongyong* preface, unlike in the *Daxue,* Zhu does not mention Fuxi, Shennong, and Huangdi as the progenitors of the Way. Instead he identifies the *content* of the Way in terms of the "sixteen-word teaching" taken from the *Shujing* 書經 (Scripture of Documents): "The human mind is precarious, the mind of the Way is barely perceptible. Be discriminating [or refined]; be one. Hold fast the Mean."[111] The terms "human mind" (*renxin* 人

---

108. de Bary and Bloom, *Sources of Chinese Tradition,* 724 (translation by de Bary). Original in Zhu, *Sishu zhangju jizhu,* 14. See also Gardner's translation in *Chu Hsi and the Ta-hsueh,* 83–86. Earlier in the preface Zhu names Fuxi, Shennong, and Huangdi as the first in the line of sages (ibid., 78).

109. *Analects* 20:1.

110. de Bary and Bloom, *Sources of Chinese Tradition,* 732 (translation by de Bary). Original in Zhu, *Sishu zhangju jizhu,* 29.

111. "Da Yu mo" (Counsels of the Great Yu), *Shujing*; Legge, *The Chinese Classics,* 3:61–62.

心) and "mind of the Way" (*daoxin* 道心, which I prefer to translate "moral mind"), were central to Zhu Xi's theory of mind and self-cultivation. This paragraph is also Zhu Xi's most prominent published use of the term *daotong*. Later in the preface, after discussing *renxin* and *daoxin* and the contributions of the earlier sages, and relating phrases in the text (which he attributes to Zisi) to the "sixteen-word teaching," Zhu says:

> Thereafter the transmission was resumed by Mencius, who was able to interpret and clarify the meaning of this text [the *Mean*] and succeed to the tradition of the early sages; but upon his demise the tradition was finally lost. . . . Fortunately, however, this text was not lost, and when the Masters Cheng, two brothers, appeared [in the Song] they had something to study in order to pick up the threads of what had not been transmitted for a thousand years, and something to rely on in exposing the speciousness of the seeming truths of Buddhism and Daoism. Though the contribution of Zisi was great, had it not been for the Chengs we would not have grasped his meaning from his words alone. But alas, their explanations also became lost.[112]

In neither of these two important texts does Zhu Xi even mention Zhou Dunyi. This is perplexing, given the much greater preponderance of texts in which he clearly identifies Zhou as the first sage of the Song. It should also be noted that in these prefaces he speaks of the Cheng brothers *together* "connecting" with or "picking up the threads" of Mencius's tradition. He ignores Cheng Yi's claim that his elder brother had been the first to do so, which, as noted above, had been the prevailing opinion in the *daoxue* fellowship until Zhu Xi's and Zhang Shi's campaign to replace Cheng Hao with Zhou Dunyi.

One possible solution to this puzzle is that Zhu Xi might have changed his mind at some point about Zhou's relationship to the Cheng brothers. But this argument is seriously weakened by the fact that after publishing the Four Books in 1190 he wrote three more pieces in which he says or implies that Zhou Dunyi recovered the *dao* before Cheng Hao and Cheng Yi (the last three items in the list above). In one of them, in fact, he uses the same

---

112. de Bary and Bloom, *Sources of Chinese Tradition*, 734 (translation by de Bary). Original in Zhu, *Sishu zhangju jizhu*, 30. Plaks considers the attribution of the *Zhongyong* to Zisi to be slightly more reliable than the attribution of the *Daxue* to Zengzi. See Plaks, *Ta Hsüeh and Chung Yung*, 118–19.

"thread" terminology that he had used in the *Zhongyong* preface, where he had said that the two Chengs "picked up the threads of what had not been transmitted for a thousand years." Now (1194), though, he writes, "The threads of the two Chengs came from our Venerable Zhou (*Zhou weng* 周翁)."[113]

A better solution to this apparent contradiction can be deduced from closer inspection of the relevant passages in the prefaces, in particular these:

> [T]he two Cheng masters of Henan appeared and connected up with the tradition from Mencius. The first truly to recognize and believe in *this work* (*cibian*), they expounded it to the world and further rearranged the fragmented text so as to bring out its essential message (*Daxue* preface).
>
> Fortunately, however, *this text* (*cishu*) was not lost, and when the Masters Cheng, two brothers, appeared [in the Song] they had something to study in order to pick up the threads of what had not been transmitted for a thousand years, and something to rely on in exposing the speciousness of the seeing truths of Buddhism and Daoism. Though the contribution of Zisi was great, had it not been for the Chengs we would not have grasped *his meaning* from his words alone (*Zhongyong* preface).

Zhu Xi is focusing here not on the central message of the *daotong*, which he identifies as the sixteen-word teaching of Yao and Shun, but rather on these particular texts, the *Daxue* and *Zhongyong*. According to Thomas Wilson, "Because Zhu Xi based his version of the Four Books on the Cheng brothers' commentaries, it was necessary to sanction their interpretation of *these works* genealogically by maintaining that they had received *this teaching* from the ancient sages."[114] Also, the Cheng brothers' work as a whole was more closely related to these two texts than was Zhou Dunyi's, although Zhou did draw on the *Zhongyong*—mainly its concept of "being authentic" (*cheng*)—for his *Tongshu*.[115] Whether or not we regard these two prefaces as contradictions of

---

113. "*Ye xiu Daozhou san xiansheng ciwen*" (Essay in homage to the reconstructed shrine to the Three Masters at Daozhou), *Wenji* 86:4049.

114. Wilson, *Genealogy of the Way*, 199; my emphasis.

115. If this explanation is not entirely convincing, we are left with something of an inconsistency in Zhu Xi's conception of the *daotong*. But that is not the only inconsistency in his writings and conversations. He never set himself the task of constructing what we would call a systematic philosophy, a *summa daologica*. All his

our general premise, the fact remains that in the vast majority of his statements on the *daotong,* and in the unanimous view of his students and later followers, Zhu Xi clearly names Zhou Dunyi the first sage of the Song.

THE PROBLEMS WITH ZHOU

Zhu Xi's elevation of Zhou Dunyi was problematic from the beginning and caused him considerable intellectual conflict, most famously with Lu Jiuyuan in the late 1180s.[116] We can identify three types of problems with Zhu's choice of Zhou: sectarian, philosophical, and historical.

Sectarian Problems

In the late 1180s Zhu Xi was compelled to defend his choice of Zhou Dunyi and his texts, primarily with the brothers Lu Jiushao 陸九韶 (1120s–1190s) and Lu Jiuyuan 陸九淵 (1139–1193). I consider their discussions a "sectarian" issue because it was an internecine conflict within a religious "fellowship" (Hoyt Tillman's term for the *daoxue* scholars of the Song, although he doesn't explicitly call it religious), and it concerned their self-definition in opposition to another religious group, the Daoists.[117] Zhu had met the Lu brothers in

---

teachings were specific to particular contexts. For example, in one of his better-known statements, he advises a student to spend half the day in "quiet-sitting" (*jingzuo*) or meditation and half the day reading books. But it is abundantly clear that this recipe was not meant as general advice to everyone; it was what the particular student needed. In other cases Zhu Xi simply contradicts himself—that is, assuming that our records of his writings and conversations are accurate.

What we should bear in mind is that, as David Hall and Roger Ames have suggested, the idea of a universally valid principle (or system) independent of particular context and circumstance—what they call "logical order"—is a Western construction. Traditional Chinese thinking tends more toward "aesthetic order" in which the meanings of words, things, and propositions emerge *from* their interrelated, particularistic contexts (Hall and Ames, *Thinking Through Confucius,* 11–25, 131–38). This theory, which I believe has wide applicability in analyses of Chinese thought, strengthens the argument given above: that Zhu's remarks about the recovery of the *dao* in the *Daxue* and *Zhongyong* prefaces were specific to those texts.

116. See Tillman, *Confucian Discourse and Zhu Xi's Ascendancy,* 216–22.

117. Ibid., 2–5. Tillman defines the *daoxue* fellowship as "a network of social relations and a sense of community with a shared tradition that distinguished them from other Confucians" (3). For discussions of the religious status of Confucianism see Adler, "Confucianism as Religion / Religious Tradition / Neither: Still Hazy after All These Years"; idem., "Divination and Sacrifice in Song Neo-Confucianism," 73–75; and idem., "Varieties of Spiritual Experience: *Shen* in Neo-Confucian Discourse," 141–42.

1175, when they had joined him for discussions of their general approaches to learning at Goose Lake Monastery, a meeting arranged by their mutual friend, Lü Zuqian.[118] In 1181, Zhu Xi had invited Lu Jiuyuan to lecture at his White Deer Grotto academy. Zhu was so pleased with Lu's lecture on "rightness versus profit" (*yi* 義 versus *li* 利) that he asked Lu to write it down for deposit in the academy library, and said that he considered Lu a "comrade" (*tongzhi* 同志).[119] But in 1187, Lu Jiushao, the elder brother, wrote Zhu a letter criticizing Zhu's use of Zhou Dunyi's *Taijitu shuo* in the *Jinsilu* (Reflections on Things at Hand, 1175), focusing on the term *wuji* 無極 in Zhou's first sentence.[120] Lu pointed out that the term did not occur in the *Tongshu*, so it must have been either someone else's term or an idea that Zhou had entertained in his youth and later rejected. The argument was then picked up by Lu Jiuyuan, who exchanged two letters each with Zhu Xi on the topic of *wuji* and *taiji* 太極.[121] Lu Jiuyuan argued that *wuji* was strictly a Daoist term that originated in the *Laozi* (chapter 28); that Zhou Dunyi had received the Diagram from Daoists; that Zhu had misinterpreted *taiji*; and several other points, including the historical problem that the Cheng brothers, who allegedly (according to Zhu) had received and propagated Zhou's vision of the *dao*, never once mentioned the Diagram, *wuji*, or *taiji* (more on this below).[122] All these points raised the question (for Lu) of Zhou's suitability to be considered the first Confucian sage since Mencius.[123]

---

118. *Nianpu*, 529; Ching, "The Goose Lake Monastery Debate (1175)"; Tillman, *Confucian Discourse*, 105–106, 203–205.

119. *Nianpu*, 688. The lecture can be found in Huang and Quan, *Song-Yuan xue'an*, 58:13b. It was based on *Analects* 4:16: "The Master said: The gentleman (*junzi*) is familiar with what is right (*yi*), just as the small man (*xiaoren*) is familiar with profit (*li*)" (trans. Dawson, *The Analects*, 14). The distinction between *yi* and *li* is also the topic of the first passage of the *Mencius*.

120. *Wuji er taiji*, or "Nonpolar and yet Supreme Polarity," in my translation (see chapter 4 and Part II below).

121. These are well summarized in Carsun Chang, *Development*, 1:146–152; Tillman, *Confucian Discourse*, 216–22; and Shu, *Zhuzi dazhuan*, 729–55.

122. The whole series of letters between Zhu and the Lu brothers is reproduced in Huang and Quan, *Song-Yuan xue'an*, ch. 58.

123. Lu could have added that the *Taijitu* was only one of several similar diagrams used by Daoists, such as the *Wujitu* (*Wuji* diagram) and the *Xiantian taiji tu* (*Taiji* diagram predating heaven). The former is identical to the *Taijitu* except for its inscriptions. In the current version of the Daoist Canon (*Daozang*), which was compiled in the Ming,

Philosophical Problems

A. C. Graham's discussion of both the philosophical and the historical issues, contained in an appendix to his first book, *Two Chinese Philosophers: Ch'eng Ming-tao and Ch'eng Yi-ch'uan* (1958), is still one of the best and most incisive treatments. First, Graham argues that the Chengs' philosophy based on *li*, a concept Zhou did not discuss systematically, was in an entirely different league from Zhou's. In contrasting Zhou's term *taiji* with the Chengs' *li* he says:

> Both words refer to a "one" behind the "many" but to call it the Supreme Ultimate [*taiji*] implies that all things come from the same source, being produced by the division of a primal unit; to call it *li*, that they are united by a single principle running through them, from which one can infer from the known to the unknown. The new term is thus both less high-sounding and more rational than the old, and calls attention to the sudden change of intellectual climate of which one is conscious in passing from Zhou Dunyi to the Chengs. . . . The philosophy of the Chengs is not a development of that of Zhou Dunyi; it is based on quite different premises.[124]

Thus, according to Graham, the equation of *taiji* and *li* is a category mistake. *Taiji* belongs to the discourse of cosmology, or the "physical" (*xing'er xia* 形而下) realm; *li* is a "metaphysical" (*xing'er shang* 形而上) term. He further says, "[T]here is nothing in the *Discussion of the Chart* [*Taijitu shuo*] to suggest that there is any difference in kind between the Supreme Ultimate producing the Yin and Yang and the Yin and Yang producing the five elements. The Supreme Ultimate ought by analogy to be the original undivided ether [*qi*]."[125] Zhou Dunyi, he says, really belongs to a group of eleventh-century thinkers who were primarily interested in the *Yijing* and the diagrams connected with it; Shao Yong was another one. The only reason why today we associate those

---

it is found in the *Yuqing wuji zongzhen wenchang dadong xianjing zhu* (vol. 103). Another point supporting the Daoist origin of the *Taijitu* is that Zhou does not mention a couple of its elements in his "Discussion" (see Part II), which one would expect him to do if he had composed the diagram.

124. Graham, *Two Chinese Philosophers*, 160, 162.

125. Ibid., 163. Graham points out that Zheng Xuan (127–200) and Liu Mu (eleventh century) had interpreted *taiji* as *qi*.

two with the Chengs and Zhang Zai is that Zhu Xi drew on all of them. In their own time they had little philosophically in common, although of course they knew each other.[126]

Given this philosophic distance between Zhou and the Chengs it should not be surprising that the Chengs occasionally contradict Zhou's views. For example, one of Zhou's fundamental principles is "emphasizing stillness" (*zhu jing* 主靜).[127] But this was too quietistic for the Chengs (and later for Zhu Xi), who were concerned to maintain the traditional Confucian emphasis on active social involvement; "stillness" was too similar to Daoist and Buddhist quietism. So they consciously reinterpreted Zhou's "stillness" as "reverent composure" (another word pronounced *jing* 敬), which can be maintained both in stillness and in activity.[128]

Historical Problems

The problems raised by Zhu Xi's claim that the Cheng brothers "received the Way" from Zhou Dunyi are numerous. Among them are these:[129]

- The Chengs never spoke of *taiji*,[130] which was the major concept that Zhu Xi adopted from Zhou; nor of the *Taijitu*, which was Zhou's

---

126. Ibid., 153.

127. See *Taijitu shuo,* translated in Part II below.

128. Graham, *Two Chinese Philosophers,* 165–66. The other example of contradiction Graham gives is not as compelling, because Zhu Xi offers a way to reconcile Zhou with the Chengs. In *Tongshu* 3 Zhou says, "loving is called humanity (*ren*)." But Cheng Yi (and later Zhu Xi) says that love is a "feeling" or "disposition" (*qing*) while humanity is part of the "nature" (*xing*). Feelings/dispositions are functions of *qi*, while the nature is the human instantiation of *li*; so to equate them would be another category mistake. However, in his commentary on the passage, Zhu Xi applies the distinction of "substance" (*ti*) and "function" (*yong*) to the two terms, saying that humanity is the substance and loving is the function (see *Tongshu* 3[c], translated in Part II). While Zhou does not make this distinction, Zhu's interpretation is at least consistent with his own theory. It does, however, require that a "substance" can be metaphysical while its "function" is physical—a point that can be debated.

129. Ibid., 159–64. See also Qian, *Zhuzi xin xue'an* 3:49–52; Zhang, *Zhou Lianxi yanjiu,* 31–32; and Wilson, *Genealogy of the Way,* 197–227.

130. Not counting an anonymous preface to Cheng Yi's *Commentary on the Yi,* which is not considered to be his. See *Er Cheng ji,* 690–91.

most famous contribution to the tradition.¹³¹ Nor did they ever (as far as we know) use the term *wuji*. In fact they did not discuss *any* of Zhou's doctrines. Nor did their students.

- Zhou did not make much use of the concept of *li* (principle or order), which was a central concept for the Chengs. It does not occur at all in the *Taijitu shuo*; in the *Tongshu* it occurs four times (in sections 3 and 13), plus once in a section title (22), which may or may not be Zhou's.¹³²

- The Chengs referred to Zhou by his personal name, Maoshu; yet Cheng Yi referred to his teacher Hu Yuan 胡瑗 as Teacher Hu (Hu *xiansheng* 先生). Moreover, Zhou changed his name from Dunshi to Dunyi in 1063 (to avoid an Imperial taboo), sixteen years after the Chengs had studied with him. The second part of his new name (Yi 頤) is the same as Cheng Yi's personal name, which would have been unlikely if Zhou had considered Cheng his disciple.

- Cheng Yi said that Cheng Hao had independently rediscovered the Way (in the Classics), and this, as we have seen, was the prevailing view at least up to the mid-twelfth century.

- Zhou was said to have received the *Taijitu* from the Daoist Mu Xiu (979–1032), who got it from Chong Fang (965–1015), who got it from the famous Daoist priest and *Yijing* expert Chen Tuan (d. 989). Zhu Xi was, for the most part, rather hostile toward Daoism.¹³³

---

131. Zhu claims that the *Taijii* Diagram and its Discussion were esoteric teachings that Zhou did reveal to the Cheng brothers, but they were unwilling to share them with their own students because they thought none could understand them. See his 1172 letter to Zhang Shi, *Wenji* 31:1341; Chan, "Chu Hsi's Completion of Neo-Confucianism," 126; Ching, *The Religious Thought of Chu Hsi*, 39.

132. The title of section 22 is *li xing ming* (principle, nature, destiny), but none of those terms occurs in the section. Zhu Xi says he "restored" the section titles from the original after Hu Hong had removed them. See below, Part II: *Tongshu* translation and the 1179 postface to the revised edition.

133. This claim originated with Zhu Zhen (1072–1138, no relation to Zhu Xi); see Zhu Zhen, *Jin Zhouyi biao* (Memorial presenting the *Zhouyi*), 1:425. For brief accounts of all these figures see Nielsen, *A Companion to* Yi Jing *Numerology and Cosmology*. For more on Chen Tuan see Livia Kohn, *Chen Tuan*. Zhu Zhen—a student of Xie Liangzuo (1050–1121), who had been a student of the Cheng brothers—was especially interested in the "images and numbers" (*xiangshu*) approach to the *Yijing*. Julia Ching

- The Chengs' immediate disciples never mentioned Zhou in their writings. No one seems to have claimed a significant role for Zhou in the Cheng school until Hu Hong, or perhaps his father, Hu Anguo.

Given all these problems and the lack of historical evidence for any philosophical link between Zhou and the Chengs, why did Zhu Xi raise Zhou Dunyi to such a position of prominence in the tradition? Why was he willing to try so transparently to explain away Zhou Dunyi's evident debts to Daoism? Why did he ignore the compelling evidence that the Cheng brothers owed nothing philosophically to Zhou? Why was he so intent on declaring Zhou to be the first Confucian sage since Mencius?

An argument could be made that, for different reasons, Zhu could not accept either of the Cheng brothers as independent revivers of the Way. First of all, as mentioned above, Cheng Yi had claimed that Cheng Hao had revived the Way, so that would eliminate Cheng Yi. The usual explanation for Zhu's rejection of Cheng Hao is that he felt that Cheng's idea that "the humane person forms one body with all things" was too idealistic.[134] But could Zhu not have argued that Cheng Yi really was the one, and that Cheng was merely being respectful to his elder brother in giving him the credit? It was Cheng Yi, after all, to whom Zhu was philosophically most indebted. This

---

summarizes the theories of the Daoist origins of the *Taijitu* in *The Religious Thought of Chu Hsi*, 235–36. The Daoist origin was supported by Qing dynasty scholars, such as Huang Zongyan (1616–1686) (*Tuxue bianhuo*, 459), and reaffirmed by modern scholars, such as Feng Youlan (Fung Yu-lan) (*History of Chinese Philosophy*, 2:442), A. C. Graham (*Two Chinese Philosophers*, 156–57), and Richard J. Smith (*Fathoming the Cosmos and Ordering the World*, 115–27).

Zhu Xi basically ignored the reputed Daoist origin of the Diagram, even when it was mentioned by opponents, such as Lu Jiuyuan. In the "Record of the reconstruction of Zhou Dunyi's study hall in Jiangzhou," translated above, he says that Zhou created the Diagram. In his biographical account of Chen Tuan and his followers he does not specifically mention any diagrams (Zhu, *Bachao mingchen yanxing lu* [Record of the words and deeds of famous officials from eight dynasties], *juan* 11.

134. Indeed, modern scholars have paid considerable attention to the philosophical differences between the two Cheng brothers, instead of lumping them together as a coherent and consistent group, as was the case in the Song-Yuan period. See, e.g., Mou, *Xinti yu xingti*, vol. 1:42–60. For Cheng Hao's sentence see Chan, *Source Book in Chinese Philosophy*, 523.

would have presented much less of a problem than those listed above. So it is difficult to accept that Zhu had no choice but to nominate Zhou Dunyi.

In modern scholarship the prevailing view has been that it was Zhou's concept of *taiji*, and the use he makes of it in the *Taijitu shuo*, that attracted Zhu to Zhou and persuaded him to give Zhou the exalted status of sole founder of *daoxue*.[135] Here is the relevant passage from the *Taijitu shuo*:

> *Taiji* in activity generates *yang*; yet at the limit of activity it is still. In stillness it generates *yin*; yet at the limit of stillness it is also active. Activity and stillness alternate; each is the basis of the other. In distinguishing *yin* and *yang*, the Two Modes are thereby established.

As is well known, Zhu interpreted *taiji* as *li*—an equation he apparently learned from Li Tong[136] (what exactly it means will be discussed in chapter 4). Since *taiji* in the *Taijitu shuo* gives rise to the *yin* and *yang* modes of *qi*, the equation of *taiji* and *li*—a rather forced one, as we have seen, and one that Zhou Dunyi never suggested—enabled Zhu Xi to forge a link between the metaphysical realm of *li* and the cosmological realm of *yin-yang qi*. In this sense *taiji* became the fundamental principle, or linchpin, of Zhu Xi's entire philosophical system. As Wing-tsit Chan concludes, "[T]he concept of the Great Ultimate [*taiji*] is indispensable to Zhu's remolding of the Neo-Confucian philosophy and he could not help taking advantage of the *Treatise* [*Taijitu shuo*] in spite of its beginning sentence."[137]

---

135. See, for example, Chan, "Chu Hsi's Completion of Neo-Confucianism," 127.

136. See *Nianpu*, 266, quoting from *Yanping dawen* (Dialogues with Li Tong), in Zhu Jieren et al., *Zhuzi quanshu*, 13:328; and Graham, *Two Chinese Philosophers*, 163.

137. Chan, "Chu Hsi's Completion of Neo-Confucianism," 116. Chan also says that "the concepts of sincerity [*cheng*, authenticity], nature, destiny [*ming*, decree], mind, Great Ultimate, etc. all originated in the *Diagram of the Great Ultimate* and the *Tongshu*," and therefore Zhou Dunyi's concepts filled gaps between the thought of Mencius and that of the Cheng brothers (ibid., 127). This, it seems to me, is an enormous exaggeration. *Cheng* was an important concept in the *Zhongyong*, although Zhou developed it further and made it the hallmark of the sage. "Nature" (*xing*) was much more developed in the *Mencius* than in Zhou's writings. *Ming* was also discussed by Mencius, and as *tianming* (Mandate of Heaven) it goes back to the *Shijing* and *Shujing*. "Mind" is more central in Mencius than in Zhou. That leaves *taiji* as the only term in Chan's list that needs to be explained.

74   RECONSTRUCTING THE CONFUCIAN DAO

However, this solution is likewise unconvincing. If Zhu Xi had simply wanted to use *taiji* to express the idea of the ultimate reality and to posit a link between *li* and *qi*, he had available to him a text whose Confucian authority was unquestioned: the *Yijing*. The *Xici* 繫辭 (Appended remarks) appendix of the *Yijing* contains the following lines:

> In change there is *taiji*, which generates the Two Modes. The Two Modes generate the Four Images, and the Four Images generate the Eight Trigrams.[138]

The *Yijing* was one of the Five (or Six) original Confucian scriptures or classics, and Zhu Xi was intimately familiar with it. Although Ouyang Xiu 歐陽修 (1007–1072) had argued that Confucius could not have written the appendices, as was traditionally believed, Zhu Xi held to the traditional view. In 1177, the same year he wrote his "Record of the reconstruction of Zhou Dunyi's library in Jiangzhou," he completed his first commentary on the *Yijing*, which unfortunately is not extant.[139] But in 1188, he published a revised version, the *Zhouyi benyi* 周易本義 (Original meaning of the *Yijing*), which covers the entire text including the appendices.[140] His comment on the lines above reads as follows:

> One always generates two; this is a natural principle (*ziranzhi li* 自然之理). Change (*yi* 易) is the alternation of *yin* and *yang*, and *taiji* 太極 is its principle. The Two Modes are the first single-line [figures] divided into *yin* and *yang*.[141] The Four Images are the next-level two-line [figures], divided into "elder" and "younger" [*yin* and *yang*].[142] The Eight Trigrams are the next-level three-line [figures], with the images of the "three powers" [heaven, earth, humanity] now

---

138. *Yijing*, *Xici* A.11.5 (Zhu, *Zhouyi benyi* 3:14b). This is the first occurrence of *taiji* in extant Chinese literature.

139. *Nianpu*, 594. Earlier biographers, such as Wang Mouhong (*Zhuzi nianpu*, 1706), say that this was actually the *Zhouyi benyi*, but Shu Jingnan refutes this.

140. Cheng Yi's commentary on the *Yi* did not include the appendices because Cheng Yi felt that they were Confucius's commentary on the main text, and so it was unnecessary (and perhaps presumptuous) to comment on them further.

141. ▬▬ and ▬ ▬

142. ▬▬▬▬ ▬▬ ▬▬ ▬ ▬ ▬▬ ▬ ▬ ▬ ▬

complete.¹⁴³ This passage really [expresses] the natural sequence by which the Sage [Fuxi] created the *Yi*; he achieved it without availing himself of the slightest bit of wisdom.¹⁴⁴

Thus, according to Zhu Xi, the *Yijing* passage, exactly like the first section of Zhou Dunyi's *Taijitu shuo*, links the metaphysical discourse of *li* with the cosmological discourse of *yin* and *yang*. If this linkage were his main concern, he could easily have used this passage as a source text. He could thereby have avoided the unpleasantness of relying so strongly on Zhou Dunyi, with his unfortunate Daoist connections and his problematic term *wuji*. So we must look elsewhere for a solution to our problem. The key lies in the one element in the *Taijitu shuo* passage that has no parallel in the *Yijing* passage: the *interpenetrating* modes of activity and stillness (*dong-jing* 動靜).

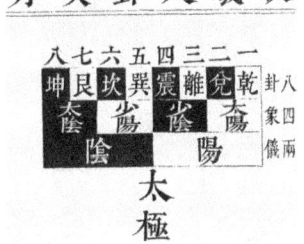

143. Zhu Xi is describing here the evolution of the eight trigrams in the "Fuxi" sequence, which is also depicted in the chart at right (one of nine appended to the beginning of his *Zhouyi benyi*). In this version, though, the individual lines are not indicated.

144. *Yijing*, *Xici* A.11.5 (Zhu, *Zhouyi benyi* 3:14b). Note again that "naturalness" explains what he describes elsewhere as the intentionality of Heaven.

Chapter Three

The Interpenetration of Activity and Stillness

In the previous chapter we saw that the strangeness of Zhu Xi's elevation of Zhou Dunyi has been discussed since the twelfth century, and that the conventional explanation for it leaves much to be desired. By situating Zhu's choice in the historical context of his life and religious practice, in this chapter we will find that a pattern emerges that makes better sense of Zhu's appropriation of Zhou.

The critical turning point in the development of Zhu Xi's mature system of thought and practice was his resolution of a problem that occupied him from about 1163 to 1169.[1] It was fundamentally a spiritual crisis concerning the methodology of self-cultivation, the process of transforming oneself into a sage (*shengren* 聖人). Sagehood was the Neo-Confucian term for what Confucius had called the "humane [*ren* 仁] person," the ethical ideal of a person who naturally and spontaneously responds to any situation in such a way as to maximize human flourishing. Zhu Xi's entire life-project was to define the best way to achieve this religious goal and to provide specific

---

1. This has been thoroughly studied, for example by Qian Mu, *Zhuzi xin xue'an*, 2:123–82; Thomas Metzger, *Escape from Predicament: Neo-Confucianism and China's Evolving Political Culture*, 93–99; Kirill O. Thompson, *An Inquiry into the Formation of Chu Hsi's Moral Philosophy*, 90–118; Chen Lai, *Zhu Xi zhexue yanjiu*, 106–33; Matthew Levey, *Chu Hsi as a "Neo-Confucian,"* 86–144; Tillman, *Confucian Discourse*, 59–64; and Rodney L. Taylor, "Chu Hsi and Meditation," 46–56.

methods to aid people in the process. But *praxis* alone was not enough for him; he always tried to provide a philosophical structure for it, a *theoria* to inform and justify the *praxis*.

My theory, in brief, is that Zhou Dunyi's *Taijitu shuo* provided the cosmological theory that supported the particular solution Zhu Xi arrived at for his method of self-cultivation. The key linkage between the theory and the practice was Zhou Dunyi's concept of the interpenetration of activity and stillness (*dong jing* 動靜), which applied both to the cosmos at large and to the mind/heart (*xin* 心).

THE PROBLEM OF MIND/HEART

The problem of mind/heart was central to Zhu's philosophical system and to the spiritual crisis he experienced in the 1160s. It is useful, especially for comparative purposes, to place it in the context of the problem of evil—a crucial question in any religious or philosophical tradition. In "Western" theology (Jewish-Christian-Islamic) this is called the problem of theodicy, or the question, "If God is good (and omnipotent), why is there evil and suffering?"[2] The analogous problem in Confucian thought is, "If human nature is good, why is there evil? Why isn't every person a sage?" Mencius answered the question by asserting that our good nature requires a nurturing environment—biological, social, cultural, and political—in order to thrive. We require adequate nourishment, a loving family life, education, and good government that supports all the rest. Otherwise the good nature can be overwhelmed by destructive outside forces, like the green shoots and trees on Ox Mountain that are constantly being eaten by grazing animals and chopped down by people.[3] We need to "preserve and nourish" (*zun yang*) the naturally occurring sprouts of our nature. The aforementioned external supports make that possible, just as seeds require water, sunlight, and protection to grow but have the principle and power of growth within them.

But that still leaves the question of human beings' differing abilities to resist such environmental forces. Simply from observation we have the sense that one person may succeed in life while another, with more or less the same level of environmental/social support, may not. The closest Mencius

---

2. The term *theodicy* was coined by Gottfried Wilhelm Leibniz (1646–1716) from the Greek words for "god" and "justice."

3. *Mencius* 6A.8.

comes to explaining this is to say that what distinguishes a "great" from a "small person" (*xiaoren*)—and in this context these are moral categories—is that the former uses his mind/heart as a guide. He further says, "The organ of the [mind/]heart can think. But it will find the answer only if it does think; otherwise, it will not find the answer."[4] In other words, achieving self-realization is a matter of will. But this simply pushes back the question, leaving us to wonder why some have stronger wills than others.

Zhu Xi, drawing heavily upon Cheng Yi and Zhang Zai, provided a solution to this problem based on the central concept in Cheng-Zhu thought, the relationship of *li* 理 (pattern/order/principle) and *qi* 氣 (psycho-physical-spiritual stuff).[5] This relationship has been the subject of much scholarly debate—again, ever since the twelfth century and continuing today—but here I will simply present my own view, and that rather briefly. Zhu Xi repeatedly argued that "*li* is never separate from *qi*."[6] This means that *qi* is always ordered by *li,* and *li* is always instantiated in *qi*. However, the nature of *li* is different from the nature of *qi,* which is to say that they are ontologically distinct. To put it over-simply, *li* is metaphysical (*xing'er shang* 形而上) and *qi* is psychophysical (*xing'er xia* 形而下, including the whole spectrum from material to spiritual). *Li* is metaphysical in the sense that it is the abstract order—or better yet, the ordering—of things, and is therefore categorically distinct from the *qi*-based existence of the things themselves.[7]

As *li* is simply the order or pattern of a thing, the purity of the thing's *qi* (the stuff that is ordered) determines how easily its pattern (*li*) can be

---

4. *Mencius* 6A.15, trans. Lau, *Mencius,* 168.

5. Daniel Gardner, based on Benjamin Schwartz, translates *qi* as "psycho-physical stuff" (*Learning to Be a Sage,* 49, n.52), but it is more precisely psychophysical-spiritual. *Qi* is the stuff of which all existing things are composed, including mind, spirit, and gods. This means that the term *spiritual* in the discussion of Zhu's spiritual crisis should not be construed as it generally has been in the Western religious and philosophical traditions, implying a categorical distinction from a "physical/material" realm. Confucian "spirit" (*shen*) must be understood as a form of *qi,* which comprehends the spectrum of matter-energy-spirit. See my "Varieties of Spiritual Experience: *Shen* in Neo-Confucian Discourse."

6. E.g., in *Yulei* 1:115–16. Therefore, Zhu cannot be called a dualist in the Platonic or Cartesian sense, as *li* has no existence apart from *qi*—unlike the eternal forms for Plato and mind for Descartes. See also note 83 below.

7. Whether this theory makes Zhu a "dualist," and if so what kind of dualist, is where much of the debate occurs, but it need not detain us here. The subject will come up again in chapter 4.

discerned. For example, the nature (*xing* 性) or principle (*li*) of water can best be discerned when it is pure. Likewise, the nature or principle of the mind/heart can best be understood when it is free of the clouding effect of selfish desires, anger, or other such phenomena. These are functions of our physicality, which Zhu Xi called the "psychophysical nature" (*qizhizhi xing* 氣質之性).[8] This self-knowledge or self-realization—the state in which one's actual, spontaneous thoughts, intentions, and desires are true expressions of our moral nature *and* are put into practice—is what Zhou Dunyi called "authenticity" (*cheng* 誠), and which he further claimed is the defining characteristic of the sage.[9]

So, Zhu Xi's explanation for people's differing abilities to realize their moral nature, even in the theoretical case of equal environmental nourishment—i.e., his solution to the Confucian problem of evil—is that each person is born with a unique endowment of *qi*, in a unique configuration of clarity and obscurity. The factors that determine this configuration or allotment of *qi* are beyond the individual's control, and so they are attributed to Heaven. Basically they comprise all the factors influencing the quality and configuration of one's *qi* at the time and place of one's birth, even including the climate and the positions of the planets (as Zhu mentions in his "Record of the reconstruction of Zhou Dunyi's library in Jiangzhou," translated in chapter 2). If Zhu had had access to our contemporary science he would undoubtedly have included one's genetic endowment and prenatal nutrition as significant factors determining the quality of one's *qi*.

There is a marked strain of optimism in Confucian thought regarding the possibility of becoming a sage or humane person. Both Mencius and Xunzi had said that any person theoretically can become a sage, although Xunzi also said that not everyone actually has the ability to do so.[10] While the Song Confucians generally followed Mencius and rejected Xunzi, Zhu Xi said that Mencius's discussion of human nature (*xing* 性) was flawed, as it applied only

---

8. He borrowed this term from Zhang Zai, who contrasted the physical nature with the "nature of Heaven and earth" (*tiandizhi xing* 天地之性), i.e., one's "original" nature (*Zhangzi quanshu,* 2:18b–19a; Chan, *Source Book,* 511).

9. *Tongshu* 1–4; drawing upon the *Zhongyong,* where *cheng* is also a prominent term. In his commentary, Zhu Xi defines authenticity as "actualized principle" (*shi li*)—i.e., the instantiation of *li* in thought and behavior (see Part II, Zhu's comments on *Tongshu* 1a and 1b).

10. Burton Watson, trans., *Hsün Tzu: Basic Writings,* 167.

to its metaphysical aspect (the "original nature," which Zhang Zai had called the "nature of Heaven and earth"). Mencius, according to Zhu, ignored the original nature's instantiation in the *qi* of the mind/heart (the psychophysical nature). And while he retained Mencius's optimism regarding the theoretical possibility of every person become a sage, he also took very seriously the difficulty of the process, which was caused by the "clouding" effect of the psychophysical nature. In this respect he was a bit more like Xunzi. Xunzi stressed the absolute need for learning and ritual in order to "transform" one's originally evil nature (*xing*) into goodness; Zhu Xi stressed the need for learning and self-cultivation in order to "transform the psychophysical" nature, that is, to clarify it so that the original moral nature can be expressed. Perhaps Zhu Xi's greater sensitivity to the difficulty of the process of self-actualization was in part a reaction to the failure of the optimistic political and institutional reforms of the Northern Song. In any case, he believed that ordinary people needed all the help they could get in the process of self-transformation/self-realization aimed at (if not actually achieving) sagehood. This was the reason for his lifelong dedication to systematizing an educational curriculum, based on the "eight items" of the *Daxue* (Great Learning), that would provide the guidance of past sages (as interpreted by himself) in this process.[11]

INTELLECTUAL AND SPIRITUAL CULTIVATION

Because of the large number of commentaries Zhu Xi wrote and his insistence on the importance of reading, his program of self-cultivation is often described as "following the path of inquiry and study" (*dao wenxue* 道問學), as opposed to "honoring the moral nature" (*zun dexing* 尊德性)—two phrases from the *Zhongyong* (section 27). In this respect he was following Cheng Yi; both Cheng and Zhu are legitimately associated with the intellectual or "rationalistic" path to sagehood. Cheng Hao and Lu Jiuyuan, on the other hand, are both associated with the more inward-oriented path of self-knowledge. According to Lu Jiuyuan, Zhu Xi himself acknowledged this distinction, admitting that

---

11. The eight items are investigating things (*ge wu* 格物), extending knowledge (*zhi zhi* 致知), making the will authentic (*cheng yi* 誠意), rectifying the mind (*zheng xin* 正心), cultivating the person (*xiu shen* 修身), regulating the family (*qi jia* 齊家), governing the country (*zhi guo* 治國), and pacifying the world (*ping tianxi* 平天下). *Daxue* 1, in *Sishu zhangju jizhu*; Chan, *Source Book*, 86–87. For my summary of Zhu Xi's methods of self-cultivation see Smith, Bol, Adler, and Wyatt, *Sung Dynasty Uses of the I Ching*, 171–72.

because of his emphasis on the intellectual dimensions of self-cultivation, some of his own students were not as good as Lu's in "putting beliefs into practice."[12] Another way to describe the distinction is in terms of the quest to understand the natural/moral order (*li*) "externally," in books, things, and human affairs versus "internally" in one's own mind/heart. Using the terminology of two of the "eight items" of the *Daxue*, the Cheng-Zhu school stressed "investigating [external] things" (*ge wu* 格物) while the Lu-Wang school emphasized "making the [internal] will authentic" (*cheng yi* 誠意). I shall refer to these two aspects of self-cultivation respectively as "intellectual cultivation" and "spiritual cultivation."[13]

While this distinction is valid as a broad generalization, it does not mean that Zhu Xi ignored the internal, spiritual approach. In fact, his "spiritual crisis" of the 1160s centered on just that aspect of self-cultivation. It involved Zhu's understanding of the second half of the first chapter of the *Zhongyong* (Centrality and Commonality):

> Before the feelings of pleasure, anger, sorrow, and joy are expressed [*weifa* 未發] it is called centrality [or equilibrium, *zhong* 中]. When these feelings are expressed [*yifa* 已發] and each and all attain due measure and degree, it is called harmony [*he* 和]. Centrality is the great foundation of the world, and harmony is its universal [or penetrating] path. When centrality and harmony are realized to the highest degree, heaven and earth will attain their proper order and all things will flourish.[14]

In his commentary on this section, Zhu Xi says (with reference to Confucius's grandson Zisi, the reputed author of the *Zhongyong*):

> [Here] it speaks of the essentials of preserving, nourishing, and examining the mind . . . [and] the meritorious achievements and transforming influence of the sage and the spirit man in their highest

---

12. Lu, *Xiangshan quanji*, 34:4b–5a; trans. Chan, *Source Book*, 582.

13. This usage of "spiritual" is consistent with my understanding of the distinction between spirituality and religion. I take spirituality to be the internal, subjective aspect of religion, including beliefs, values, and the experiential dimension. Religion, the broader category, also includes ritual and the social dimension (see p. 10).

14. Trans. Chan, *Source Book*, 98, substituting "centrality" for "equilibrium" and "expressed" for "aroused."

degree. Zisi's hope was that the student should hereby return to search within himself to find these truths, so that he might remove his selfish desires aroused by external temptations, and realize in full measure the goodness which is natural to him.[15]

We are clearly dealing here with the internal, subjective dimension of self-cultivation, which was just as important to Zhu as the intellectual dimension of investigating the principles of things. The key terms in which he discussed the problem came from the *Zhongyong* passage above: *weifa* ("not yet expressed") / *zhong* (centrality) and *yifa* ("already expressed") / *he* (harmony). The underlying question was this: In which of these two "phases" of mind/heart can the principle (*li*) of being human, otherwise known as human nature (*renxing* 人性), best be seen and understood: the centrality (*zhong*) before feelings are expressed (*weifa*), or the harmony (*he*) of properly expressed (*yifa*) feelings? Should spiritual cultivation be directed at the mind/heart in its still phase or in its active functioning?[16] I shall henceforth refer to this as the *zhong/he* problem.

This was the question that Zhu Xi grappled with in the 1160s. At the beginning of this period he was under the influence of Li Tong, whom he had first visited in 1153 and with whom he studied until Li's death in 1163. Two months after Li Tong died, Zhu met Zhang Shi, a member of the "Hunan school" and a former student of Hu Hong. These two relationships were the most significant influences on Zhu Xi's struggle with the problem of spiritual cultivation.

---

15. Zhu, *Zhongyong zhangju*, in *Sishu zhangju jizhu*, 33; trans. Chan, *Source Book*, 98.

16. Thomas Metzger has discussed this question thoroughly in *Escape from Predicament*, where he enumerates five "naturally given phases of the mind" in Zhu Xi's thought: (1) "total stillness," in which the mind has access to the "good cosmic force" represented by "Heaven" (*tian*); (2) "sensation of an outer object" or stimulus (*gan*); (3) "imminent issuance (*weifa*)," i.e., the point at which feelings and other responses to stimuli are "not yet expressed" and are in perfect "equilibrium" (*zhong*); (4) "incipient issuance (*ji*)"; and (5) "accomplished issuance (*yifa*)," i.e., the "already expressed" feelings and other mental activities, which should be but are not necessarily in "harmony" (*he*) with the still, unexpressed phases of the mind (87). I have discussed the third of these (incipience) in Smith, Bol, Adler, and Wyatt, *Sung Dynasty Uses of the I Ching*, 190–99; and Adler, "Response and Responsibility: Chou Tun-i and Neo-Confucian Resources for Environmental Ethics." Here I am simplifying the discussion to Metzger's phases (3) and (5), because *weifa* (*zhong*) and *yifa* (*he*) are the terms in which Zhu Xi and his colleagues discussed the problem in question.

Li Tong, as mentioned in chapter 1, had been a student of Luo Congyan, who had been a student of Cheng Yi and later of Cheng's student Yang Shi.[17] Luo Congyan and Li Tong had both taught the practice of "quiet-sitting" (*jingzuo* 靜坐), a form of meditation undoubtedly influenced by Chan "sitting-meditation" (*zuochan* 坐禪, or *zazen* in Japanese).[18] This form of spiritual cultivation was supported by Zhou Dunyi's statement, "The sage ... emphasizes stillness (*zhu jing* 主靜),"[19] and it is possible that Zhou also practiced quiet-sitting.[20] Yet, as we shall see, Cheng Yi refused to accept Zhou's concept of "emphasizing stillness" at face value, choosing to interpret "stillness" as "reverent composure" (another word pronounced *jing* 敬).

The whole subject of stillness or quietude was problematic for the Confucians of both the Northern and Southern Song, because it smacked of Buddhist and Daoist quietism. Buddhism, of course, taught not only the quietistic practice of meditation but also the renunciation of ordinary life to live in a monastery. The terms used for becoming a monk or nun in China were "leaving the family" (*chu jia* 出家), or sometimes "leaving the world" (*chu shi* 出世). This was tantamount, in the eyes of many Confucians, to a renunciation of Chinese culture and even of life itself.[21] The key Buddhist term *nirvana* (extinction),[22] too, had strongly negative connotations from the Confucian perspective, as did the important Mahayana concept of "emptiness" (*kong* 空) and the word *wu* 無 (nonexistence) in such Chan terms as "no-mind" (*wuxin* 無心) and "no-thought" (*wunian* 無念).[23] Daoism had its own term for emptiness or vacuity, *xu* 虛, which the partisan Confucians often equated with the Buddhist concept of emptiness (although they are actually quite different), and also stressed "nonexistence" (*wu*).[24] And the Song dynasty saw a significant

---

17. Huang and Quan, *Song-Yuan xue'an,* 15:1a–2a, 25:1a–b.

18. See Okada Takehiko, *Zazen to Seiza*; Taylor, *The Confucian Way of Contemplation*; *Yulei* 38:379–84.

19. See Part II below, *Taijitu shuo,* section G. Zhu Xi brings the concept of emphasizing stillness into his interpretation of the *Tongshu* also (see below, *Tongshu* sections 13 and 40).

20. Taylor, *The Confucian Way of Contemplation,* 36–41.

21. See the discussion above in chapter 1.

22. Chinese *nieban* (a transliteration), or *mie* (translation of *nirodha*, or "extinction").

23. See Yampolsky, *The Platform Sutra,* sections 17, 31.

24. E.g., in the *Laozi,* "non-action," "no-knowledge," and "returning to *wuji.*"

growth in Daoist monasticism, modeled after Buddhist monasticism, with the advent of the Quanzhen (Complete Perfection) school.

All this is simply to point out that the question Zhu Xi was grappling with—whether *li* could best be understood in the still or the active phase of mind—was fraught with sectarian difficulty. It was precisely in the problematic space between traditional Confucian "activism" and Buddhist/Daoist "quietism" that Zhu Xi had to work out the solution to his spiritual crisis.

The practice of quiet-sitting was a major aspect of the problem, because Zhu was seeking not only a theoretical way of bridging the still and active phases of mind but also a practical means. Quiet-sitting had a long pedigree in China, with some forms of meditation dating back at least to the late Warring States period; for example, Zhuangzi's "sitting and forgetting" (*zuowang* 坐忘) and fasting the mind (*xinzhai* 心齋), and the *Guanzi*'s "maintaining the One" (*shouyi* 守一) and "concentrating the mind" (*zhuanxin* 專心).[25] Nevertheless, the incorporation of quiet-sitting into Song Confucian practice was almost certainly a response to the popularity of Buddhism, even though most Song Confucians took pains to distinguish it from Chan sitting-meditation. Zhu Xi, for example, said:

> Quiet-sitting should not be like entering *samadhi* (*ruding* 入定) in *zazen,* cutting off all thoughts. Just collect the mind and don't let it go and get involved with idle thoughts. Then the mind will be profoundly unoccupied and naturally concentrated. When something happens, it will respond accordingly. When the thing is past it will return to its [still] depth.[26]

Despite the negative overtones of "stillness" from a Confucian perspective, Zhu Xi considered it essential to incorporate a theory of stillness/activity or centrality/harmony into his system, and most importantly to incorporate that theory into the practice of self-cultivation. He frequently used terminology

---

25. Watson, *The Complete Works of Chuang Tzu,* 57, 90; Roth, *Original Dao,* 82–83, 107, 155, 167. It should be noted, however, that all we have of these early forms of meditation are textual references. While some scholars, such as Roth, believe that there must have been lineages of teachers who transmitted the actual practices, I know of no concrete evidence for them. See Paul R. Goldin's review of *Original Dao* in *Sino-Platonic Papers* 98 (Jan. 2000): 100–108.

26. *Yulei* 12:379.

from the *Xici* appendix of the *Yijing* to discuss the phases of mind/heart, especially *Xici* A.10.4: "*jiran budong, gan er sui tong*" 寂然不動, 感而遂通 ("silent and inactive; when stimulated it then penetrates").[27] Although the referent in the text is the *Zhouyi* 周易 itself in its "spiritual" mode as an oracle, Zhu Xi comments on it, "The mystery of the human mind/heart, in its stillness and activity, is also like this."[28] This line from the *Yijing*, then, could be interpreted to indicate the connection between the still and active phases of mind/heart. Zhu took it to mean that even in its completely still phase, the mind/heart could be fully responsive. Spontaneous, moral responsiveness to both natural and social relations (especially the latter) was a signature characteristic of the sagely mind.[29] Therefore, "quiet and inactive; when stimulated it then penetrates" was a picture, so to speak, of the goal of self-cultivation, a goal described in terms of the relationship—a nondual relationship, as we shall see—of activity and stillness.

Zhu's use of terminology from the *Yijing* to discuss this relationship is not surprising. "Activity" and "stillness" (*dong jing*) themselves were closely connected with the *Yijing*: they are the primary cosmological manifestations of the *yin-yang* polarity, whose oscillating flow is described in the opening passage of Zhou Dunyi's *Taijitu shuo*.[30] Shao Yong, whose philosophy was strongly based on the *Yijing,* had also described the cosmogonic process in terms of the stillness/activity polarity. In one of his diagrams he illustrates the evolution of stillness and activity into eight subdivisions,

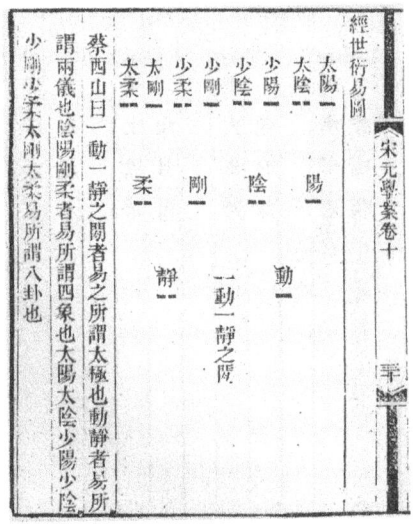

FIGURE 3.1 Shao Yong's *Jingshi yanyi tu*

---

27. *Wenji* 67:3256; Zhu, *Zhouyi benyi* 3:12b.

28. *Zhouyi benyi* 3:13a.

29. See Adler, "Response and Responsibility: Chou Tun-i and Neo-Confucian Resources for Environmental Ethics."

30. See chapters 2 and 4.

which Zhu Xi and his followers interpreted as *Taiji* unfolding into the Eight Trigrams. In a process paralleling the unfolding of *taiji* into the "Two Modes," "Four Images," and Eight Trigrams in *Xici* A.11.5, Shao's diagram begins with the alternation of activity and stillness, which unfolds into *yang, yin,* firm (*gang* 剛), and yielding (*rou* 柔), which in turn each divide into "young" and "mature" phases that clearly parallel the Eight Trigrams. In the reproduction of the chart above, the comment is by Zhu Xi's friend Cai Yuanding 蔡元定 (1135–1198), with whom he collaborated on the *Yixue qimeng* (Introduction to the Study of the *Yi*). The first sentence of the comment says, "The relationship of activity and stillness is what the *Yi* calls *taiji*."[31]

With the goal of sagehood defined in terms of bridging the still and active phases of mind,[32] the problem for Zhu Xi was how to achieve it; or, shifting back to the *Zhongyong* terminology, "how to make the principle of equilibrium (*zhongzhi li* 中之理) manifest in outer actions."[33] It was a matter of enabling one's experienced mental functioning and one's moral activity (*de xing*) to authentically (*cheng*) reflect the goodness inherent in the human mind in the form of its principle or nature, the principle of being human. This is obviously the crux of the problem of Confucian self-cultivation, in that one's Heaven-endowed moral potential (*de*) is the creative power to transform oneself into a sage and ultimately to transform or "pacify (balance) the world" (*ping tianxia* 平天下). For someone as conscious as Zhu Xi of the *difficulty* of gaining access to the inborn moral nature, given the opposing forces he saw in his day, it was a problem whose solution was critical to his entire project.[34]

---

31. See Huang and Quan, *Song-Yuan xue'an,* 10:21b; Birdwhistell, *Transition to Neo-Confucianism,* 240; Wu Kang, *Shaozi Yixue,* 17. The diagram is called the *Jingshi yan yi tu,* which might be translated as the "The *Huangji jingshi*'s diagram of the evolution of the *Yi*." *Huangji jingshi shu* (Royal Ultimate for Governing the World) is the title of Shao's magnum opus, where the diagram originally appeared (although it is missing from the Sibu beiyao edition). It is also found in Hu Guang, *Xingli daquan shu,* 8:1b and Li Guangdi, *Xingli jingyi,* 3:1a. For Shao Yong's conception of *taiji* see below, chapter 4, note 81.

32. Metzger, op. cit., 90.

33. Ibid., 94, quoting Zhu Xi from Qian Mu, *Zhuzi xin xue'an,* 2:152.

34. These opposing forces included, on the individual psychophysical level, the clouding effect of one's psychophysical nature (*qizhizhi xing*); on the political level, the failure during the Northern Song, despite the best efforts of his predecessors, to put into effect a humane government (*ren zheng*); and on the social level the insidious popularity of Buddhism and Daoism during the Song.

It was also a problem that Chan Buddhists were simultaneously dealing with. The rivalry between Dahui Zonggao 大慧宗杲 (1089–1163) and Hongzhi Zhengjue 宏智正覺 (1091–1157), the two most prominent Chan Buddhists of the Song, centered on the question whether the fundamental, prelinguistic level of mind (one's Buddha-nature) could be apprehended in "silent illumination" (*mo zhao* 默照, Hongzhi's method) or the active engagement with *gong'an* 公案 (*kōan*s); the issue here was very closely parallel to the difference between Li Tong's approach and that of the Hunan school.[35]

Zhu Xi's efforts to develop a satisfactory solution to the problem went through three stages, beginning with his several extended visits and regular exchanges of letters with Li Tong from 1153 to 1163.[36] Li's views of stillness or quietude and the importance of quiet-sitting in the practice of self-cultivation were, as we have seen, highly susceptible to the criticism that they were significant steps down the slippery slope to Buddhism and Daoism. Nevertheless, through Li Tong's influence Zhu Xi came to the view that the mind's access to centrality, and hence to the mind's creative principle, had to be gained directly by practicing quiet-sitting and focusing on the mind in its still phase.[37]

---

35. See Morten Schlütter, *How Zen Became Zen: The Dispute over Enlightenment and the Formation of Chan Buddhism in Song-Dynasty China*, chs. 5–7. The dispute continued in Japanese Zen: Dōgen Kigen (1200–1253), the founder of the Sōtō sect in Japan, brought Hongzhi's method to Japan and renamed it "just sitting" (*shikan taza*), while Dahui's method was practiced by the Rinzai school in Japan. As Hakuin Ekaku (1686–1769), the systematizer of the *kōan* method, describes his method in his autobiography (he is actually quoting someone else, but he agrees):

[My practice is not] going off to some mountain and sitting there on a rock or under a tree like a piece of wood "quietly illuminating" yourself. [It is] something you are totally immersed in, without a moment's interruption or pause, in all your daily activities—walking, standing, sitting, or lying down. That is why it is said that practice concentrated in activity is a hundred thousand times superior to practice performed in a state of inactivity. (Norman Waddell, trans., *Wild Ivy: The Spiritual Autobiography of Hakuin Ekaku*, 101)

36. The precise chronology of this process depends largely upon the dating of Zhu Xi's letters to Zhang Shi. Here I am simply following Shu Jingnan's dating in *Zhuzi nianpu changbian*. For a thorough examination of the dating question (written before Shu's work) see Matthew Levey, *Chu Hsi as a "Neo-Confucian,"* 298–365. See also Chen Lai's dating of Zhu's letters in *Zhuzi shuxin biannian kaozheng*.

37. This stage is sometimes referred to as his agreement with the Daonan school. "Daonan" (*dao*-south) refers to Yang Shi and his followers, including Li Tong, because Yang claimed to have brought the Cheng brothers' *dao* south (see chapter 1).

Li Tong died in 1163; two months later Zhu Xi met Zhang Shi, and the following year Zhu and Zhang began discussing the Hunan school's theory of *zhong* and *he*.[38] In the third month of 1166, after further communication by letter with Zhang Shi, Zhu edited and published Zhou Dunyi's *Tongshu* and began a correspondence with Lin Piao about Zhou's theory of *taiji*. The close sequence of his involvement with the *zhong/he* problem and with Zhou Dunyi's works suggests that they might have been related in his thinking.

That year (1166) began the period of Zhu's most intense struggle with the *zhong/he* problem, although he was simultaneously working on other projects, such as his commentary on *Mencius* and his compilation of the conversations (*yulu*) and "surviving works" (*yishu*) of the Cheng brothers.[39] In the sixth month of 1166 Cai Yuanding came to study with Zhu, beginning a relationship that became more a friendship than a teacher-student relationship, and played a significant role in Zhu's eventual resolution of the *zhong/he* problem.[40] That same month he corresponded several times with Zhang Shi on the problem, and three months later he first realized the importance of Cheng Yi's theory of "emphasizing reverent composure" (*zhu jing*), which later became the key to his final resolution of the problem.[41] His correspondence with Zhang Shi continued into the following year.

In the eighth month of 1167, Zhu went to Tanzhou (modern Changsha) to visit Zhang Shi, and stayed for about three months.[42] According to Li Fangzi (Zhu's student and one of his earliest biographers), their discussions during this period focused on *taiji*.[43] But they clearly discussed the *zhong/he* problem as well, because during this visit Zhu was persuaded by Zhang to accept the Hunan school's theory. This was the second stage in the development of his thinking. The Hunan school supported the view that only in activity, both mental and physical, could the creative power of Heaven be experienced; that stillness or centrality/equilibrium was to be found within the activity of daily life. For example, Zhang Shi's teacher, Hu Hong, in a discussion with a student, had cited Mencius's dialogue with King Xuan of Qi (*Mencius* 1A.7)

---

38. *Nianpu,* 305, 311, 330.
39. Ibid., 359–60, 390.
40. Ibid., 353.
41. Ibid., 355–58, 360–63.
42. Ibid., 370–80.
43. Ibid., 373.

in which they discuss the king's compassion for an ox about to be sacrificed. Hu Hong said, "When the King of Qi saw the ox and could not bear its being slaughtered, that was the sprout of the originally good mind seen in the midst of desire for profit." Zhang Shi cited this comment in an essay he wrote in 1166.[44] As Metzger describes the issue discussed by Zhang and Zhu, Zhang Shi

> suggested that accomplished issuance [*yifa*] is all that exists, that it is an indivisible process, and that in its very indivisibility it comprehends the equilibrium of imminent issuance [the *zhong* of *weifa*]. To apprehend equilibrium [*zhong*], therefore, was to revise and broaden our understanding of accomplished issuance [*yifa*], looking in it, so to speak, rather than behind it for *zhong*. The advantage of this view was that by locating *zhong* in a completely manifest form of experience, it not only directed moral effort toward the proper Confucian business of "daily affairs," rather than to the unworldly realm of Buddhism, but also raised hopes that *zhong* could be more easily apprehended.[45]

The implication of this position was that quiet-sitting and the effort to apprehend the mind in perfect stillness were misguided; thus it directly challenged what Zhu Xi had learned from his revered teacher, Li Tong. Note, however, that there is a sectarian element in Zhang Shi's reason: the need to avoid Buddhist unworldliness.

A taste of Zhu Xi's spiritual practice at this time is conveyed by a letter he had written to Zhang Shi the year before his 1167 visit, in Thomas Metzger's translation:

> From the time one has life, one has some kind of knowledge. Affairs and things come into his life, and he responds to and is in contact with them without a moment's rest. His thoughts are changing continuously until he dies. Essentially this state of affairs does not come to a halt for even an instant. Thus it is for the whole world. Yet sages and superior men have spoken of what is called the equilibrium of imminent issuance (*weifazhi zhong* 未發之中), and the

---

44. Schirokauer, "Chu Hsi and Hu Hong," 484.

45. Metzger, *Escape from Predicament*, 96.

state of total stillness without movement (*jiran budong* 寂然不動). How can we reasonably suppose that they regarded the concrete flow of daily affairs as accomplished issuance, and a temporary interruption of this flow, some point lacking contact with affairs, as the time of imminent issuance?

When I tried to think of it in this way, I only found moments without awareness, during which false and dark notions would clog up my mind, hardly the substance of pure consciousness responding to things. Moreover, as soon as I became conscious of any feeling just at that subtle moment of incipience, then this consciousness itself was just a recurrence of accomplished issuance, not what is referred to as total stillness. One may say that the more I sought it, the less I could see it.

So I withdrew from this course and looked for it by examining daily affairs. I considered the fact that any case of becoming aware of an object and empathetically pervading it with one's response, that is, any instance of becoming conscious of something after coming into contact with it, can reasonably be regarded as an indivisible whole. In its inexhaustibility, the process of responding to things is the concrete possibility in terms of which the will of heaven is realized and things come into being without end. Even as things arise and are destroyed ten thousand times a day, the ultimate substance of total stillness is never anything but totally still. What is called imminent issuance [*weifa*] is simply like this.[46]

Thus, Zhu at this point agreed with Zhang that it was pointless to seek a state of perfect stillness. Since the conscious mind can never be perfectly still—that is, the only possible perfect stillness is found in "moments without awareness"—one can only seek for one's moral nature in activity. In an essay he wrote several years later (1172) describing this stage in his thinking he said:

When I heard that Zhang Qinfu [Zhang Shi] had received the teachings of Master Hu [Hong] of Hengshan, I went to inquire about them. Qinfu informed me about what he had heard, which

---

46. *Wenji* 30:1315; trans. Metzger, *Escape from Predicament*, 96–97. Metzger and Levey (336) date this letter to 1168; I am using Shu Jingnan's dating (*Nianpu* 355), with which Chen Lai agrees (35).

was new to me. I retired to ponder it deeply, nearly forgetting to sleep and eat. One day I sighed and said, "Although people from childhood assume that activity and stillness are different, in fact they are in essence nothing but the already expressed (*yifa*); we can never experience the unexpressed (*weifa*) itself." From this point I no longer had doubts, and I took the meaning of the *Zhongyong* to be nothing other than this.[47]

Having solved (he thought) the *zhong/he* problem, in the fourth month of 1168 Zhu wrote in his postface to the *Chengshi yishu* 程氏遺書 (Surviving works of the Chengs):

> Those who read this book will really be able to emphasize reverent composure to establish the basis (*zhu jing yi li qi ben* 主敬以立其本) and to fully investigate *li* to advance their knowledge (*qiong li yi jin qi zhi* 窮理以進其知).[48]

Zhu here is alluding to Cheng Yi's dictum, "Self-cultivation requires reverent composure; the pursuit of learning depends on the extension of knowledge";[49] thus, self-cultivation (here indicating the narrower sense of spiritual cultivation) is the basis or root (*ben*) of learning. Spiritual cultivation is internal; objective learning, or intellectual cultivation, is external. This suggests that at this time he was concerned with establishing an experiential basis in practice for the realization of *li*, and that he knew that Cheng Yi's notion of reverent composure was the key.[50]

But in 1169 he had a further, decisive realization of the significance of reverent composure. Zhu was discussing the *zhong/he* issue with Cai Yuanding when he "suddenly doubted" the Hunan theory.[51] He says,

---

47. "Zhong-he jiushuo xu" (Preface to the old theory of equilbrium and harmony), *Wenji* 75:3634; *Nianpu* 406.

48. *Nianpu*, 390; *Wenji* 75:3625. "To fully investigate *li* to advance their knowledge," echoes the *Daxue*, "investigating things to extend knowledge" (*gewu zhizhi*).

49. *Yishu* 18, in *Er Cheng ji*, 188.

50. In the following month Zhang Shi wrote an essay entitled *Gen zhai ming* (Record of hard fasting), in which he too argues that *gongfu* (moral cultivation) must be the basis of learning (*Nianpu*, 394).

51. *Wenji* 75:3634.

> So I again took up the writings of the Chengs, emptied my mind and calmed my *qi*, and reread them. I hadn't gotten further than a few lines when the congealment loosened and the ice melted. From that point I understood the fundamental nature of the feelings and nature and the subtle meanings of the sages and worthies.[52]

This has been called his "sudden enlightenment of the new theory of *zhong* and *he*,"[53] the final resolution of the problem and the inception of his "mature theory." Zhu explained his new theory immediately after this event in an essay entitled "Discussion of *yifa* and *weifa*," and in a shorter version of it, the "First letter to the gentlemen of Hunan on centrality and harmony."[54] In the letter he first explains that, before studying with Li Tong, he had accepted Cheng Yi's teaching that "whenever we talk about the mind, we refer to the state after feelings are aroused." Therefore, he says,

> I looked upon the mind [*xin*] as the state after feelings are aroused and upon nature [*xing*] as the state before the feelings are aroused. However, I have observed that there are many incorrect points in Master Cheng's works. I have therefore thought the matter over, and consequently realized that in my previous theory not only are the [contrasting] terms "mind" and "nature" improper but the efforts in my daily task [*riyong gongfu* 日用功夫] also completely lack a great foundation. Therefore the loss has not been confined to the meanings of words.[55]

In other words, he realized that it was incorrect to imply a dualistic relationship between mind and nature. The identification of *weifa* with nature (*xing*) and *yifa* with mind (*xin*) is a false distinction; in fact, as Cheng Yi himself had said, "the mind is one," and it is never in a state of total stillness. Furthermore, this has not only theoretical but also practical implications for his "daily practice" of self-cultivation:

---

52. *Wenji* 75:3635. Note his meditative approach to reading, an important aspect of his "methodology of reading" (*dushu fa*).

53. *Nianpu*, 406.

54. *Nianpu*, 407–408. The essay is found in *Wenji* 67:3266–69; the letter in *Wenji* 64:3130–31, and fully translated by Chan, *Source Book*, 600–602.

55. Chan, *Source Book*, 600.

> Right along, in my discussions and thinking, I have simply considered the mind to be the state after the feelings are aroused, and in my daily efforts I have merely considered examining and recognizing the clues [of activities or feelings] as the starting points [i.e., focusing on the incipient beginnings of mental activity]. Consequently I have neglected one aspect of the effort of daily self-cultivation [*pingri hanyang yiduan gongfu* 平日涵養一段功夫], so that my mind was disturbed in many ways and lacked the quality of depth or purity. Also, when it was expressed in speech or action, it was always characterized by a sense of urgency and an absence of reserve, and there was no longer any disposition of ease or profoundness [because he was focusing on mental activity, not stillness]. For a single mistake in one's viewpoint can lead to as much harm as this. This is something we must not overlook.[56]

It is clear in this part of the letter how the issue concerns the practical problem of self-cultivation as much as it concerns theory. Rather than accepting a dualistic model of the mind/heart, Zhu chooses to discuss it in terms of its substance (*ti* 體) and function (*yong* 用):

> [B]efore there is any sign of thought or deliberation and prior to the arrival [stimulus] of external things, there is the state before the feelings of pleasure, anger, sorrow, and joy are aroused [*weifa*]. At this time, the state is identical with the substance [*ti*] of the mind, which is absolutely quiet and inactive [*jiran budong*], and the nature endowed by Heaven should be completely embodied in it. Because it is neither excessive nor insufficient, and is neither unbalanced nor one-sided, it is called equilibrium [*zhong*]. When it is acted upon and immediately penetrates all things [*gan er sui tong*], the feelings are then aroused. In this state the functioning [*yong*] of the mind can be seen. Because it never fails to attain the proper measure and degree and has nowhere deviated from the right, it is called harmony [*he*].[57]

---

56. Ibid., 601–602, slightly modified (Chan omits "one aspect" in the second sentence).
57. Ibid., 600–601.

So instead of Cheng Yi's simple distinction between the nature (*xing*) as the unexpressed centrality and the mind (*xin*) as the expressed harmony, Zhu Xi makes it a tripartite relationship based on the substance-function rubric and Zhang Zai's dictum, "The mind/heart connects the nature and feelings" (*xin tong xing qing* 心統性情):[58]

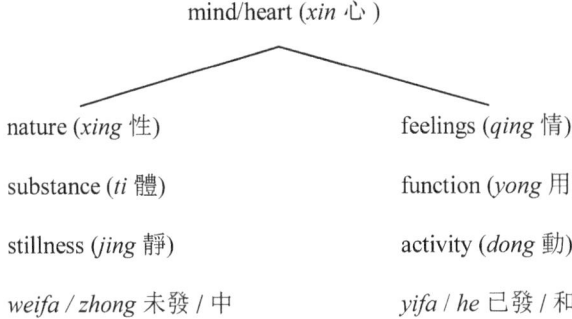

The substance-function (*ti-yong*) rubric in Chinese thought is used "to describe phenomena which, while logically distinguishable, cannot actually exist apart from one another,"[59] such as a lamp and its light,[60] or human nature and feelings.[61] In terms of the philosophical understanding of the mind, the *ti-yong* rubric preserves the unity or continuity of mental states and processes while introducing a meaningful distinction between the still and active phases.

But there remains a problem in terms of the practical implications for self-cultivation. As he continues in the "First letter to the gentlemen of Hunan on centrality and harmony":

> However, the state before the feelings are aroused cannot be sought and the state after they are aroused permits no manipulation.[62]

---

58. *Zhangzi quanshu* 14:2a; Chan, *Source Book,* 517.

59. Philip J. Ivanhoe, "*Ti* and *yong*," in Craig, ed., *Routledge Encyclopedia of Philosophy*. Matthew Levey emphasizes this point in *Chu Hsi as a "Neo-Confucian,"* 146–80.

60. Yampolsky, trans., *The Platform Sutra of the Sixth Patriarch,* 137.

61. *Yulei* 5:215.

62. Chan, *Source Book,* 601.

The *weifa* (unexpressed) state "cannot be sought" because the act of seeking it makes it *yifa* (expressed). And the *yifa* state "permits no manipulation" because whatever underlying errors there may be, such as some selfish desire motivating the act of self-examination, have already been acted upon. Zhu finds the solution to this dilemma in Cheng Yi's teachings:

> In the final analysis what he said was no more than the word "reverent composure" (*jing*). This is why he said, "Reverent composure without fail is the way to attain equilibrium."[63]

Jing (sometimes translated as "seriousness" or "reverence") was classically defined as the properly respectful and reverent attitude one should have when performing a sacrifice, but the Neo-Confucians extended it beyond that context. Cheng Yi had said, "[T]he effort to maintain reverent composure joins the states of activity and stillness at their point of intersection."[64] This was the key both to Zhu's adoption of the term as the foundation of mental cultivation and, as we shall see, to his particular interest in Zhou Dunyi. As he continues in his letter to the gentlemen of Hunan:

> So long as in one's daily life the effort at reverent composure and spiritual cultivation (*hanyang* 涵養) is fully extended and there are no selfish human desires to disturb it, then before the feelings are aroused [*weifa*] it will be as clear as a mirror and as calm as still water, and after the feelings are aroused [*yifa*] it will attain due measure and degree without exception. This is the essential task in everyday life. As to self-cultivation when things occur [i.e., in response to external stimuli] and seeking understanding through inference when we come into contact with things, this must also serve as the foundation. If

---

63. Chan 1963, 601, quoting *Henan Chengshi yishu*, 2A:44, and substituting "reverent composure" for "seriousness." The *Yishu* contains the bulk of the Chengs' teachings on *jing*, and Zhu Xi had compiled the text in 1168, the year before this letter was written. It was Zhu's work on this text that therefore precipitated the resolution of his crisis. See Van Ess, "The Compilation of the Works of the Ch'eng Brothers," 295–98.

64. Zhu Xi quotes this in his "Discussion of Master Cheng's nourishing and contemplation" (*Wenji* 67:3269). For more on *jing* see Graham, *Two Chinese Philosophers*, 67–73; Chan, *Source Book*, 522, 547, 593, 785; and Chan, trans., *Neo-Confucian Terms Explained*, 100–104. See also *Yulei* 12:369–79; Qian, *Zhuzi xin xue'an*, 2:298–335; Yoshikawa and Miura, *Shushi shu*, 115–19.

we observe the state after the feelings are aroused, what is contained in the state before the feelings are aroused can surely be understood in silence.⁶⁵

In other words, the relationship between the stillness and activity of the mind, or the *weifa* and *yifa* states of the feelings, or centrality and harmony, can be described as *interpenetration*. That is, stillness and centrality can be found within harmonious activity, and harmonious or moral activity can be found in stillness—as long as one maintains the attitude of reverent composure. Stillness in the midst of moral activity can be understood as a sense of calm purpose combined with a sense of the ultimate significance (or ultimate concern, to use Paul Tillich's term) of one's engagement in the process of moral transformation. These are both implied by the word *jing* (reverent composure). Activity in the midst of stillness can be understood in the sense that in a practice such as quiet-sitting, or even in sleep, one is nourishing one's Heaven-endowed moral potential. An example of this would be Mencius's description of the restorative effects of the "night *qi*" (*ye qi* 夜氣) in his famous Ox Mountain allegory:

> If, in spite of the respite a man gets in the day and in the night and of the effect of the morning air (*danzhi qi* 但之氣) on him, scarcely any of his likes and dislikes resemble those of other men, it is because what he does in the course of the day once again dissipates what he has gained. If this dissipation happens repeatedly, then the influence of the air in the night (*ye qi*) will no longer be able to preserve what was originally in him, and when that happens, the man is not far removed from an animal. . . . Hence, given the right nourishment (*yang*) there is nothing that will not grow, and deprived of it there is nothing that will not wither away.⁶⁶

In his commentary on this passage Zhu Xi quotes the *Yijing*'s statement (as quoted by Cheng Hao) that the noble person (*junzi*) uses "reverent composure to straighten oneself internally" (*jing yi zhi nei* 敬以直內).⁶⁷ And in a remark

---

65. Chan, *Source Book,* 601, slightly modified.
66. *Mencius* 6A.8, trans. D. C. Lau, *Mencius,* 165.
67. Zhu, *Sishu jizhu, Mengzi* 6:7b. The original text is in the *Wenyan* commentary on line two of the hexagram Kun; see Zhu, *Zhouyi benyi,* 1:12b. Cheng Hao's reference to the line is from *Henan Chengshi yishu,* 1:21. See also Chan, trans., *Reflections on*

collected in Zhu's *Classified Conversations,* he says, "To see [an example of] 'emphasizing stillness,' look at the 'night *qi*' (*ye qi*) section [of *Mencius,* i.e., 6A.8]."⁶⁸ So it is clear that he regards sleep as an example of Zhou Dunyi's "cultivating stillness," and that he understands cultivating stillness, following Mencius and presumably including quiet-sitting, as active spiritual cultivation (*hanyang*) or "nourishment" (the same *yang*). Thus *jing* implies both "activity in stillness" and "stillness in activity."

In one remarkable essay, the "Discussion of *Taiji*" (*Taiji shuo* 太極說), Zhu Xi clearly demonstrates the relevance of Zhou Dunyi's concept of *taiji*—and therefore the relevance of Zhou himself—to his mature theory of spiritual cultivation. As far as I know this essay was not published, but it was undoubtedly circulated to his students (who numbered in the thousands over the course of his lifetime) and his friends. (Section letters are for reference only.)

Discussion of *Taiji* (*Taiji shuo* 太極說) by Zhu Xi

[A] "Activity and stillness have no starting point; *yin* and *yang* have no beginning;"⁶⁹ this is the Way of Heaven. Beginning in *yang,* completing in *yin,* rooted in stillness, flowing in activity; this is the human Way. But since *yang* returns to its root in *yin* and stillness returns to its base in activity, [human beings'] activity and stillness also have no starting points, and their *yin* and *yang* also have no beginnings. So humans are never separate from Heaven, and Heaven is never separate from humans.

[B] "*Yuan* 元 and *heng* 亨 are the penetrating [quality] of authenticity" is activity; "*li* 利 and *zhen* 貞 are the recovery of authenticity" is stillness.⁷⁰ *Yuan* (originating) is the starting point of activity, yet it is

---

Things at Hand, 126, where it is mistakenly translated as "Seriousness [*jing*] is to straighten the external life." It is correctly translated on p. 139, where Cheng Hao quotes the full line, "Seriousness is to straighten the internal life and righteousness [*yi*] is to square the external life."

68. *Yulei* 94: 3139. Here he is referring to Zhou's doctrine of emphasizing stillness, but since he followed Cheng Yi in interpreting Zhou's "stillness" as "reverent composure," as we have just seen, this is really about the latter.

69. Quoting Cheng Yi, in *Er Cheng ji, Jing shuo,* 1:1029.

70. Quoting Zhou Dunyi, *Tongshu* 1. *Yuan heng li zhen* is the hexagram text of Qian, the first hexagram of the *Yijing.* Zhu Xi's commentary on the two sentences in the

rooted in stillness. *Zhen* (being correct) is the material of stillness, yet it is expressed in activity. The alternation of activity and stillness (*yidong yijing* 一動一靜) is an endless cycle. So *zhen* [even though it is is the material of stillness] is how myriad things achieve their ends and achieve their beginnings [hence stillness is creative]. Thus, although humans cannot be inactive, "establishing the peak of being human (*renji* 人極)" requires "emphasizing stillness."[71] Only by emphasizing stillness can their expression in activity always be measured and never lack their fundamental stillness.

[C] Stillness is how the nature (*xing* 性) is established; activity is how the endowment (*ming* 命) proceeds. But in fact stillness is the cessation of activity. Therefore the alternation of activity and stillness is always the procession (*xing* 行) of the endowment, and its procession through activity and stillness is the reality of the nature. Therefore [the *Zhongyong*] says, "What heaven endows (*ming*) is called the nature (*xing*)."[72]

[D] The unexpressed (*weifa* 未發) feelings are the nature; this is what is called "centrality/equilibrium (*zhong* 中), the great root of all under heaven."[73] The expressed (*yifa* 已發) nature is the feelings;[74] when they are all measured they are called "harmony (*he* 和), the pervasive way of all under heaven."[75] This is all the natural [Way] of heaven. The wondrous virtue of the nature and feelings is the mind/heart (*xin* 心).[76] What brings about centrality and harmony,

---

Tongshu is: "*Yuan* is originating, *heng* is penetrating, *li* is carrying out, *zhen* is being correct: the Four Virtues [characteristic powers] of Qian. 'Penetration' (*tong*) is just at the point when it appears and is bestowed on things, the 'issuing' of goodness. 'Recovery' (*fu*) is when each one receives it and stores it within, the 'fulfillment' of the nature" (*Zhou Lianxi ji*, 5:3b). For a discussion of *yuan, heng, li,* and *zhen* as the Four Virtues of Qian, see Shchutskii, *Researches on the I Ching*, 136–44.

71. These two phrases both come from the second half of the *Taijitu shuo*.

72. *Zhongyong* 1.

73. Ibid.

74. Not mind, as Cheng Yi had said.

75. Ibid.

76. An allusion to Zhang Zai's dictum, "The mind/heart connects the nature and the feelings."

establishes the great root, and makes the pervasive Way proceed is the rulership (*zhuzai* 主宰) of heavenly principle.⁷⁷

[E] Being still and lacking any impropriety is the centrality/equilibrium of the nature; this is "silent inactivity" (*jiran budong* 寂然不動).⁷⁸ Being active and in equilibrium is the feelings being expressed correctly; this is "penetrating when stimulated."⁷⁹ That which is always aware in stillness and always stopped (still) in activity is the mystery of the heart/mind: silent and yet stimulated, stimulated and yet silent.⁸⁰

The remarkable thing about this "Discussion of *Taiji*," of course, is that "*taiji*" is not even mentioned in it! The fact that it is called a discussion of *taiji* shows how central that concept is to Zhu Xi's system, as the essay systematically relates a substantial number of the key terms in that system. The essay shows how the human being is an integral part of the natural world, reflecting the Way of heaven; both follow the fundamental principle of ceaseless *yin-yang* alternation (section A). The terms *activity* and *stillness*, which are the first manifestations of *taiji* according to Zhou Dunyi's *Taijitu shuo*, are woven throughout the essay, linking together other key terms from the *Tongshu, Yijing,* and *Zhongyong* (the four texts most closely associated with Zhou Dunyi). Section B quotes a line from the *Tongshu* that links together the cosmic/natural principles of Qian (the first hexagram of the *Yijing*)—in Zhu's own interpretation, of course—with being authentic (*cheng* 誠), the identifying characteristic of the sage according to Zhou Dunyi. The effect of this is to deepen the meaning of the natural-human linkage posited in section A by suggesting that the linkage is constituted not only by the formal continuity of *yin-yang* alternation but also by the underlying principle of natural/moral creativity. By "natural/moral creativity" I mean the unceasing creativity of the natural world, suggested by Cheng Yi's phrase "unceasing birth and growth" (*sheng sheng buxi* 生生不息),⁸¹ and the moral creativity by which human beings "author" themselves by fulfilling the moral potential

---

77. *Li* comprehends both phases, stillness and activity (etc.).
78. See *Tongshu* 4, quoting *Yijing, Xici* A.10.4.
79. Ibid.
80. *Wenji,* 67:3274.
81. *Henan Chengshi yishu,* 15:149), based on the *Yijing*'s line, "Birth and growth are called the Way" (*Xici* A.5.6).

inherent in the natures—a fulfillment described by the term *being authentic,* which Zhu Xi defined as "actualizing principle" (*shi li* 實理).[82] Thus, these two forms of creativity are manifestations of the single pattern/principle/ order of the cosmos.

Section C further links activity and stillness with *xing*: the nature or principle of being human, which we fulfill in differing degrees depending upon our environmental influences and the quality of our *qi*; and *ming*: the "givenness" or facticity of that endowment, which define the unalterable limitations we are born with. Section D sets *xing* (nature) in another dyadic relationship, this time with *qing* 情—the feelings or dispositions, which are functions of the physical nature—and correlates *xing* and *ming* with the terms *weifa/zhong* and *yifa/he,* the terms with which Zhu struggled in the 1160s. This section shows that the essay, although undated, must have been written after the final resolution of his spiritual crisis, because here he implicitly rejects Cheng Yi's theory that *weifa/zhong* refers to the nature and *yifa/he* refers to the mind. Zhu instead follows Zhang Zai's dictum that "[t]he mind/heart connects the nature and the feelings/dispositions" (*xin tong xing qing* 心統性情).

The last sentence of section E reinforces this rough dating in referring to activity (being aware) in stillness and stillness (being stopped) in activity; "silent and yet stimulated, stimulated and yet silent." I therefore take this essay as strong confirmation that Zhu Xi's understanding of *taiji*, and therefore the significance of Zhou Dunyi to him, revolved around *taiji*'s relationship to the problem of spiritual cultivation that occupied him in the 1160s.

In Zhu Xi's view—or more precisely, his own personal practice—"activity in stillness" and "stillness in activity" provide the *experiential* common ground linking the still and active phases of the mind. The still and active phases therefore have a nondual relationship as different but inseparably linked phases of the one undivided mind.[83] Thus, both quiet-sitting and active study and

---

82. See his commentary on the *Tongshu,* sections 1–3, in *Zhou Lianxi ji,* 5:2a–17b.

83. I use "nonduality" here in the sense of the *yin-yang* model: the difference between them is real, but they cannot exist separately and each implies the other. This differs from the *advaita* form of nondualism found in Sankara (eighth century CE), which is really monism (all differences are illusory). It is closer to the later Vedantic philosopher Ramanuja (eleventh century CE), whose philosophy is called *viśiṣṭādvaita,* or "qualified non-dualism." See Radhakrishnan and Moore, *A Sourcebook in Indian Philosophy,* 506–55. Nondualism in this sense is perhaps the most fundamental pattern in traditional Chinese thought, clearly present in Confucianism, Daoism, Chinese Buddhism, and popular religion.

engagement in affairs are legitimate and necessary methods of self-cultivation, and *both* provide access to the creative, transformative power of Heaven.[84] More importantly for our purposes, Zhu sees them not merely as complementary opposites but as *mutually interpenetrating* phases of the mind/heart. This is where Zhou Dunyi's writings become relevant, for they provide the philosophical/cosmological grounding for this experiential discovery.

INTERPENETRATION

The relationship between activity and stillness is outlined by Zhou Dunyi in the first section of the *Taijitu shuo* and in section 16 of the *Tongshu*, both of which will be discussed further in chapter 4.

Taijitu shuo:

Nonpolar and yet Supreme Polarity (*wuji er taiji* 無極而太極)! Supreme Polarity in activity generates *yang*; yet at the limit of activity it is still. In stillness it generates *yin*; yet at the limit of stillness it is also active. Activity and stillness alternate; each is the basis of the other. In distinguishing *yin* and *yang*, the Two Modes are thereby established.[85]

Tongshu 16: Activity and Stillness (*dong jing* 動靜)

Activity as the absence of stillness and stillness as the absence of activity characterize things (*wu* 物). Activity that is not [empirically] active and stillness that is not [empirically] still characterize spirit (*shen* 神). Being active and yet not active, still and yet not still, does not mean that [spirit] is neither active nor still.

[Zhu's comment:] There is stillness within activity, and activity within stillness. For while things do not [inter-]penetrate (*tong* 通) [i.e., they are limited by their physical forms], spirit subtly [penetrates] the myriad things.

---

84. This point raises an important question regarding the consistency of Zhu Xi's philosophical position. If *li*, in its instantiation as human nature (*xing*), is ontologically distinct from *qi* and the dispositional/affective aspect of mind (*qing*), how can the latter be transformed by the former? How can the mind unite and control human nature and the dispositions (*xin tong xing qing*), as Zhang Zai had first claimed? How can the "human mind" (*renxin*) ever come to reflect the "moral mind" (*daoxin*)?

85. *Zhou Lianxi ji*, 1:2a.

The *yin* of water is based in *yang*; the *yang* of fire is based in *yin*. The Five Phases are *yin* and *yang*. *Yin* and *yang* are the Supreme Polarity. The Four Seasons revolve; the myriad things end and begin [again]. How undifferentiated! How extensive! And how endless!

[Zhu's comment:] Substance is fundamental and unitary; hence "undifferentiated." Function is dispersed and differentiated; hence "extensive." The succession of activity and stillness is like an "endless" revolution. This continuity refers to (the relationship of) substance and function. This section clarifies the ideas of the [*Taiji*] Diagram, which should be consulted.⁸⁶

Zhu's application of the substance-function (*ti-yong* 體用) distinction to stillness and activity draws attention to their inseparability; *yong* is the function *of the substance*.⁸⁷ More precisely in this case, the relationship of activity and stillness is not only temporal alternation but also *ontological interpenetration*. That is, the *nature* of activity includes stillness and vice versa. Thus, in other comments Zhu says:

On *Taijitu shuo*:

The original ground (*chu ben* 初本) of the *yang* produced by activity is stillness. Likewise, for stillness there must be activity. This is what is meant by "activity and stillness without end."⁸⁸

Within the stillness of *yin* is the basis of *yang* itself; within the activity of *yang* is the basis of *yin* itself. This is because activity necessarily comes from stillness, which is based in *yin*; and stillness necessarily comes from activity, which is based in *yang*.⁸⁹

The material of water is *yin*, yet its nature is based in *yang*. The material of fire is *yang*, yet its nature is based in *yin*.⁹⁰

---

86. Ibid., 5:33b–34b. Zhu strongly believed that the *Taijtu shuo* and the *Tongshu* displayed a consistent philosophical vision, despite the fact that the latter does not mention the key terms *wuji* and *taiji*. In his commentaries on both texts (see below, Part II) he consistently connects each with the other.

87. See above, p. 95.

88. Ibid., 1:7b.

89. Ibid., 1:7b.

90. Ibid., 1:12a.

On *Tongshu* 16:

"Being active and yet not active, still and yet not still, does not mean that [spirit] is neither active nor still" (from *Tongshu* 16). This refers to the metaphysical order (*xing'er shangzhi li* 形而上之理). This order is spiritual and unfathomable. When it is active, it is simultaneously still. Therefore [Zhou] says "no activity." When it is still, it is simultaneously active. Therefore [Zhou] says "no stillness." Within stillness there is activity, and within activity there is stillness. When still it is capable of activity, and when active it is capable of stillness. Within *yang* there is *yin,* and within *yin* there is *yang*. The permutations are inexhaustible.[91]

The idea of metaphysical interpenetration is a prominent doctrine in Huayan Buddhism, and it is quite possible that Zhu Xi was aware of it. He had been a serious student of the Chan teacher Daoqian 道謙 from 1144 until the latter's death in 1152.[92] Daoqian had been a student of the great Chan master Dahui Zonggao 大慧宗杲, and after Daoqian's death Zhu visited Dahui in 1155.[93] Since Chan Buddhism was strongly influenced by Huayan philosophy and Zhu Xi was an avid reader, we certainly cannot rule out the possibility that he read some Huayan texts as well as Chan.

The relevant idea in Huayan Buddhism is *wu-ai* 無礙, literally "non-obstruction," as expressed in the doctrines *li-shi wu-ai* 理事無礙 (the non-obstruction of principle and phenomenon) and *shi-shi wu-ai* 事事無礙 (the non-obstruction of phenomenon and phenomenon).[94] *Li-shi wu-ai* means that since all phenomena are empty of "own-being" (i.e., they are interdependent), each phenomenon or thing fully manifests the ultimate principle (namely emptiness); hence the "non-obstruction" (or interpenetration) of principle and phenomenon. *Shi-shi wu-ai* goes a step farther: each thing fully *contains* the reality of every other thing (the principle of emptiness); hence the mutual non-obstruction or interpenetration of every thing with every other thing. This is the point of the "Jewel-net of Indra" image in the *Huayan (Avatamsaka)*

---

91. Ibid., 5:35a.
92. *Nianpu,* 87, 103, 107, 116, 138, 151, 153.
93. Ibid., 189. See also chapter 1.
94. Gimello, *Chih-yen,* 454–510; Chang, *The Buddhist Teaching of Totality,* 141–71, 207–23.

Sutra: there is a multifaceted jewel at every intersection of thread in the net, and every jewel reflects every other jewel.[95] The formal structure of this argument is basically the same as the argument I have outlined here for the interpenetration of activity and stillness.

Zhu Xi uses basically the same terminology of "non-obstruction" in reference to the relationship between *wuji* and *taiji*:

> "Nonpolar, yet Supreme Polarity" explains existence [polarity or differentiation] within non-existence [nonpolarity or undifferentiation]. If you can truly see it, it explains existence and non-existence, or vice versa, neither obstructing the other (*dou wu fang-ai* 都無妨礙).[96]

As we shall see in chapter 4, Zhu Xi understood *taiji* to be the most fundamental cosmic ordering principle/pattern, which is, to be specific, the principle of *yin-yang* polarity. In other words, the simplest, most basic ordering principle in the Chinese cosmos is the differentiation of unity into bipolarity (not duality).[97] *Wuji er taiji*, then, means that this most fundamental principle, bipolarity—despite its evident "twoness" and its role as the ultimate source of multiplicity—is itself, as a rational ordering principle, essentially *un*differentiated.[98] *Wuji er taiji* is "the undifferentiated principle of differentiation," or "the formless basis of form." In fact, the line might better be understood as a topic heading rather than an exclamatory sentence. As Zhu frequently affirmed, "Principle is one" or "unitary." Since any concrete instance of differentiation or polarity embodies this integral, nonpolar principle, the two—nonpolarity and ultimate polarity—themselves have a relationship of interpenetration. Hence, every concrete thing embodies both polarity (as its order or pattern) and nonpolarity

---

95. For a stimulating discussion of this image see Francis Cook, "The Jewel Net of Indra," in Callicott and Ames, *Nature in Asian Traditions of Thought*.

96. *Zhou Lianxi ji*, 1:6a.

97. I use "principle" here not in the sense of a "transcendent" principle that exists independently of things and imposes order on them, but rather in the sense of an "emergent" principle or pattern that arises *from* the contingent flow of events. This is consistent with Hall and Ames's notion of "aesthetic order," although they reserve the word *principle* for what they call "logical order" (Hall and Ames, *Thinking Through Confucius*, 15–16).

98. He affirms this in his comment on *Tongshu*, section 16: "'Undifferentiated (*hun*)' refers to the Supreme Polarity" (additional comment 6; see Part II).

(as the unity of that principle), or differentiation and undifferentiation, or multiplicity and unity. Zhu's use of the term *non-obstruction* in this context is very close to the Buddhist concept, and suggests that metaphysical interpenetration is significant in understanding the importance of *wuji* and *taiji* in his system. The interpenetrating (non-obstructing) relationship of *wuji* and *taiji* served as a model for the interpenetrating relationship of stillness and activity. As Cheng Chung-ying put it, "*Taiji* is nothing other than the permanent union of the moving forces of *yin-yang* [which are] immanent in *taiji* and are immanent in each other."[99]

The practice of self-cultivation was the purpose of Zhu Xi's entire philosophical and educational system. Everything in it should be understood in that light. And he was never satisfied until he could establish a solid philosophical grounding for that practice. Accordingly, Zhu found in Zhou Dunyi's discussions of the interpenetration of activity and stillness, based on the interpenetration of *wuji* and *taiji*, exactly the underpinning he needed for the methodology of self-cultivation that he worked out through his struggle with the problem of centrality and harmony. His statement in the 1169 letter to the gentlemen of Hunan, "If we observe the state *after* the feelings are aroused, what is contained in the state *before* the feelings are aroused can surely be understood in silence" (quoted above) is an example of this *praxis* that required a supporting *theoria*—preferably a cosmological theory, since like all Confucians (except Xunzi) he believed that their ethics and moral psychology were grounded in the natural world. What he found in Zhou's *Taijitu shuo* and *Tongshu* fit that bill.

To conclude, it is useful to look at Zhu's comments on section 20 of the *Tongshu*, which is entitled "Learning to be a Sage" (*shengxue* 聖學), where he integrates Cheng Yi's concept of "reverent composure" (*jing* 敬) with Zhou's concept of activity and stillness. Cheng Yi himself had made the connection in saying that "the effort to maintain reverent composure joins the states of activity and stillness at their point of intersection."[100] Zhu Xi developed the connection in terms of Zhou's notion of "unity" (*yi* 一), which he discusses in terms of Cheng's characterization of *jing* as a state of mind that "emphasizes

---

99. Cheng, "Categories of Creativity in Whitehead and Neo-Confucianism," 551.

100. See Zhu's "Discussion of Master Cheng's nourishing and contemplation" (*Wenji* 67:3269), quoted above.

unity."[101] Zhu Xi further applies Cheng Yi's concept of *jing* to Zhou Dunyi's teaching on stillness in such a way as to minimize the latter's Daoist and Buddhist implications. The text reads:

Can Sagehood be learned?

Reply: It can.

Are there essentials (*yao* 要)?

Reply: There are.

I beg to hear them.

Reply: To be unified (*yi*) is essential. To be unified is to have no desire. Without desire one is vacuous when still (*jing xu* 靜虛) and direct in activity (*dong zhi* 動直). Being vacuous when still, one will be clear (*ming* 明); being clear one will be penetrating (*tong* 通). Being direct in activity one will be impartial (*gong* 公); being impartial one will be all-embracing (*pu* 溥). Being clear and penetrating, impartial and all-embracing, one is almost [a sage].[102]

Zhu Xi claims that what Zhou Dunyi meant here by "desirelessness" (*wuyu*) is the same as what Cheng Yi meant by *jing* or reverent composure—thus redefining in Confucian terms a proposition with obvious Buddhist and Daoist resonances—because both terms were defined in terms of unity or unification.[103] Zhu discusses two senses of "unity" here. In metaphysical

---

101. Graham, *Two Chinese Philosophers*, 68–70.

102. *Zhou Lianxi ji*, 5:38b. Note the similarity of the term *direct in activity* (*dong zhi*) to the important term in section 14 of the *Platform Sutra, direct mind* (*zhi xin*) (Yampolsky, *The Platform Sutra of the Sixth Patriarch*, 136, where it is translated as "straightforward mind").

103. Although Zhu Xi, like the Buddhists, acknowledged the potential for evil (or suffering) in human desire (*renyu*), he taught that desires should be not eliminated but selectively cultivated and trained to accord with the Way. Only selfish desires (*siyu*) should be eliminated. The basic Buddhist approach was to extinguish all desire or "thirst" (*tanha*), at least insofar as it is based on ignorance (*avidya*). The most prominent Daoist claim about desirelessness was found in the first chapter of the *Laozi*.

terms, he identifies unity with the Supreme Polarity inherent in the mind.[104] In terms of self-cultivation, he says that both Zhou and Cheng interpret "unity" of mind as a "clear-sighted unity, not a muddle-headed unity," and not "lumping everything together."[105] It is neither concentration on one thing to the exclusion of all else, nor concentration on unity and neglect of diversity. Both the one and the many are preserved.

Zhu Xi considered the state of mind described by the terms *unity* and *reverent composure* to be the spiritual basis of self-cultivation, including intellectual cultivation (investigating things and extending knowledge), spiritual cultivation (rectifying the mind), and moral activity (in the family, community, and state)—i.e., the whole spectrum outlined by the "eight items" of the *Great Learning*. It is a state of composure that remains unchanged by external stimuli and yet enables one to respond to them—a state of equipoise and fluid responsiveness.[106] This condition is independent of the mind's content or activity at any particular moment. In the absence of stimuli the mind characterized by reverent composure is equable yet poised to respond; when stimulated it responds immediately ("direct activity") because it is not preoccupied with private motivations or with fixed concentration. Since it is not preoccupied with anything it cannot be disturbed. *Jing* is the experiential ground or orientation for both mental activity and stillness. As a student put it to Zhu Xi in a question:

> "Vacuous when still" [in *Tongshu* 20, above] means the mind is like a clear mirror or still water, without the slightest bit of selfish desire added to it. Thus its activity completely follows the outflowing of

---

104. In his published commentary on the first line of section 20 he says, "The truth of the Nonpolar (*wuji*) and the origin of the Two Modes and the Four Images are not external to this mind, and in the realm of daily functioning itself there is no separation from the power to use them" (*Zhou Lianxi ji*, 5:39a). In his commentary on the first line of section 22 of the *Tongshu* he says, "Were it not for the perfect intelligence of the Supreme Polarity of the human mind, how would one be able to discern it?" (ibid., 6:1b).

105. *Zhou Lianxi ji*, 5:39b. This, incidentally, is also a major emphasis of Chan and Zen teachers, such as Hongzhi Zhengjue (1091–1157)—Zhu Xi's contemporary—and the great Japanese Zen master Dōgen Kigen (1200–1253), who studied and practiced in China under Hongzhi's third-generation successor, Tiantong Rujing (1163–1228).

106. For a discussion of responsiveness in Neo-Confucian discourse, see Adler, "Response and Responsibility."

the natural order (*tianli* 天理), without the slightest selfish desire disturbing it. "Vacuous when still" is its substance; "direct in activity" is its function.[107]

Zhu Xi replies:

> If things [i.e., incoming stimuli] come and get the better of it [the mind], then it is full. If it is full, it will be obscured; if obscured then blocked. Directness in activity is simply having absolutely no obstruction (*ai* 礙) in its activity.[108]

Thus, the quality of the mind in its still phase determines the quality of its activity—in particular its capacity for "directness in activity" or immediate, intuitive response to changing events. The purpose of "emphasizing stillness" is to "nourish activity."[109] In this way Zhu Xi, with the help of Cheng Yi and Zhang Zai, "saves" Zhou Dunyi from Daoist and Buddhist quietism and establishes a Confucian brand of quietism that fundamentally entails activity. This was a middle ground between the "quietistic" application of Zhou's thought he had learned from his teacher, Li Tong, and the emphasis on activity and the active mind that was taught by the Hunan school. It was the solution to his spiritual crisis, and it may be the best explanation for his curious appropriation of Zhou Dunyi and for the use he made of Zhou's ideas—in particular the concept of polarity as the key to understanding *taiji*.

---

107. *Zhou Lianxi ji,* 5:40a; *Yulei* 94:3163–64.

108. Ibid. Note again Zhu's use of the term *ai* (obstruction), discussed above in connection with Huayan Buddhism.

109. *Yulei,* 71:2855.

Chapter Four

Taiji as "Supreme Polarity"

Zhu Xi achieved the final resolution of his spiritual crisis in the third month of 1169. The first piece he wrote following that was the essay "Discussion of *yifa* and *weifa*" on the expressed and unexpressed phases of mind/heart, followed shortly by the "First letter to the gentlemen of Hunan on equilibrium and harmony," a shortened form of the essay. As we saw in the previous chapter, the solution he found was to see that *yifa* / *zhong* 已發 / 中 and *weifa* / *he* 未發 / 和 are interpenetrating phases: activity in stillness and stillness in activity. This allowed him to synthesize the approaches to spiritual cultivation that he had learned from Li Tong and the Hunan school into a new approach—a true synthesis.

In the sixth month of 1169 he published a revised edition of Zhou Dunyi's *Taijitu shuo* and *Tongshu* (without commentaries), known as the Jian'an edition after the place of publication. Of course he must have been working on this for some time before it was published. We do not know exactly when he began this project, but it seems fair to say that it was the next thing he worked on after the essay and letter on *yifa* and *weifa*, and I take that to be significant.[1] My hunch is that he immediately realized that

---

1. According to Shu Jingnan, in the fourth month of 1169 Zhu sent the surviving writings of Cheng Hao to Zhang Shi. This is the only text mentioned between the *Yifa weifa shuo* and the *Taijitu shuo* and *Tongshu* (*Nianpu*: 406–12).

Zhou's writings provided a philosophical basis for the method of spiritual *praxis* that he had just discovered. His realization was no doubt facilitated by his recent and ongoing conversations and correspondence with Zhang Shi, who had picked up an appreciation of Zhou Dunyi from his teacher Hu Hong, and was considered something of an expert on Zhou.² Nevertheless, there is no evidence that the discovery of Zhou's relevance to Zhu Xi's religious *praxis* was anything but Zhu's alone. This connection between Zhu's thought and practice constitutes a much stronger explanation than has hitherto been proposed for Zhu's otherwise odd choice of Zhou Dunyi as the first Confucian sage of the Song.³

TABLE 4.1. Zhu Xi's editions of Zhou Dunyi's works

Year/month	
1166/3	Publishes *Tongshu* 通書 (Changsha edition, no commentary)
1169/6	Revises and publishes *Taijitu shuo* 太極圖說 and *Tongshu* (Jian'an edition, no commentary)
1170/spring	Completes draft of *Taijitushuo jie* 太極圖說解 (commentary)
1173/4	Postface to *Taijitushuo jie*
1179/5	Revises and publishes *Taiji* and *Tongshu* (Nankang ed., no commentary)
1187/9	Completes *Tongshu jie* 通書解
1188/2	Sends *Taijitushuo jie* (and *Ximing jie* 西銘解) to students

---

2. Tillman and Soffel, "Zhang Shi's Philosophical Perspectives on Human Nature, Heart/Mind, Humaneness, and the Supreme Ultimate," 135.

3. Tillman and Soffel (ibid.) represent the hitherto standard explanation, focusing solely on philosophy:

> Hu Hong certainly inspired Zhang's initial interest in the [*Taiji*] diagram. His interest further developed due to his exchanges with Zhu Xi and Lü Zuqian as they realized its usefulness in providing an ontological and cosmological foundation for their *moralist teachings*, which had been developed from classical texts like the *Mencius* and the *Zhongyong* (emphasis mine).

This chapter examines a corollary of this hypothesis: the meaning of *taiji* 太極 in Zhu Xi's system. Throughout these chapters, I have been using "Supreme Polarity," the translation I first proposed in the second edition of *Sources of Chinese Tradition* in 1999.[4] In this chapter, through a close examination of Zhu's commentaries and other statements on the *Taijitu shuo* and *Tongshu*, I will set out the fuller basis for my argument that scholars should jettison the "standard" English translation of *taiji* as "Supreme (or Great) Ultimate" and replace it with "Supreme Polarity," and the same for its correlate, *wuji* 無極 ("Nonpolar").[5]

The first half of Zhou's "Discussion of the *Taiji* Diagram" (*Taijitu shuo*), beginning with the supremely enigmatic exclamation that we will discuss later in this chapter, reads as follows (divided into sections for later reference):[6]

[A] Nonpolar and yet Supreme Polarity (*wuji er taiji* 無極而太極)!

[B] The Supreme Polarity in activity generates *yang*; yet at the limit of activity it is still. In stillness it generates *yin*; yet at the limit of stillness it is also active. Activity and stillness alternate; each is the basis of the other. In distinguishing *yin* and *yang*, the Two Modes are thereby established.

[C] The alternation and combination of *yang* and *yin* generate water, fire, wood, metal, and earth. With these five [phases of] *qi* harmoniously arranged, the Four Seasons proceed through them.

[D] The Five Phases are the unitary *yin* and *yang*; *yin* and *yang* are unified in the Supreme Polarity; the Supreme Polarity is fundamentally Nonpolar. [Yet] in the generation of the Five Phases, each one has its nature.[7]

---

4. de Bary and Bloom, eds., *Sources of Chinese Tradition,* 2nd ed., vol. 1: 673–76, and in Part II below.

5. An earlier version of this chapter, "On Translating *Taiji*," written in 2009, will appear in David Jones and He Jinli, eds., *Rethinking Zhu Xi: Emerging Patterns Within the Supreme Polarity*.

6. *Zhou Lianxi ji,* 1:2a.

7. In other words: seen as a whole system, the Five Phases (*wuxing*) are based on the *yin-yang* polarity; the *yin-yang* polarity is the Supreme Polarity; and the Supreme Polarity is fundamentally nonpolar. However, taken individually as temporal phases, the Five Phases each have their own natures (as do *yin* and *yang*).

[E] The reality of Nonpolarity and the essence of the Two [Modes] and Five [Phases] mysteriously combine and coalesce. "The Way of *Qian* 乾 becomes the male; the Way of *Kun* 坤 becomes the female";[8] the two *qi* stimulate each other, transforming and generating the myriad things.[9] The myriad things generate and regenerate, alternating and transforming without end.[10]

Putting aside for the moment the difficulty of the first line, the gist of this philosophical cosmogony has been generally agreed upon since the twelfth century. It depicts a universal creative principle or force (*taiji*) that unfolds or evolves into a bipolar state of creative tension, which in turn further differentiates into the multiplicity of the phenomenal world, each particular entity of which is said to contain in full the original creative principle. The remaining portion of the text claims that human beings are endowed with the finest and most potent form of the fundamental psychophysical-energetic stuff of the cosmos (*qi* 氣), and that the "sage" represents the highest perfection of this moral, anthropocosmic potential. In Zhou's other major work, the *Tongshu* (Penetrating Writing, or Penetrating the *Yi*), he continues this line of argument by further developing the moral psychology of the sage, with important references back to the cosmology of the *Taijitu shuo*.[11]

As we have seen in chapter 2, the usual explanation for Zhu Xi's interest in the *Taijitu shuo* hinges on his claim, which he probably learned from his teacher, Li Tong, that "*Taiji* is simply a word for *li* 理."[12] He takes great pains

---

8. *Yijing* (Scripture of Change), *Xici* (Appended Remarks), A.1.4; in *Zhouyi benyi*, 3:1b. Qian and Kun are the first two hexagrams, symbolizing pure *yang* and pure *yin*, or Heaven and Earth, respectively.

9. Paraphrasing *Yijing*, *Tuan* commentary to hexagram 31 (Xian): "The two *qi* stimulate and respond in mutual influence, the male going beneath the female.... Heaven and Earth are stimulated and the myriad things are transformed and generated" (*Zhouyi benyi*, 2:1a-b).

10. Cf. *Xici* A.5.6, "Generation and regeneration are what is meant by change (*yi*)" (*Zhouyi benyi*, 3:6a).

11. Zhu Xi claimed that the original title of *Tongshu* was *Yitong* (Penetrating the *Yi*), and this has been accepted by most scholars because the text relies extensively on the *Yi*. Wing-tsit Chan, for example, translates *Tongshu* as "Penetrating the *Book of Changes*" (*Source Book*, 460). For Zhu Xi's argument see *"Zaiding Taiji Tongshu houxu"* (Postface to Revised *Taijitu shuo* and *Tongshu*), in *Wenji*, 76:3652. Zhu also argued that the *Tongshu* was essentially an expansion and explanation of the *Taijitu shuo*; see *Zhou Lianxi ji* 5:1a, 4a; and *Yulei*, 94:3144.

12. *Yulei*, 1:114.

to stress also that *taiji* is not a concrete thing: "*Taiji* is simply the principle of two *qi* and five phases; it is not a thing on its own."¹³ This means that *taiji* belongs to the realm "above form" (*xing'er shang* 形而上); it is metaphysical. The two modes of *qi* (*yin* and *yang*) and the Five Phases, which are also modes of *qi*, belong to the realm "within form" (*xing'er xia* 形而下); they are physical. But the two realms are linked by Zhou Dunyi's statement that "*Taiji* in activity generates *yang*." This, according to Zhu Xi's interpretation, means that *li* in some sense generates *qi*: "*Taiji* generates *yin* and *yang*; *li* generates *qi*. Once *yin* and *yang* are generated, then *taiji* is within them. And *li*, likewise, is within *qi*."¹⁴

The claim that *li* generates *qi* presents something of a philosophical problem for Zhu Xi, because he also repeatedly stresses that *li* and *qi* are never separate; *qi* is always ordered by *li*, and *li* cannot exist on its own apart from *qi*: "In the world there is never *qi* without *li* and never *li* without *qi*."¹⁵ So how can *li* generate *qi*? Doesn't the act of "generation" (*sheng* 生, literally, "giving birth to") imply that *li* exists temporally before *qi*? The issue can be partially solved by asserting that *li* has *logical* priority over *qi*, but not *temporal* priority. As Zhu Xi says, "There being this principle there is then (*bian* 便) this *qi*, but the principle is the basis (*ben* 本), so because of (or "from," *cong* 從) the principle we can speak of *qi*."¹⁶ In other words, we can conceive of *li* without *qi* in the sense that we can think about patterns and principles apart from their instantiation in things; but we cannot conceive of *qi* without *li*, or completely chaotic matter-energy, because even a homogeneous mass of unspecified stuff has some characteristics, such as density. Therefore, according to this interpretation, "*Taiji* in activity generates *yang*" means that *yang qi* exists *because of* the principle of activity that is part of *taiji*; hence the logical priority of *li*.¹⁷

---

13. *Yulei*, 94:3116.

14. In *Zhou Lianxi ji*, 1:7b.

15. *Yulei*, 1:114.

16. Ibid.

17. Fung Yu-lan says that *li* does not *exist* (*cunzai*) apart from *qi*, but it does *subsist* (*qianzai*); see Fung, *History*, 2:535. (My copy of the original Chinese text, in one volume, is a pirated Taiwanese version dating from the years when mainland books were prohibited in Taiwan, so it has no publishing information, but this passage is on p. 896.) The relevant definition of "subsist" is "to be logically conceivable as the subject of true statements" (*Merriam-Webster Collegiate Dictionary*, eleventh ed.) Still, this does not explain how to get from subsistence to existence.

This, according to the consensus of scholars, is the key to Zhou Dunyi's importance to Zhu Xi. Zhou Dunyi's depiction of *taiji* provides Zhu with the critical link between the metaphysical realm of *li* and the physical realm of *qi*. *Taiji* is thus the linchpin holding together the two halves of Zhu Xi's entire philosophical system: *li* and *qi*, human nature (*xing* 性) and feelings/dispositions (*qing* 情), moral mind (*daoxin* 道心) and human mind (*renxin* 人心), heavenly principle (*tianli* 天理) and human desire (*renyu* 人欲).

The first appearance of *taiji* in an extant text is in the *Xici* 繫辭 (Appended Remarks, also called the *Dazhuan* 大傳 or Great Treatise) appendix of the *Yijing* (Scripture of Change), which probably dates to the fourth or third century BCE and was the most important *Yijing* appendix for the Song Confucians. It primarily discusses the philosophy of change underlying the *Yijing* as a divination system.[18] The *Xici* passage reads:

> Therefore in change there is *taiji*, which generates the Two Modes. The Two Modes generate the Four Images, and the Four Images generate the Eight Trigrams.[19]

---

18. See Gerald Swanson, "The Concept of Change in the Great Treatise," and Willard Peterson, "Making Connections: 'Commentary on the Attached Verbalizations' of the Book of Change."

19. *Zhou Yi, Xici* A.11.5 (*Zhouyi benyi*, 3:14b). In most translations the opening phrase is "In the *Changes* . . . ," referring either to the scripture itself or to the system of change underlying it. This passage was also the basis of Shao Yong's philosophy.

It is possible that the word *taiji* in the *Xici* was a later interpolation. This is the only appearance of *taiji* in the "traditional" text of the *Yi*, which is that of Wang Bi (226–249 CE), who wrote an extremely influential commentary on it (*Zhouyi Wang-Han zhu*; trans. by Richard John Lynn in *The Classic of Changes*. In 1973 a collection of texts written on silk was discovered in a tomb at Mawangdui (near present-day Changsha, Hunan province), which was sealed in 168 BCE. It included a version of the *Yijing* that has been dated to around 200–190 BCE, more than four hundred years older than Wang Bi's version. And in the Mawangdui version of the *Xici* the word *taiji* does not appear; the line reads, "This is why the *Changes* has great constancy (*daheng* 大恆)" (trans. Edward L. Shaughnessy, *I Ching*, 198–99). (The Mawangdui text also differs in the sequence of hexagrams and has different names for about half of them—including the first two, Qian and Kun [ibid., 16], which are called *Jian* ["The Key"] and *Chuan* ["The Flow"] in Shaughnessy's translation [ibid., 17].)

However, the Han dynasty "apocryphal" text, *Yiwei Qian zuodu* 易緯乾鑿度 (Apocryphon to the *Yi*: Chiseling Open the Regularity of Qian), uses *taiji* in a manner quite similar to the *Xici*:

> Master Kong said: "Change (*yi*) begins in *taiji*. *Taiji* divides into two, thus generating Heaven and Earth. Heaven and Earth are measured by spring,

The Two Modes are the single undivided line ══ (called "firm" and symbolizing *yang*) and the divided line ▬ ▬ (called "yielding" and symbolizing *yin*). The Four Images are the four two-line combinations of firm and yielding: ⚏ (younger *yang*), ⚌ (elder *yang*), ⚎ (younger *yin*), and ⚏ (elder *yin*). The Eight Trigrams are all the possible three-line combinations: ☰ (Qian, Heaven), ☱ (Dui, Lake), ☲ (Li, Fire), ☳ (Zhen, Thunder), ☴ (Sun, Wind), ☵ (Kan, Water), ☶ (Gen, Mountain), and ☷ (Kun, Earth). So the passage describes a cosmogony, based on the fundamental principle of *yin-yang* bipolarity, unfolding from the unitary *taiji*, which is inherent in the cosmological process of change and transformation. It is worth noting here that *change* is the fundamental state, which does not need to be explained—exactly the opposite of Platonic metaphysics, in which *being* is more real than *becoming*.

Taiji occurs in the *Zhuangzi, Huainanzi, Shiji, Chunqiu fanlu* (once in each), eight times in the *Han shu,* and once in the *Hou Han shu.*[20] After the Han it became a standard term in Daoism. That is the most relevant context for this study because Zhou Dunyi most likely received the *Taiji Diagram* from Daoist circles, as was claimed by Zhu Zhen (1072–1138).[21] Isabelle Robinet has thoroughly examined the Daoist meanings of *taiji* in this period.[22] According to Robinet, *taiji* was the name of one of the Daoist heavens,[23] and thus was prefixed to the names of many Daoist immortals, or divinities, and to the titles of the texts attributed to them. It was sometimes identified with Taiyi, the Supreme One (a Daoist astral divinity), and with the pole star (*jixing* 極星).[24] From this it came to be associated with the

---

autumn, winter, and summer, thus generating the Four Seasons. The Four Seasons each have the divisions of *yin* and *yang,* or firm and yielding, thus generating the Eight Trigrams." (*Yijing jicheng* ed., vol. 157, 6)

20. According to *Chinese Text Project,* http://ctext.org/pre-qin-and-han, accessed May 12, 2009. This list does not include Han dynasty Daoist texts or apocrypha to the *Yi.*

21. See above, chapter 2, note 133.

22. Isabelle Robinet, "The Place and Meaning of the Notion of *Taiji* in Taoist Sources Prior to the Ming Dynasty." See also her entries on the "*Taiji tu*" and "*wuji* and *taiji*" in Pregadio, ed., *The Encyclopedia of Taoism,* vol. 2: 934–36; 1057–59.

23. See also Fabrizio Pregadio, *Great Clarity: Daoism and Alchemy in Early Medieval China,* 47.

24. Yu Fan (164–233), a Han dynasty *Yijing* expert in the "images and numbers" (*xiangshu*) tradition, said, "*Taiji* is *Taiyi*, which divides into heaven and earth, thus generating the Two Modes" (quoted in Nielsen, *Companion,* 229, 315–17), echoing *Xici* A.11.5. Zheng Xuan (127–200), another *xiangshu* expert, identified *Taiyi* with the pole star (ibid., 229, 333–34). For more on Taiyi as a divinity see Isabelle Robinet, *Taoist Meditation: The Mao-shan Tradition of Great Purity,* 134–38.

idea of the heart or center (*xin* 心).²⁵ But its primary associations were with Daoist cosmogonic schemes, where it usually denoted a stage of chaos later than *wuji* ("unlimited"),²⁶ a state in which *yin* and *yang* have differentiated but have not yet become manifest. It thus represented a "complex unity," or the unity of potential multiplicity. It carried connotations of a turning point in a cycle, an end point before a reversal, and a pivot between bipolar processes. In Daoist *neidan* meditation, or physiological alchemy, it represented the energetic potential to reverse the normal process of aging by cultivating within one's body the spark of the primordial *qi*, thereby "returning" to the primordial, creative state of chaos from which the cosmos evolved. The *Taiji* Diagram in Daoist circles, when read from the bottom upward, was originally a schematic representation of this process of "returning to *wuji*" (*Laozi* 28), that is, returning to the undifferentiated state.²⁷ As Robinet summarizes it, "*taiji* is a limit in the sense that it is the beginning and the end of the world, a turning point.... The *taiji* is the limit and the juncture between the two worlds, the noumenal world that 'antedates Heaven' [*xiantian* 先天] and the phenomenal world that is 'after Heaven and Earth' [*houtian* 後天]."²⁸

This dual characterization of *taiji*—as the limit and the juncture or turning point—is central to my argument. Both "limit" and "juncture" derive from the literal meaning of the word *ji* 極: the "ridgepole" of a house. The ridgepole is, of course, the highest point of the structure, and therefore the vertical limit of the space within. It is from this image that the colloquial meaning of *ji* is derived: the farthest point, the extreme, the endpoint, the ultimate point. This is the meaning that is captured by the standard English translation of *taiji* as "Supreme (or Great) Ultimate." But the ridgepole also divides the roof into two complementary parts. My contention is that the idea

---

25. Cheng Yi affirmed this in his discussion of the *Xici*; see *Er Cheng ji, Jing shuo*, 1:1027.

26. *Wuji* is an almost exclusively Daoist term that is found in *Laozi* 28, *Zhuangzi* 6, and *Liezi* 5. In Daoist texts it came to denote a state of primordial chaos, prior to the differentiation of *yin* and *yang*, and sometimes equivalent to *dao*. This more developed sense is consistent with its usage in *Laozi* 28, and with the more general sense of *wu* in *Laozi* as the state of "nonexistence" that precedes "existence" (*you*, e.g., ch. 40) and/or is interdependent with it (ch. 2).

27. See Judith A. Berling, "Paths of Convergence: Interactions of Inner Alchemy, Taoism, and Neo-confucianism," 128–31; and Chang Chung-yüan, *Creativity and Taoism*, 165–66.

28. Robinet, "*wuji* and *taiji*," in Pregadio, *Encyclopedia of Taoism*, 1058.

of "juncture" or "turning point" needs to be more explicit in a translation of *taiji* in order to accurately convey the meaning of *taiji*, especially as Zhu Xi understood it.[29]

The nearly universal use of "Supreme Ultimate" by scholars writing in English in the past century can be traced back to J. Percy Bruce's 1923 book, *Chu Hsi and His Masters*—the first book in English on Zhu Xi. Derk Bodde, translating FungYu-lan's *History of Chinese Philosophy* in 1953, followed Bruce's lead, as did Carsun Chang in *The Development of Neo-Confucian Thought* (1957). Wing-tsit Chan, whose *A Source Book in Chinese Philosophy* (1963) is still a well-respected resource (deservedly so) for English translations from Chinese philophical texts, used "Great Ultimate." But the majority of scholars still use "Supreme Ultimate," probably to preserve the distinction between *da* (great) and *tai* (greatest, extremely).[30] Following is a list of all the major Western-language translations I have found of the *Yijing* (only those that include the *Xici* appendix) and the *Taijitu shuo*, with their terms for both *wuji* and *taiji*:

	Wuji	Taiji
Jean Baptiste de Régis (d. 1738)[31]		summus terminus
Thomas McClatchie (1876)[32]		Great Extreme
Georg von der Gabelentz (1876)[33]	Ohne Prinzip	Urprinzip

---

29. Centrality was also a prominent layer of meaning of the closely related term *huangji* ("royal ultimate"), from the *Hongfan* (Great Plan) chapter of the *Shujing*. Zhu Xi makes this connection more than once; see below, pp. 131–32.

30. Actually, both the Mawangdui and the traditional Wang Bi versions of the *Yi* use *da* instead of *tai* in the *Xici* A.11 passage (Mawangdui: *daheng* [see note 17 above], Wang Bi: *daji*). Zhu Xi, in his commentary on the (Wang Bi) *Yi*, says that *da* should be read as *tai* (*Zhouyi benyi*, 3:14b), as did Wang Bi's follower Han Kangbo (332–380) (*Zhouyi Wang-Han zhu*, 7:9b).

31. P. [Jean Baptiste de] Régis, trans., *Y-King: Antiquissimus Sinarum Liber Quem ex Latina Interpretatione,* 2:514. For Régis's date of death see Nicolas Standaert, *The Interweaving of Rituals: Funerals in the Cultural Exchange Between China and Europe,* 277, n. 71.

32. Rev. Canon [Thomas] McClatchie, *A Translation of the ConfucianYijing or the "Classic of Change,"* 322.

33. Georg von der Gabelentz, *Thai-kih-thu, des Tscheu-Tsï,* 31.

Angelo Zottoli (1880)[34]		summum terminum
Paul-Louis-Félix Philastre (1885)[35]		extrême origine
Stanislas Le Gall (1894)[36]		grande extrême
Charles Joseph de Harlez (1897)[37]		premier principe
James Legge (1899)[38]		Great Extreme, Grand Terminus
J. Percy Bruce (1923)[39]	Infinite	Supreme Ultimate
Alfred Forke (1938)[40]	Prinzip des Nichtseins	Urprinzip
Henri Maspero (1940?)[41]	Sans-Faîte	Grande-Faîte
Richard Wilhelm (1924)[42]		großen Uranfang
Derk Bodde (1953)[43]	Ultimateless	Supreme Ultimate
Chow Yih-ching (1954)[44]	Sans-faîte	Faîte Suprême

---

34. P. Angelo Zottoli, S. J., *Cursus Litteraturae Sinicae*, vol. 3: *Studium Canonicorum*, 579.

35. P.-L.-F. Philastre, trans., *Le Yi King, ou Livre des Changements de la Dynastie des Tsheou*, 2:523.

36. Stanislas Le Gall, S. J., *Le Philosophe Tchou Hi: Sa Doctrine, Son Influence*, 32–34, 99–119. This is not a translation of either the *Yijing* or the *Taijitu shuo*; Le Gall translates *juan* 49 of Li Guangdi, ed., *Zhuzi quanshu* (Zhu Xi's "Complete Works"), which is a classified compilation of passages from Zhu's *Yulei* and *Wenji* and not to be confused with the 2002 work by the same title edited by Zhu Jieren et al. The second section of chapter 49 is on *taiji*.

37. Charles Joseph de Harlez, *Le Yi-King*, 117.

38. James Legge, trans., *The I Ching: The Book of Changes*, 2nd ed. Legge inexplicably uses "Great Extreme" in his Introduction (12) and "Grand Terminus" in the text of the *Xici* (373).

39. J. Percy Bruce, *Chu Hsi and His Masters*, 24–25, 30, 126–55; also Bruce, trans., *The Philosophy of Human Nature* (a translation of *juan* 42 of *Zhuzi quanshu*), 291–95.

40. Alfred Forke, *Geschichte der Neueren Chinesischen Philosophie*, 48.

41. Henri Maspero, *Le Taoïsme et les Religions Chinois*, 86. Maspero defines *taiji* as "nom de l'union du *Li* et du *Qi*; Grande-Faîte" (639). Although Maspero did not translate either the *Yijing* or the *Taijitu shuo*, I include him here because of his influence on later scholars. Chow, for example, cites him as an authority (*La Philosophie Morale*, 154, n.1).

42. Richard Wilhelm, trans., *I Ging: Das Buch der Wandlungen*, 295. Cary F. Baynes's English translation of Wilhelm's German is "Great Primal Beginning" (Richard Wilhelm, trans., *The I Ching or Book of Changes*, 3rd ed., 318).

43. Fung, *History*, 2:435. In vol. 1, Bodde uses "Great Ultimate" (384).

44. Chow Yih-ching, *La Philosophie Morale dans le Néo-Confucianisme (Tcheou Touen-yi)*, 41–72, 154–62.

Joseph Needham (1956)[45]	That which has no Pole	Supreme Pole
Carsun Chang (1957)[46]	Ultimate of Nothingness	Supreme Ultimate
Wing-tsit Chan (1963)[47]	Ultimate of Non-being	Great Ultimate
Wu Jing-nuan (1991)[48]		Great Axis
Richard John Lynn (1994)[49]		great ultimate
Richard Rutt (1996)[50]		Ultimate Limit
Edward Shaughnessy (1996)[51]		great extreme

As is evident from the table above, only four of the twenty-one translators listed have followed the "juncture" thread of *taiji*'s meaning: Henri Maspero (1940?), Chow Yih-ching (1954), Joseph Needham (1956), and Wu Jing-nuan (1991). One of the primary meanings of the word *faîte* used by Maspero and Chow is "ridgepole," so it is the most literal translation of *ji*. Chow explains that it is "the summit of a building, the furthest point above which one cannot climb. In philosophical language this word therefore figuratively indicates the first principle or the first cause."[52] So, while Chow preserves the imagery of the ridgepole, he still wants to extend it to the more abstract notion of principle. Needham maintains the concrete imagery with "Supreme Pole," explaining that *ji* is "not merely any boundary, but a polar or focal point on a boundary. . . . *ji* was from of old the technical term for the astronomical pole. Around the Pole Star all man's universe revolved."[53] But "Supreme Pole" is problematic, because Zhu Xi repeatedly insists that *taiji* is not a concrete thing. So "pole" will not do, but "polarity" is consistent with Zhu's equation of *taiji* and *li*, or principle/pattern/order.

---

45. Joseph Needham, *Science and Civilisation in China, vol. 2: History of Scientific Thought*, 460–67.

46. Chang, *Development*, 1:142.

47. Chan, *Source Book*, 463. Chan used "Great Ultimate" consistently in his many other writings on Neo-Confucianism.

48. Wu Jing-Nuan, trans., *Yi Jing*, 271.

49. Richard John Lynn, trans., *The Classic of Changes: A New Translation of the I Ching as Interpreted by Wang Bi*, 55, 65.

50. Richard Rutt, trans., *The Book of Changes (Zhouyi): A Bronze Age Document*, 418.

51. Shaughnessy, *I Ching*, 330, n. 83.

52. "Le faîte est le sommet d'un bâtiment, le point extrême au-dessus duquel on ne peut monter. En langage philosophique ce mot figuré indiquerait donc le principe premier ou la cause première" (Chow, *La Philosophie Morale*, 155 n. 1).

53. Needham, *Science and Civilisation in China*, vol. 2, 464.

As we shall see, the great preponderance of evidence from Zhu Xi's writings supports the idea that *taiji* is the principle or pattern of polarity. As Zhu clearly states in his commentary on the *locus classicus* of *taiji* in the *Xici*, "Change is the alternation of *yin* and *yang*. *Taiji* is this [or its] principle (*li*)."[54] It is called "supreme" (*tai*) because it is the most fundamental ordering principle of the entire cosmos. As for the other key term in the opening sentence of Zhou Dunyi's *Taijitu shuo*, *wuji* as "nonpolar" follows logically from *taiji* as polarity. *Wuji* means undifferentiated; *taiji* is the simplest principle of differentiation or ordering, the *yin-yang* polarity. (We shall return later to Zhu Xi's interpretation of Zhou's first sentence, "*Wuji er taiji*.")

Before setting out the positive evidence for this argument, let us first examine the justification for translating *taiji* as "Supreme/Great Ultimate." The following passage from Zhu Xi's *Classified Conversations*, in Wing-tsit Chan's translation, is sometimes used to illustrate or justify this interpretation:

> The Great Ultimate is similar to the top of a house or the zenith of the sky, beyond which point there is no more. It is the ultimate of principle. Yang is active and yin is tranquil. In these it is not the Great Ultimate that acts or remains tranquil. It is simply that there are the principles of activity and tranquility. Principle is not visible; it becomes visible through yin and yang. Principle attaches itself to yin and yang as a man sits astride a horse. As soon as yin and yang produce the Five Agents, they are confined and fixed by physical nature and are thus differentiated into individual things each with its nature. But the Great Ultimate is in all of them.[55]

The words translated by Chan as "top" and "zenith" in the first sentence are both *ji*. Hence, we have here again the dual connotations of "limit" and "juncture" mentioned by Robinet: the highest point in the house but also the division between the two halves of the roof; the highest point in the heavens but also the pole star around which the heavens revolve.[56] But here

---

54. Zhu, *Zhouyi benyi*, 3:14b.

55. Chan, *Source Book*, 641; quoting Li Guangdi, *Zhuzi quanshu*, 49:13a. The passage comes from *Yulei*, 41:3126.

56. To be precise, of course, the pole star is the highest point in the sky only at the North Pole.

the former meaning, that of the ultimate limit, is emphasized by the additional phrase, "beyond which point there is no more."

The idea of an ultimate limit fits with the colloquial usage of *ji,* both in the Song and today, in the adverbial sense of "very" or "most": for example, *ji hao* 極好 ("very good" or "the best"), *ji da* 極大 ("the biggest"). This colloquial connotation is the governing image in the translations "supreme ultimate" and "great ultimate." It is a linear image: the point beyond which there is no more; the highest, greatest point on a linear scale; the last stop on the line; the final frontier; the highest, best principle. As Zhu Xi says, "*Taiji* is simply the extreme utmost (*jizhi* 極至), but it has no location. [It is] the highest (*zhigao* 至高), the most mysterious (*zhimiao* 至妙), the most essential (*zhijing* 至精), the most spiritual (*zhishen* 至神), [but] with no location."[57] "*Taiji* is simply the finest and best moral principle";[58] "the perfectly pure and good nature (*xing*) is what is meant by *taiji*."[59] Therefore there is no denying the idea of the highest or the farthest as *part* of the meaning of *taiji*.

However, the Song Confucians did not necessarily think as much as we in the West in *linear* terms. For them, the governing image was that of *yin-yang* circulation or complementarity.[60] Therefore, we must be careful not to impose a foreign way of thinking on their words. As Roger Ames has written, "[O]ur existing formula of terms for translating the core [Chinese] philosophical vocabulary is freighted with a cosmology not its own, and thus perpetuates a pernicious cultural reductionism."[61] In our case, to ignore the nonlinear aspect of the "ridgepole" image obscures the fact that the farthest point is also the *center* of a bipolar and/or circulating pattern. The farthest point is not the last stop on a one-way line; it is one extreme of a bipolar

---

57. *Yulei,* 94: 3120.

58. *Yulei,* 94: 3122.

59. *Yulei,* 94: 3140.

60. I am making no claim here about the Chinese conception of time, nor am I suggesting Whorfian limitations to Chinese thought or rationality. I am simply noting the greater emphasis in Chinese thought on the principle of bipolar alternation, as evidenced by the ubiquity of the *yin-yang* concept.

61. Roger Ames, "Translating Chinese Philosophy," in *An Encyclopedia of Translation: Chinese-English, English-Chinese,* ed. Chan Sin-wai and David E. Pollard, 731. For another useful collection of articles on translation issues (not all concerning Chinese), see Cornellia N. Moore and Lucy Lower, eds., *Translation East and West: A Cross-Cultural Approach.*

pattern or process of alternation. As Cheng Yi's student Yang Shi (1053–1135) put it, nicely combining the two aspects of the image:

> Centrality (*zhong* 中) is the utmost extreme (*zhiji* 至極) of the Way.[62] Therefore centrality is called *ji* 極 [here "the ultimate" would be an appropriate translation]. The ridgepole of a house is also called *ji*, because it is both the center and highest part.[63]

Zhu Xi himself sometimes used, and even defined, *ji* as "ultimate," as mentioned just above. But that does not mean that he conceived it in a linear fashion. In his commentary on the *Yijing* we can see how he understood the idea of "extremity" as part of an alternating, polar process. In the *Xici* appendix there is the line:

> Change and transformation (*bianhua* 變化) are images of advance and retreat. The firm and yielding [lines] are images of day and night. The activity of the six lines are the Way of the Three Extremes (*san ji* 三極).[64]

Zhu Xi comments on this:

> The yielding changes and becomes firm; at the extreme (*ji* 極) of its retreat it advances. The firm transforms and becomes yielding; at the extreme of its advance it retreats. Upon changing into the firm then there is the *yang* of day. Upon transforming into the yielding then there is the *yin* of night.[65]
>
> The first two of the "six lines" are earth; the third and fourth are the human; the fifth and top are heaven. "Activity" means change and transformation. "Extreme" (*ji* 極) means utmost (*zhi* 至). "Three Extremes" means the utmost principle (*zhi li* 至理) of Heaven, earth,

---

62. *Zhong* also has the connotation of "hitting the mark" or "getting it just right." But in view of the last sentence of this quotation I think "centrality" is appropriate here. Both the literal meaning and the connotation are implied by the notion of "being centered" as a psychological state.
63. *Yang Guishan xiansheng quanji* (Complete writings of Yang Shi), 14:8b.
64. *Yijing*, *Xici* A.2.4 (*Zhouyi benyi* 3:3a).
65. Note the parallel with the beginning of the *Taijitu shuo*.

and the human. Each of these "three powers" is the unitary *taiji* (Supreme Polarity).[66]

Thus, *ji* here is defined as *zhi* (utmost), but clearly in the sense of the extreme point in a cyclic or alternating *yin-yang* process.

Applying this insight to Zhu Xi's understanding of *taiji* clarifies a great deal and adds meaningful content to what can be a rather empty placeholder of a term. For what exactly does "supreme ultimate" mean? How can "the ultimate" be modified? Does it imply that there is an "inferior ultimate"? Scholars explaining Zhu Xi's concept, following his equation of *taiji* with *li*, typically say something to the effect that *taiji* means "the principles of all things."[67] Fung Yu-lan, for example, says, "The Supreme Ultimate, therefore, consists of the Principles or *li* of all things in the universe, brought together into a single whole (*tiandi wanwuzhi lizhi zonghe* 天地萬物之理之總和)."[68] He draws this conclusion from the following dialogue in Zhu Xi's *Classified Conversations*:

> *Zhonglü said*: *Taiji* is the utmost principle of the human mind.
>
> *Reply*: Everything has this *ji*, which is the extreme utmost of moral principle.
>
> *Jiang Yuanjin said*: For example, the humanity of the ruler and the reverent composure (*jing* 敬) of the subject are this *ji*.
>
> *Reply*: This is the *ji* of one thing. The principle of all things in heaven and earth (*zong tiandi wanwuzhi li* 總天地萬物之理) is *taiji*.[69]

---

66. *Yijing*, *Xici* A.2.4 (*Zhouyi benyi* 3:3a). The "three powers" (*san cai*) are Heaven, earth, and humanity. Here again Zhu is echoing the *Taijitu shuo*.

67. Chan, *Source Book*, 639. A decade later Chan wrote that *taiji* is "the highest principle of each and every thing" and "at once the one universal principle and the sum-total of all principles" (Chan, "Chu Hsi's Completion," 114, 115). "The one universal principle" is consistent with my interpretation. He also says here, coming close to my interpretation, "Chu Hsi always saw the Great Ultimate, or principle in its ultimate state, as embodying *yin* and *yang*, that is, the operation of myriad things" (115). But he doesn't follow through on this observation, and in fact there is a difference between "embodying *yin* and *yang*" and actually being the principle of *yin* and *yang*.

68. Fung, *History*, 2:537 (Chinese version, 899).

69. *Yulei*, 94:3127.

Note that Fung (accurately translated here by Derk Bodde) refers to "the Principles [plural] or *li* of all things." But in Zhu Xi's remark, *zong* more likely modifies "things in heaven and earth" than "principle." Therefore, Zhu Xi is speaking of a unitary principle, not all principles; Fung's paraphrase is mistaken on this point. Elsewhere Zhu says,

> *Taiji* is not a separate thing. It is *yin-yang* and is within *yin-yang*. It is the Five Phases and is within the Five Phases. It is the myriad things and is within the myriad things. It is nothing but one principle (*yige li* 一個理). Since it is the extreme utmost [i.e., the ultimate, most fundamental principle] we call it *taiji*.[70]

So it is clear that we are talking about a single principle, not a collection of principles; the single, most fundamental ordering principle. And that principle is *yin-yang* bipolarity.

Turning now to the positive evidence for the claim that *taiji* means "supreme polarity," I will focus first on Zhu Xi's most prominent published comments on the term, accompanied by further statements on those comments from his conversations and letters. We begin with his published commentary on the *locus classicus*, the *Xici* appendix to the *Yijing*, which was quoted above ("Therefore in change there is *taiji*, which generates the Two Modes. . . ."). Zhu Xi's comment on this in his *Zhouyi benyi* 周易本義 (Original Meaning of the *Scripture of Change*) is:

> One always generates two; this is a natural principle. Change is the alternation (*bian* 變) of *yin* and *yang*. *Taiji* is this [or its] principle.[71]

This is a straightforward statement that clearly says more than "*taiji* is principle"; it says that *taiji* is a *specific* principle: the principle of *yin-yang* polarity. Discussing the *Xici* passage in a letter, Zhu Xi wrote:

> "'Change' (*yi* 易) is alternating change (*bianyi* 變易),"[72] combining the meanings of the "alternation of activity and stillness"[73] and the

---

70. Hu, *Xingli daquan shu*, 26:6b.

71. *Zhouyi benyi*, 3:14b.

72. Quoting Cheng Yi's preface to his *Yi zhuan* (Commentary on the *Yi*), in *Er Cheng ji*, 689.

73. *Xici* A.5.1, in *Zhouyi benyi*, 3:5a.

expressed (*yifa*) and unexpressed (*weifa*) [phases of mind]. *Taiji* is the mystery of nature and feelings, the principle of the alternation of activity and stillness and the expressed and unexpressed. Thus "In change there is *taiji*" means that activity and stillness, "closing and opening,"[74] always has this principle.[75]

Although *taiji* became a very common term in Daoism during the period from the Han through the Song, as we have seen, the next significant text for Zhu Xi was Zhou Dunyi's *Taijitu shuo*, the relevant section of which has already been quoted at the beginning of this chapter. Before turning to Zhu Xi's commentary on it, it is worthwhile first to summarize Zhou Dunyi's own interpretation of the term. Most scholars agree that Zhou's concept of *taiji* seems to have been strictly cosmological, not metaphysical. Graham argues that *taiji* for Zhou was something like undifferentiated *qi*, as it was for Zheng Xuan 鄭玄 (127–200) and Zhou's contemporary Liu Mu 劉牧 (1011–1064).[76] I prefer to say that Zhou thought of *taiji* as the energetic potential of *qi* to divide into the *yin* and *yang* modes—the incipient bipolarity of undifferentiated *qi*. This explains Zhou's statement in the *Taijitu shuo*: "The Five Phases are the unitary *yin* and *yang*; *yin* and *yang* are the unitary Supreme Polarity; the Supreme Polarity is fundamentally Nonpolar."[77] That is, undifferentiated *qi* more likely correlates with *wuji*, not *taiji*. It is also important to note that Zhou did not explicitly make use of the concept of *li*, which was the innovation of his nephews, the Cheng brothers, possibly influenced by Huayan Buddhism.[78]

Zhu Xi, as we have noted, claimed that *taiji* is just another name for the most fundamental form of *li*. This was a major breakthrough, enabling him to philosophically link the cosmological discourse of those Northern Song thinkers who drew inspiration from the *Yijing* and its associated diagrams

---

74. *Xici* A.11.4, in *Zhouyi benyi*, 3:14a.

75. Letter to Wu Huishu, in *Wenji*, 42:1909. Note here the linkage of *taiji* with the *weifa/yifa* or *zhong/he* problem discussed in the previous chapter.

76. Graham, *Two Chinese Philosophers*, 155, 163. See also Chan, *Source Book*, 639. For Liu Mu see Nielsen, *Companion*, 160–61.

77. He also says, in the *Tongshu*, "*Yin* and *yang* are *taiji*" (section 16).

78. As noted in the previous chapter, *li* was used by Huayan Buddhists to mean specifically the principle of emptiness. Zhou uses *li* in two sections of the *Tongshu* (3 and 13), but not with the meaning given it by the Chengs.

with the new metaphysical discourse of the Cheng brothers.[79] Yet, as was mentioned above, it was problematic.

Granting that Zhou Dunyi's concept of *taiji* differed importantly from Zhu Xi's, it seems to me significant that the second sentence of the *Taijitu shuo*—where one would expect there to be a clarification of the enigmatic opening exclamation—immediately discusses the bipolar relationship of activity and stillness ("*Taiji* in activity generates *yang*; yet at the limit of activity it is still . . ."). In other words, the polarity model of *taiji* makes it clear in what way the second sentence actually clarifies the first. The English translations of the "Supreme Ultimate" sort fail to clarify the logical connection between the two sentences. While Zhou Dunyi is not talking about the abstract or metaphysical *principle* of *yin-yang* alternation, he is clearly identifying *taiji* with the bipolar alternation of activity/*yang* and stillness/*yin*. In section 16 of the *Tongshu* he says flatly, "*Yin* and *yang* are *taiji*."[80] And later in the *Taijitu shuo* we read, "The Five Phases are the unitary *yin* and *yang*; *yin* and *yang* are the unitary *taiji*; *taiji* is fundamentally Nonpolar." This begins to hint at Zhu Xi's later view: just as the Five Phases are a further developmental stage or unfolding of *yin* and *yang*, so too *yin* and *yang* are the natural expression of bipolarity, and bipolarity itself is an integral, unified concept. In these passages we have (1) the direct equation of *yin* and *yang* with *taiji* and (2) the implication that the "dual" nature of *taiji*/bipolarity is somehow also *nondual*.[81]

What does this mean in terms of Zhu Xi's interpretation, based on the equation of *taiji* and *li*? Zhu Xi's published commentary on the enigmatic opening sentence of the *Taijitu shuo* (A above) reads as follows:

> "The operation of Heaven above has neither sound nor smell,"[82] and yet it is the pivot (*shuniu* 樞紐) of the actual process of creation and the basis of the classification of things. Thus it says, "Nonpolar and yet Supreme Polarity!" It is not that there is nonpolarity outside of the Supreme Polarity.[83]

---

79. See Graham, *Two Chinese Philosophers,* 159–60, 168.

80. *Zhou Lianxi ji,* 5:34a.

81. Zhou Dunyi's contemporary Shao Yong also spoke of *taiji* in terms of *yin* and *yang*, but with a significant difference: he said that *taiji* generates *yin* and *yang* "without activity" (*budong*), while Zhou said that *taiji* "in activity generates *yang*." See Shao Yong, *Huangji jingshi shu,* 8B:23a; and Chan, *Source Book,* 492.

82. *Zhongyong* 33 (last line), quoting *Shujing* (Scripture of Odes), no. 235.

83. *Zhou Lianxi ji,* 1:5a.

Just as *taiji* is not a concrete thing, neither is *wuji*; it simply indicates the "unitariness" of principle.⁸⁴ But what is most significant here is the word *pivot*, especially given its prominent location in the first sentence of Zhu's published commentary on the *Taijitu shuo*. "*Shu*" 樞 is also the word used by Zhuangzi, in the second chapter of his work, where he refers to "the axis of *dao*" (*daoshu* 道樞), the central point where "'this' and 'that' no longer find their opposites."⁸⁵ Zhu's first sentence here means that the creative principle and ground of being—what he elsewhere calls the "principle of Heaven" or "natural principle" (*tianli* 天理)—is characterless or undifferentiated and yet contains within it the potential for change and differentiation. Like a pivot point, it is dimensionless yet constitutes the central axis of change and differentiation. This is Zhu Xi's statement of the perennial, cross-cultural problem of the relationship between "the one" and "the many": the paradox that Zhou attempts to express (according to Zhu) with the enigmatic "*Wuji er taiji*."⁸⁶ Zhu expands on the notion of "pivot" in the following statement from his *Classified Conversations*:

> Originally, the word *ji* was taken from from the meaning of *shuji* 樞極 [axis-pole, or pole star]. The Sage [Confucius] called it *taiji* to indicate the basis of heaven and earth; Master Zhou followed this and also called it *wuji* in order to emphasize the mystery of what "has neither sound nor smell."⁸⁷

He also says:

> "*Wuji*" simply means formless principle. *Taiji* is simply the principle of two *qi* and Five Phases; it is not a thing on its own.⁸⁸

---

84. Zhu makes this point repeatedly in conversations; see, for example, *Yulei* 94:3116.

85. Burton Watson, trans., *The Complete Works of Chuang Tzu*, 40; Wang Xianqian, ed., *Zhuangzi jijie* (Collected explanations of the *Zhuangzi*), 10. Recall that "center" (*zhong*) was one of the traditional meanings of *ji*.

86. For a discussion of "the one and the many" problem in the Chinese context, see Rudolf Wagner, *Language, Ontology, and Political Philosophy in China: Wang Bi's Scholarly Exploration of the Dark (Xuanxue)* (Albany: State University of New York Press, 2003), 121–53. One might also draw an analogy here with the Judeo-Christian-Islamic paradox of God as the unmoved mover, or uncreated creator.

87. *Yulei*, 94:3117. The reference to Confucius is based on Zhu's erroneous belief that Confucius wrote the "Ten Wings" or appendices of the *Yijing*, where *taiji* first appeared (in the *Xici* appendix).

88. *Yulei*, 94:3116.

Zhu's published comment on the next few sentences of the *Taijitu shuo* (B) reads as follows:

> That in Supreme Polarity there is activity and stillness is the flowing forth of what is given (*ming* 命) by Heaven. It is what is meant by "the alternation of *yin* and *yang* is called the Way."[89]

Here he is specifying the content of *taiji* as activity and stillness. In a further conversation on the same passage he says:

> Within Heaven and Earth, there is only the bipolar (*liang duan* 兩端) activity and stillness, in an endless cycle; there is absolutely nothing else. This is called change. And since there is activity and stillness, there is necessarily the principle of activity and stillness. This is called the Supreme Polarity.[90]

This is one of Zhu Xi's most explicit statements that *taiji* is the principle of activity and stillness. While he never explains exactly *how* a metaphysical principle can cause physical change, the point here is his clear statement that *taiji* is the principle of activity and stillness, or the principle of bipolar change.[91]

Zhu's published comment on section C of the *Taijitu shuo* is:

> In Supreme Polarity there is [the principle of] the alternation of activity and stillness, and the Two Modes are distinguished; with *yin* and *yang* the alternation and combination of the Five Phases are set.[92]

---

89. *Zhou Lianxi ji*, 1:6b, quoting *Yijing, Xici* A.5.1, which is also quoted in Zhou's *Tongshu*, 1.

90. *Zhou Lianxi ji*, 1:7b.

91. The third sentence is based on Cheng Yi's dictum, "Where there is a thing there must be a principle" (*Henan Chengshi yishu*, 18, in *Er Cheng ji*, 193; cf. Chan, *Source Book*, 563). On the causation problem (see note 15 above), even Wing-tsit Chan, for whom Zhu Xi was the highest exemplar of Chinese philosophers, admitted, "As to how the Great Ultimate can produce the two material forces (yin and yang), Chu's answer is vague" (ibid., 639).

This clearly implies that the alternation of activity and stillness is the first or most fundamental manifestation of *taiji*. If *taiji* meant the sum total of all principles, why would activity and stillness be singled out?

In an exchange on section E of the *Taijitu shuo* and the key term *weifa* (unexpressed [mind]) from the *Zhongyong* we read:

> *Li asked:* Are "the reality of the Nonpolar" (*wujizhi zhen* 無極之真) and "the equilibrium of the unexpressed [feelings]" (*weifazhi zhong* 未發之中) the same or different?
>
> *Reply:* The reality of the Nonpolar includes activity and stillness; the equilibrium of the unexpressed refers only to stillness. *Taiji* is simply the extreme utmost (*jizhi*), but it has no location. [It is] the highest (*zhigao*), the most mysterious (*zhimiao*), the most essential (*zhijing*), the most spiritual (*zhishen*), [but] with no location. Lianxi feared that people would say that *taiji* had form, so he said "*wuji er taiji*." Within this *wu* there is the principle of the utmost extreme (*zhijizhi li* 至極之理). It is like *huangji* 皇極 ("royal ultimate"), which is the hub of the universe but has no location. It is neither here nor there; it is only at the center, where everything comes together. He then pointed to the peak of the house (*wuji* 屋極) and said: It's not even there.[93]

It is tempting to suspect that in the last sentence Zhu Xi was actually speaking tongue-in-cheek, by pointing to the very object (the ridgepole) that gave *taiji* its root meaning. "*Huangji*" is a term from the *Hongfan* 洪範 (Great Plan) chapter of the *Shujing* (Scripture of Documents), where it refers to the ruler as the ultimate standard. In the official Tang dynasty commentary on the *Shujing*, Kong Yingda 孔穎達 (574–648) says, "*Huang* means 'great' (*da* 大); *ji* means 'central' (*zhong* 中)."[94]

In his essay "Analysis of *huangji*" (*Huangji bian* 皇極辯), Zhu says:

---

92. *Zhou Lianxi ji,* 1:11b.

93. *Yulei,* 94:3120.

94. See Ruan Yuan, ed., *Shisan jing zhushu,* 189. For translations of the *Hongfan* see Legge, *The Chinese Classics,* vol. 3, *Shoo King,* 324; and Chan, *Source Book,* 8–11. See also Nylan, *The Shifting Center,* 68.

> *Huang* is a designation of the ruler; *ji* means the utmost extreme, a name for the norm or standard (*biaozhun* 標準). This is always at the center of a thing, and is what those all around hope to use to rectify themselves. Therefore to take the extreme (*ji* 極) as the standard (*zhun* 準) of the center is acceptable, but to take it simply as the center is unacceptable. It is like the North Star as the peak of heaven (*tianji* 天極), or the ridgepole as the peak of a house (*wuji* 屋極); their meanings are the same.[95]

Note that Zhu here does define *ji* as "utmost extreme," which is its colloquial meaning. But as in the previous quote, he combines this with the sense of *ji* as a center—not in a spatial sense, but in a normative sense. This is the aspect of *taiji* that is lost by translating it as "Supreme Ultimate."[96]

Zhou Dunyi's other major work, the *Tongshu*, contains only one mention of *taiji*, in the important section (16) entitled Activity and Stillness (*dong jing*):

> The *yin* of water is based in *yang*; the *yang* of fire is based in *yin*. The Five Phases are *yin* and *yang*. *Yin* and *yang* are the Supreme Polarity.[97]

Here again is a direct equation of *yin-yang* and *taiji*, in a section whose main point is that activity and stillness, *yin* and *yang*, operate not only in cyclical alternation but also in interpenetration (*yin* within *yang* and vice versa). In section 1 of the *Tongshu*, Zhou Dunyi quotes a line from the *Xici* (A.5.1): "The alternation of *yin* and *yang* is called the Way." In a conversation on this line Zhu says, "'The alternation of *yin* and *yang* is called the Way' is the Supreme Polarity."[98] Thus, Zhou identifies *yin-yang*—the bipolar alternation

---

95. *Wenji* 72, 3454. See again Yang Shi's statement above about *zhong* (centrality/equilibrium) and *ji*. Yu Yingshi discusses this at length, in the context of Song political culture, in *Zhu Xi de lishi shijie*, 533–77.

96. Zhang Shi used similar language to explain *taiji*. In his comment on *Xici* A.11.5, the *locus classicus* of the term, Zhang Shi says that *taiji* is the centrality (*zhong*) or unity (*yi*) of the "three powers" (*sancai*), or the Ways of heaven, earth, and humanity; he too compares it with the "royal ultimate" (*huangji*), just as Zhu Xi did (*Zhang Shi quanji*, 1:11–12). This is consistent with the notion that *taiji* is not the endpoint of a linear process but rather the midpoint or juncture of a bipolar process. For more on Zhang Shi's understanding of *taiji*, see Tillman and Soffel, "Zhang Shi's Philosophical Perspectives," 134–39.

97. *Zhou Lianxi ji*, 5:34a.

98. *Yulei*, 74:2523 and *Zhou Lianxi ji*, 5:5b.

of *qi*—as *taiji*, while Zhu abstracts from *yin-yang* its principle or pattern and identifies that as *taiji*. The difference between these is the *li-qi* distinction of the Cheng brothers, which allowed for a qualitative leap to a level of abstraction not found in the other Northern Song Confucians.

In section 22 of the *Tongshu*, Zhou Dunyi says, "The manifest and the subtle: without intelligence one cannot perceive them." Zhu Xi's published comment on this line is:

> This discusses *li*. Yang is bright and *yin* is dark. Were it not for the perfect intelligence of the Supreme Polarity of the human mind, how would one be able to discern it?[99]

This requires a bit of interpretation. The Supreme Polarity of the human mind is the principle or order inherent in the mind that enables it to apprehend principle or order in external things. The fact that Zhu associates the manifest and the subtle with *yang* and *yin* suggests that this is the specific principle inherent in the mind that enables one to know the manifest and the subtle. Section 22 of the *Tongshu* also contains this passage:

> The Two [Modes of] *qi* and the Five Phases transform and generate the myriad things. The five are the differentia (*shu* 殊) and the two are the actualities (*shi* 實); the two are fundamentally one. Thus the many are one, and the one actuality is divided into the many. Each one of the many is correct; the small and the large are distinct.

Zhu Xi's comment on it:

> The Two [Modes of] *qi* and the Five Phases are that by which Heaven bestows the myriad things and generates them. From the product (*mo*) we can deduce the origin (*ben*); thus the differentiation of the Five Phases [as product] is the actuality of the two *qi* [as origin], and the actuality of the two *qi* [as product] in turn is based on the polarity of the unitary order/principle (*yi lizhi ji* 一理之極) [as origin].[100]

What Zhu is saying here is that the Five Phases are a further differentiation of *yin-yang qi*, and *yin-yang qi* is a manifestation of the unitary principle of

---

99. *Zhou Lianxi ji*, 6:1a.

100. *Zhou Lianxi ji*, 6:11a.

bipolarity. The latter step (and perhaps the former) is an example of the doctrine Zhu Xi adopted from Cheng Yi, "Where there is a thing there must be a principle."[101] Note how much less specific meaning would be conveyed by translating the last clause as "the actuality of the two *qi* is based on the *ultimacy* of the unitary principle." The actuality (*shi*) of the two *qi* is the principle of bipolarity, not some vague ultimacy, all-inclusiveness, or finality.

I have focused here on Zhu Xi's published commentaries on the *Yijing* and Zhou Dunyi's two major works, along with his conversations with students about those works and commentaries, and his essay on *taiji* (in chapter 3). Many other quotes can be found in Zhu's writings and conversation in which *taiji* is specifically identified as or associated with the principle of *yin-yang* polarity; just about every time the subject of *taiji* comes up the conversation concerns activity and stillness, *yin* and *yang*, or bipolarity in general.[102] For example, "What makes *taiji* what it is is nothing other than the Two Modes, Four Images, and Eight Trigrams."[103] Translating *taiji* as "Supreme/Great Ultimate" fails to account for this.

Zhu Xi's students and followers clearly understood their master's view, and continued to propagate it. For example, one of Zhu's prominent disciples was Chen Chun 陳淳 (1159–1223), who wrote:

> *Taiji* simply means principle. Why is principle called *ji*? *Ji* means reaching the ultimate, because it is in the focal point (center, *zhong*) or axis (*shuji*). *Huangji* (royal ultimate), *beiji* (North Pole), etc., all have the meaning of being the focal point. But *ji* should not be understood [literally] as the center. The greatest extent of anything is always at its center/focal point. Things from all directions reach their ultimate point here and cannot go any further. Take the ridgepole of a roof. It is called the *wuji* 屋極 (terminus of a building). It is simply the converging point of all building materials from the various directions, reaching their terminus at this center.[104]

---

101. Note 91 above.

102. See *Yulei* 75 (on *Xici* A), *Yulei* 94 (on Zhou), and Li Guangdi, *Zhuzi quanshu* 49 (on human nature and principle).

103. *Yulei* 75:2567.

104. Modified from Wing-tsit Chan's translation, *Neo-Confucian Terms Explained*, 117. Original in Yang Jia, ed., *Jinsilu jijie / Beixi ziyi*, *Ziyi* B:10a (p. 35); and Hu Guang, *Xingli daquan shu*, 26:9a.

Chen Chun here reiterates what Zhu Xi had said in his *Huangji bian* (Analysis of *huangji*, quoted above). He clearly emphasizes the meaning of *ji* as juncture or center—not in spatial terms (hence his caution that *ji* should not be understood as the literal, geometric center) but in terms of the principle of polarity, like the ridgepole of the house and the pole star: the focal point or center of gravity—the "heart" (*zhongxin* 中心) of a thing, where it is most pure. And finally, Rao Lu 饒魯, a student of Zhu Xi's son-in-law and leading disciple, Huang Gan, wrote:

> The term *taiji* expresses the majesty of natural principle (*tianli*). The word *ji* means axis or pivot (*shu* 樞), knot or node (*niu* 紐), root (*gen* 根), or basis (*di* 柢); as we say in common speech, *shuji* 樞極 [axis], or *genji* 根極 [root]. . . . The word *tai* means so great that nothing can be added, and expresses the fact that it is the Great Pivot and the Great Basis of the universe. All things, however, which bear this name, such as the North (celestial) Pole, the South (celestial) Pole, the ridge of a house, the Capital of Shang, or the four compass-point directions, have visible forms and locations to which we can point, but this *ji* alone is without form, and has no relation to space. Master Zhou therefore added the term *wu* (*wuji*), expressing the fact that it is not (confined to) any form such as that of a nodal pivot or a basic root, yet nonetheless is really the Great Nodal Pivot and the Great Basic Root of the universe.[105]

To recapitulate, translating *taiji* as "Supreme/Great Ultimate" does express its colloquial meaning ("great extreme"), but it completely misses the significance of the term as it was used in the Daoist tradition and in the Cheng-Zhu school of Confucianism. "Supreme Polarity" and its correlate for Zhou Dunyi's *wuji*, "Nonpolar(ity)," convey the crucial idea that *yin-yang* polarity is the most fundamental ordering principle or *li*, according to Zhu Xi and his followers, and is first manifested as the polarity of activity and stillness. The centrality of *yin-yang* polarity in Chinese thought is indeed well known. As Robert Neville puts it, "The Chinese tradition in its most ancient roots conceives of the elementary units of reality as changes from *yin* to *yang*

---

105. Translation by Needham, *Science and Civilisation in China,* 2:465, slightly modified. Rao Lu was also known as Rao Shuangfeng. See Huang and Quan, *Song-Yuan xue'an,* chs. 63, 83.

or vice versa."[106] And as Zhu Xi says in his commentary on the *Taijitu shuo* (section C), "[N]othing happens that is not the Way of *yin* and *yang*. As for what makes them *yin* and *yang*, nothing happens that is not the original nature of the Supreme Polarity."[107] This interpretation *includes* the colloquial meaning of the term: polarity is the "ultimate" principle in the sense that one can go no farther in explaining a phenomenon. It is the first ordering principle and therefore the last step in an explanation. This is why we do occasionally find the language of finality or ultimacy in Cheng-Zhu discussions of *taiji* (for example, Chen Chun's above). But the crucial point is that *taiji* is primarily the unitary principle that contains the possibility of differentiation and change. Like the literal image of a supreme ridgepole, *taiji* is both the highest, farthest point and (more significantly) the pivot or axis of the Way.

---

106. "Units of Change—Units of Value," 145–46.

107. *Zhou Lianxi ji,* 1:11b.

Conclusions

Zhou Dunyi has been universally depicted as the forerunner of the Cheng-Zhu school of "Neo-Confucian" thought and practice ever since the late twelfth century. Virtually every history of this movement, in both East Asian and Western scholarship, has begun with Zhou Dunyi and his *Taijitu shuo* (Discussion of the *Taiji Diagram*), explaining (1) that this short text provided the cosmological underpinning of Neo-Confucian thought; (2) that Zhou Dunyi was the teacher of the Cheng brothers, around whom the movement coalesced; and (3) that it was then "completed" (whether or not that word is used) by Zhu Xi, the great synthesizer.

What is almost always left out of this scenario is the fact that Zhou Dunyi's role in the Cheng-Zhu school was entirely the construction of Zhu Xi nearly one hundred years after Zhou died. Until then Zhou was a distinctly minor figure, and the prevailing consensus among Confucian literati was that Cheng Hao had been the first to revive the Confucian *dao* in the Song. The question that has never been satisfactorily answered is *why* Zhu Xi retrospectively chose Zhou Dunyi, against vociferous opposition, to initiate the revival of the Confucian *dao* after its long eclipse since the time of Mencius. The assumption has been that this could be explained philosophically: that Zhou's concept of *taiji* provided a philosophical link between the cosmological discourse of *qi* and the metaphysical discourse of *li*. This is a correct observation (i.e., it did provide such a link), but it is not a sufficient explanation of Zhu Xi's choice. As shown at the end of chapter

3, the concept of *taiji* was also found in the *Xici* appendix of the *Yijing*, a text whose Confucian legitimacy was questioned by no one. Zhou Dunyi, on the other hand, was widely known as a Daoist-leaning thinker with little or no following among Confucians, despite his brief time as teacher of the teenage Chengs.

My argument here has been that Zhou Dunyi's thought provided an underpinning not for Zhu Xi's philosophy but for his religious practice. Specifically, Zhou's theory of the interpenetration of activity (*dong*) and stillness (*jing*) enabled Zhu Xi to show that his mature theory of mental/spiritual cultivation was confirmed as correct because it mirrored the fundamental principle immanent in the natural world. It is a mistake, therefore, to seek a purely philosophical explanation of Zhu Xi's selection of Zhou Dunyi as the first Confucian sage of the Song. It is tempting to say that Zhu Xi was more like a theologian than a philosopher in the Western sense, but this does not go far enough. Although he has been compared with Thomas Aquinas as a "great synthesizer," in another respect he was actually more like a Benedict of Nursia (Saint Benedict, 480–547), in that he was chiefly concerned with facilitating the religious *practice* of Confucian self-cultivation for himself and his many followers, not with building a philosophical "theology" (or "daology").[1] Zhu's elevation of Zhou Dunyi was entirely the result of his dogged pursuit of a satisfactory and philosophically justifiable method of practicing what Mencius had described 1,500 years before: "If you fully explore your mind, you will know your nature. If you know your nature, you know Heaven. To preserve your mind and nourish your nature is to serve Heaven."[2] In Cheng-Zhu terminology this meant becoming aware of the substance (*ti*) or principle/order (*li*) of one's mind, which is the moral nature (*xing*). This was extremely difficult, according to Zhu Xi, because desires and feelings inevitably arise when the mind is active, and they cloud the inherent principle/order of the mind. Zhou Dunyi's concept of "activity in stillness and stillness in activity"

---

1. In other important respects Zhu Xi and Benedict were of course very different. Neither Zhu Xi nor any Confucian would countenance monasticism, which was the context of Benedict's religious practice. And Benedict's "Rule," or monastic code, emphasized institutional structure and code of conduct more than individual spiritual practice, which was Zhu Xi's focus. Still, both emphasized practice over theory. For one of many comparisons with Aquinas, see Siu-chi Huang, "Chu Hsi's Ethical Rationalism," 175. For Benedict, see Alston, "Rule of St. Benedict."

2. *Mencius* 7A1, trans. Charles A. Muller; http://www.acmuller.net/con-dao/mencius.html.

implied that both phases of the mind are immanent, and therefore can be known by the active mind. This was the reason why Zhu Xi elevated him to the position of founding father of the Cheng-Zhu school.

The tendency to view Zhu Xi through a philosophical rather than a religious lens has roots in late nineteenth and early twentieth-century China. Before the late nineteenth century, the distinction between "philosophical" and "religious" would have been difficult to express in China. The modern Chinese words for "philosophy" and "religion" were both originally Japanese neologisms coined in the late nineteenth century by translators of Western texts and treaties who felt that the Japanese language lacked precise equivalents. In the case of "religion," they apparently felt that Christianity belonged to a different category of things than Buddhism and Shinto, perhaps because of its exclusivism and its stronger emphasis on belief. The words they invented, which were quickly adopted by the Chinese, were *tetsugaku* (Chinese *zhexue* 哲學) for philosophy and *shūkyō* (Chinese *zongjiao* 宗教) for religion. The former was not a bad choice, as it literally means "wise learning." The latter, though, introduced problems that are still causing cross-cultural difficulties in discussing Chinese religion. *Zongjiao* can be translated literally as "sectarian teaching," which has a narrower range of connotations than "religion," especially as religion is understood today in global and comparative contexts. This is one of the reasons why Confucianism is not usually placed in that category by Chinese and Japanese. Another byproduct of the tendency to see Christianity as the model for what a religion should look like is the assumption that religions necessarily have institutional bases that are separate and distinct from society at large. Confucianism in Chinese history, though, has been more like what C. K. Yang called "diffused religion," in which religious practice takes place in "secular" settings (e.g., the family and the academy).[3]

In the early twentieth century the influence of the "New Culture movement" and the "May 4th generation" of Chinese scholars had profound effects on both East Asian and Western scholarship on Confucianism and Zhu Xi. The New Culture movement at the beginning of the twentieth century was an attempt to modernize China by adopting certain features of Western Enlightenment culture, notably Western science, technology, and democracy; by reforming political institutions and establishing a republic to replace the system of imperial rule, which ended in 1911; by language reform (using

---

3. See C. K. Yang, *Religion in Chinese Society*. For more extended discussions of the word *zongjiao* see Anthony C. Yu, *State and Religion in China*, 9–16; and Adler, "Confucianism as Religion / Religious Tradition / Neither."

the spoken language rather than the old literary language, commonly called "classical Chinese," for all writing); etc.[4] The term *May 4th generation* refers to May 4, 1919, when demonstrations by university students in Beijing (and later throughout the nation) began against the Treaty of Versailles, which gave parts of Shandong province that had been controlled by Germany to Japan. The nationalistic character of this movement gradually merged with the modernizing agenda of the New Culture movement, and the term *May 4th generation* now more or less stands for both.

The aspect of this movement that is relevant to scholarly perspectives on Zhu Xi is its uncritical acceptance of the Enlightenment preference for reason over religion. For the majority of Chinese intellectuals, religion represented tradition and philosophy represented modernity.[5] Two members of the May 4th generation are familiar to all Western students of Chinese thought: Fung Yu-lan (Feng Youlan, 1895–1990) and Wing-tsit Chan (1901–1994). They were two of the most influential historians of Chinese philosophy in the twentieth century, and Feng was also a philosopher himself in the Zhu Xi tradition. An implicit agenda in both of their careers was to demonstrate that Chinese philosophy deserved to be taken seriously by the global scholarly community; this would contribute to the acceptance of China as a modern nation. Wing-tsit Chan, in particular, occasionally expressed disdain for religion—for example, in regard to the Daoist religion that began in the second century CE, which he considered a degeneration of the lofty philosophy of Laozi and Zhuangzi. (Later in his career he appeared to be more accepting of religion, as in his essays, "Chu Hsi's Religious Life" [1983] and "Memory, Dreams, Divination, and Popular Beliefs" [1988].)[6]

Another factor contributing to the bias for philosophy over religion among historians of Chinese thought is the fact that the academic study of

---

4. See de Bary and Lufrano, eds., *Sources of Chinese Tradition*, 2nd ed., vol. 2, ch. 33.

5. There were also those who felt that tradition and modernity could be reconciled, such as the reformer Kang Youwei (1858–1927), who was older than the May 4th generation and wanted to make Confucianism the state religion. Contemporary scholars, such as Tu Weiming, critique the dualism of the tradition-modernity model, and, like Kang Youwei but in different ways, see possibilities for their reconciliation. Many non-Western nations have adopted aspects of modernity (e.g., market economies, democracy) but have creatively adapted them to their traditional forms of culture, creating new syntheses. See, e.g., Tu, "Introduction," in Tu, ed., *Confucian Traditions in East Asian Modernity*.

6. In *Chu Hsi: Life and Thought*, 139–61, and *Chu Hsi: New Studies*, 106–25.

religion, as distinct from theology, did not fully develop until roughly the 1960s. The anthropological study of religion had begun in the late nineteenth century, and the sociology of religion in the early twentieth, but neither of these approaches focus on religious thought. Theology of course does focus on thought, but, unlike religious studies, does so from the perspective of a particular religious tradition, accepting its fundamental truth-claims, such as the existence of God.

Since the 1990s this bias has begun to fade in Chinese scholarship. Even in the 1980s one of the deans of the study of religion in China, Ren Jiyu (1916–2009), had begun to argue that Confucianism should be considered a religious tradition. However, for Ren this was an indictment of Confucianism; he held to the Marxist-Maoist view that religion was a tool of oppression used by the landowning class in China to keep the peasantry from demanding adequate living conditions. Ren's views continued to be propagated later by several of his former students. But in the 1990s an alternative view began to appear: that yes, Confucianism is a religion, but that this is not necessarily a bad thing. These points have been vigorously argued, for example on the Web site Confucius2000.com. So today it is not difficult to find Chinese scholars whose approach to Confucianism is generally in tune with that of religious studies scholars outside China.[7]

Nevertheless, the result of the previously mentioned factors is that the academic study of Confucianism, both in East Asia and in the West, has largely been the province of intellectual historians and historians of philosophy not specifically trained in the relatively new field of religious studies. Moreover, many of those who do acknowledge a religious dimension to Confucian thought neglect the *praxis* dimension. Yet one of the hallmarks of East Asian religion is its relatively greater emphasis on the ritual, experiential, and social dimensions than on the doctrinal dimension.[8] As Ian Reader has cogently argued in regard to contemporary Japanese religion, *action* is more important than *belief*,[9] and this is also generally true of Chinese religion.[10] As mentioned

---

7. Two books in English appeared in 2013, both telling this story: Anna Sun, *Confucianism as a World Religion,* and Yong Chen, *Confucianism as a Religion.*

8. I am using Ninian Smart's terminology, the seven dimensions of religious worldviews: mythic, ritual, doctrinal, ethical, social, experiential, and artistic (material). See Smart, *Dimensions of the Sacred.*

9. Reader, *Religion in Contemporary Japan,* 13–15.

10. In this respect Zhu Xi was exceptional in demanding coherence between action and belief.

above, Christianity places much more emphasis on the doctrinal dimension, on belief. Since Christianity is often uncritically presumed to be the model of what "a religion" should look like by both Western and Asian scholars, those who may not make a conscious effort to question their own assumptions on such matters are often unwilling or unable to acknowledge the religious dimensions of Confucianism.

Zhu Xi's emphasis on practice over doctrine may be why, great synthesizer that he was, he never attempted to write a systematic overview of his ideas, a *Summa Daologica,* if you will. His mission was to train people to live according to the Dao. For the literati (intellectuals) of his time this required three types of practice: *intellectual cultivation* (learning the principles of things—the natural/moral order—by reading books, studying history, and handling daily affairs;[11] *spiritual cultivation* ("rectifying the mind," "making the will authentic," "quiet-sitting," etc.); and, perhaps most importantly, *practice*: putting into effect in social relations and formal rituals what one has learned. All three of these constituted Zhu Xi's religious practice.[12]

It was by looking at Zhu Xi's thought in the context of his religious practice—specifically his spiritual cultivation—that I discovered the two central pillars of my argument: (1) the close parallel between Zhu's solution to his "spiritual crisis" of the 1160s and his interpretations of Zhou Dunyi's writings (the interpenetration of activity and stillness), and (2) the fact that immediately after writing the *Yifa weifa shuo* (Discussion of *yifa* and *weifa*), outlining his final theory on the subject of that crisis, he turned to work on Zhou's writings. The "*ji-chou* enlightenment 己丑悟," Zhu's final resolution of the *weifa-yifa* problem, occurred in the third month of 1169, and he first

---

11. This was a formula Zhu Xi adopted from Cheng Yi. See Zhu, *Daxue huowen.*

12. Zhu's synthesis also included elements for what we might call non-literati, such as his book on *Family Rituals (Jia li)*, which became the standard authority on ancestor worship, puberty rituals, weddings, and funerals throughout the imperial period. See Patricia Buckley Ebrey's companion volumes, *Chu Hsi's Family Rituals* and *Confucianism and Family Rituals in Imperial China.* For a discussion of later Chinese and Japanese assessments of Song Confucianism as "empty learning" (*xuxue / kyōgaku* 虛學) as opposed to Qing dynasty and twentieth-century "practical learning" (*shixue / jitsugaku* 實學), see de Bary's "Introduction" to de Bary and Bloom, eds., *Principle and Practicality,* 1–4. These more recent views of Zhu Xi, which de Bary correctly observes "speak for their own time and its dilemmas, not for a past from which they have already been considerably distanced" (2), may be yet another factor in the modern tendency to ignore the *praxis* dimension of Zhu Xi's project.

wrote the *Yifa weifa shuo* and the letter to the "gentlemen of Hunan" (a shortened form of the essay) to explain it. Three months later he published his revision of Zhou Dunyi's *Taijitu* and *Tongshu* (the Jian'an edition, without commentary). Zhu's mother died three months after that, and he buried her in the first month of 1170. That spring he completed his draft of the *Taiji tushuo jie* (Commentary on the *Taijitu shuo*), although the postface wasn't written until 1173 and it wasn't published until 1188. In the seventh month of 1170 he moved his father's tomb. (I mention these important family matters because they undoubtedly slowed his scholarly output in 1169 and 1170.) Toward the end of 1173 he completed the draft of the *Yi-Luo yuan-yuan lu*, his history of the Cheng school, placing Zhou Dunyi at the head. This was the beginning of his campaign to create the figure of Zhou Dunyi as the first sage of the Song, followed shortly by the anthology *Jinsilu* (Reflections on Things at Hand) in 1175, also leading off with Zhou Dunyi. He continued to write on Zhou for the next twenty years—a total of twenty-two pieces between 1169 and 1194.

Zhu Xi's construction of the figure of Zhou Dunyi was also the reconstruction of the Confucian *dao*, which Mencius had called the Way of the Sages. In the narrowest sense, it was a revision of the generally accepted lineage of past Sages, the *daotong* (succession of the Way). But in placing the constructed figure of Zhou Dunyi where he did, Zhu also made Zhou's texts and the ideas in them canonical, in the sense of a rule or standard. What Zhou added to the normative Cheng-Zhu understanding of *dao* was the idea that the most fundamental ordering principle (*li*) was *yin-yang* polarity, which is first manifested as the alternation of activity and stillness in the philosophical cosmogony of the *Taijitu shuo*. Zhu Xi followed through on this principle quite consistently, as, for example, in his "Discussion of *Taiji*" and just about every time he discussed *taiji*. This focus on *yin-yang* was also the basis of his interpretation of the *Yijing*: in his 1188 commentary on that text, the *Zhouyi benyi* (Original meaning of the *Zhouyi*), his hermeneutical first principle is to focus on the *yin-yang* meanings of the hexagrams in order to discover the primordial Sage Fuxi's original intent in creating the *Yi*. (Fuxi, according to the tradition, created only the hexagram divination system, with no textual content, and the hexagram lines alone signify nothing other than *yin* and *yang*.)

The effect of this emphasis on stillness-activity and *yin-yang* is to reinforce the implicit Confucian claim—present in the tradition since before Confucius's time in the concept of the "mandate of Heaven" (*tianming*)—that moral principle is natural principle. We tend to associate the idea that morality is natural with Mencius, who of course made it quite explicit. But it can be considered the key identifying characteristic of Confucian thought, especially in relation to classical Daoism (the *Laozi* and *Zhuangzi*), in which human values are merely unnatural conventions. In the Song period competition with Buddhism, the claim that social and family values were rooted in the natural world was used to refute the validity of Buddhist monasticism. Song Confucians also tried to use it to refute the Mahayana concept of emptiness—although in that case they were arguing against a straw man, as the concept of emptiness does not mean nothingness.

Zhu Xi's appropriation of Zhou Dunyi demonstrates not only the integration of metaphysics, cosmology, and ethics in Song Confucian ("Neo-Confucian") thought. It also demonstrates how this was a comprehensive religio-philosophical tradition, embodying not only theory but also practice.

Part II

Translations of Zhou Dunyi's Major Works and Zhu Xi's Commentaries, with Further Discussions by Zhu Xi and His Students

Introduction

According to the epitaph of Zhou Dunyi written shortly after his death by his friend Pan Xingsi 潘興嗣 (1023–1100), Zhou's written works included

> the "Supreme Polarity Diagram" (*Taijitu* 太極圖), a "Discussion of the *Yi*" (*Yishuo* 易說), "Penetrating the *Yi*" (*Yitong* 易通) in several tens of sections (*pian* 篇), and ten books (*juan* 卷) of poetry. These are now stored at his home.[1]

This presents us with several problems. What about the *Taijitu shuo*? Did Pan mean to include it under the title *Taijitu*? Or is it what he called the *Yishuo*? And if not, where is the *Yishuo*? And finally, was the *Tongshu* originally called *Yitong*?

To take the easiest problem first, it has been universally assumed ever since at least Zhu Xi's time that *Yitong* was the original title of the *Tongshu*. In fact, it is a more appropriate title, and some contemporary authors call our text by that original name.[2] My view on the other two titles is that "*Taijitu*" covered both the diagram and the explanation, and that *Yishuo* was a

---

1. Pan Xingsi, "Lianxi xiansheng muzhi ming," in *Zhou Lianxi ji*, 10:20b.
2. E.g., Bounghown Kim, *A Study of Chou Tun-i's Thought*, chs. 5–6; and Bent Nielsen, *A Companion to Yi Jing Numerology and Cosmology*, 338. A literal translation of *Tongshu* would be either "Penetrating writing" or "Penetrating the book." Another strategy is to call it *Yi tongshu*, or "Book penetrating the *Yi*."

commentary on the *Yi* that has been mostly lost, except for remarks on nine hexagrams that were incorporated into the *Tongshu* (sections 31, 32, and 40). It would make sense that Zhou had written a commentary on the *Yi*, as he drew on it extensively in both the *Taijitu shuo* and the *Tongshu*.

The Cheng brothers presumably had copies of Zhou's works, as according to an account written in 1144 by Qi Kuan 祁寬, at least two of their students passed them on to other scholars.[3] One of these students was Hou Zhongliang 候仲良 (who was also a nephew of the Chengs), who passed them on to Zhu Zhen (the source of the claim that the *Taiji* Diagram came from Daoists). Hou also became a teacher of Hu Hong, so that may be how Hu received them. As we saw in chapter 2, Hu Hong was apparently the first to claim that Zhou Dunyi perceived the Way directly.

Zhu Xi first read the *Taijitu shuo* and the *Tongshu* at the age of twenty-three, four years after receiving the *jinshi* degree, during a period in which he was seriously studying both Buddhist and Daoist texts. He later said he did not understand it at that time. He took it up again eight years later, compiling Zhou's surviving texts and sending them to his teacher Li Tong. For the next few years, until Li Tong's death in 1163, Zhou's texts were among the topics they discussed in person and in letters. During his several months' visit with Zhang Shi in 1167, Zhou's concept of *taiji* was one of the topics they focused on. In the third month of 1169 he had his "sudden enlightenment" on the *zhong/he* problem (see chapter 3 above). Three months later he published the *Taijitu shuo* and the *Tongshu* texts themselves, without commentaries (the 1169 Jian'an edition; his postface is translated below). He must have been simultaneously working on a commentary, since he finished the first draft in the spring of 1170. The fact that he published Zhou's texts immediately after resolving the *zhong/he* problem, while he was in the process of writing a commentary, suggests some sense of urgency in making the texts available for people to read. He apparently completed the commentary in 1173, when he wrote a postface (*houji*) to it, but he did not publish it at that time. In 1179 he received an old family edition of Zhou's *Taiji* and *Tongshu* from Jiujiang, where Zhou had lived in retirement. Making corrections based on these texts, he published a new edition of them (the 1179 Nankang edition; postface also translated below).[4] Between 1185

---

3. Qi Kuan, *"Tongshu houba"* (Colophon to the *Tongshu*, 1144), in *Zhou Lianxi ji*, 7:12a-b.

4. He lists nineteen differences between the old family edition and the one he had previously used, which he refers to as the Yanping edition, in *"You Yanping ben"* (*Zhou Lianxi ji*, 7:3b–4a).

and early 1189, he carried on the exchange of letters with the Lu brothers about Zhou's writings, especially the *Taijitu shuo*. He finally published the commentary translated here in 1188.

The main source text for these translations, *Zhou Lianxi xiansheng quanji* 周濂溪先生全集 (Complete collection of Zhou Dunyi's works), in thirteen chapters (*juan* 卷), was compiled by Zhang Boxing 張伯行 (1652–1725) in 1708, and was included in his collection, *Zhengyi tang quanshu* 正誼堂全書 (Library of Zhengyi Hall).[5] It includes all of Zhou Dunyi's surviving works, Zhu Xi's published commentaries on them, lengthy selections from Zhu Xi's *Classified Conversations* (*Zhuzi yulei* 朱子語類) and his *Collected Papers* (*Hui'an xiansheng Zhu wengong wenji* 晦庵先生朱文公文集), and various pieces about Zhou written by others.[6] I have also included some selections from Zhu's *Classified Conversations* that are not included by Zhang in his compilation. For these I have used the edition of the *Zhuzi yulei* included in Zhu Jieren, Yan Zuozhi, Liu Yongxiang, eds. *Zhuzi quanshu* 朱子全數 (Zhu Xi's complete works, 2002) in twenty-seven volumes.

Three editions of Zhang Boxing's compilation have been used: (1) the unpunctutated Baibu congshu jicheng edition; (2) a reprint of an unidentified punctuated woodblock edition, with the same pagination as (1), published under the title *Taijitu xiangjie* 太極圖詳解 (Detailed Discussion of the Supreme Polarity Diagram);[7] and (3) the punctuated Congshu jicheng 叢書集成 edition, entitled *Zhou Lianxi ji* 周濂溪集.[8] In addition, for Zhou's texts and Zhu's published commentaries, I have consulted Chen Keming 陳克明, ed., *Zhou Dunyi ji* 周敦頤集 (Collection of Zhou Dunyi),[9] which contains no supplementary discussions from the *Classified Conversations* or the *Collected*

---

5. Zhang Boxing was a high official of the Qing dynasty, becoming president of the Ministry of Ritual (*Libu*) in 1723. At the time he compiled the *Zhou Lianxi xiansheng quanji* he was governor of Fujian province. He was a devoted follower of Zhu Xi, and in 1878 he was enshrined in the Confucian temple. See Dean R. Wickes, "Chang Po-hsing," and Jonathan Spence, "Chang Po-hsing and the K'ang-hsi Emperor." The latter is a critical examination of Zhang's official career, suggesting that in his later years Zhang suffered from extreme paranoia.

6. A very similar collection of Zhou's works was compiled by Dong Rong (1711–1760) in 1756, entitled *Zhouzi quanshu* (Master Zhou's complete works), in twenty two chapters.

7. Beijing: Xuefan chuban she, 1990. The foreword to this book, by Sun Guozhong 孫國中, justifies its publication in service of Marxist-Leninist thought.

8. Taibei: Taiwan Commercial Press, 1966.

9. Beiing: Zhonghua shuju, 1990.

Papers. I have encountered no significant differences among these editions. However, in his quotations of passages from Zhu Xi's *Classified Conversations* and other texts, Zhang Boxing sometimes differs slightly from the originals I have consulted, but without changes in meaning.

My translations include the complete texts of Zhou Dunyi's works, Zhu Xi's complete (published) commentaries, and a significant selection of Zhu Xi's discussions with his students on the original texts and the commentaries, mostly taken from the *Zhuzi yulei*. I have not translated all of the supplementary discussions that Zhang Boxing includes in his compilation, although I have included more than those specifically relevant to the argument of this book. The result reflects my judgment of what is significant and interesting, which includes, in addition to the content of the selections, the glimpse they provide into the learning environment established by Zhu Xi and his students.

Chapter Five

The Supreme Polarity Diagram

(*Taijitu* 太極圖)

INTRODUCTION

One of the distinctive aspects of the Song dynasty revival of Confucianism was a surge of interest in the use of *tu* 圖 ("diagrams") as means of conveying the subtler meanings of the Way that can elude discursive expression. As Wang Bo 王柏 (1197–1274) put it, "[T]he meaning(fullness) of one single *tu* can not be exhausted by millions of words."[1] The historian Zheng Qiao 鄭樵 (1104–1162) likewise subordinated the written word to *tu* by correlating diagrams with *jing* 經 (warp, scripture), which are invariable, while writing (*shu* 書) was correlated with *wei* 緯 (weft, apocrypha, variable).[2]

The category of *tu* included two genres: (1) diagrammatic or schematic and (2) representational. Both of them were "instructive images conveying skilled specialist knowledge."[3] The latter genre included representations of such things as technical devices or farming methods. The former genre,

---

1. From Wang Bo's preface to his *Yanji tu* (Diagrams on the Fathoming of Incipience), 1a; translated by Michael Lackner, "Diagrams as an Architecture by Means of Words," 345. Wang Bo was a third-generation disciple of Zhu Xi (through Huang Gan and He Ji) (ibid., 347).

2. Francesca Bray, "Introduction," 39.

3. Ibid., 3.

which was the chief interest of the Song Confucians, included two subtypes: (1) cosmological and (2) exegetical. Cosmological *tu* included the *Taijitu*, diagrams based on the *Yijing* or the Five Phases, and so forth. Exegetical *tu* were word-based devices used to express and understand the meaning of texts or passages from texts, and were often designed in stemmatic fashion, like genealogical charts. Zhu Xi, for example, composed such a diagram to explain the meaning of his "Discussion of humanity" (*Renshuo* 仁說).[4]

Confucians had traditionally placed greater faith than Daoists and Buddhists in the capacity of words to fully express the *dao*. Daoists since the *Laozi*, and Mahayana Buddhists at least since Nagarjuna, had always stressed the limitations of rational discourse. The Daoist use of charms and talismans (*fu* 符) and the Buddhist use of mandalas were precursors to the Song Confucian use of *tu*. But the most direct influence on the Confucians was the *Yijing*, which of course has graphic imagery (trigrams/hexagrams) at its core. The *Yi* in fact has been called "*tu par excellence*."[5] It was also associated with various numerological/cosmological diagrams, such as the *Hetu* 河圖 ([Yellow] River Diagram) and *Luoshu* 洛書 (Luo [River] text).[6]

The fascination with *tu* was an important part of the renewed interest in the *Yijing* as a source of cosmological insight, one of the chief characteristics of the Song revival of Confucianism. The interest in *tu* flourished throughout the Song and Yuan dynasties, but began to decline during the Ming (1368–1644). From the sixteenth century onward, Confucian thinkers tended to reverse Wang Bo's and Zheng Qiao's way of thinking about the priority of *tu* over words (*yan* 言) or writing (*shu*), and began to think of pictorial representation (*hua* 畫) as more subtle and refined than *tu*.[7] During the Qing dynasty (1644–1911), the *kaozheng* 考證 (evidential research) movement's rejection of the authenticity of the cosmological *tu* associated with the *Yijing* was part of the general demise of traditional Chinese cosmology.[8]

---

4. Ibid., 36, and Lackner, "Diagrams as an Architecture by Means of Words," 348–52. Zhu Xi's *Renshuo tu* is in *Yulei* 105:3454–55. The *Renshuo* itself is in *Wenji* 67:3279–81.

5. Ibid., 346.

6. See the "Record of the Reconstruction of Zhou Dunyi's Library/study (*shutang*) in Jiangzhou," chapter 2 above.

7. Bray, "Introduction," 45–49.

8. Hu Wei, *Yitu mingbian* (Analysis of the Diagrams of the *Yi*); John Henderson, *The Development and Decline of Chinese Cosmology*; idem., "Chinese Cosmographical Thought," 225–27.

Although the prevailing theory regarding the origin of the *Taijitu* in Zhu Xi's time (and still today) was that Zhou Dunyi had received it from Daoist sources, Zhu and his followers insisted that Zhou had composed it himself. Zhu Xi could not accept Zhu Zhen's theory of the diagram's Daoist origin because it would have undermined his claims about the uniqueness of the Confucian *dao* (as we have seen in chapter 1) and the singular importance of Zhou Dunyi (chapter 2). Zhou Dunyi's creation of the *Taijitu* was a kind of "revelation," part of his "reception of the propagation of the *dao* conferred by Heaven,"[9] which confirmed the objective truth of Confucian values.

The *Taiji* Diagram is included several times in the current Daoist Canon (*Daozang* 道藏), which was compiled in the Ming 明 dynasty (1368–1644). One of them is identified as "Mr. Zhou's *Taijitu*," and is accompanied by his *Taijitu shuo*.[10] There are also at least half a dozen similar diagrams.[11] The two most similar are the *Taiji* Preceding Heaven Diagram (*Taiji xiantian tu* 太極先天圖) and the *Wuji* Diagram (*Wuji tu* 無極圖), both of which have been extensively studied since the Qing dynasty (1644–1911) for their possible connection with Zhou Dunyi's *Taiji Diagram*.[12]

---

9. "Record of the Reconstruction of Zhou Dunyi's Library/study (*shutang*) in Jiangzhou," chapter 2 above.

10. In "Diagrams of the *Zhouyi*" (*Zhouyi tu* 周易圖), ch. 1:1b–2a (*Dongzhen bu* 洞真部, *Lingtu lei* 靈圖類). The diagram is also found in *Yuanshi wuliang durenpin miaojing tongyi* 元始無量度人上品妙經通義, 1:1a; *Yuanshi wuliang durenpin miaojing neiyi biao* 元始無量度人上品妙經內義, 6b; *Dayi xiangshu junshen tu* 大易象數鈎深圖, 1:1a.

11. For five of them and a good but brief discussion of the *Taijitu* in a Daoist context see Robinet, "*Taiji tu*." In the *"Wuming lun"* (Discourse on the Nameless) by He Yan (c. 207–249) there is a passage (with no diagram) that could be interpreted as a description of something like level B of the *Taijitu*, depicting the interaction of *yin* and *yang*: "It is like *yang* within *yin*, and *yin* within *yang*. The summer sun is *yang*, yet the evening and the winter sun are both *yin*; the winter sun is *yin*, and yet the morning and the summer sun are both *yang*. Both are different from what is near and the same as what is distant." That is, in summer (*yang*) the evenings are *yin* like winter, and in winter (*yin*) the mornings are *yang* like summer. This is quoted in Zhang Zhan's commentary on the *Liezi* (Chen Chun, ed., *Liezi Zhan zhu*, 4:4b). There were three earlier compilations of the Daoist Canon: in the fifth, eighth, and eleventh centuries (the last under early Song rule).

12. For a summary of this scholarship see Kim, *A Study of Chou Tun-i's Thought*, 118–43. See also Fung Yu-Lan, *History of Chinese Philosophy* 2: 438–42; and Julia Ching, *The Religious Thought of Chu Hsi*, 15–20. 235–41.

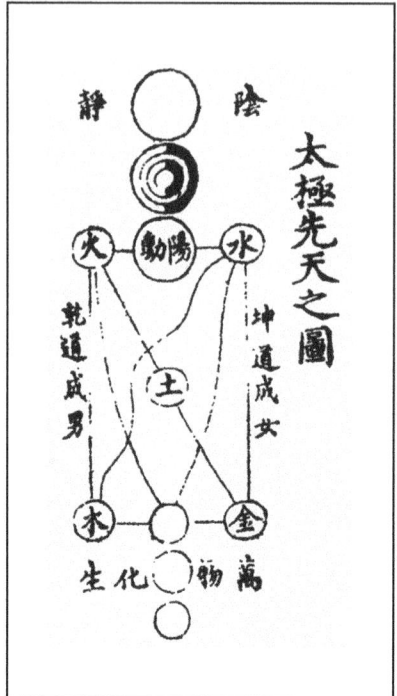 

FIGURE 5.1 *Taiji* Preceding Heaven Diagram (*Taiji xiantian tu*). From "Diagrams of the Mysterious True Origin Scripture of the Great Cavern of the Highest Quarter" (*Shangfang dadong zhenyuan miaojing tu* 上方大洞真元妙經圖), in *Zhengtong daozang*, vol. 437. Described in Schipper and Verellen, *The Taoist Canon*, 1220–1221.

FIGURE 5.2 *Wuji* Diagram (*Wuji tu*). From Wei Qi 衛琪, "Commentary on the Jade Purity Non-polar Comprehensive Truth Great Cavern Immortals Scripture according to Wenchang" (*Yuqing wuji zongshen Wenchang dadong xianjing zhu* 玉清無極總真文昌大洞仙經註, 1309), in *Zhengtong daozang*, vol. 103. Described in Schipper and Verellen, *The Taoist Canon*, 707–708.

The question how the *Taiji* Diagram was transmitted to Zhou Dunyi has been vigorously debated since the twelfth century. As noted in the previous chapters, the most prominent theory is that of Zhu Zhen 朱震 (1072–1138), who said that it was given to Zhou by Mu Xiu 穆修 (979–1032), a mid-level government official, who died when Zhou was fifteen; Mu Xiu had received it from Chong Fang 种放 (956–1015), a former official who became a Daoist recluse; and he in turn had received it from the well-known Daoist master

Chen Tuan 陳搏 (d. 989).[13] Chen Tuan is also credited with having transmitted a number of other diagrams, including several based on the trigrams and hexagrams of the *Yijing* that were popularized by Shao Yong and Zhu Xi.[14] Zhu Zhen put forth this theory, however, in 1134, sixty-one years after Zhou Dunyi had died, and his sources for it are unknown, so its reliability is debatable.[15] Likewise, the specific historical connections among the various similar diagrams are still topics for debate.

In addition to the obvious Daoist connections, another possible strand of influence on the *Taijitu* comes from Buddhism. Zhou Dunyi is known to have had Buddhists among his teachers and friends; the most commonly mentioned is Shou Ya 壽崖 of Helin Temple in Runzhou (Jiangsu province), where Zhou Dunyi lived for a couple years in his early twenties.[16] According to Chao Yuezhi 晁說之 (1059–1129), Shou Ya taught Zhou, but what he taught is unknown and whether Zhou was even considered a Buddhist layman is doubtful.[17] Like most if not all Confucian literati of the Song, Zhou moved in the same circles as Buddhist literati, and several others are known to have

---

13. See Nielsen, *Companion,* 29 (Chen Tuan), 33 (Chong Fang), 179 (Mu Xiu). Also on Chen Tuan see Kohn, *Chen Tuan,* and Smith, *Fathoming the Cosmos,* 115–20. An alternate version of the *Wujitu* (same diagram with different labels) is found in Huang Zongyan, *Tuxue bianhuo,* 456 (Robin Wang reproduces and translates this one in *Yinyang,* 219). Huang traces it back to Heshang Gong, the early commentator on the *Laozi,* and says that Wei Boyang included it in his *Cantongqi,* although it is not in the extant edition.

14. The most important of these was the Diagram Preceding Heaven (*Xiantian tu*), also known as the Fuxi sequence, which was used by both Shao Yong and Zhu Xi. See chapter 2 for the significance of Fuxi to Zhu Xi. For a chart illustrating the whole geneaology of Chen Tuan's influence on Song *Yijing* studies see Huang Zongyan, *Zhouyi xunmen yulun,* 403.

15. Kim, *A Study of Chou Tun-i's Thought,* 105.

16. See Huang and Quan, *Song-Yuan xue'an,* 12:29b, 30b; and Du Zheng, *Nianpu,* in *Zhou Lianxi ji,* 10:3b. Late in his life Zhou apparently had anti-Buddhist feelings, as in 1071 he criticized Han Yu (768–824) for having donated a gift to a Buddhist temple (Chan, "Chou Tun-i," 280).

17. See Kim, *A Study of Chou Tun-i's Thought,* 144–52. Huang Zongyan, writing in the seventeenth century, says that Shou Ya was also involved in the transmission of *Yijing*-related diagrams and that Chong Fang passed down the *Xiantian tu* to both Mu Xiu and Shou Ya. See Hu Hong's "Preface to Master Zhou's *Tongshu,*" translated above in chapter 1, where Hu does not mention Shou Ya.

had interactions with him.[18] But the only specific Buddhist influence on the *Taijitu* that has been suggested is that of Guifeng Zongmi 圭峰宗密 (781–841), who is a "patriarch" (lit. "ancestor") of both the Huayan and Chan schools. In the most commonly used edition of his "Preface to the Collected Writings on the Source of Chan" there is a diagram depicting the stages of enlightenment whose uppermost element, representing the *ālayavijñāna* (storehouse consciousness) is almost identical to the second level of the *Taijitu*

(note that it lacks the small circle in the center, which Zhu Xi says represents *taiji*):[19]

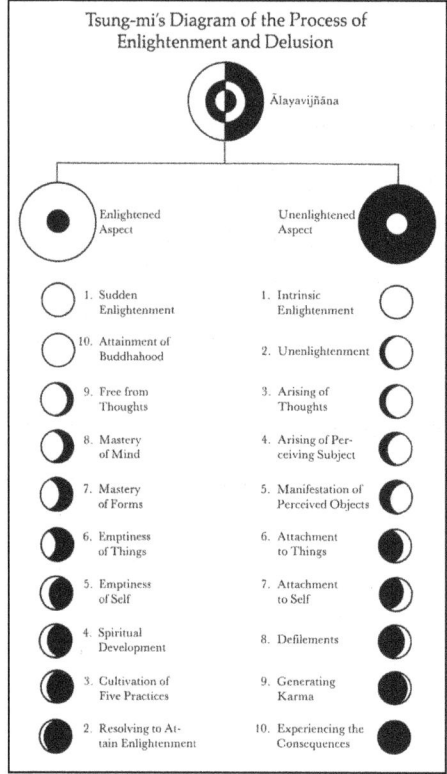

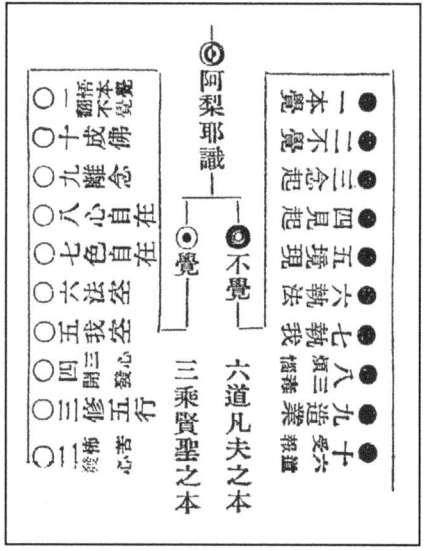

FIGURE 5.3

---

18. E.g., Huanglong Huinan, Huanglong Zuxin, Donglin Changzong, Foyin Liaoyuan. See Anon., "*Zhou Dunyi de fojiao yinyuan*," and Qian Mu, *Zhuzi xin xue'an*, 1:19–20.

19. From Gregory, "Sudden Enlightenment Followed by Gradual Cultivation," 291. Original in *Taishō shinshū daizōkyō'* v. 48, 410–11.

However, this diagram, which is found at the end of Zongmi's "Preface" in the Taishō canon and is dated 1303, is not found at all in extant earlier versions of the text: one found in the "library cave" of the Mogao cave temple complex at Dunhuang, dated 952; and two later Korean editions of the text, both based on a Song version.[20] This suggests the possibility that the diagram was a later addition to Zongmi's text, perhaps influenced by the *Taijitu* instead of vice versa. So, while Zhou Dunyi was probably influenced in his thinking by Buddhism (see Introduction to the *Taijitu shuo*), the available evidence points to a purely Daoist origin for the *Taijitu*.

Nevertheless, Zhu Xi is quite emphatic that Zhou Dunyi composed the *Taijitu* himself, as he states in the first sentence of the preface below. In a letter to Huang Gan he contrasts the *Taijitu* with the "Prior Heaven Diagram" (*Xiantiantu* 先天圖), which was popularized by Zhou's contemporary Shao Yong. This diagram, according to Zhu Zhen, had also been passed through Chen Tuan, but it was traditionally attributed to the mythic sage Fuxi (it depicts the *Yijing* hexagrams in binary order, or the "Fuxi sequence"):

> The Prior Heaven was Fuxi's original diagram; [Shao] Kangjie did not create it himself. Although it is wordless, it is all-inclusive. Every word and meaning in the *Yi* flows out from it. But the *Taiji* [Diagram] was created by [Zhou] Lianxi himself; it brings to light the general outline and ideas of the *Yi*.[21]

Of course, Zhu Xi could not allow that the *Taijitu* had Daoist origins, as that would have supported the Lu brothers' argument that Zhou Dunyi did not belong in the *daotong*.

The historical connection between Zhou's *Taijitu* and the familiar *taiji* or *yin-yang* diagram

often seen today (on T-shirts, jewelry, etc.) is not as direct as one might assume. Although the second level of Zhou's diagram resembles it somewhat, it clearly lacks the dynamism of the interlocking swirls. Zhou's picture of *yin* and *yang* is actually composed of the trigrams *kan* ☵ (water) and *li* ☲ (fire) bent into semicircles. These two trigrams had great significance in Daoist alchemy,

---

20. Gregory, *Tsung-mi*, 196; Kim, *A Study of Chou Tun-i's Thought*, 158–59.
21. *Wenji* 46: 2155.

where they were the prime symbols of *yin* and *yang*—further supporting the Daoist provenance of the *Taijitu*. The earliest known depiction of the dynamic, swirly *yin-yang* circle comes from a text dating to the 1370s, the *Liushu benyi* 六書本義 (Original meaning of the six writings) by Zhao Huiqian 趙撝謙 (1351–1395), where it is combined with the Eight Trigrams and called the "River Chart spontaneously [generated] by Heaven and Earth":[22]

FIGURE 5.4 Original version (Louis, "The Genesis of an Icon," 171). See also Hu Wei, *Yitu mingbian*, 84.

FIGURE 5.5 Modern version

By the Ming dynasty, as François Louis has shown, this diagram had become an iconic representation of the basic principle of Chinese cosmology, the immanent creativity of *taiji*.

In the following translation of Zhu Xi's explanation of Zhou Dunyi's *Taijitu* I have included all of Zhang Boxing's comments, because they clarify Zhu Xi's many allusions to correlative cosmology. Notes not identified as Zhang's are mine. The bracketed letters to the left of the chart are for reference in the text.

---

22. See François Louis, "The Genesis of an Icon: The *Taiji* Diagram's Early History." This article is about the diagram shown above, not Zhou Dunyi's *Taijitu*.

The Supreme Polarity Diagram

[Preface by Zhu Xi:][23]

Master Zhu said: The Supreme Polarity Diagram was created by Master Lianxi. Master Zhou's [original] name was Dunshi and his style name was Maoshu. Later, to avoid [Emperor] Yingzong's name, he changed [his own] to Dunyi. His family lived along Lian Stream (Lianxi) in Rongdao County in Daozhou. He was broadly learned and energetic in practice, and he heard the Way early. In handling affairs he was firm and determined; he had the style of a man of old. In governing he was careful to take reciprocity seriously and was fully devoted to moral principle. He created the Supreme Polarity Diagram, the *Penetrating Writing* (*Tongshu*), and the *Penetration of the Yi* (*Yitong*), altogether several tens of chapters. Emotionally he was light-hearted, his manners were exceedingly pleasant, and he especially enjoyed fine landscapes. At the base of Mt. Lu there was a stream where the master enjoyed sitting at the edge, so he called it Lianxi (Waterfall Stream) and built his study on its bank.

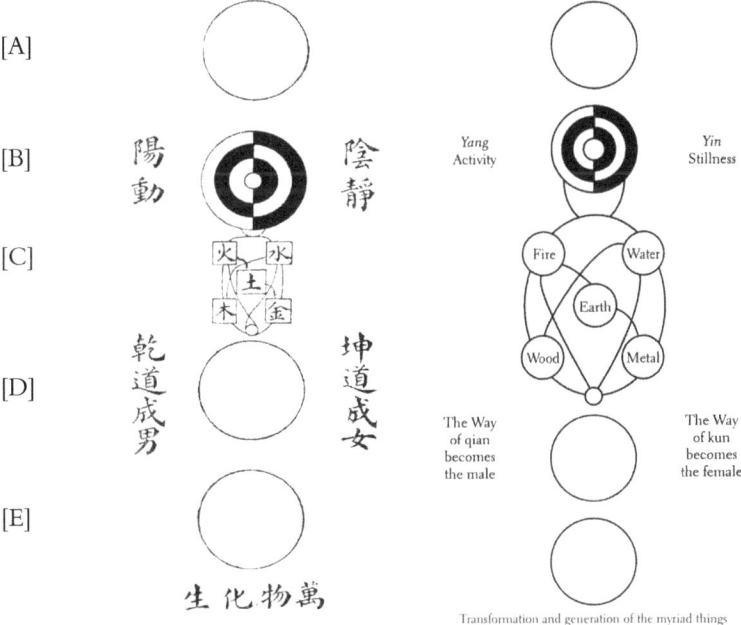

---

23. This was actually not written as a preface; it was excerpted by Zhang Boxing from Zhu Xi's *Yi-Luo yuan-yuan lu* (Record of the origins of the Luoyang school) and placed before the Diagram. Zhu Jieren, Yan Zuozhi, Liu Yongxiang, eds., *Zhuzi quanshu* (Zhu Xi's Complete Works), vol. 12, 923–25.

Master Zhu's Explanation of the Diagram
(*Zhuzi tu jie* 朱子圖解)

[A] ○

This stands for "Nonpolar (*wuji*) and yet Supreme Polarity (*taiji*)!" [*Taijitu shuo*], which is the fundamental substance (*benti*) by which *yang* [arises] from activity and *yin* from stillness.[24] But it [*wuji-taiji*] is not separate from *yin* and *yang*;[25] it is precisely *yin* and *yang* that indicates the fundamental [substance].[26] It is only for the sake of speech that they are distinguished from [lit. not mixed with] *yin* and *yang*.[27]

[B] ◉

This is the active *yang* and still *yin* of ○ [*wuji/taiji*]. The central [inner] ○ is the fundamental substance.[28] ☾ is the activity of *yang*; the functioning of ○ is how it operates. ☽ is the stillness of *yin*; the substance of ○ is how it is established. ☽ is the basis of ☾, and the ☾ is the basis of ☽.

[C]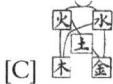

This is *yang* changing and *yin* combining to generate water, fire, wood, metal, and earth. This ╲ is *yang* transforming, and this ╱ is *yin* combining.

---

24. [Zhang Boxing: *Taiji* is *li*; *yin-yang* is *qi*. What enables *qi* to be active and still is the *li* as master (*zai* 宰).]

25. [Zhang: The Way (*dao* 道) is not separate from implements (*qi* 器).]

Alluding to *Yijing*, *Xici* A.12.4: "What is above form (*xing'er shang* 形而上) is called the Way; what is within form (*xing'er xia* 形而下) is called implements" (*Zhouyi benyi* 3:16a).

26. [Zhang: The Way within implements.]

27. [Zhang: The Way is the Way; implements are implements. Already in the above three sentences the necessity to see in terms of unity and multiplicity is clarified.]

28. [Zhang: This is the *taiji* of the first paragraph.]

Water 水 is the flourishing of *yin*;²⁹ therefore it resides on the right.³⁰ Fire 火 is the flourishing of *yang*;³¹ therefore it resides on the left.³² Wood 木 is the fragility of *yang*;³³ therefore it is below fire.³⁴ Metal 金 is the fragility of *yin*;³⁵ therefore it is below water.³⁶ Earth 土 is blended *qi*;³⁷ therefore it resides in the center. The connection between water and fire above by the ⌣ is *yin* [water] based in *yang* [fire] and *yang* based in *yin*.³⁸

With water there is wood, with wood there is fire, with fire there is earth, with earth there is metal, and metal returns to water [liquid]. Like a beginningless circle, the five *qi* are arranged and the four seasons proceed.³⁹

[A-B-C]

"The Five Phases are the unitary *yin* and *yang*" [*Taijitu shuo*]; there is nothing other than these five manifestations [of *qi*] and two actualities.⁴⁰ "*Yin* and *yang*

---

29. [Zhang: In autumn *yin* appears and in winter *yin* flourishes.]
30. [Zhang: The place of north.]
31. [Zhang: In spring *yang* appears and in summer *yang* flourishes.]
32. [Zhang: The place of south.]
33. [Zhang: When *yang* first appears it is fragile.]
34. [Zhang: The place of east.]
35. [Zhang: When *yin* first appears it is fragile.]
36. [Zhang: The place of west.]
37. [Zhang: The four (above states of) *qi* blended.]
38. See *Tongshu* 6[e].
39. This is the "mutual production" sequence of the Five Phases, possibly dating back at least to Dong Zhongshu's *Chunqiu fanlu* 春秋繁露 (Luxuriant gems of the *Spring and Autumn Annals*) in the second century BCE.
40. [Zhang: Water, fire, wood, metal, and earth each has its polarity.] Zhang alludes to the later sentence in the *Taijitu shuo*, "each one has its nature" (quoted in this paragraph). So polarity (*ji* 極) here implies that each has a specific configuration of the *yin-yang* polarity.

[Zhang: *Yin* and *yang* together are a balanced polarity (*zhong ji* 中極). But the polarities of the Five Phases are also the polarities of *yin* and *yang*. It is not there in

are the unitary Supreme Polarity" [*Taijitu shuo*], without distinction [lit. no this and that] between essential and gross, root and branch.[41] "The Supreme Polarity is fundamentally Nonpolar" [*Taijitu shuo*] means that "the operation of Heaven above has neither sound nor smell."[42] "In the generation of the Five Phases, each one has its nature" [*Taijitu shuo*] means that the manifestations of *qi* and differences in its materiality each, no doubt have their own ○.[43] ⟲ This is how the Nonpolar, the two [*qi*], and five [phases] "mysteriously combine" [*Taijitu shuo*], without doubt.[44]

[D] ○

Qian is male and Kun is female; in terms of the transformations of *qi*,[45] each has its unique nature, yet male and female are "the unitary Supreme Polarity" [*Taijitu shuo*].

---

the Five Phases there is something that is lacking from *yin* and *yang*.] In other words, the Five Phases are simply further iterations of the fundamental *yin-yang* polarity.

41. [Zhang: "Essential" means the Supreme Polarity and "gross" means *yin* and *yang*; *li* is the root and *qi* is the branch. But while there are these differentia of essential and gross, root and branch, the reality is undifferentiated into distinctions such as this and that.]

42. [Zhang: The Way, which is above forms (metaphysical), is fundamentally nonspatial and ineffable (lit. cannot be spoken of in terms of named characteristics).] *Zhongyong* 33 (last line), quoting *Shijing*, no. 235. Zhu Xi quotes this again in the first line of his commentary on the *Taijitu shuo*.

43. [Zhang: The Supreme Polarity is not a nonexistent thing; all things contain it. Therefore it does not depend on borrowing.] Each thing has its own unique nature, symbolized by the separate, non-overlapping circles of the Five Phases.

44. [Zhang: *Li* and *qi* blend together and mysteriously combine, and only then are able to generate the myriad things.]

45. [Zhang: Generating by receiving the natural *qi* of heaven and earth is called "the transformations of *qi*."] I.e., *qi* is inherently dynamic and creative. The phrases in the Diagram, "The Way of Qian becomes the male" (left) and "The Way of Kun becomes the female" (right) come from *Yijing, Xici* A.1.

[E] ◯

"The myriad things transform and generate";[46] in terms of the transformations of form,[47] each has it own nature, yet the myriad things are "the unitary Supreme Polarity."[48]

"Only humans receive the finest and most spiritually efficacious [*qi*]" [*Taijitu shuo*]; what is meant by "human" ◯ [human ultimate] lies simply in this.[49] Thus form (*xing*) is the character of ☽,[50] and spirit (*shen*) is the expression of ☾.[51] The fivefold nature is the virtues of 火 水 / 土 / 木 金 ;[52] good and bad is the distinction of male and female;[53] and the myriad events are the images of the myriad things.[54] This is how the activity of Heaven puts in order

---

46. *Yijing, Xici* A.1, the phrase at the bottom of the Diagram.

47. [Zhang: In the human world, things are generated when they receive the *qi* of heaven and earth and then interact and stimulate each other; this is called "the transformations of form."]

48. [Zhang: Up to this point the discussion analyzes the substance of the Diagram. From here on it fully extends the ideas based on the Diagram.] The preceding three sections are about the relationship between unity and multiplicity. They exemplify Cheng Yi's doctrine, often quoted by Zhu Xi, "Principle (*li*) is one; its manifestations are many." In other words, the differentiations of *yin*, *yang*, and the Five Phases are real, yet they are fundamentally one in substance (*ti*).

49. This refers to level D of the diagram (male and female).

50. [Zhang: Receiving the Supreme Polarity and the *qi* of *yin* stillness.] ☽ is defined in the second paragraph as the still *yin*, which is associated with concrete form.

51. [Zhang: Receiving the Supreme Polarity and the *qi* of *yang* activity.] ☾ is defined above as the active *yang*, which is associated with spirit.

52. [Zhang: Receiving the Supreme Polarity and the *li* of the Five Phases.]

53. [Zhang: *Yang* is good, *yin* is bad.] "Good and bad is the distinction of male and female" reflects the essentialized view of male and female first introduced by Dong Zhongshu in the second century BCE, which deeply affected gender relations thereafter in China. See Chan Sin Yee, "The Confucian Conception of Gender in the Twenty-First Century," and Adler, "Daughter/Wife/Mother or Sage/Immortal/Bodhisattva? Women in the Teaching of Chinese Religions."

54. [Zhang: Heaven's ability to transform and generate things, humans' ability to differentiate the myriad events.]

the interactive process,⁵⁵ and what good fortune and misfortune, repentance and regret, follow in life.⁵⁶

Only the Sage receives the refined, undivided essence⁵⁷ and is able to complete the substance and function of ○ [*wuji-taiji*].⁵⁸ In this way, the alternation of activity and stillness reaches its peak (*ji*),⁵⁹ and all situations under Heaven "stimulate and penetrate" (*gantong*) the centrality (*zhong*) of the "silent and inactive" (*jiran budong*).⁶⁰

Now, hitting the mark (*zhong*)⁶¹ is humanity (*ren*)⁶² and stimulation,⁶³ and is represented by the ☾ [the active *yang*];⁶⁴ the functioning of ○ [*wuji-taiji*]

---

55. [Zhang: Physical nature (per se) is unordered; moral nature is unmixed (i.e., purely good).]

56. [Zhang: In following with *li* there is good fortune; in going against *li* there is misfortune. Repentance comes from bad fortune and hastens good fortune. Regret comes from good fortune and tends toward misfortune.] Good fortune and misfortune, repentance and regret are some of the oldest oracular formulas in the *Yijing* (Scripture of Change).

57. [Zhang: The Sage receives the finest, purest, unmixed, most unified, and undivided (portion) of the two *qi* and Five Phases that Heaven produces. This is what makes him unique among humans.]

58. [Zhang: All humans embody the principle of activity and stillness. The Sage completes the virtue of activity and stillness.]

59. [Zhang: Following with *yin* and *yang* accords with the natural order (*tianli*).] This is an instance of the use of *ji* in its colloquial meaning (see chapter 4). The idea is that the Sage brings to fruition the moral potential of the natural world.

60. [Zhang: In the nature of ordinary people, the physical endowment is unbalanced and impure, so they cannot overcome errors. The nature of the Sage is clear and unified, enabling him to quietly stimulate the myriad affairs without obstruction.] "Stimulate and penetrate" and "silent and inactive" allude to *Yijing, Xici* A.10.4, which expresses Zhu's understanding of the ideal interpenetration of stillness and activity (see chapter 3).

61. [Zhang: Centrality is ritual propriety, correlated with fire.]

62. [Zhang: Humanity is correlated with wood.]

63. [Zhang: Wood and humanity in terms of the seasons are spring. Fire and ritual propriety in terms of the seasons are summer. Spring and summer are the time of the growth and flowing of the creative process. Humanity and ritual propriety are the human mind's mechanism for displaying *li* through stimulation.]

64. [Zhang: Following the pattern of *yang*'s activity.]

is how it operates.⁶⁵ Correctness (*zheng*)⁶⁶ is rightness (*yi*)⁶⁷ and silence, and is represented by the ☽ [the still *yin*];⁶⁸ the substance of ○ [*wuji-taiji*] is how it is established.⁶⁹ Centrality and correctness, humanity and rightness, are the pure, complete substance,⁷⁰ yet stillness is always the master of it.⁷¹

So the human ○ is established accordingly,⁷² and ⊚ there is nothing in heaven and earth, the sun and moon, the four seasons, ghosts and spirits, that can oppose him [i.e., he is fully in accordance with natural/moral principle].⁷³

---

65. [Zhang: Spreading out is the function.]
66. [Zhang: Correctness is wisdom, correlated with water.]
67. [Zhang: Rightness is correlated with metal.]
68. [Zhang: Following the pattern of *yin*'s stillness.]
69. [Zhang: Harvesting and storing is the substance.]
70. [Zhang: Although hitting the mark and humanity are correlated with active functioning, and correctness and rightness are correlated with still substance, nevertheless the four are all the virtues of the nature and are thoroughly contained within the Sage's complete substance.]
71. [Zhang: Ordinary people, due to the injury to their natures caused by feelings and desires, often act deficiently. The Sage maintains the centrality (*zhong*) of the *weifa* (unexpressed feelings) in the harmony (*he*) of his *yifa* (expressed feelings/mental activity], and therefore always makes stillness the master (see chapter 3).] The point of this paragraph is (1) human moral behavior, described in terms of the stillness and activity of the human mind, is an expression of the fundamental *yin-yang* character of the natural world; (2) these phases are the substance and function of *wuji-taiji*; and (3) the stillness of the unexpressed feelings, which reflects the inherent goodness of human nature, must guide and harmonize the activity of the expressed feelings. This is how Zhu Xi interprets Zhou Dunyi's claim in the *Taijitu shuo* [G] that the Sage "emphasizes stillness."

"Hitting the mark" (lit. "centrality") and "correctness" are also associated with the *Yijing*, where they refer to characteristics of hexagram lines. "Central" means the middle positions of the two component trigrams (i.e., positions 2 and 5 of the hexagram); "correct" means a *yin* (broken) line in an odd position and a *yang* (unbroken) line in an even position.

72. [Zhang: "Cultivating the Way is called education" (*Zhongyong* 1).]

The superior person's caution and fearfulness is how he cultivates this and has good fortune.[74] The petty person's recklessness and depravity is how he perverts this and has misfortune.[75]

The Ways of Heaven, earth, and humans are each the one ○ [*wuji-taiji*]. *Yang* [Heaven], firmness [earth], and humanity [humans], represented by ☾, are the origin of things.[76] *Yin,* the yielding, and rightness, represented by ☽, are the end of things.[77] This is what is meant by change, and the Way of the three ultimates (*san ji*) [Heaven, earth, humans] is established therein.[78] In reality there is just one ○.[79] Thus, "In change there is the Supreme Polarity" is the meaning of ◉.[80]

---

73. [Zhang: Heaven and earth, the sun, moon, and four seasons, ghosts and spirits have nothing that is not the two [modes of *qi*] and the five [phases] mysteriously combining and constituting [things]. The Sage completes the substance and function of the Supreme Polarity, and so throughout the universe what can oppose it him? The *Zhongyong*'s statement, "Heaven and earth are established, the myriad things are nourished," is correct (*Zhongyong* 2). This is the moral order (*daoli*).]

74. [Zhang: This is learning how to know what is beneficial and to put it into effect to serve the functioning of one's material endowment. The elementary learner questions this, but the achievement is great. This is how one can cultivate oneself and have good fortune.]

75. [Zhang: Under stimulation by things the desires act up and one does not understand moderation. Then the human desires become reckless and the natural order (*tianli*) is extinguished. This is how one perverts oneself and has bad fortune.]

76. [Zhang: "Nonpolar and yet Supreme Polarity!" (*Taijitu shuo*).]

77. [Zhang: "Supreme Polarity is fundamentally nonpolar" (ibid.).] "Firmness" (*gang* 剛) and "yielding" (*ruo* 弱) refer to the solid and broken hexagram lines, respectively. In the *Yijing* they are called the Way of earth; *yin* and *yang* are the Way of Heaven; humanity (*jen*) and rightness (*yi*) are the Way of humans [referring to *Shuogua* 2 (*Zhouyi benyi* 4:1b)].

78. I use "three ultimates" here instead of "three polarities" because the term is an allusion to the term *human ultimate* (*ren ji* 人極) in the *Taijitu shuo*. "Ultimate" makes more sense than "polarity" in that case, because it refers to the Sage as the ideal human. But in fact all three can be understood as three fundamental configurations of the *yin-yang* polarity.

79. [Zhang: The myriad principles are none other than one principle.]

80. [Zhang: The Supreme Polarity is nothing other than *yin* and *yang*.]

Chapter Six

Discussion of the Supreme Polarity Diagram
(*Taijitu shuo* 太極圖說)

INTRODUCTION

Zhou Dunyi's "Discussion of the Supreme Polarity Diagram" is his most famous work. But as documented in the previous chapters, its fame stems entirely from Zhu Xi's choice to reject the prevailing view that Cheng Hao had revived the Way in the Song and to place Zhou in that position, despite Zhou's reliance on Daoist concepts. The most problematic passages for some of Zhu Xi's colleagues, such as the Lu brothers (see chapter 2), were section A (particularly the term *wuji* 無極, or "nonpolar") and section G (the phrase *zhu jing* 主靜, "emphasizing stillness"). But once Zhu Xi's reconstruction of the Confucian *dao* 道 and the *daotong* 道統 was canonized in 1241, this text became the universally acknowledged basis of "Neo-Confucian" cosmology.[1] It provided the cosmological grounding for the Cheng-Zhu philosophy based on *li* 理 (commonly but misleadingly called *lixue* 理學, or the "study of principle"), by positing *taiji* 太極 as the crucial link between *li* and *qi* 氣 (see chapter 4).

I include here an unannotated copy of Zhou Dunyi's text before the annotated commentary. In the annotated version, the bracketed letters and numbers are for reference only. The numbers identify "additional comments"

---

1. In 1241, Zhou Dunyi, Zhang Zai, the Cheng brothers, and Zhu Xi were officially installed in the Confucian temple.

by Zhu Xi and his students included in Zhang Boxing's *Zhou Lianxi ji* (not all are included here, hence some numbers are missing); most of them are taken from the *Zhuzi yulei*. Following them in most sections I add more additional comments from the *Yulei*, identified with bullet points.

Discussion of the Supreme Polarity Diagram
(*Taijitu shuo* 太極圖說)

Nonpolar and yet Supreme Polarity!

The Supreme Polarity in activity generates *yang*; yet at the limit of activity it is still. In stillness it generates *yin*; yet at the limit of stillness it is also active. Activity and stillness alternate; each is the basis of the other. In distinguishing *yin* and *yang,* the Two Modes are thereby established.

The alternation and combination of *yang* and *yin* generate water, fire, wood, metal, and earth. With these five [phases of] *qi* harmoniously arranged, the Four Seasons proceed through them. The Five Phases are the unitary *yin* and *yang*; *yin* and *yang* are the unitary Supreme Polarity; the Supreme Polarity is fundamentally Nonpolar. [Yet] in the generation of the Five Phases, each one has its nature.

The reality of Nonpolarity and the essence of the Two [Modes] and Five [Phases] mysteriously combine and coalesce. "The Way of Qian becomes the male; the Way of Kun becomes the female"; the two *qi* stimulate each other, transforming and generating the myriad things. The myriad things generate and regenerate, alternating and transforming without end.

Only humans receive the finest and most spiritually efficacious [*qi*]. Once formed, they are born; when spirit is manifested, they have intelligence; when their fivefold natures are stimulated into activity, good and evil are distinguished and the myriad affairs ensue.

The sage settles these [affairs] with centrality and correctness, humanity and rightness (the Way of the sage is simply humanity and rightness, centrality and correctness) and emphasizes stillness. (Without desire, [he is] therefore still.) In so doing, he establishes the peak of humanity. Thus, the sage's "virtue equals that of Heaven and Earth; his clarity equals that of the sun and moon; his timeliness equals that of the four seasons; his good fortune and bad fortune equal those of ghosts and spirits." The noble person cultivates these and has good fortune. The petty person rejects these and has bad fortune.

Therefore, [the *Yi*] says, "Establishing the Way of Heaven, [the sages] speak of *yin* and *yang*; establishing the Way of earth they speak of yielding and firm [hexagram lines]; establishing the Way of humanity they speak of humanity and rightness." It also says, "[The sage] investigates beginnings and follows them to their ends; therefore he understands death and birth."

Great indeed is [the *Scripture of*] *Change*! Herein lies its perfection.

FIGURE 6.1 First page (recto and verso) of Zhu Xi' commentary on the *Taijitu shuo*, from Zhang Boxing's *Zhou Lianxi ji*; showing Zhou's opening statement (*Wuji er taiji*), Zhu's commentary, Zhang Boxing's note (smaller characters), and Zhang's selections from Zhu Xi's *Classified Conversations*.

Master Zhu's Commentary on the Discussion of the Supreme Polarity Diagram
(*Zhuzi Taijitu shuo jie* 朱子太極圖說解)

[*Zhou Dunyi's text*][2]

[A] Nonpolar (*wuji* 無極) and yet Supreme Polarity (*taiji* 太極)![3]

[*Zhu Xi's published commentary*]
"The operation of Heaven above has neither sound nor smell,"[4] and yet it is the pivot (*shu-niu* 樞紐) of the actual process of creation and the basis of the classification of things. Thus, it says, "Nonpolar and yet Supreme Polarity!" It is not that there is nonpolarity outside of the Supreme Polarity.[5]

[*Zhu Xi's additional comments*]
[1] *Ji* 極 is the polar extremity (*jizhi* 極至) of the moral order (*daoli* 道理). The principle of all things in Heaven and Earth is *taiji*. *Taiji*

---

2. *Zhou Lianxi ji*, 1:5a–35a. Additional comments by Zhu Xi are taken from ibid. (identified with bracketed numbers) and the *Zhuzi yulei* (bullet points). I have not included Zhang Boxing's annotations to this text, as they are not particularly helpful.

3. The line reads simply, "*Wuji er taiji.*" Since *er* can mean "and also," "and yet," or "under these circumstances," the precise meaning of the line is far from clear. Another possible translation would be, "The Supreme Polarity that is nonpolar!" For Zhou Dunyi, it may have been simply an expression of awe and wonder at the paradoxical nature of the ultimate reality, specifically its interpenetration of unity and multiplicity (see the discussion in chapter 3). Zhu Xi interprets it (below) in terms of *li* (principle/pattern/order), a concept that plays virtually no role in Zhou's thought (see chapter 2).

4. *Zhongyong* 33 (last line), quoting *Shijing*, no. 235.

5. Grammatically, "the pivot" here refers to "the operation of Heaven," but as explained in chapter 2 it also refers to *taiji* as "Supreme Polarity." Thus, *taiji* is the principle (*li*) of the creative process inherent in the natural world. "Heaven" connotes both naturalness and creativity. The latter is symbolized by the first hexagram of the *Yijing* (*Qian*): "The movement of Heaven is to create" (*Yijing*, *Xiang zhuan* (Commentary on the images); *Zhouyi benyi* 1:4a). It is its bipolarity that both "powers" its creativity and makes it "rational" (capable of being classified). The connection with *wuji*, as Zhu further explains in the additional comments, is simply to stress the "unitary" or undifferentiated nature of *taiji* as principle (see chapter 4). That is, *wuji* is the unitariness of *taiji/li*.

is just the unitary real principle that runs through them and unifies them.[6]

[4] *Wuji er taiji* correctly means that there is no specific form but there is specific moral principle.

[5] Calling it "nonpolar (*wuji*)" correctly clarifies its nonspatial form. It exists prior to things, and yet at no time is it not established after the existence of things. It exists outside of *yin-yang*, and yet at no time does it not operate within things. It penetrates and connects the "complete substance"; there is nothing in which it does not exist.

[6] [Master Zhou] does not say, "Nonpolar, then Supreme Polarity." This would make it equivalent to a thing, which could not be the basis of the myriad transformations. [Likewise he] does not say, "Supreme Polarity, then Nonpolarity." This would make it sink into empty silence, and it would be unable to be the basis of the myriad things. It is just this sentence [of Zhou's] that makes evident what he says below [section E] about its being essential, mysterious, and limitless, and addresses what he says about the multitudinous moral principles.[7] Everything is arranged, nothing is out of order. Now, this is right in front of our eyes, yet from antiquity to the present, it has not been seen through.

[8] "The operation of Heaven above has neither sound nor smell" explains nonexistence [of characteristics] within existence [of Heaven]. "Nonpolar, yet Supreme Polarity" explains existence [polarity, or differentiation] within nonexistence [nonpolarity, or undifferentiation]. If we could actually see it, it would explain existence and nonexistence—first one, then the other, neither one obstructing (*fang-ai*) [the other].[8]

---

6. "Actualized principle" (*shi li*) is also Zhu Xi's definition of *cheng* (being authentic); see his comments on *Tongshu*, sections 1a and 2a (below).

7. Zhou Dunyi never speaks of "multitudinous moral principles," so Zhu Xi here is referring to his own interpretation. He uses the term in his commentary on *Tongshu* 2(e), but the idea of principle runs throughout both commentaries.

8. See the discussion of this passage in chapter 3.

[9] *Rao Shuangfeng* 饒雙峯[9] *said*: Heaven and Earth, through *yin-yang* and the Five Phases, close and open without limit, and this principle governs closing and opening. It is like the hinge (*shu-niu*) of a door. Male and female creatures generate and generate [produce and reproduce] without end,[10] and this principle is the basis of generation and regeneration [or life and growth], like the root of a tree. In reference to human beings, it is that by which the myriad good qualities are generated and the myriad affairs are settled. There is nothing that lacks this principle as its root and its hinge. If students understand its meaning and apply it daily, and with dignified stillness nourish themselves when [their feelings are] not yet aroused, and examine themselves after [their feelings are] aroused, then some of them might be able to silently understand the mystery of this principle.[11]

• As for *"wuji er taiji,"* fearing that people would consider *taiji* to be a thing with form and shape, [Master Zhou] also said *wuji* to say that it is simply principle.[12]

• *"Wuji er taiji"* simply means formless principle. *Taiji* is simply the principle of two *qi* and Five Phases; it is not a thing on its own. In reference to principle we cannot call it existing; in reference to things we cannot call it not existing.[13]

• Originally, the word *ji* was taken from from the meaning of *shuji* (endpoint/extreme of pivot/hinge). The Sage [Confucius][14] called it *taiji* to indicate the basis (*gen*) of heaven and earth; Master Zhou

---

9. Rao Shuangfeng (Rao Lu 饒魯) was a student of Zhu Xi's son-in-law and disciple, Huang Gan (Huang Mianzhai). See Huang Zongxi and Quan Zuwang, comps., *Song-Yuan xue'an* (Scholarly record of the Song and Yuan dynasties), chs. 63, 83.

10. *Sheng sheng buxi* 生生不息, a phrase first used by Cheng Yi; see *Henan Chengshi yishu*, 15:149. In section E below Zhou Dunyi says, "The myriad things generate and regenerate, alternating and transforming without end."

11. Rao Shuangfeng illustrates here how Zhu Xi's early successors clearly understood *taiji* as "polarity." Cf. the other quote of his at the end of chapter 4.

12. *Yulei* 94:3116.

13. I.e., as principle it has no independent existence; it does have existence in things. Ibid.

14. Referring here to Confucius as the reputed author of the *Xici* appendix of the *Yijing*, where the term *taiji* was first used.

followed this and also called it *wuji* in order to emphasize the mystery of what "has neither sound nor smell" [i.e., undifferentiation].[15]

- *Taiji* has no place, no form, no position where it can be put. We speak of it in terms of the unexpressed moment, but the unexpressed is just stillness. Activity and stillness, *yin* and *yang*, are all within form (*xing'er xia* 形而下, i.e., physical). Activity is the activity of *taiji*, and stillness is the stillness of *taiji*, but activity and stillness are not *taiji*. This is why Master Zhou only spoke of it [*taiji*] in terms of *wuji*. (It lacks form but has principle.) We definitely cannot call the unexpressed *taiji*, but it contains pleasure, anger, sorrow, and joy. Pleasure and joy are *yang*, and anger and sorrow are *yin*. The four at first are unexpressed, yet principle is already contained in them.[16]

- *Question*: In "*wuji er taiji*," *ji* means polar extremity, beyond which is nothing. *Wuji* is the utmost of nonexistence. In utmost nonexistence lies utmost existence; therefore, [Zhou] says "*wuji er taiji*." *Reply*: The foundation (*ben* 本) is just *taiji*, but originally there are no things, so he says "*wuji er taiji*." If he had [only] said *wuji* this would have been fine, but *taiji* [alone] would not do.[17]

- *Taiji* is not a distinct thing. It is *yin-yang* and is in *yin-yang*; it is the Five Phases and is in the Five Phases, it is the myriad things and is in the myriad things. It is simply a principle (*yige li* 一個理). Since it is their polar extremity, it is called Supreme Polarity.[18]

---

15. *Yulei* 94:3117. For Zhu's comment on "*taiji*" in the *Xici* appendix of the *Yijing*, see chapter 2. This is a response to the Lu brothers, who argued that Confucius used the term *taiji* but not *wuji*.

16. *Yulei* 94:3120. This passage relates *taiji* to the *weifa/zhong–yifa/he* problem, which was the issue underlying Zhu's "spiritual crisis" (see chapter 3). It also addresses the fundamental problem of how metaphysical principle (*li*) can produce physical things (*qi*), which some see as a weakness in Zhu Xi's system (see chapter 4).

17. *Yulei* 94:3121. Note that Zhu Xi here is correcting the questioner's understanding of the two terms, which seems to envision a linear model.

18. By saying that *taiji* is "simply *a* principle" Zhu Xi implies that it is not a general name for the totality of all principles, as some have alleged; it is specifically the principle of *yin-yang* polarity, as argued in chapter 4. He repeats this below in section C, additional comment 5. I translate *zhiji* as "polar extremity" to be consistent with my interpretation of *taiji*; likewise, I translate *jizhi* (the same two characters reversed) as "utmost pole" (section E below, first additional comment). But both terms could also be translated more colloquially and simply as "extreme."

[*Zhou Dunyi's text*]

[B] The Supreme Polarity in activity generates *yang*; yet at the limit (*ji*) of activity it is still. In stillness it generates *yin*; yet at the limit of stillness it is also active. Activity and stillness alternate; each is the basis of the other. In distinguishing *yin* and *yang*, the Two Modes are thereby established.[19]

[*Zhu Xi's published commentary*]
That in Supreme Polarity there is activity and stillness is the flowing forth of what is given by Heaven. What is meant by "the alternation of *yin* and *yang* is called the Way,"[20] and "being authentic is the foundation of the sage"[21] is the Way of the ends and beginnings that are given (decreed) to things.[22] Its activity is [what is referred to by the sayings,] "the penetrating [quality] of authenticity,"[23] "what continues it is good,"[24] and "what the myriad things rely on for their beginnings."[25] Its stillness is [what is referred to by the sayings,] "the recovery of authenticity,"[26] "what completes it is human nature,"[27] and the myriad things "each correct in its nature and endowment."[28]

"At the limit of activity it is still . . . at the limit of stillness it is active. Activity and stillness alternate; each is the basis of the other." This is how the endowment (*ming*) flows forth endlessly. "In activity it generates *yang*; in stillness it generates *yin*. . . . In distinguishing *yin* and

---

19. The Two Modes, in the context of the *Yijing*, refer either to *yin* and *yang*, or to the "firm" (solid) and "yielding" (broken) lines making up the trigrams and hexagrams, or to stillness and activity (see chapter 3).

20. *Tongshu* 1, quoting *Yijing, Xici* A.5.1. Throughout Zhu Xi's commentaries on the *Taijitu shuo* and the *Tongshu* he details their correspondences with each other.

21. *Tongshu* 1.

22. "The Way of ends and beginnings" paraphrases *Tongshu* 16 (g). This sentence is discussed below in additional comments 9 and 10.

23. *Tongshu* 1.

24. Ibid., quoting *Xici* A.5.2.

25. Paraphrasing *Tongshu* 1, which quotes *Yijing, Tuan* commentary on hexagram 1.

26. *Tongshu* 1.

27. Ibid., quoting *Xici* A.5.2.

28. *Tongshu* 1, quoting *T'uan* commentary on hexagram 1.

yang, the Two Modes are thereby established." "Distinguishing" is how each is correctly defined without overlap.

Thus, the Supreme Polarity is fundamentally mysterious; activity and stillness are the "mechanism" (*ji* 機) on which it "rides" (*cheng* 乘) [the opportunity for it to manifest itself]. The Supreme Polarity is the formless [metaphysical] Way; *yin* and *yang* are the formed [concrete] implements.[29] In this way, observing from what is evident, [one can see that] while activity and stillness are not simultaneous, and *yin* and *yang* are not the same, nevertheless there is nowhere that the Supreme Polarity does not exist in them.[30] Observing it in terms of its subtlety, it is full of profundity, and the principle of activity and stillness, *yin* and *yang*, is completely contained in it. Though you push forward [into the past] you cannot see their original coming together; pull back [into the future] and you cannot see a final separation. Therefore, Master Cheng [Yi] said, "Activity and stillness have no ends, *yin* and *yang* have no beginnings."[31] Were it not for those who understood the Way, how could we know it?

[*Zhu Xi's additional comments*]

[1] Within Heaven and Earth, there is only the principle of activity and stillness in an endless cycle; there is absolutely nothing else. This is called change. And since there is activity and stillness, there is necessarily the principle of activity and stillness. This, then, is called the Supreme Polarity.[32]

[2] Supreme Polarity generates *yin* and *yang*, and *li* generates *qi*. Once *yin* and *yang* are generated, then Supreme Polarity is within them. And *li*, likewise, is within *qi*.

---

29. Alluding to *Yijing, Xici* A.12.4: "What is above form (*xing'er shang*) is called the Way; what is within form (*xing'er xia*) is called implements" (*Zhouyi benyi* 3:16a). *Xing'er shang* is the modern Chinese word for "metaphysical."

30. This concerns the "nonduality" of *yin-yang* and stillness-activity pairs: the difference between them is real, but they are united in being the two inseparable poles of *taiji*.

31. From *Henan Cheng shi jing shuo* (Discussions of the classics by the Chengs of Henan), 1:1029; in *Er Cheng ji* (Collection of the two Chengs), and in *Er Cheng quanshu* (Complete collection of the two Chengs), *Sibu beiyao* ed., 1:2a.

32. This is one of Zhu Xi's clearest statements that *taji* is the specific principle of bipolarity.

[3] Supreme Polarity is distinguished simply by *yin* and *yang*. This embraces all things under Heaven.[33]

[4] Activity and stillness, *yin* and *yang,* are within form. But activity [according to Zhou] is the activity of Supreme Polarity, and stillness is likewise the stillness of Supreme Polarity. Nevertheless, activity and stillness are not Supreme Polarity.[34]

[5] "The Supreme Polarity in activity produces *yang*" does not mean that after there is activity then *yang* is produced. Rather, once there is activity, this is classified as *yang*; and once there is stillness, this is classified as *yin*. The original ground (*chu ben* 初本) of the *yang* produced by activity is stillness. Likewise, for stillness there must be activity. This is what is meant by "activity and stillness without end." Moreover, if you look at where it says "[Supreme Polarity] in activity generates *yang*," this is actually *that by which* there is activity—it is produced from stillness. And stillness, above, is likewise produced from activity. This principle is simply that of cyclical production.[35]

[6] Within the stillness of *yin* is the basis of *yang* itself; within the activity of *yang* is the basis of *yin* itself.[36] This is because activity necessarily comes from stillness, which is based in *yin*; and stillness necessarily comes from activity, which is based in *yang*.

[7] *Yin* and *yang* are merely *qi*. When *yin qi* flows forth it becomes *yang,* and when *yang qi* congeals it becomes *yin*. They are not really two distinct things.

[8] *Question:* "The alternation of *yin* and *yang* is called the Way"—is this Supreme Polarity? *Reply:* *Yin* and *yang* are simply *yin* and *yang*. The Way is Supreme Polarity—that by which there is the alternation of *yin* and *yang*.[37]

---

33. *Yulei* 94: 3115.
34. I.e., activity and stillness are physical (*qi*), while *taiji* is metaphysical (*li*).
35. Partly from *Yulei* 94: 3124.
36. Metaphysical interpenetration.
37. This seems to be from *Yulei* 94:3145, but the phrase after the dash is not there. Instead, Zhu quotes Cheng Yi saying, "That by which there is the alternation of *yin* and *yang* is the Way." Zhang Boxing might have conflated this passage with *Yulei* 74:2523, where Zhu says, "'The alternation of *yin* and *yang* is called the Way' is the Supreme Polarity."

[9] *Question* on "Being authentic is the Way of the ends and beginnings that are given (*ming*) to things." *Reply*: Being authentic is to actualize principle. Everywhere the generation (*sheng* 生) of things follows this process. The myriad things taking form throughout Heaven and earth are this process.[38]

[10] Speaking in terms of *li*, Heaven and earth are completely real (*shi* 實) and without error for a single moment. Therefore, from antiquity until the present, not a single thing has not been real, and within every thing, from beginning to end, is the action of real principle (*shi lizhi suowei* 實理之所為). Speaking in terms of mind, the mind of the sage is also completely real and without error for a single moment. Therefore, from birth to death not a single event (*shi* 事) has not been real, and within every event, from beginning to end, is the action of real mind. This is the meaning of "Being authentic is the end and beginning of things."[39]

[. . . .][40]

• Master Zhou and Kangjie [Shao Yong] both discussed *taiji* and *yin-yang* as they are found in the *Yi*. Master Zhou said, "*Taiji* in

---

38. This exchange about a sentence in Zhu Xi's commentary (above) also relates to the *Tongshu*, in which *cheng* is a central topic. It shows that *li* should not be interpreted as static "principle/pattern/order" but rather as the dynamic *ordering* of things; the dynamism inherent in *qi*; the principle of life and growth or generation and regeneration (*sheng sheng*; see below, section E).

39. Quoting *Zhongyong* 25 (Sishu jizhu ed., 17b). This section is a further elaboration of the meaning of *cheng* (being authentic), and is also an implicit refutation of the Buddhist concept of "emptiness" (*kong* 空). Although emptiness in Mahayana Buddhism does *not* mean voidness or nothingness (it really means emptiness of independent, autonomous existence, i.e., interdependence), the Confucians of the Cheng-Zhu school consistently depicted it in that way, using the word *shi* (full, real, actual) as the opposite of *kong* (emptiness).

40. Zhang Boxing includes a total of twenty-seven additional comments in this section, more than twice as many as any other section (the average of all the others is seven). Although this of course directly reflects only Zhang's judgment of this section's importance, I think it also accurately reflects the importance of *yin-yang* bipolar alternation in Zhu Xi's system; he had a lot to say about it. This is related to the fact that in his *Classified Conversations* (*Zhuzi yulei*, compiled in 1270), roughly 11 percent of the total number of pages are devoted to discussions of the *Yijing*, which of course is based on the *yin-yang* polarity.

activity generates *yang*; in stillness generates *yin*." This means that the activity of *taijii* is *yang*, at the extreme of activity is stillness, and stillness is *yin*. When there is activity there is the *taiji* of *yang*, and when there is stillness there is the *taiji* of *yin*. So *taiji* is within *yin* and *yang*. "In change there is *taiji*, which generates the Two Modes" [in the *Yijing*]⁴¹ is the first place where the actual principle (*shili* 實理) is discussed. This theory of generation [or creativity] means inherent generation [creativity]. *Taiji* has always been within *yin* and *yang*. But when we speak of a sequence there must be this actualized principle, and as soon as there is *yin* and *yang*, this principle is unified. However, when we examine it in things, then *yin-yang* contains *taiji*. Extending it to its roots, then *taiji* generates *yin-yang*.⁴²

• *Question about* "In change there is *taiji*, which generates the Two Modes; the Two Modes generate the Four Images, and the Four Images generate the Eight Trigrams." *Reply*: This is *taiji*, but in terms of the drawing of the trigrams. Before the trigrams were drawn, *taiji* was just a chaotic moral principle containing within it *yin* and *yang*, firm and yielding [lines], odd and even; there is nothing it did not contain. When the solid and broken lines are drawn, that is the Two Modes. When a further solid line is added, that is *yin* with *yang* [and so on . . .]; these are the Four Images.⁴³

• "In activity it generates stillness, in stillness it generates activity": activity is the activity of *taiji*, and stillness is the stillness of *taiji*.⁴⁴

• "Activity and stillness alternate; each is the basis of the other:" stillness in activity, activity in stillness, opening and closing, going and coming, without any cessation.⁴⁵ "In distinguishing *yin* and *yang*, the Two Modes are thereby established": the Two Modes are heaven

---

41. *Xici* A.11.5.

42. *Yulei* 75:2564 (comment on *Xici* A.11.5). The idea of *taiji* as the principle of creativity has been discussed by Cheng Chung-ying, "Categories of Creativity in Whitehead and Neo-Confucianism." See also Joseph A. Adler, "The Great Virtue of Heaven and Earth: Deep Ecology in the *Yijing*."

43. *Yulei* 75:1565.

44. *Yulei* 94:3118.

45. Note that Zhu Xi goes beyond Zhou Dunyi here to say that the relationship is not only temporal alternation but also metaphysical interpenetration (see chapter 3).

and earth; this is different from the idea of the two modes in the drawing of the trigrams/hexagrams.[46]

[*Zhou Dunyi's text*]

[C] The alternation and combination of *yang* and *yin* generate water, fire, wood, metal, and earth. With these five [phases of] *qi* harmoniously arranged, the Four Seasons proceed through them.

[*Zhu Xi's published commentary*]

As there is [the principle of] Supreme Polarity, there is the alternation of activity and stillness, and the Two Modes are distinguished.[47] As there is *yin* and *yang*, the alternation and combination of the Five Phases are contained [therein]. But the material of the Five Phases is contained in earth, and *qi* is what circulates through heaven. Speaking of the generation sequence (*shengzhi xu* 生之序) in terms of their material (*zhi* 質) we should say, "Water, fire, wood, metal, and earth," with water and wood

---

46. *Yulei* 94.3118.

47. This could be interpreted as an example of Zhu Xi making the problematic leap from the metaphysical (*taiji*, which is *li*) to the cosmological or physical (the alternation of activity and stillness, which occurs in the realm of *qi*), as discussed in chapter 3. But in his first exchange of letters with Lu Jiuyuan, Lu asks him about two passages from the *Xici* appendix of the *Yijing*: "What is above form (*xing'er shang*) is called the Way" (A.12.4) and "The alternation of *yin* and *yang* is the Way" (A.5.1). Since the Way (*dao*) is nearly synonymous with *li* and is therefore "above form" or metaphysical, Zhu agrees with the face value of the first statement but not the second. He replies:

> How can the alternation of *yin* and *yang* be above form? The correct way to interpret the alternation of *yin* and *yang* is to classify it as formed implements (*qi* 器 implements; what *Xici* A.12.4 calls "within form" [*xing'er xia*]). However, that by which (*suoyi*) it is the alternation of *yin* and *yang* [i.e., its principle] is the substance of the Way (*dao ti*). So when we speak of the utmost extreme (*zhi ji*) of the substance of the Way we call it *taiji*; when we speak of the flowing out (*liuxing* 流行) of *taiji* we call it the Way. Although they are two names, they are a fundamentally nondual substance (*chu wuliang ti* 初無兩體) (*Wenji* 36:1568).

Therefore, in the present passage, the alternation of activity and stillness must mean "that by which" there is alternation of activity and stillness, their principle—which, as we have seen in chapter 4, is *taiji*.

as *yang*, and fire and metal as *yin*.⁴⁸ Speaking of the circulation sequence (*xingzhi xu* 行之序) in terms of *qi* we should say, "wood, fire, earth, metal, and water," with wood and fire as *yang*, and metal and water as *yin*.⁴⁹ In terms of their connection (*tong* 統), *qi* is *yang* and material is *yin*. In terms of their alternation, activity is *yang* and stillness is *yin*.

Thus, the alternation of the Five Phases is inexhaustible, so nothing happens that is not the Way of *yin* and *yang*. As for what makes them *yin* and *yang*, nothing happens that is not the original nature of the Supreme Polarity. How can there be any deficiency or discontinuity!

[*Zhu Xi's additional comments*]

[4] The material of water is *yin*, yet its nature is rooted in *yang*. The material of fire is *yang*, yet its nature is rooted in *yin*. Water is dark on the outside and bright on the inside; this is its basis in *yang*. Fire is bright on the outside and dark on the inside; this is its basis in *yin*. This is [demonstrated by the fact that] within the activity of *yang* in the Supreme Polarity Diagram is a dot, and within the stillness of *yin* it is clear.

[5] Supreme Polarity is simply a principle.⁵⁰ Spinning about, it divides into the two *qi*. The activity within is *yang*, and the stillness is *yin*. It also divides in the five *qi*, and separates into the myriad things.

---

48. The "generation sequence" and "circulation sequence" (next sentence) refer to the River Chart (*Hetu* 河圖), which Zhu Xi later discussed fully in the first chapter of his *Yixue qimeng* (Introduction to the study of the *Yi*, 1186). The generation sequence is based on the numerical order of the numbers depicted in the chart (1 through 5). The discussion also presumes the general cosmological principle that odd numbers are *yin* and even numbers are *yang* (see also *Yijing, Xici* A.9 [*Zhouyi benyi* 3:9b]). "Water and wood as *yang*, and fire and metal as *yin*" is partly counterintuitive (especially fire as *yin*), but it is based on the numbers associated with these phases in the *Hetu* (see additional comment 6 below).

49. Unlike the generation sequence, the circulation sequence is based on the logic of the Five Phases, and is identical with the old "mutual generation" (*xiang sheng* 相生) sequence, possibly dating back to Zou Yan (third century BCE): wood generates fire when burned, fire generates earth in the form of ashes, earth generates metals in the form of ores, metal generates "water" or liquid when melted (or dew forms on cold metal). The association of wood and fire with *yang*, and metal and water with *yin*, makes more intuitive sense than the associations of the generation sequence (previous note).

50. "Simply a principle" (*yige li*), namely the principle of bipolarity, not a general name for the totality of all principles (see chapter 4).

[6] *Question on* "Speaking of the generation sequence in terms of their material." Why is it that the [Taiji] Diagram does not indicate this sequence? And why are water and wood called *yang* and fire and metal called *yin*? *Reply*: The 1 of Heaven generates water, the 2 of earth generates fire, the 3 of Heaven generates wood, the 4 of earth generates metal. Thus 1 and 3 are *yang*; 2 and 4 are *yin*. [Analogous question on the circulation sequence.] *Reply*: This is in terms of the Four Seasons: spring and summer are *yang*; autumn and winter are *yin*.

[*Zhou Dunyi's text*]

[D] The Five Phases are the unitary *yin* and *yang*; *yin* and *yang* are the unitary Supreme Polarity; the Supreme Polarity is fundamentally Nonpolar. [Yet] in the generation of the Five Phases, each one has its nature (*xing* 性).[51]

[*Zhu Xi's published commentary*]

With the Five Phases in place, production and flourishing are in place and everything is complete. Therefore, this infers the basis (*tui ben* 推本) and clarifies the completely unitary substance, which is nothing but the mystery of the nonpolar. Yet the mystery of the nonpolar has always been contained within each thing.[52]

Now, the Five Phases are different material, the Four Seasons are different *qi,* yet nothing can be other than *yin* and *yang*. *Yin* and *yang* have different positions, activity and stillness occur at different times, yet nothing can be apart from the Supreme Polarity. As for what makes it the Supreme Polarity, from the beginning it can be said that it has no sound and smell; this is the fundamental substance of the nature [of humans and things]. Under heaven, how can there be things apart from their nature?

But the generation of the Five Phases accords with the received inequalities of their physical material (*qizhi* 氣質). This is what is meant by "each one has its nature." As each has its nature, the complete substance

---

51. In other words: seen as a whole system, the Five Phases are based on the *yin-yang* polarity; the *yin-yang* polarity is the Supreme Polarity; and the Supreme Polarity is fundamentally nonpolar. However, taken individually as temporal phases, the Five Phases each have their own natures, as do *yin* and *yang*.

52. "The basis" is the underlying principle, which is the "substance." In other words, this section emphasizes the unitary principle running through the multiplicity of phenomena.

of the whole Supreme Polarity is contained within each and every thing, and we can see that there is nowhere that this nature does not exist.[53]

[*Zhu Xi's additional comments*]

[2] *Question* about "in the generation of the Five Phases, each one has its nature." Are their principles the same? *Reply*: They are the same, and their physical material is different. *Question*: Since you say that their physical material is different, then their principles do not interpenetrate. *Reply*: Definitely. Humanity cannot produce rightness, and rightness cannot produce humanity.[54]

[3] The physical nature is simply principle fallen (*duo* 墮) into the midst of physical material. Therefore it accords with the physical material and becomes a [particular] nature. If Master Zhou's statement "each having its nature" meant that originally there was no fundamental nature (*benranzhi xing* 本然之性), then where would the physical nature (*qizhizhi xing*) come from?[55]

[5] *Question on* "Each has its nature." Certainly this refers to the physical material of the Five Phases. But in water soaking downward, fire burning upward, wood being crooked or straight, metal bending and changing, and earth being sown and harvested;[56] these can only be seen in their physical nature, the inequalities of their endowments. How then can we see "the complete substance of *taiji* that is

---

53. Here Zhu Xi is emphasizing that the unitariness of the principle/pattern/order that runs through all things does not mean that their differences are not real; both the one and the many are fully real. This idea is also central in the Chinese schools of Mahayana Buddhism. See Adler, "Synthesis: 'The One and the Many' in the *Lotus Sutra* and Zhu Xi."

54. The apparent contradiction between the first answer and the second can be explained by assuming that in the first Zhu is referring to the universal order of things, while in the second he is referring to specific principles. In other words, this is an application of Cheng Yi's dictum, "Principle/order is one, its manifestations are many."

55. Here again, Zhu is explaining the interface of the unitary principle or nature of the cosmos with the particular principles or natures of individual things. Zhu accepted Cheng Yi's dictum, "Nature is the same as principle" (*xing ji li*), so the one/many issue applied in the same way to both terms.

56. These characteristics of the Five Phases are from the "Great Plan" (*Hong fan*, section 3) chapter of the *Shujing*.

contained within each and every thing," and "the nature that exists everywhere"? *Reply*: Physical material is *yin-yang* and the Five Phases. The nature is the complete substance of *taiji*. But in discussing the physical nature, even though this complete substance sinks (*duo*) into the midst of physical material, it is not different from the unitary nature.

• "The Five Phases are simply *yin* and *yang*; *yin* and *yang* are simply the Supreme Polarity; the Supreme Polarity is fundamentally Nonpolar." This means that there is never a time when there is *yin* and *yang* and no *taiji*.[57]

[*Zhou Dunyi's text*]
[E] The reality of Nonpolarity and the essence of the Two [Modes] and Five [Phases] mysteriously combine and coalesce. "The Way of Qian 乾 becomes the male; the Way of Kun 坤 becomes the female";[58] the two *qi* stimulate each other, transforming and generating the myriad things.[59] The myriad things generate and regenerate (*sheng sheng* 生生), alternating and transforming without end.[60]

[*Zhu Xi's published commentary*]
Under heaven there are no things outside the nature (*xing*), and there is nowhere that the nature does not exist.[61] That by which the nonpolar, the two [*yin-yang*], and the five [phases] pervade everywhere is what is meant by "mysteriously combine." "Reality" means that in terms of principle

---

57. *Yulei* 94:3118.

58. *Yijing*, *Xici* A.1.4 (*Zhouyi benyi*, 3:1b). Qian and Kun are the first two hexagrams, symbolizing pure *yang* and pure *yin*, or Heaven and Earth, respectively.

59. Paraphrasing *Yijing*, *Tuan* commentary to hexagram 31 (Xian 咸): "The two *qi* stimulate and respond in mutual influence, the male going beneath the female. . . . Heaven and Earth are stimulated and the myriad things are transformed and generated" (*Zhouyi benyi*, 2:1a-b).

60. Cf. *Xici* A.5.6, "Generation and regeneration are what is meant by *yi* (change)" (*Zhouyi benyi*, 3:6a).

61. Zhu is connecting this section with the previous one by bringing in "the nature," which is the "principle" (*li*) of a thing.

it is without error.⁶² "Essence" means that in terms of *qi* it is nondual (*bu er* 不二). "Coalesce" means to gather, as *qi* gathers to become forms. Thus, with the nature as master [of a thing] and *yin-yang* and the Five Phases as its orderly variations, each [thing] coalesces according to its kind to become forms.⁶³ The creative *yang* becomes the male and the Way of the father; the obedient *yin* becomes the female and the Way of the mother. This is the origin of people and things as they are generated by the transformations of *qi*. As *qi* gathers to become things, the forms interact and the *qi* stimulates, and so through the transformation of forms people and things are generated and regenerated and change and transformation occur without end.⁶⁴

From the perspective of male and female, the male and female each has its nature, yet the male and female are the unitary Supreme Polarity. From the perspective of the myriad things, the myriad things each have their natures, yet the myriad things are the unitary Supreme Polarity. Speaking of them combined, the myriad things together embody the one Supreme Polarity; speaking of them separately, each thing contains the one Supreme Polarity. What I mean by saying [above], "Under heaven there are no things outside the nature, and there is nowhere that the nature does not exist" can be seen in its entirety even more so in this. Master Zisi said, "[I]f the noble person speaks of its greatness, there is nothing in the world capable of bearing it up, while if he speaks of its smallness, there is nothing in the world capable of breaking it down."⁶⁵ This is what it means.

---

62. "Without error" (*wu wang* 無妄) also means something like "without absurdity," so what Zhu Xi means is that reality is fully rational or capable of being understood. *Wu wang* is also hexagram 25 in the *Yijing*.

63. Chen Lai points out that the phrase "the nature as master" comes from Hu Hong's *Zhi yan* (Understanding words). Chen Lai, *Zhu Xi zhexue yanjiu*, 5.

64. "The *qi* stimulates" (*qi gan* 氣感) refers to the mutual stimulation and response (*gan ying* 感應) or interdependence of all things in terms of the inherent dynamism or energetic potential of *qi*. "Generated and regenerated" (*sheng sheng* 生生) is an allusion to *Xici* A.5, "Generation and regeneration [or life and growth] are called change (*yi*)" (*Zhouyi benyi* 3:6a).

65. Quoting the *Zhongyong* (Centrality and Commonality), ch. 12, trans. Irene Bloom, in *Sources of Chinese Tradition*, ed. de Bary and Bloom, 2nd ed., vol. 1, 335. The paragraph suggests the "holistic" character of traditional Chinese cosmology: the whole

[*Zhu Xi's additional comments*]

[1] *Question*: When Master Zhou spoke of "the reality of Nonpolarity" he did not mention Supreme Polarity. Why? *Master Zhu replied*: The reality of Nonpolarity already has Supreme Polarity within it. The word *reality* is this Supreme Polarity.

[2] The sentence, "The reality of Nonpolarity and the essence of the Two [Modes] and Five [Phases] mysteriously combine and coalesce" is very mysterious. It is *qi* and *li* combining to become the nature.[66]

[3] What accounts for the creativity (*zaohua* 造化) of the Way of Heaven's flowing out and nourishing of the myriad things is nothing but *yin-yang* and the Five Phases. And what we call *yin-yang* and the Five Phases requires that there be *li* and then (*er hou* 而後) *qi*. The generation of things is the gathering of this *qi*, and only then is there form. Thus, the generation of humans and things must receive this *li*; and only then (*ran hou* 然後) do they have the nature that soundly accords with humanity, rightness, ritual propriety, and wisdom.[67] They must receive this *qi*; only then do they have a body consisting of the *hun* 魂 and *po* 魄,[68] five organs, and hundred structures. This is just what Master Zhou calls "the essence of the Two [Modes] and Five [Phases] mysteriously combining and coalescing."

[. . . .]

- *Li* 李 *asked*: Are "the reality of the Nonpolar" and "the centrality of the unexpressed" [from *Zhongyong* 1] the same or different? *Reply*: The reality of the Nonpolar includes activity and stillness; the centrality

---

is more than the sum of its parts (i.e., something new emerges, at a higher level of organization, when all the parts are present and functioning as they should), and each part contains or reflects the whole (i.e., a bodily organ, such as the heart, is defined in terms of its function—pumping blood—in the whole organism). The Huayan Buddhist doctrine of mutual "nonobstruction" (or interpenetration) and the image of the Jewel Net of Indra is another expression of this way of thinking (see chapter 3 above).

66. By "the nature" Zhu means its two aspects, the original (moral) nature (*ben xing* 本性) and the physical nature (*qizhizhi xing* 氣質之性).

67. Mencius's "four constant virtues" (*Mencius* 2A.6 and 6A.6). Zhu is using temporal-sounding language here (*er hou, ran hou*), but in the context of his other discussions of *li* and *qi* it is clear that he is referring to logical, not temporal, priority.

68. The *yang* and *yin* souls.

of the unexpressed refers only to stillness. *Taiji* is simply the polar extremity (*jizhi*), but it has no location. The highest (*zhigao* 至高), the most mysterious, the most essential, the most spiritual, have no location. Lianxi feared that people would say that *taiji* had form, so he said "*wuji er taiji.*" Within this *wu* there is the principle of the utmost pole (*zhiji*). It is like *huangji* 皇極 (royal ultimate), which is the hub of the universe, but has no location. It is neither here nor there; it is only at the center, where everything comes together. *He then pointed to the peak of the house (wuji 屋極) and said*: It's not even there.[69]

[*Zhou Dunyi's text*]

[F] Only humans receive the finest and most spiritually efficacious [*qi*].[70] Once formed, they are born; when spirit (*shen* 神)[71] is manifested, they have intelligence; when their fivefold natures are stimulated into activity, good and evil are distinguished and the myriad affairs ensue.[72]

[*Zhu Xi's published commentary*]

This says that ordinary people contain the principle of activity and stillness, yet they commonly lose it in activity.[73] Now, when human beings are born, none lack the Way of Supreme Polarity. Thus, people individually receive the finest of the physical interaction of *yin-yang* and Five Phases, and therefore their mind/hearts are the most spiritually efficacious and

---

69. *Yulei* 94:3120. See the discussion of this passage in chapter 4.

70. I translate *ling* 靈 as "spiritually efficacious," but a more concise rendering would be "numinous."

71. The word *shen* can refer either to a deity or to the finest form of *qi* (psychophysical substance), which is capable of penetrating and pervading things and accounts for human intelligence. See *Tongshu* (below), chs. 3, 4, and 16; and Adler, "Varieties of Spiritual Experience."

72. The fivefold nature consists of the "five constant virtues," which correspond to the Five Phases. The five are Mencius's four—humanity (*ren* 仁), rightness (*yi* 義), propriety (*li* 禮), wisdom (*zhi* 智)—plus trustworthiness (*xin* 信). For incipient activity and the differentiation of good and evil, see *Tongshu* (below), section 3.

73. Both good and evil arise in activity.

they have the means not to lose the entirety of their nature. This is called the mind/heart of Heaven and earth and the peak of humanity.[74]

However, form is generated in *yin* and spirit arises in *yang*; the nature of the five constant [virtues] stimulates things and acts; the goodness of *yang* and the evil of *yin* are differentiated by kind; and so the different aspects of the fivefold nature are scattered among myriad affairs. Thus, the transformation and generation of the myriad things from the two *qi* and Five Phases is like this in humans. Were it not for the sage's ability to settle the complete substance and Supreme Polarity, with the activity of desires and being overcome by feelings interacting to produce benefit and harm, there would be no peak of humanity and we would be "not far removed from animals."[75]

[*Zhu Xi's additional comments*]

[1] The two *qi* and Five Phases interact in myriad changes. Thus, in the generation of humans and things[76] there are inequalities in their purity and coarseness. In terms of the unitary *qi*, humans and things are both generated by receiving this *qi*. In terms of purity and coarseness, humans get the correct (*zheng* 正) and penetrating (*tong* 通) *qi*, while things get the *qi* that is partial (*pian* 偏) and blocked (*sai* 塞). Only humans get the correct [*qi*], so their *li* is penetrating and not blocked. Things get the partial [*qi*], so their *li* is blocked and unaware. . . .[77]

[4] *Question on* "when their fivefold natures are stimulated into activity, good and evil are distinguished." *Reply*: The nature of Heaven and earth is principle/order. As soon as there are *yin-yang* and Five

---

74. *Renji* 人極, lit. peak of being human; see section G below.

75. A reference to *Mencius* 6A.8. Zhu is saying here that the appearance of evil in human activity and feelings is a natural occurrence, and that reliance on the sages is necessary to overcome it.

76. From the following discussion it is clear that Zhu is thinking of "living things."

77. The rest of this passage gives examples of the similarities and differences between humans and animals, including some interesting observations of quasi-moral behavior in birds (who "know filiality") and otters (who "know ritual"). For more on this see Kim, *The Natural Philosophy of Chu Hsi*, 175–77, 194–97.

Phases, there is the physical nature. In this there is differentiation of dark and clear, thick and thin.

[8] *Yin* and *yang* refer to activity and stillness. In terms of good and evil, this is the moral order (*daoli* 道理). When followed by humans this is how it can be seen.

[*Zhou Dunyi's text*]

[G] The sage settles these [affairs] with centrality (*zhong* 中) and correctness (*zheng* 正), humanity (*ren* 仁) and rightness (*yi* 義) (the Way of the sage is simply humanity and rightness, centrality and correctness) and emphasizes stillness (*zhu jing* 主靜).[78] (Without desire, [he is] therefore still.)[79] In so doing he establishes the peak of humanity (*renji* 人極).[80] Thus, the sage's "virtue equals that of Heaven and Earth; his clarity equals that of the sun and moon; his timeliness equals that of the four seasons; his good fortune and bad fortune equal those of ghosts and spirits."[81]

---

78. "Centrality" (*zhong*) and "correctness" (*zheng*) are qualities of *Yijing* hexagram lines: positions two and five are "central" to the two component trigrams; a line is "correct" if it is a *yang* (solid) line in an even numbered position (2, 4, 6) or a *yin* (broken) line in an odd numbered position (1, 3, 5). A line that is both central and correct (i.e., a *yang* line in position two or a *yin* line in position five) is usually auspicious. See Nielsen, *A Companion to Yi Jing Numerology and Cosmology*, 338. "Centrality" is also translated as "equilibrium" in the context of the *weifa/yifa* or *zhong/he* problem (see chapter 3). "Emphasizing stillness" (*zhu jing*) is one of the phrases that greatly troubled many of Zhu Xi's colleagues, as it smacked of Daoist and Buddhist quietism (see chapter 3).

79. The two parenthetical notes are by Zhou; they are taken from *Tongshu*, sections 6 and 20. The terms *without desire* and *emphasizing stillness* were questionable to many Confucians, who usually preferred to speak of limiting desires (especially selfish desires), but not eliminating them. Both terms had Buddhist as well as Daoist connotations.

80. *Renji*, lit. peak of being human, using the same term *ji* that elsewhere is translated as "polarity." See the discussion in chapter 4, especially on the imagery of the peak of a roof or the zenith of the heavens. The term is an allusion to "three peaks/ ultimates" (*sanji*) in *Xici* A.2.4: "The activity of the six lines symbolizes the Way of the three ultimates" (*Zhouyi benyi* 3:3a). The three ultimates are understood by everyone from Han Kangbo to Zhu Xi (ibid.) to be Heaven, Earth, and Humanity. For Han's commentary see Wang Bi and Han Kangbo, *Zhouyi Wang-Han zhu*, 7:2a; and Lynn, *The Classic of Changes*, 50.

81. *Yijing*, *Wenyan* appendix, under Qian; *Zhouyi benyi*, xx.xx.

[*Zhu Xi's published commentary*]
This says that the sage completes the virtues of activity and stillness yet is always based in stillness. While humans [all] receive the finest *qi* of *yin-yang* and the Five Phases at birth, the sage at birth gets the finest of the finest. Thus, in acting he is centered [or in a state of equilibrium] and at rest he is correct, his expressions (*fa* 發) [of feeling] are humane and his decisions are right.[82] In the alternation of activity and stillness he is thoroughly in possession of the means to complete the Way of Supreme Polarity without deficiency. In regard to "the activity of desires and being overcome by feelings, interacting to produce benefit and harm" [from the previous section of commentary] he is settled.

But stillness is the return to authenticity and the reality of the nature. Were it not for this mind/heart's silent, desireless stillness, how could it respond to the changes of the myriad things and events and unify the activity of all under heaven?[83] Thus, the sage is central and correct, humane and right; his activity and stillness flow cyclically, and so in his activity he necessarily emphasizes stillness.[84] This is how he achieves the central position, and heaven and earth, sun and moon, four seasons, and ghosts and spirits cannot oppose him.

So it is necessary that the substance be established before the function proceeds. It is like what Master Cheng [Hao] said about Qian and Kun, activity and stillness: "Without focusing on unity one cannot proceed directly; without uniting everything one cannot express oneself broadly."[85] This is also the idea.[86]

---

82. Zhu's use of the term *expressions* (*fa*) here suggests that he is linking Zhou Dunyi's use of "centrality" (*zhong*), based on the *Yijing*, to the "*zhong/he* or *weifa/yifa*" problem based on the *Zhongyong* (see chapter 3).

83. In other words, equilibrium (*zhong*) in stillness is necessary to ensure harmony (*he*) in activity. In this respect stillness is of primary importance; hence it is "emphasized (*zhu*)."

84. The interpenetration of activity and stillness (chapter 3).

85. *Er Cheng ji, Yishu* 11:129.

86. Note that Zhu's entire commentary on this section attempts to justify the "emphasis on stillness."

[*Zhu Xi's additional comments*]

[1] The sage at birth receives a complete endowment [of *qi*]. His constitution (*qizhi*) is clear and pure, completely ordered (*li*). He is one with Heaven without depending at all upon cultivation.[87]

[2] The sage in every respect, inside and out, is entirely bright and penetrating. Although his form is that of a person, it is entirely natural order (*tianli* 天理).

[3] The section on the sage establishing the peak of humanity does not discuss humanity, rightness, ritual, and wisdom [Mencius's "four constant virtues"]; instead, it discusses humanity, rightness, centrality, and correctness. Centrality and correctness are ritual and wisdom; centrality and correctness are even closer. Centrality is the point where ritual becomes proper. Correctness is the point where wisdom is exactly correct. Centrality is the peak (*ji* 極) of ritual; correctness is the substance of wisdom.[88]

[5] Although human nature is the same [in everyone], there must be different emphases in the endowment of *qi*. When wood-*qi* predominates, then the mind/heart of pity and grief will be greater and the mind/heart of shame and dislike, deference and yielding, and right and wrong will be blocked and not expressed.[89] When metal-*qi* predominates, then the mind/heart of shame and dislike will be greater and the mind/heart of pity and grief, deference and yielding, and right and wrong will be blocked and not expressed. The same is true for water and fire [*qi*]. Only when *yin* and *yang* combine their virtues and the fivefold nature is complete is there centrality and correctness, which is being a sage.

[7] *Question about* "centrality and correctness, humanity and rightness, and emphasizing stillness." Centrality and humanity are activity; correctness and rightness are stillness. As the Teacher [Zhu Xi] has explained [above], "Were it not for this mind/heart's desireless stillness, how could it respond to the changes of the myriad things

---

87. Cf. Zhu's arguments for including Zhou Dunyi in the *daotong* despite his not having had any notable teachers: the greatest sages are born, not made (see chapter 2).

88. For more discussion on this point see *Yulei* 94: 3135–36.

89. These are the four "beginnings" or "seeds" of virtue in *Mencius* 2A.6 and 6A.6.

and events and unify the activity of all under heaven?" Now, in this mind's silent, desireless stillness, if one desired to see what was correct and right, how would one see? *Reply*: One simply sees the definite substance of principle (*lizhi ding ti* 理之定體).[90]

[9] The two words "emphasizing stillness" refers to what a sage does. They continue from the previous passage, where he "settles these [affairs] with centrality and correctness, humanity and rightness," in order to clarify "centrality" among the four. It is like being a guest and a host oneself. In view of this, the student should apply effort in a definite sequence. One should first establish a foundation and then examine oneself; then there will be progress. What is meant by stillness is not to apply absolutely no effort. If one does it like this one can apply effort.[91]

[. . . .]

[*Zhou Dunyi's text*]
[H] The noble person cultivates these and has good fortune. The petty person rejects these and has bad fortune.

[*Zhu Xi's published commentary*]
Because of the sage's [possession of the] complete substance of Supreme Polarity, [in his] alternating between activity and stillness there is nothing that is not the peak of centrality and correctness, humanity and rightness. And this is done naturally, without artificial cultivation. Not until reaching this level of cultivation does the noble person have the means to experience good fortune. Without knowing these [centrality and correctness, humanity and rightness] the petty person corrupts them and experiences bad fortune. The difference between cultivating them and corrupting them lies in the gap between reverent composure (*jing* 敬) and indulgence (*si* 肆). With reverent composure one's desires are

---

90. The questioner is asking how one could know the correctness and humanity of the still phase of mind, since this knowing would be mental activity. Zhu's reply is far from satisfactory.

91. I.e., "emphasizing stillness" clarifies "centrality/equilibrium," which must come before harmonious activity. But this is a stillness that can include certain forms of mental activity, such as the nourishing function of sleep (discussed in chapter 3).

few and principle is clear; as they become fewer and fewer to the point where there are none, then one is "unoccupied when still and direct in activity," and "sagehood can be learned."[92]

[*Zhu Xi's additional comments*]
[3] In terms of events (*shi* 事) there is activity and there is stillness. In terms of mind's circulation and penetration, moral effort (*gongfu* 工夫) from the beginning is uninterrupted, but stillness is its basis. This is the idea of what Master Zhou called "emphasizing stillness." But speaking of stillness [by itself] is one-sided, so Master Cheng only spoke of "reverent composure."

[4] The word *stillness* in Lianxi's phrase "emphasizing stillness" can be regarded as just "reverent composure." He also says, "without desire [he is] therefore still." If this were taken as vacuous stillness (*xujing* 虛靜), I fear people would go after Buddhism and Daoism.
[. . . .]

[*Zhou Dunyi's text*]
[I] Therefore, [the *Yi*] says, "Establishing the Way of Heaven, [the sages] speak of *yin* and *yang*; establishing the Way of Earth they speak of yielding and firm [hexagram lines]; establishing the Way of Humanity they speak of humanity and rightness."[93] It also says, "[The sage] investigates beginnings and follows them to their ends; therefore he understands death and birth."[94]

[*Zhu Xi's published commentary*]
Yin and *yang* become the images by which the Way of Heaven is established. The firm and yielding become the material by which the Way of earth is established. Humanity and rightness are the virtues by which the human Way is established. The Way is simply unitary, but it makes itself visible along with [the unfolding of] events. Thus, there is

---

92. Both phrases from *Tongshu* 20.
93. *Yijing, Shuogua* (Remarks on Trigrams), 2 (*Zhouyi benyi*, 4:1b).
94. *Yijing, Xici*, A.4.2 (*Zhouyi benyi*, 3:4a-b).

the distinction of the three realms [Heaven, earth, humans], and within each there is the further differentiation of substance (*ti* 體) and function (*yong* 用). Its actuality/reality (*shi* 實) is the unitary Supreme Polarity.

Yang, firmness, and humanity are the beginning of things; *yin*, yielding, and rightness are the end of things. If we are able to them to their beginnings and understand how they are generated, then we can turn to their ends and understand how they die. This is the ineffable mystery (*buyanzhi miao* 不言之妙) of the orderly process of creation, flowing from past to present, throughout heaven and earth. When the Sage [Fuxi] created the *Yi*, his general idea was nothing but this, and so [Zhou Dunyi] refers to it [the *Yi*] as verification of his theory.

[*Zhu Xi's additional comments*]

[1] *Yin* and *yang* refer to *qi*. The firm and yielding can be seen when there is material form. Humanity and rightness [exist] when *qi* has gathered into form and *li* is contained therein. But it is all one. [On the level of] *yin* and *yang*, within *yang* there is *yin* and *yang*. [On the level of] the yielding and firm, within *yin* there is *yin* and *yang*. [On the level of] humanity and rightness, the *yin* and *yang qi* gathers to become the firm and yielding material, and this [natural/moral] order first becomes the peak of the human Way.[95] Humanity is *yang* and firm; rightness is *yin* and yielding. Humanity chiefly produces, and rightness chiefly gathers. Therefore, they are classified accordingly [as *yang* and *yin*]. *Someone asked* about Yang Ziyun's [Yang Xiong's 揚雄] statement, "The noble person is yielding in regard to humanity and firm in regard to rightness."[96] We can probably select from his idea what is compatible and what is useful. *Reply*: The substance of humanity is firmness and its function is yielding; the substance of rightness is yielding and its function is firmness.

---

95. I think this sentence means that the unitary principle or order (*li*), which defines the ultimate goal of human life, combines both the "Heavenly" order of *yin* and *yang* and the "earthly" order of firm and yielding lines. In other words, principle (*li*) ultimately is the natural/moral order, and it is reflected or "imaged" (*xiang* 象) in the *Yijing*.

96. Yang Xiong (53 BCE-18 CE), *Fayan* (Model sayings), 12:1.

[4] Among the four [virtues of] humanity, rightness, ritual, and wisdom, humanity and rightness are complementary and critical. Humanity is humanity, but ritual is humanity's manifestation. Rightness is rightness, but wisdom is the source of rightness. This is like spring, summer, autumn, and winter; although they are four seasons, nevertheless spring and summer are both classified as *yang*, and autumn and winter are both classified as *yin*. The Way of Heaven and earth is not dualistic (*bu liang*); so we cannot conclude that because there are four "beginnings" (*duan* 端) they are dualistic.[97]

[. . . .]

[*Zhou Dunyi's text*]

[J] Great indeed is [the *Scripture of*] *Change*! Herein lies its perfection [*zhi* 至].

[*Zhu Xi's published commentary*]

The *Yi* as a book is exceedingly great and comprehensive, but in speaking of its utmost extreme [*zhi ji* 至極, i.e., its ultimate meaning], this Diagram exhausts it. How deep is its meaning! In my limited experience I have heard that when the Cheng brothers were studying under Master Zhou, Master Zhou personally handed down this Diagram. Many of the Chengs' statements about the nature and the Way of Heaven came from this. But when they died they had not yet clarified this Diagram to others, and so its meaning necessarily became obscured. Still, students cannot fail to understand it.

[*Zhu Xi's additional comments*]

[1] The *Taiji* Diagram simply clarifies the general outline and meaning of the *Yi*.

[2] "Great indeed is the *Yi*!" just refers to [the previous passage] from *yin* and *yang*, firm and yielding, humanity and rightness to "investigates beginnings and follows them to their ends; therefore

---

97. The "four beginnings" (*si duan*) are Mencius's term for the innate feelings that, when cultivated, lead respectively to the "four virtues" mentioned here. Zhu Xi here is again explaining why Zhou Dunyi mentions only two of them, as he did in section G.

he understands death and birth." Human life and death is just the bending and stretching, coming and going of yin and yang qi.[98]

[3] *Question*: What did Yichuan [Cheng Yi] follow in seeing the Way? *Reply*: He was able to get it from the Six Scriptures. But also, when he was with Lianxi [Zhou Dunyi], he could see the great moral order (*daoli*). . . .

[4] In the "Discussion of the *Taiji* Diagram" the changes of yin and yang and the Five Phases are not uniform. The two Chengs followed this in first inferring the [idea of] physical nature (*qizhizhi xing*).[99]

[5] *Question*: The Teacher [Zhu Xi] has said that the Masters Cheng did not hand down the *Taiji* Diagram to their disciples, probably because there was no one who was able to receive [understand] it. But why is it that in Confucius's school it was never mentioned to Yan and Zeng?[100] *Reply*: How do you know they did not discuss it? . . .

[6] The *Taiji* Diagram has never been hidden from people. But the only people who understood *taiji* were some in the Chan school, who miraculously were able to use it. They spoke about *taiji* without knowing that it was called *taiji*.[101] The natural order (*ziranzhi li* 自然之理) of Heaven and earth and the myriad things, from antiquity to the present, has been mishandled but not broken. The term *wuji* (nonpolar) is Master Zhou's penetrating insight into the substance of the Way, repeatedly producing the constant virtues. Going forward

---

98. A good example of Zhu's naturalism. Even the "mysteries" of birth and death can be understood in terms of the *yin-yang* theory of change embodied in the *Yi*.

99. By "not uniform" Zhu means that Zhou Dunyi implies that *qi* appears in gradations of quality, for example when he says that "only humans receive the finest and most spiritually efficacious" (section F). There is, however, no evidence that the Chengs were influenced by this (see chapter 2).

100. Two of Confucius's most important disciples: Yan Hui (see *Tongshu*, sections 10, 23) and Zeng Can or Master Zeng (Zengzi), the reputed author of the *Daxue* (Great Learning).

101. This is one of the highest compliments Zhu Xi ever paid to Chan Buddhism; perhaps he is thinking of his former Buddhist teachers, Daoqian and Dahui (see chapter 1). I suspect that he is alluding to the Mahayana concept of Buddha-nature (*fo xing*) or Dharma-body (*fa shen*), either of which in some respects can be considered analogous to his concept of *taiji*.

courageously, he explained it to people who did dare to speak of moral principle. He caused later scholars to clearly see the mystery of *taiji*, which is not classified as either being or nonbeing, and is not located anywhere. It is truly a secret not transmitted since the sages.

[. . . .]

Final notes (*hou ji* 後記)[102]

When I wrote this discussion (*shuo* 說)[103] I recorded it by sending it to Zhang Jingfu [Zhang Shi] of Guanghan. Jingfu sent me a letter, saying, "In the discussions and dialogues in the writings of the two masters [Cheng brothers] there are many mentions of being disciples [of Zhou Dunyi]. They frequently discussed the *Western Inscription* [of Zhang Zai], but there was never one word about the [*Taiji*] Diagram. You say that this must be because of its obscure ideas,[104] which it certainly has. But what do you mean by 'obscure ideas'"?

I think that the Diagram uses images to fully express its ideas, which analyze the obscure and subtle; this is why Master Zhou felt compelled to create it.[105] Contemplating the ideas that he personally handed down, he probably thought that only the Cheng brothers were equal to them. As for the Chengs not discussing [the Diagram], I suspect that there was no one [among their students] able to receive [understand] it. Being unable to silently understand the explicit meaning [*biao*, lit. outward manifestation] of the words and ideas, their minds would have jumped to the mystery of [Buddhist] emptiness (*kong*), which enters the ear and leaves the mouth [without understanding]; words would not overcome this injury. (In recent years I have experienced this inadequacy.)[106] Observing [Cheng Yi's] response to Zhang Hongzhong's essay, written after he completed

---

102. This section actually follows the "Appended arguments" (next section) in *Zhou Lianxi ji,* but it seems to make more sense to place it immediately following Zhu's commentary. In *Zhou Lianxi ji* it has no title, but in *Zhuzi quanshu* (13:79) and in Shu, *Nianpu* (488) it is entitled "Final notes" (*houji*). It was written in 1173, immediately after Zhu completed his draft of the commentary (which was not published until 1188).

103. Referring to Zhu's published commentary.

104. Above, p. 194, penultimate sentence of commentary.

105. Note that Zhu rejects the claim that Zhou received the Diagram from Daoists.

106. This is Zhu's own note.

his *Commentary on the Yi,* I am deeply troubled that there was no one to receive [the Diagram]. Their discussion of Hengqu's [Zhang Zai's] theory of the "pure and vacuous, one and great" [i.e., the Supreme Vacuity, *taixu* 太虛] in the *Record of Looking East (Dongjianlu* 東見錄), says that people would have looked elsewhere [i.e., to Buddhism] if they did not just speak about reverent composure. So their ideas can also be seen.[107]

For example, the *Western Inscription* [by Zhang Zai] pushes people toward Heaven, using what is near to clarify what is distant, in the most intimate aspects of students' daily functioning. It is not like this text [the *Taijitu shuo*], which details the origins of the nature and the given (*xing ming* 性命) and outlines their progress in stages, but which one cannot readily put into words. Confucius spoke elegantly in the *Shi* 詩 [Scripture of Poetry/Songs], the *Shu* 書 [Scripture of Documents], and the several *Li* 禮 [Record of Ritual, Rites of Zhou, and Etiquette and Ritual], but in the *Yi* he was concise; this is the idea.[108] Master Han [Yu] said, "Yao and Shun benefitted the people greatly; Yu's concern for the people was deep."[109] I think that Master Zhou and the Chengs were also like this. When I replied to Jingfu [Zhang Shi] I wrote to this effect.

Qiandao 乾道 period, *gui-si* 癸巳 year [1173], 4th month

---

107. The *Dongjianlu* is a collection of the Cheng brothers' conversations, not attributed to either one specifically, compiled by Lü Yushu (呂與叔), a student first of Zhang Zai and then, after his death, the Cheng brothers. It now comprises the second and third sections of the *Er Cheng ji* (Complete Collection of the Cheng Brothers). For Lü Yushu see *Song-Yuan xue'an,* 31:10b–19a. The statement Zhu is referring to is this:

> When Hengqu taught people, he originally said that contemporary scholars were extremely obstinate. So in explaining the "pure and vacuous, one and great," he could only hope that people would not go elsewhere [i.e., to Buddhism]. Today we only speak about reverent composure. (*Er Cheng ji,* 34 [*juan* 2A])

The idea is that Zhang Zai's theory of the "Supreme Vacuity" (*taixu*) was dangerously close to the Buddhist theory of emptiness (*kong*), and might therefore mislead people. But the Cheng brothers corrected that by focusing on reverent composure (*jing*), in effect shifting the focus from airy metaphysics to concrete practice. Zhu Xi is saying here that the same caution led the Chengs not to discuss Zhou Dunyi's theory of *taiji* and the text translated here with their students, and that accounts for its absence in their writings and recorded sayings.

108. That is, the *Taijitu shuo* is written gnomically, in brief but profound statements, and is therefore very difficult to understand.

109. Han Yu, *Changli xiansheng ji,* 21 ("Dui Yu wen").

Appended arguments[110]

[1] When I wrote this explanation,[111] my reading of books was extremely conflicted and my argumentation was confused, as if my interaction [with the text] was unsuccessful. Therefore, I discussed it in general terms. As for most of the difficulties, some say that we should not divide the good nature into *yin* and *yang*; some say we should not divide the Supreme Polarity's *yin* and *yang* into the Way and implements; some say we should not divide humanity and rightness, centrality and correctness into substance and function; some say we should not say that each thing contains the one Supreme Polarity. There are also those who say that [Cheng Yi's doctrine] "Substance and function have a single source"[112] does not enable us to say that function proceeds only after substance is established. There are those who say that humanity being the unified substance does not just refer to the activity of *yang*. And there are those who say that the distinction of humanity and rightness, centrality and correctness should not revert to these categories.

The theories of these numerous people are all reasonable (principled). But in regard to their ideas about the sages and worthies, they all get one [aspect] and ignore the rest. The entirety of the substance of the Way is purely one: the distinctions of essential and gross, root and branch, inner and outer are clearly within it; there can be not the slightest discontinuity (gap). These words of the Sages and worthies, some departing from and some agreeing with [each other], some different and some the same, are

---

110. This section follows immediately after Zhu's commentary on the *Taijitu shuo* in *Zhou Lianxi ji* and in *Zhuzi quanshu* (2002), vol. 13. In the former it is called "Appended discriminations" (*fu bian* 附辨), and there are spaces between the subsections I have numbered, suggesting that they come from various sources. In the latter the section is simply introduced by "*Lun yue* 論曰" (Discussions say), but there is a note saying that in *Zhou Lianxi ji* the title is "Appended arguments/disputations" (*fu bian* 附辯); also the formatting suggests that it is one continuous piece (*Zhuzi quanshu*, vol. 13:76). Shu Jingnan includes excerpts from it with the title, "*Taijitu shuo* arguments/disputations" (*Zhuzi nianpu changbian*, 487).

111. Referring to Zhu's commentary, which was completed in 1173 but not published until 1188.

112. Referring to Cheng Yi's statement that "substance and function have a single source; the evident and subtle have no gap," in the Preface to his commentary on the *Yijing*. See *Yizhuan xu*, in *Er Cheng ji* (Complete Collection of the Cheng Brothers) (Beijing: Zhonghua shuju, 1981), 689.

the totality of the substance of the Way. Today's followers understand the "purely" [one] being great and enjoy saying it, yet they do not understand the "clearly" [within it], which has never departed from it.[113] In this way, believing in unity but doubting differences, being pleased with agreement but hating difference, their discussions all sink into partiality; they disappear without a bit of praise, like feet without inches. How mistaken!

[2] As for the relation between goodness and the nature, we cannot say they are two things. But to connect them: goodness refers to the transformations of *yin* and *yang*; what realizes/actualizes it is the nature, which refers to the human endowment. The transformation and flow of *yin* and *yang*, which is without beginning and inexhaustible,[114] is the activity of *yang*. The finite human endowment, which cannot be changed, is the stillness of *yin*. Discussing it like this, how can there be no division into two?[115] But the goodness of the nature is above form (metaphysical); *yin* and *yang* are within form. How can Master Zhou's idea mean that goodness is *yang* and the nature is *yin*? He only speaks of their distinction, so we must classify them in this way.

[3] It is certain that *yin-yang* and *Taiji* cannot be spoken of as two principles. But *Taiji* is imageless, and *yin-yang* are *qi*, so how can there not be hierarchical differentiation?[116] This is how there is a distinction between the Way and implements. Therefore, Master Cheng said, "The theory of what is above form being the Way and what is within form being implements must be put forth. But implements are also the Way, and the Way is also implements." Taking this idea and extending it would not be a biased [approach].

[4] Humanity and rightness, centrality and correctness are all the one principle, yet there are actually some who are uncomfortable with their

---

113. That is, they understand the unity of the Way but do not understand that this unity and its different manifestations are not two different levels of reality. There is a parallel here with the last lines of the first chapter of the *Laozi*: "These two are the same; / when they appear they are named differently. / This sameness is the mystery; / mystery within mystery, / the door to all marvels" (Muller trans.)

114. Reading *you qiong* 有窮 as *wu qiong* 無窮.

115. That is, the *yin-yang* distinction is a real one.

116. See Tomoeda Ryutaro's translation of these two sentences in Wing-tsit Chan, ed., *Chu Hsi and Neo-Confucianism* (Honolulu: University of Hawaii Press, 1986), 159.

division into substance and function. But humanity is the growth of goodness; centrality is the assembling of excellence; rightness is the appropriateness of benefit; correctness is the substance of uprightness. As for origination and flourishing (*yuan heng* 元亨), they are the penetrating [quality] of authenticity; benefit and uprightness (*li zhen* 利貞) are the return to authenticity. So how can we say that there is no distinction of substance and function!

[5] The myriad things are all generated from the one Supreme Polarity, yet there are those who question what we say about each thing containing [the Supreme Polarity]. But natural principle is wholly contained within each thing with no overlap and no conflict, unifying them into a class [*zong* 宗, lit. lineage] and assembling them under a head [*yuan* 元, lit. origin]. So then how can we not say that each contains the one Supreme Polarity!

[6] As for the statement that substance and function have a single source, what Master Cheng said is rather fine. His statement, "Substance and function have a single source" refers to the subtlest principle, vast and selfless, the myriad images brilliantly contained in it. His statement, "No gap between the evident and the subtle" refers to the perfectly evident images of every event and every thing: this principle existing everywhere. In reference to principle, substance is prior to function, because as soon as we mention substance, the principle of function is already contained in it. This is how they have "a single source." In reference to events, the evident is prior to the subtle; once there is an event, the substance of principle can be seen. This is how there is "no gap."[117] So, as for the "single source," how can we say it spreads without [distinctions of] fine and coarse or first and last? And when we say that the substance is established and then the function proceeds, we likewise cannot deny that first there is one and then the other.

[7] "Humanity is the unified substance" is what Master Cheng meant by saying "Special words include the four." But his words were, "The head (*yuan* 元) of the four virtues is specifically humanity among the five constant [virtues]. Speaking of it individually [lit. partially], it is [just] one thing; speaking of it as the whole [lit. special], it includes the four." So this is how humanity includes the four; it is certainly never apart from

---

117. See Tomoeda's translation of the preceding four sentences in ibid., 160.

the partial way of speaking of it as one thing, and there was never any nonrecognition [on the part of Master Cheng] of the one thing referred to individually. So it is permissible to use shorthand "special words" for the unified substance.

Similarly, this Diagram is a "special word" that matches humanity and rightness, compares them to centrality and correctness, and classifies them as *yin-yang* and firm-yielding. . . .

[8] In general, in this text Master Zhou's words and ideas are highly clear and completely successful, and their principles are thoroughly fine and comprehensive. Readers who are able to empty their minds, unify their thoughts, and return to the depth [of their minds] without first getting confused by language, will be not far from getting Master Zhou's mind, and will have no fear of getting tangled up in speech.

Chapter Seven

Penetrating the Scripture of Change
(*Tongshu* 通書)

INTRODUCTION

The *Tongshu* is less well-known than the *Taijitu shuo* but is no less important for an understanding of both Zhou Dunyi's thought and Zhu Xi's reasons for installing Zhou in the *daotong* lineage. The two works are very different in format: the *Taijitu shuo* is a single coherent essay, while the *Tongshu* as we have it today (in Zhu Xi's rescension) is composed of forty shorter, aphoristic, mostly independent pieces.[1] Furthermore, the central idea of the former (*taiji*) is found only once in the latter, and the central idea of the latter (*authenticity*) is entirely absent from the former. Nevertheless, there are several important overlaps and no significant inconsistencies between the two texts, and I agree with Zhu Xi that they are products of the same author. Zhu Xi considers them to be completely interrelated, and throughout his commentaries he identifies terms and passages from one that explain or are explained by the other. In some of these cases, however, the correlation makes sense only in terms of his own interpretation of their meaning.

While the *Taijitu shuo* is a philosophic cosmogony, situating human beings and in particular sages in the metaphysical and cosmological natural order, the *Tongshu* focuses in more detail on sagehood. Relying on both the

---

1. Three topics are divided into two sections each (1–2, 24–25, 38–39), and one into three (17–19).

Yijing and the *Zhongyong* (Centrality and commonality), it defines sagehood as "being authentic" (*cheng* 誠). This term, usually but inadequately translated as "sincerity," has both a psychological and metaphysical meaning. On the simplest level it means having consistency between one's inner state and one's outward behavior. On this level "sincerity" is a somewhat superficial but adequate translation. However, even in the *Zhongyong* it is clear that *cheng* has a deeper meaning than "sincerity," and for this reason I translate it as "being authentic," in the sense of being real or genuine, true to one's innate moral nature.[2] *Zhongyong* 20 says:

> Being authentic is the Way of Heaven. To think how to be authentic is the way of man. He who is authentic is one who hits upon what is right without effort and apprehends without thinking. He is naturally and easily in harmony with the Way. Such a man is a sage.[3]

To be authentic is both to be true to one's inner moral nature and also to be *real* (*shi*), which means to be fully embedded in the Way, or to be fully aligned with *li,* the natural/moral order. Therefore Zhu Xi defines being authentic as "actualizing principle" (*shi li* 實理), or actualizing the natural/moral order. In the case of human beings it means to fully manifest the principle of being human, which is the moral or fundamental nature (*ben xing* 本性). To suggest this range of meanings in the translation below I translate *li* sometimes as "principle" and sometimes as "order."

Zhou Dunyi, following the *Zhongyong,* defines sagehood as being authentic. He develops the concept further, relating it to the capacity to understand one's inner mental states in their "incipient" (*ji* 幾) phases, just as they are emerging from stillness into activity (section 3).[4] Thus, stillness and activity are one of the important links between the *Tongshu* and *Taijitu*

---

2. I try to avoid "authenticity" when possible because the reification of an abstract concept, which is implied by turning an adjective into a noun, is more fitting in a Greek-derived philosophical context (e.g., by deriving "the good" from "good") than in the Chinese.

3. Trans. Wing-tsit Chan, *A Source Book in Chinese Philosophy,* 107, substituting "authentic/authenticity" for "sincere/sincerity."

4. For a full discussion of "incipience," see Smith, Bol, Adler, and Wyatt, *Sung Dynasty Uses of the I Ching,* 190–99.

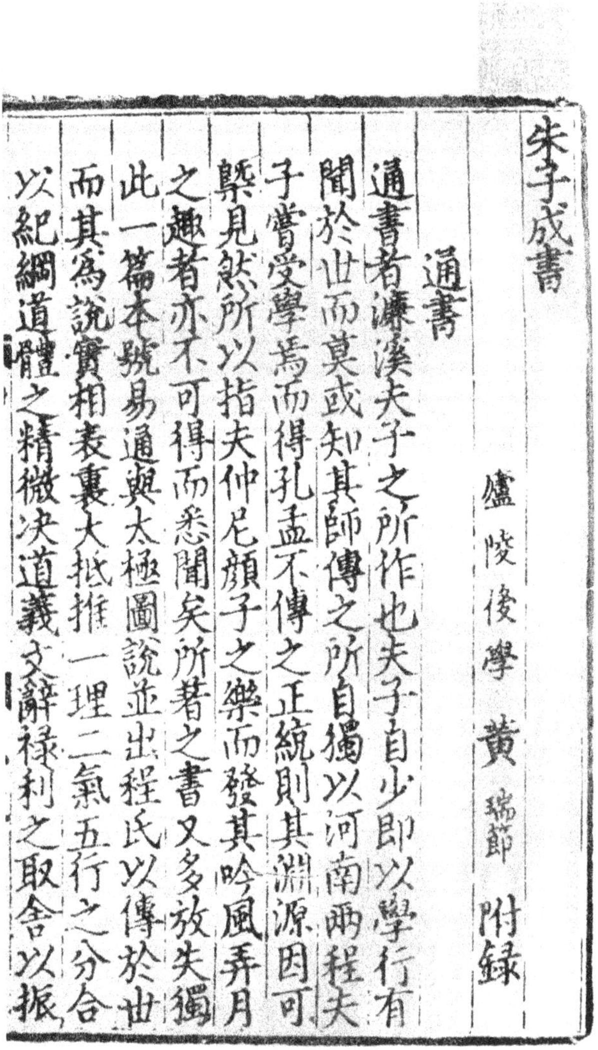

朱子成書

盧陵後學黃瑞節附錄

通書

通書者濂溪夫子之所作也夫子自少即以學行有聞於世而莫或知其師傳之所自獨以河南兩程夫子嘗受學焉而得孔孟不傳之正統則其淵源因可槩見然所以指夫仲尼顏子之樂而發其吟風弄月之趣者亦不可得而悉聞矣所著之書又多放失獨此一篇本號易通與太極圖說並出程氏以傳於世而其爲說實相表裏大抵推一理二氣五行之分合以紀綱道體之精微決道義文辭祿利之取舍以振

FIGURE 7.1 First page of the preface to Zhu Xi's commentary on the *Tongshu*, published between 1335 and 1340 by Huang Ruijie. From the collection of the Shanghai Library, printed as a frontispiece to *Zhuzi quanshu* (2002).

shuo, but in this text it is more in the context of moral psychology rather than cosmology. These ideas are developed mostly in sections 1–4, 16, and 20, which I consider the most important ones. Section 16, in particular, amplifies Zhou Dunyi's concept of the "interpenetration" of stillness and activity, which, as we saw in chapter 3, is the key to Zhu Xi's appropriation of Zhou.

In several sections (10, 23, and 29) Yan Hui 顏回 or Master Yan (Yanzi 顏子, also called Yan Yuan 顏淵), is singled out a prime example of sagehood, as "second only to Confucius" (23d), for his extreme dedication to learning—specifically, learning to become a sage. This reverence for Master Yan was shared by Cheng Yi, who wrote a famous essay called "On what Master Yan loved to learn."[5] It seems very likely that Cheng Yi picked up this attitude toward Yan Hui when he and his brother were studying with Zhou as teenagers. The other sections of the *Tongshu* cover a variety of Confucian topics and *Yijing* hexagrams (probably taken from Zhou's lost "Discussion of the *Yi*" [*Yishuo* 易說]), and there are two short sections (38–39, which were probably combined originally) on Confucius himself.[6]

According to Zhu Xi, Zhou's original text had titles for each section, but Hu Hong had removed them and substituted "Master Zhou says" for each. Hu also, says Zhu, changed the order of the sections.[7] Zhu Xi says he corrected both of these mistaken emendations, but he does not say where he got the section titles (he never met Hu Hong). He most probably made them up, because in at least one case (section 22, "Principle, nature, and endowment" [*Li xing ming* 理性命]) the title clearly reflects Zhu's interpretation more than Zhou's words themselves.

I include here an unannotated translation of Zhou Dunyi's text before the fully annotated translation and commentary. Most of the internal quotations are from the *Yijing*, and are identified in the annotated translation.

---

5. *Zhou Lianxi ji* 7:1a-b; trans. Chan, *Source Book*, 547–50.

6. The sections with the most additional comments selected by Zhang Boxing are 1–2, which are both on authenticity and were probably originally combined (twenty-three comments), 3 (authenticity, incipience, and virtue: nineteen), 23 (Master Yan: fifteen), and 22 (principle, nature, and endowment: nine). The average number of comments in all the other sections is two each.

7. See Zhu's two postfaces (1169 and 1179) below, and his additional comment [1] under section 22.

Penetrating the Scripture of Change
(*Tongshu* 通書),[8] by Zhou Dunyi

1. BEING AUTHENTIC (A)

Being authentic is the foundation of the sage. "Great indeed is the originating [power] of Qian! The myriad things rely on it for their beginnings." It is the source of being authentic. "The way of Qian transforms and each receives its correct nature and endowment." In this way authenticity is established. Being "pure and flawless" it is perfectly good. Thus: "The alternation of *yin* and *yang* is called the Way. That which issues from it is good. That which completes [constitutes] it is human nature." *Yuan* and *heng* are the penetrating [quality] of authenticity. *Li* and *zhen* are the recovery of authenticity. Great indeed is change, the source of human nature and endowment!

2. BEING AUTHENTIC (B)

Being a sage is nothing more than being authentic. Being authentic is the foundation of the Five Constant [Virtues] and the source of the Hundred Practices. It is imperceptible when [one is] still, and perceptible when one is active; perfectly correct [in stillness] and clearly pervading [in activity]. When the Five Constants and Hundred Practices are not authentic, they are wrong, blocked by depravity and confusion. Therefore one who is authentic has no [need for] undertakings. [Being authentic is] perfectly easy, yet difficult to practice. When one is determined and precise, there is no difficulty with it. Therefore, [Confucius said], "If in one day one could subdue the self and return to propriety, then all under Heaven would recover their humanity."

3. AUTHENTICITY, INCIPIENCE, AND VIRTUE

In being authentic there is no [intentional] acting. In incipience there is good and evil. As for the [Five Constant] Virtues, loving is called humanity, being appropriate is called rightness, being ordered/principled is called ritual propriety, being penetrating is called wisdom, and preserving is called honesty.

One who is by nature like this, at ease like this, is called a sage. One who recovers it and holds onto it is called a worthy. One whose subtle signs

---

8. *Zhou Lianxi ji,* chs. 5–6.

of expression are imperceptible, and whose fullness is inexhaustible, is called spiritual.

4. SAGEHOOD

"Completely silent and inactive" means being authentic. "Penetrating when stimulated" means being spiritual. That which is active but not yet formed, between existing and not existing, is incipient. Authenticity is essential [pure], and therefore clear. Spirit is responsive, and therefore mysterious. Incipience is subtle, and therefore obscure. One who is authentic, spiritual, and incipient is called a sage.

5. CAUTIOUS ACTIVITY

To be active and correct is called the Way. To be functioning and harmonious is called virtue. To rebel against humanity, to rebel against rightness, to rebel against ritual propriety, to rebel against wisdom, and to rebel against honesty is to be completely depraved. To be depraved in one's activity is abuse. To do so to an extreme is injury. Therefore the noble person is cautious in activity.

6. THE WAY

The Way of the Sages is nothing more than humanity and rightness, centrality and correctness. Preserve it and it will be valuable. Practice it and it will be beneficial. Enlarge it and it will match Heaven-and-earth. How can it not be easy and simple? How can it be difficult to know? By not preserving it, not practicing it, and not enlarging it.

7. THE TEACHER

Someone asked: "Who makes all under Heaven good?" Reply: "The teacher." "What do you mean?" "[He is one whose] nature is simply in equilibrium between firm and yielding good and evil." "I do not understand." Reply: "Firmness is good when it is right [or appropriate], direct, decided, dignified, capable and certain. It is evil when it is violent, narrow, and limited. Yielding is good when it is compassionate, docile, and mild. It is evil when it is weak, indecisive, and treacherous."

Only centrality is harmonious and "moderately regulated." This is "the all-encompassing Way of the world." It is the activity of the sage. Therefore, the sage establishes education, to enable common people to change their evil [tendencies], and on their own to reach equilibrium and stay there. Therefore, "those who first become aware awaken those who become aware later," the unenlightened seek from the enlightened, and the Way of instruction is established. With the Way of instruction established, then good people will proliferate. When good people proliferate, then the Court will be correct and all under Heaven will be well governed.

8. GOOD FORTUNE

In human life, it is unfortunate not to hear about one's errors. To lack shame is a great misfortune. Only with a sense of shame can one be taught. If one hears about one's errors, then one can become a worthy.

9. THINKING

The "Great Plan" says: "[The virtue of] thinking is called perspicacity. . . . Perspicacity makes one a sage." To be without thinking is the foundation. When thinking is penetrating, this is its function. When there is incipient activity on the one hand, and authentic activity on the other, with no thinking and yet penetrating everything, one is a sage.

If one does not think, then one cannot penetrate subtleties. If one is not perspicacious, then one cannot penetrate everything. Thus, [the ability] to penetrate everything arises from penetrating subtleties, and [the ability] to penetrate subtleties arises from thinking. Therefore, thinking is the foundation of the sage's achievement and the opportunity for good fortune or misfortune. The *Yi* says, "The noble person perceives incipience and acts, without waiting all day." It also says, "Knowing incipience is his spirituality."

10. BEING INTENT ON LEARNING

The sage emulates Heaven. The worthy emulates the sage. The literatus emulates the worthy. Yi Yin and Yan Yuan [Master Yan] were great worthies. Yi Yin was ashamed that his prince was not Yao or Shun. If one person did not attain his rightful place, it was like being whipped in the marketplace. Yan Yuan "did not transfer his anger and did not repeat an error," and "for three months did nothing contrary to humanity."

Be intent on having Yi Yin's intention, and learn what Yan Yuan learned. If you exceed this you will be a sage. If you reach it you will be a worthy. Even if you do not reach it you will not miss out on an honorable reputation.

11. COMPLIANCE AND TRANSFORMATION

Heaven generates the myriad things through *yang*, and fulfills the myriad things through *yin*. Generating is humanity; fulfilling is rightness. Therefore, when a sage is above [on the throne], he nourishes the myriad things with humanity and corrects the myriad people with rightness.

The Way of Heaven proceeds and the myriad things comply [with it]. The virtue of the sage cultivates [others] and the myriad people are transformed. Great compliance and great transformation leave no visible trace. Since no one understands them, they are considered spiritual. Therefore everything under Heaven is originally contained in every person. How can the Way be distant? How can its methods be numerous?

12. GOVERNMENT

Teaching by speaking directly to everyone is not sufficient even in a village of ten households. How much more difficult in an extensive empire with millions of people! I say: Purify the mind/heart, that is all. "Purify" means to do nothing contrary to the four [virtues of] humanity, rightness, propriety, and wisdom, whether in activity or when still, in one's speech, appearance, seeing, and hearing. When his mind/heart is pure, then worthy and talented men will assist him. When worthy and talented men assist him, the empire will be well governed. Purifying the heart/mind is indeed essential. Employing worthy men is urgent.

13. RITUAL AND MUSIC

Ritual is order. Music is harmony. *Yin* and *yang* are harmonious only when ordered. Then the ruler is [truly] ruler, the minister is minister, father is father, son is son, elder brother is elder brother, younger brother is younger brother, husband is husband, and wife is wife. The myriad things are harmonious only when each achieves this order. Therefore, ritual is first and music follows.

14. STRIVING FOR ACTUALIZATION

For actualization to dominate [one's work] is good. For name [fame] to dominate is shameful. Therefore, the noble person advances his virtue and cultivates his work with unceasing diligence, striving for the dominance of actualization. If his virtue and affairs are not prominent, he apprehensively fears that others will know [about it]; he wants to distance himself from shame.

The inferior person, on the other hand, is simply hypocritical. Therefore, the noble person is always at ease, while the inferior person is always anxious.

15. LOVE AND REVERENT COMPOSURE

[What if I] do not measure up to a good person?
If you do not measure up, then learn to do so.
Question: [What if] there is a bad person?
If he is not good, then inform him that he is not good. Furthermore, exhort him, saying, "Suppose you change; you will then become a noble person."

If one person is good and two are not good, then learn from the one and exhort the two. If someone says, "This person has done something that is not good, but it is not a great evil," then say, "Who makes no errors? How do we know that he cannot change? If he changes, then he can become a noble person. Not changing results in evil. Evil is what Heaven hates. How can he not fear [Heaven]? How do we know that he cannot change?" Therefore, the noble person possesses all goodness, and there is no one who does not love and revere him.

16. ACTIVITY AND STILLNESS

That which has no stillness in activity and no activity in stillness is a thing. That which has no activity in activity, and no stillness in stillness, is spirit. It is not the case that having no activity in activity and having no stillness in stillness is neither activity nor stillness. Things, then, are not penetrating. Spirit renders the myriad things subtle.

The *yin* of water is based in *yang*; the *yang* of fire is based in *yin*. The Five Phases are *yin* and *yang*. *Yin* and *yang* are the Supreme Polarity. The Four Seasons revolve; the myriad things end and begin [again]. How undifferentiated! How extensive! And how endless!

17. MUSIC (A)

The ancient sages and kings systematized the ritual procedures and reformed education. The Three Bonds were corrected, the Nine Divisions were arranged, the hundred surnames [i.e., all people] were in great harmony, and the myriad things were all in accord. They created music to give expression to the airs of the eight [directional] winds and to pacify the dispositions of all under Heaven.

Therefore, the sounds of music are placid and not distressing, harmonious and not licentious. When they enter the ear they move the heart/mind;

[yet] they are entirely placid and harmonious. Being placid, they calm the desirous heart/mind. Being harmonious, they ease the fierce heart/mind. To be easygoing and evenly balanced is the height of virtue. In the transformation of all under Heaven, government is perfected. This is what is meant by the Way that matches Heaven-and-earth, the ultimate of antiquity.

Later generations have neglected ritual. Their governmental measures and laws have been in disorder. Rulers have indulged their material desires without restraint, and consequently the people below them have suffered bitterly. Rulers have claimed that ancient music is not worth listening to and replaced it by or changed it into modern music, which is seductive, licentious, depressive, and complaining. It arouses desires and increases bitterness without end. Therefore, there have been cases of people destroying their rulers, casting away their fathers, taking life lightly, and ruining human relations, and it has been impossible to put an end to such atrocities. Alas! Ancient music appeased the heart but modern music enhances desires. Ancient music spread a civilizing influence, but modern music increases discontent. To hope for perfect government without restoring ancient ritual and changing modern music is to be far off the mark.

18. MUSIC (B)

Music is based in government. When government is good and the people are at peace, then the minds/hearts of all under Heaven are harmonious. Therefore, the sages created music to give expression to these harmonious hearts/minds. When it spreads throughout Heaven-and-earth, the *qi* of Heaven-and-earth is stimulated and there is great harmony throughout. When Heaven-and-earth are harmonious, then the myriad things are compliant. Therefore, the ancestral and natural spirits will approach [when sacrifices are offered], and birds and beasts will be tame.

19. MUSIC (C)

When the sound of music is quiet then the listener's mind is pacified. When the music's lyrics are good then the singer is respectful. Thus, styles shift and customs change. The influence of weird sound and passionate lyrics is also like this.

20. LEARNING TO BE A SAGE

Can sagehood be learned?
Reply: It can.

Are there essentials?
Reply: There are.
I beg to hear them.
Reply: To be unified is essential. To be unified is to have no desire. Without desire one is vacuous when still and direct in activity. Being vacuous when still, one will be clear; being clear one will be penetrating. Being direct in activity one will be impartial; being impartial one will be all-embracing. Being clear and penetrating, impartial and all-embracing, one is almost [a sage].

21. BEING IMPARTIAL AND CLEAR

One who is impartial toward oneself will be impartial toward others. There has never been one who was not impartial toward oneself and yet was able to be impartial toward others. When one is not perfectly clear then doubts arise. Clarity is the absence of doubts. To say that being able to doubt is clarity is a thousand miles off the mark.

22. PRINCIPLE, HUMAN NATURE, AND ENDOWMENT

The manifest and the subtle: without intelligence one cannot perceive them. There is firm good and firm evil, and the same for yielding. Rest in the mean between them. The two [modes of] *qi* and the five phases transform and generate the myriad things. The five differentia are the two realities, and the two are fundamentally one. Thus, the many are one, and the one reality is divided into the many. Each one of the many is correct; the small and the large are distinct.

23. MASTER YAN

Master Yan "had only one dish [of rice] to eat, only one gourdful [of water] to drink, and he lived in a squalid lane. Others could not have endured such distress, yet it did not alter his happiness." Now, wealth and honor are what people love. Yet Master Yan, neither loving nor seeking them, took pleasure in being humble. What was in his mind? In the world there is extreme honor and extreme wealth, which can be loved and sought after. Yet he [Master Yan] was one who differed from others in seeing what was great and ignoring what was petty. Seeing what was great, his mind was at peace. With his mind at peace, nothing was insufficient. With nothing insufficient, then wealth and honor, poverty and humble station were all the same [to him]. Being all the same, then he was able to transform and equalize [others, i.e., regard others as equal]. Thus, Master Yan was second only to the Sage [Confucius].

24. TEACHERS AND FRIENDS (A)

The most revered thing in the world is the Way; the most honored is virtue; the most rare [difficult to attain] is the human being. What is rare about the human being is having the Way and virtue in one's own body. Without teachers and friends, it is impossible to seek out and obtain in one's own body that which makes the human being the most rare.

25. TEACHERS AND FRIENDS (B)

Morality is valued and honored only when it is possessed by a person. People at birth are ignorant. As they grow, if they have no teachers and friends they become stupid. This is why morality acquires honor and reverence when it is possessed by a person in reliance on teachers and friends. Is the meaning [of teachers and friends] not important? Is it not a pleasure to associate with them?

26. TRANSGRESSIONS

Zhong You [Zilu] was happy to hear about his transgressions, and his good name [reputation] was inexhaustible. Today, when people transgress, they are not happy for others to correct them. It is like concealing one's illness and avoiding a doctor, preferring to harm oneself without being aware of it. Alas!

27. POWER

The empire is simply power. Power is either weak or strong. Extreme strength cannot be overcome. If one recognizes its strength and promptly opposes it, one can [succeed]. As for the effort of overcoming [strength], if one does not recognize it early the effort will not be easy. When effort is exerted without success, it is due to Heaven. When it is not recognized or no effort is made, it is due to the person. Is it due to Heaven? Then how can a person find fault?

28. LITERARY EXPRESSION

Writing is the vehicle of the Way. When the wheels and shafts of a carriage are ornamented but cannot be used, the ornamentation is in vain. How much more so an empty carriage! Literary expression is an art. The Way and virtue are real. If one is devoted to what is real and expresses it artistically in writing, its beauty will be loved. Being loved, it will be transmitted, and worthies will be able to learn it and achieve its object. This is education. Thus, it is said, "When one's words are not written, they will not go far." But the unworthy will not learn it even if father and elder brother are nearby, or teachers and tutors exhort them. Even if forced, they will not comply. They do not know how to devote themselves to the Way and virtue; they lower themselves to being experts in literary expression. This is nothing more than art [i.e., it does not express concrete reality]. Alas! This is a long-standing defect.

29. THE COMPREHENSIVENESS OF THE SAGE

"To those who are not eager to learn I do not explain anything, and to those who are not bursting to speak I do not reveal anything. If I raise one angle and they do not come back with the other three angles, I will not repeat myself" (*Analects* 7:8). The Master said, "I wish to do without speech. . . . What ever does Heaven say? Yet the four seasons run their course through it and all things are produced by it" (*Analects* 17:17). So then, were it not for Master Yan, the Sage's comprehensiveness might not have been seen. Master Yan was the one who brought out the Sage's comprehensiveness and taught ten thousand generations without limit. Was he not equally profound? The ordinary person, having heard or understood one thing, is anxious that others will not quickly know he has it. To be in haste to be known by others by reputation is very superficial.

30. ESSENCE AND COMPREHENSIVENESS

The essence of the Sage was displayed in the drawing of the hexagrams [of the *Yi*]. The comprehensiveness of the Sage is expressed by means of the hexagrams. Were the hexagrams not drawn, the essence of the Sage could not have been seen. Were it not for the hexagrams, it would almost be impossible to know about the comprehensiveness of the Sage. How can the Yi merely be the source [first] of the Five Scriptures? It is the mystery of Heaven and Earth, ghosts and spirits!

31. QIAN [Heaven, hexagram 1], SUN [Decrease, hexagram 41], YI [Increase, hexagram 42], AND ACTIVITY

"The noble person is creatively active and unceasing in being authentic." But he must "control his anger and repress his desires," and move toward the good and correct his transgressions before he can reach his goal. Among the functions of Qian this is the best. Of the greatness of Sun and Yi, nothing surpasses this. The Sage's meaning is profound indeed! "The auspicious, the inauspicious, repentance and regret arise from activity." Alas! The auspicious is only one [of the four]. Can we not be careful about activity?

32. JIAREN (Family Members, hexagram 37), KUI (Opposition, hexagram 38), FU (Return, hexagram 24), AND WUWANG (No Error, hexagram 25)

There is a foundation for ruling the world; it is called the [individual] person. There is a model for ordering the world; it is called the family. The foundation must be proper; the proper foundation is nothing but the authentic mind. The model must be good; the good model is nothing but harmonious relations. The family is difficult [to regulate], while the empire is easy. For the family is close, but the state is distant. If family members are separated, it is surely caused by the wife. Thus, Kui (Opposition) comes after Jiaren (Family Members). "When two women live together, their wills do not go together." This is why Yao "sent down his two daughters to Guirui" [to marry] Shun, to determine whether to abdicate to him, saying "I will test him." Thus, to see how one rules the empire, observe his family. To see how he rules his family, observe his personal life. When his personal life is proper, we say his mind is authentic. An authentic mind is simply one that turns away from activity that is not good. Activity that is not good is error. When error is turned around, there is no error. With no error, one is authentic. Thus, Wuwang (No Error) follows Fu (Return) and says, "The former kings vigorously nourished the myriad things according to the season." How profound!

33. WEALTH AND HONOR

The noble person takes agreement with the Way as honor, and personal peace as wealth. Therefore, he is always at peace, with nothing lacking. He regards ceremonial carriages and caps as small change; he regards gold and jade as dust. The weight [of his riches] cannot be exceeded.

34. BEING SUPERFICIAL

The Way of the Sages enters through the ear, is preserved in the mind/heart, is comprehended in one's moral behavior, and is enacted in one's affairs and undertakings. Those who engage merely in literary expression are superficial.

35. DELIBERATION AND DISCUSSION

Being perfectly authentic, one acts. Acting, one changes. Changing, one transforms. Thus, it is said, "Deliberate before speaking; discuss before acting. By such deliberation and discussion one can complete one's transformation."

36. PUNISHMENT

Heaven gives birth to the myriad things in the spring and ceases in the autumn. Not to cease after things have come alive and been completed would be going too far. Therefore, comes the autumn for completion. The sage models Heaven in governing and nourishing the myriad people. He regulates them with punishment. As the people flourish, their desires become active and their feelings overwhelming, and benefit and harm come into conflict. If not stopped, there would be injury and destruction and no more human relations. Therefore, they receive punishment to regulate [their behavior]. Feelings are unreliable [false] and obscure; they change in a thousand ways. They can only be regulated with centrality and correctness, clarity and intelligence, firmness and decisiveness. Song [Conflict, hexagram 6] says, "It is beneficial to see the great man," for "the firm [line] has gained the central position." Shihe [Biting Through, hexagram 21] says, "It is beneficial to use litigation" to "clarify through activity." Ah! Throughout the empire, those who control punishment direct the lives of the people. In appointing them to their position, can one not be careful?

37. BEING IMPARTIAL

The Way of the sage is perfectly impartial. Someone said, "What does that mean?" I replied, "Heaven and Earth are perfectly impartial."

38. CONFUCIUS (A)

The *Spring and Autumn* [*Annals*] rectifies the Kingly Way and clarifies the great models [of the past]. Confucius compiled it for the kings of later generations. The rebellious ministers and wicked sons who were put to death in the past are a means of arousing fear in those to come. It is fitting that for ten thousand generations without end, kings have sacrificed to Confucius to repay his inexhaustible virtue and achievement.

39. CONFUCIUS (B)

Confucius was the only one whose Way and virtue were lofty and abundant, whose educational influence was unlimited, and who could truly form a trinity with Heaven and Earth and be equal to the Four Seasons.

40. MENG [Ignorance, hexagram 4] AND GEN [Keeping Still, hexagram 52]

"The ignorant youth seeks me out," and I "correct" him and "determine his course of actions," as in divination. Divination is beseeching the spirits. [To ask] a second or third time is a violation. In that case, I make no pronouncement. "Below the mountain issues forth a spring"; still [mountain] and clear [water]. When disturbed, [the water] is mixed up; when mixed up, it is not clear. Be cautious! This means [to follow] the "timely mean"! "Keep the back still," for the back is not seen. When still, one can stop [at the right point]. To stop is not to act [deliberately]. To act [deliberately] is not to stop [at the right point]. This Way is profound!

[*Author's Note*] In the annotated translation below, the subsections of Zhou Dunyi's text, as arranged by Zhu Xi, are identified by bracketed lower-case letters. The additional comments added by Zhang Boxing, mostly taken from Zhu Xi's *Classified Conversations* (*Yulei*) but a few from his *Collected Papers* (*Wenji*), are numbered in brackets (not all are translated here). I also include a few additional comments taken from the *Yulei*, identified by bullet points. Zhang Boxing inserts one note at the beginning of each section, which I include here as a footnote. A few sections (26, 37, and 38) have no commentary, and five (24, 25, 28, 39, and 40) have no additional comments.

Commentary on the *Tongshu*
(*Tongshu zhu* 通書註),[9] by Zhu Xi

PART ONE

[*Zhu Xi's Preface*][10]

The *Tongshu* is a book written by Master Lianxi (Lianxi Fuzi 濂溪夫子). The Master's family name was Zhou 周, his personal name was Dunyi 惇頤,

---

9. This is the title given it by the editors of *Zhuzi quanshu* (2002), but in most editions it is simply entitled *Tongshu*.

10. This is called a postface in Zhu Xi's *Collected Papers* (*Wenji*, 81:3856) and *Zhou Dunyi ji* (Zhonghua shuju edition), but in *Zhou Lianxi ji* and *Zhuzi quanshu* (vol. 13) it is called and printed as a preface. Also, the frontispiece reproduced above (p. 205) of the twenty-seven-volume *Zhuzi quanshu* (2002) is a page from an edition printed between 1335 and 1340 showing this as the preface.

and his style name (*zi* 字) was Maoshu 茂叔.¹¹ From his youth he was well known to the generation for his learning and conduct, yet no one knows where his teaching tradition came from. It is only because the two Masters Cheng from Henan [Cheng Hao and Cheng Yi] got their learning from him and received the orthodox succession (*zheng tong* 正統) that had not been handed down since Confucius and Mencius that its origins can be inferred.¹² But how he was directed to what Confucius and Master Yan enjoyed [i.e., learning to be a sage]¹³ and came to be interested in "singing of the wind and moon"¹⁴ we also cannot entirely determine.

Many of the books he wrote have been scattered and lost, except for this one, originally called *Yitong* 易通 (Penetrating the *Yi*), which was issued together with the "Discussion of the Supreme Polarity Diagram"¹⁵ and handed down to posterity by the Chengs. In regard to his theory, [these texts] really complement each other. Generally speaking, they extend the differentiation and integration of the unitary principle (*li* 理), the two modes of psychophysical substance (*qi* 氣), and the Five Phases (*wuxing* 五行) systematically into the subtle and manifest [aspects] of the substance of the Way. They determine the choices involved in ethical behavior, literary expression, and material profit, thereby reinvigorating the low level of common scholarship. His discussions of the methods by which to enter into virtue and the tools by which to manage the world are both cogent and terse; they are not empty words. His broad principles and general applications are unmatched by any scholars since the Qin and Han [dynasties, 221 BCE–220 CE]; likewise, the thoroughness of his reasoning and the profundity of his ideas are beyond what recent scholars have been able to glimpse.

---

11. This sentence is missing in *Zhuzi quanshu* (2002), vol. 13: 95. Zhu Xi here uses a different character (惇) for Dun than is normally used (敦).

12. Zhu Xi's use of the term *zheng tong* here is another example of his challenge to imperial moral authority. *Zheng tong* was traditionally used in reference to the legitimate succession of dynasties receiving the Mandate of Heaven. See chapter 2, notes 27 and 45.

13. Master Yan is Yan Hui, aka Yan Yuan. See sections 10, 23, and 29 below.

14. "*Yinfeng nongyue* 吟風弄月." According to Hu Hong in his Preface to the *Tongshu* (translated in chapter 1), Cheng Hao used this phrase about Zhou Dunyi. See also Zhu Xi, *Yi-Luo yuan-yuan lu*, ch. 1, and *Henan Chengshi yishu* (*Er Cheng ji* ed.), 3:59, where it is not attributed to either brother specifically. It became a standard characterization of Zhou Dunyi.

15. I.e., the *Taijitu* and *Taijitu shuo* were originally appended to the end of the *Tongshu* (see below).

Therefore, when the Cheng brothers died, there were few who transmitted [his teachings]. Those who knew them could only consider his purposes lofty and distant. In my early years, I was fortunate to receive his bequeathed writings and tried to read them. At first I did not understand at all what he was saying. Worse yet, I could not even punctuate them. In my thirties I had the opportunity to go study with Teacher Yanping 延平先生 [Li Tong 李侗], and then I began to learn about 10 to 20 percent of [Zhou's] theory. In recent years, after delving into it for a long time, I have gotten it, if only roughly. Although I do not presume to understand the broad principles and general applications, nevertheless within the words and sentences of the text one can really see the surpassing thoroughness of his reasoning and the surpassing profundity of his ideas, which will not delude us.

Since I first read this until the present, how many years and months has it been? Suddenly it is more than three decades. I regret the increasing distance from the former philosopher, and I fear that his marvelous ideas will not be transmitted. Without regard for my limitations, I have quickly done a commentary. Although my knowledge is common and shallow and inadequate to bring out the Master's intricacies, nevertheless I have begun to penetrate the general meaning, so that later gentlemen may chance to do better.

> Respectfully recorded by the later scholar Zhu Xi, on the *jia-chen* 甲辰 day of the ninth month of the *ding-wei* 丁未 year of the Chunxi 淳熙 reign [1187].[16]

---

16. [Zhang Boxing's note: This preface was the last thing written by Master Hui'an (Zhu Xi) in his collected commentary on the *Tongshu*. No one has determined in what year the Teacher first collected the *Tongshu*. In his postface the Teacher says: "The Changsha edition was the last to appear, and so that is the one I have compiled. I have examined the other editions in the most careful detail, but they seem to be incomplete. . . ." In the *ji-chou* year of the Qiandao period (1169) he revised the old text; this is the Jian'an edition. Up to the *ji-hai* year of the Chunxi period (1179), for a total of eleven years, he went back and added still more corrections; this is the Nankang edition. In another eight years, in the *ding-wei* year (1187), he redid the commentary, and this compilation was first arranged. The present edition takes only that one as correct, and this preface was placed specially at its head. Several colophons are placed at the end.]

The colophons include those by Hu Hong (translated in chapter 2), Qi Kuan (discussed in the Introduction to Part II), and Zhang Shi, plus Zhu Xi's comparison of the Zhou family edition he received in 1179 with Li Tong's edition and Cheng Yi's "Essay on what Master Yan loved to learn" (*Zhou Lianxi ji* 7:1a–5b).

[*Zhou Dunyi's text and Zhu Xi's published commentary*]

1. BEING AUTHENTIC (A) (*Cheng shang* 誠上)[17]

[a] Being authentic (*cheng* 誠) is the foundation of the sage (*shengren* 聖人).

> "Being authentic" means being perfectly actualized/real (*shi* 實) and without error; it is the correct principle/order (*li* 理) that Heaven bestows and things receive. All people have it, yet what makes the sage a sage is nothing other than the fact that he alone is able to complete it. This book and the Supreme Polarity Diagram complement each other. "Being authentic" is the same as what is called [in the Diagram] the Supreme Polarity.[18]

[b] "Great indeed is the originating [power] of Qian 乾! The myriad things rely on it for their beginnings."[19] It is the source of being authentic.

> The two sentences above explain it [being authentic] in reference to the *Yi*. "Qian" [hexagram 1] is the pure *yang* hexagram. Its meaning is vigor. It is another name for the virtue/power (*de* 德)[20] of Heaven. "The originating" means the beginning. To "rely on" means to take. This refers

---

17. [Zhang Boxing: This section discusses the Supreme Polarity (*taiji*) as actualized principle (*shi li* 實理), originating in Heaven and bestowed upon human beings; the great source of human nature and endowment (*xing ming* 性命).]

18. The connection between the originating power of Qian and authenticity is their *creativity*. Being authentic means to actualize one's moral nature, i.e., to "create" oneself as a fully human being. For the connection between being "real" or "solid" and "without error," see Zhu's commentary on *Taijitu shuo,* sections B (additional comment 10) and E (commentary). Cheng Yi's comment on the *Wu-wang* (No error) hexagram of the *Yijing* (#25) is, "Having no error is being perfectly authentic" (*Yichuan Yizhuan* [*Er Cheng ji* ed.], 822).

19. *Yijing, Tuan* commentary on hexagram 1 (Qian). See Zhu Xi, *Zhouyi benyi* (The Original Meaning of the *Scripture of Change*), 1:3a.

20. In most cases the term *virtue* will be used to translate *de*. However, it should be borne in mind that the connotation is not strictly moral, but also includes the specific power that characterizes a thing (similar to the Latin *virtus*). Thus, the "Four Virtues" of the hexagram Qian (see 1f below) are the four essential characteristics of Qian.

to the originating [power] of the way of Qian. It is what the myriad things take as their beginning. The actualized order (*shi li* 實理) flows out to be bestowed as the foundation of the human being, like water's having a source. It is the same as the "activity of *yang*" in the [*Taiji*] Diagram.[21]

[c] "The way of Qian transforms and each receives its correct nature (*xing* 性) and endowment (*ming* 命)."[22] In this way authenticity is established.

The above sentence is also from the text of the *Yi*. What Heaven bestows is "endowment"; what things receive is their "nature." This says that if the myriad things each receive their endowment correctly through the transformation of the way of Qian, then the actualized order is there as the ruler of each individual thing. This is the same as the Diagram's [term] "stillness of *yin*."[23]

[d] Being "pure and flawless"[24] it is perfectly good.

"Pure" means unadulterated. "Flawless" means without fault. This says that what Heaven bestows and things receive are in all cases the fundamental nature of the actualized order, containing no adulterations of evil.

[e] Thus: "The alternation of *yin* and *yang* is called the Way. That which issues from it is good. That which completes [constitutes] it is human nature."[25]

This is also from the text of the *Yi*. "*Yin* and *yang*" are *qi*, that which is within form [i.e., physical]. That by which there is "alternation of *yin*

---

21. The fact that *li* is frequently said to "flow out" (here *liu chu* 流出, but sometimes *liu xing* 流行) shows that *li* is not static pattern or principle, but rather the dynamic patterning or ordering of things as they come into being and continue to change.
22. *Yijing*, *Tuan* commentary on hexagram 1 (*Zhouyi benyi* 1:3a).
23. "Ruler" (*zhu*) in the sense of a ruling principle.
24. *Yijing*, *Wenyan* commentary on hexagram 1 (*Zhouyi benyi*, 1:7b).
25. *Yijing*, *Xici* A.5.1 (*Zhouyi benyi*, 3:5a).

and *yang*" is *li* (principle/order), which is above form [i.e., metaphysical]. The "Way" means the same as principle/order. "That which issues from it" means when *qi* appears but there is nothing yet constituted [i.e., no particular things yet formed]. "Good," then, is a name for when the order is in operation but there is nothing yet established. This falls under the category of *yang*; it is the source of being authentic. When "completed," things are already constituted; in "human nature" the order is already established. This falls under the category of *yin*; it is the establishment of being authentic.

[f] *Yuan* 元 and *heng* 亨 are the penetrating [quality] of authenticity. *Li* 利 and *zhen* 貞 are the recovery of authenticity.[26]

"*Yuan*" is originating, "*heng*" is penetrating, "*li*" is carrying out, "*zhen*" is being correct: the Four Virtues [characteristic powers] of Qian. "Penetrating" (*tong* 通) is just at the point when it appears and is bestowed on things, the "issuing" of goodness.[27] "Recovery" (*fu* 復) is when each one receives it and stores it within, the "completion" of its nature. In the Diagram this is the nature of the Five Phases.

[g] Great indeed is change, the source of human nature and endowment!

"Change" (*yi* 易) is the term for interchange and substitution. The hexagrams and lines are established merely from this. The interchange of *yin* and *yang* within Heaven-and-earth, and the alternation of bestowing and receiving in the flow of the actualized order in its midst, are also like this.[28]

---

26. "*Yuan heng li zhen*" is the complete text of hexagram 1 (Qian) of the *Yijing*. It is usually parsed as subject-predicate subject-predicate, but the four terms are also called the "four virtues" of Qian. For a good discussion see Shchutskii, *Researches on the I Ching*, 136–47 (Shchutskii thinks that the four terms are archaic mantic formulas whose original meanings were lost).

27. For this and the next sentence, cf. the previous passage.

28. Zhu's point here is that the fundamental nature of things is inherent in their transformative processes; ontology is inherent in cosmology.

[*Zhu Xi's additional comments*]

[1] Without the *Tongshu*, how could Master Zhou teach others how to understand the Supreme Polarity Diagram that he bequeathed? Therefore, the Diagram was first clarified by the *Tongshu*.

[2] The first half of the *Tongshu* explains the "Discussion of the Supreme Polarity [Diagram]." This moral ordering [proceeds] from one to two and from two to five. For example, "In being authentic there is no acting" [one]; "In incipience there is good and evil" [two]; and the [five] "Virtues" [in sections 2 and 3] readily correspond with the Supreme Polarity, *yin* and *yang*, and the Five Phases. One must see these details.[29]

[4] *Question on* "Being authentic is the foundation of the sage." *Reply*: This refers to the basis of ability. That by which the sage is a sage is simply by being authentic.[30]

[5] *Someone asked* about Mr. Lü [Dalin 呂大臨]'s statement, "Being authentic is the actuality (*shiran*) of order/principle."[31] *Reply*: In a word, being authentic is being actualized (*shi*). This is how Mr. Lü discusses it. It is the same as Master Zhou's saying, "Being authentic is the foundation of the sage," which refers to the actualized order. For example, Master Zhou's saying, "Being a sage is nothing more than being authentic," is the same as what the *Zhongyong* [Centrality and commonality] calls "the most perfectly authentic one under Heaven." This means that the person actually possesses this order. What Wengong 文公 [Sima Guang 司馬光] said about being authentic is the same idea as what the *Daxue* says about being authentic: it means that the person actualizes his mind/heart and does not delude himself.

[9] *Question about* "The alternation of *yin* and *yang* is called the Way. That which issues from it is good. That which fulfills/constitutes it is human nature." *Reply*: "The alternation of *yin* and *yang*" is the principle/order of Heaven-and-earth. It is like "Great indeed is the originating power of Qian! The myriad things rely on it for their beginnings." "That which issues from it is good" means "the Way of

---

29. *Yulei* 94:3144.
30. *Yulei* 94:3144.
31. In Huang and Quan, *Song-Yuan xue'an*, 31:16a (p. 536). Lü Dalin (1046–1092) was a student of Zhang Zai and the Cheng brothers whom Zhu Xi greatly admired.

Qian transforms and each receives its correct nature and endowment." "That which completes it is human nature." This section is a discussion of the idea that Heaven-and-earth bring into being the myriad things.

[. . . .]

[11] "The alternation of *yin* and *yang* are called the Way" is the Supreme Polarity. "That which issues from it is good" is simply the idea of "generating and regenerating" (*sheng sheng* 生生), which falls under the category of *yang*. "That which completes it is human nature" is the idea that "each receives its correct nature and endowment," which falls under the category of *yin*. . . .

[19] *Zhiqing* 直卿 [Huang Gan 黃幹][32] *asked about* "*Li* and *zhen* are the recovery of authenticity," giving the example of the Teacher's comment below that "'recovery' is like storing away." *The Teacher replied:* "Recovery" is just coming back. This is a sentence that Master Zhou added. Confucius [in the *Xici* 繫辭] merely said, "The transformation of the way of Qian [is how] each [thing receives] its correct nature and endowment."[33]

[. . . .]

[*Zhou Dunyi's text and Zhu Xi's published commentary*]

2. BEING AUTHENTIC (B) (*Cheng xia* 誠下)[34]

[a] Being a sage is nothing more than being authentic.

> That by which the sage is a sage is no more than his completing the actualized order. This is the same as what is called [in the Diagram] the Supreme Polarity.[35]

---

32. Huang Gan (1152–1221) was one of Zhu Xi's leading pupils and his son-in-law.

33. *Yulei* 94:3147.

34. [Zhang: This section discusses the sage's completion of this actualized order, which is the foundation of the Five Constants and the Hundred Practices.]

35. This is a case of Zhu Xi stretching the meaning of Zhou Dunyi's text, in part to account for the fact that *taiji* occurs only once in the *Tongshu* and *cheng* is not found in the *Taijitu shuo*. In a broad sense, however, since Zhu's definitions of *taiji* and *cheng* are both more or less synonymous with *li* (the former more than the latter), there is a certain validity to the equation.

[b] Being authentic is the foundation of the Five Constant [Virtues] and the source of the Hundred Practices.[36]

> The "Five Constants" are humanity, rightness, propriety, wisdom, and faithfulness. They are the natures of the Five Phases. The "Hundred Practices" are being filial, being fraternal, being loyal, being compliant, etc. They are the images of the myriad things.[37] When one has completed the actualized order, then the Five Constants are not deficient and the Hundred Practices are cultivated.

[c] It is imperceptible[38] when [one is] still, and perceptible[39] when one is active; perfectly correct [in stillness] and clearly pervading [in activity].

> At the *yin* point of stillness, authenticity is certainly never nonexistent; we merely call it imperceptible because it is unformed. [Likewise,] it is not that authenticity exists only after reaching the *yang* point of activity; we simply call it perceptible because it can be perceived. [But even] when still and imperceptible it is perfectly correct. Only after it is active and perceptible can its clarity and penetration be perceived.[40]

[d] When the Five Constants and Hundred Practices are not authentic, they are wrong, blocked by depravity and confusion.

> If not authentic, the Five Constants and Hundred Practices all lack actuality/reality. This is what is meant by "without authenticity there would be nothing."[41] In stillness to be incorrect is to be "depraved." In activity to be "unclear and unpenetrating" is to be "confused" and "obstructed."

---

36. The "Five Constants" are Mencius's four basic virtues plus faithfulness/honesty (*xin*). The "hundred practices" simply means all moral behavior.
37. Note again the parallel with the *Taijitu shuo*.
38. *Wu*, lit. "nonexistent."
39. *You*, lit. "existent."
40. This is the first appearance in the *Tongshu* of the stillness-activity dyad.
41. *Zhongyong* 25 (*Zhongyong zhangju*, 17b).

[e] Therefore one who is authentic has no [need for] undertakings (*shi* 事).

> Being authentic, the multitude of principles are naturally at the ready (*bei* 備). Without depending on effort or thinking, one easily complies with the Way of the Mean.[42]

[f] [Being authentic is] perfectly easy, yet difficult to practice.

> Since the actualized order is natural, it is "easy." Since human artificiality counterfeits it, it is "difficult."

[g] When one is determined and precise, there is no difficulty with it.

> To be "determined" is the decisiveness of *yang*. To be "precise" is the preservation of *yin*. With the courage of decisiveness and the certainty of protection, human artificiality cannot counterfeit it.

[h] Therefore [Confucius said], "If in one day one could subdue the self and return to propriety, then all under Heaven would recover their humanity."[43]

> To subdue and cast out egotism and return to follow the natural [Heavenly] order is the most difficult thing in the world. However, the opportunity can be decided in one day, and it can be followed to the point of all under Heaven recovering their humanity. Being determined and precise is as easy as this.

> [*Zhu Xi's additional comments*]
>
> [1] *Question* on "Being authentic is the foundation of the Five Constants." *Reply*: Being authentic is to penetrate the foundation.[44]
>
> [2] The second section on being authentic discusses the Supreme Polarity being present in human beings.[45]

---

42. Paraphrasing *Zhongyong* 20: "He who is authentic hits the Mean without effort, apprehends without thinking, and easily complies with the Way of the Mean. This is a sage" (*Zhongyong zhangju*, 15a).
43. *Analects* 12:1.
44. *Yulei* 94:3148.
45. *Yulei* 94:3149.

[3] *Question on* "Being authentic is the foundation of the Five Constant [Virtues]." Is this the same as this actualized order, which can be subdivided into the functions of these five? *Reply*: Yes.[46]

[. . . .]

[*Zhou Dunyi's text and Zhu Xi's published commentary*]

3. AUTHENTICITY, INCIPIENCE, AND VIRTUE (*Cheng ji de* 誠幾德)[47]

[a] In being authentic there is no [intentional] acting (*wuwei* 無為).

> The actualized order is natural (*ziran* 自然). How can there be any [intentional] acting? It is the same as the Supreme Polarity.[48]

[b] In incipience (*ji* 幾) there is good and evil.[49]

> Incipience is the imperceptible [beginning] of activity. It is that according to which good and evil are differentiated (*fen* 分). For at the imperceptible [beginning] of activity in the human mind/heart, the natural order (*tianli* 天理) will certainly be found right there; yet human desires (*renyu* 人欲) will also have sprouted within it. This is an image of *yin* and *yang*.

[c] As for the [Five Constant] Virtues, loving is called humanity (*ren* 仁), being appropriate is called rightness (*yi* 義), being ordered/principled (*li* 理)

---

46. *Yulei* 94:3149.

47. [Zhang: This section uses authenticity, incipience, and virtue to clarify the sequence of entering the Way, which is the path set out upon together by sages, worthies, and the spiritual.]

48. Note that Zhu Xi here embraces, or perhaps co-opts, the Daoist term *wuwei* by using another term from the *Laozi, ziran* (natural, spontaneous).

49. An alternative translation would be "[In authenticity there is] incipient good and evil." Again, I am following Zhu Xi's interpretation. In his comments (below), he consistently treats *ji* (incipience) as an independent subject, never an adjective, and never connecting it grammatically with the *cheng* (authenticity) of the previous line, as Wing-tsit Chan does (*Source Book*, 466).

is called ritual propriety (*li* 禮), being penetrating is called wisdom (*zhi* 智), and preserving is called honesty (*xin* 信).

> The Way apprehended by the mind/heart[50] is called "virtue." In its differentiation (*bie* 別) there are the applications (*yong* 用) of these five [virtues], and we name their substances (*ti* 體) accordingly. They are precisely the natures of the Five Phases.[51]

[d] One who is by nature like this, at ease like this, is called a sage.

> The "nature" is obtained alone from Heaven. "At ease" means originally complete in the self. "Sage" is a designation for one who has enlarged and transformed it [the self]. This is one whose authenticity is entirely established, whose incipiencies are all clear, and whose virtues are complete, all without depending on study and effort.[52]

[e] One who recovers it and holds onto it is called a worthy.

> "Recover" means to come back and reach for it. "Hold onto" means to protect and support it. "Worthy" is a designation for one whose talent and virtue surpass others. This is one who thinks about being authentic and looks into incipiencies in order to fulfill his virtue and to have the means to preserve it.

[f] One whose subtle signs of expression (*fa* 發) are imperceptible, and whose fullness is inexhaustible, is called spiritual (*shen* 神).

> When one's subtle signs of expression are mysterious and imperceptible, and one's fullness is all-encompassing and inexhaustible, then that is the mysterious functioning and unknowability of the sage.

---

50. Some editions have "body/self" (*shen* 身) instead of "mind/heart."
51. I.e., they elucidate the discussion of the Five Phases in the *Taijitu shuo*.
52. I.e., the sage transforms himself effortlessly.

[*Zhu Xi's additional comments*]

[2] [In the sentence] "In being authentic there is no acting," "being authentic" is the actualized order and "no acting" is like [the term] "silently inactive (*jiran budong* 寂然不動)."[53] The actualized order must connect activity and stillness, yet its fundamental substance is without activity. [In the sentence] "In incipience there is good and evil," "incipience" is the first subtle sign of activity. With activity (*dong* 動) there is [intentional] acting (*wei* 為), and good and evil take shape. In being authentic there is no acting, so it is simply good. Since in activity there is acting, there is good and there is evil.[54]

[3] *Zeng* 曾 asked about "In being authentic there is no acting; in incipience there is good and evil." *Reply*: Being authentic is actualized order. There is nothing that is done. It is just [what is meant by] "What Heaven endows is called the nature," and "When pleasure, anger, pity, and joy are not yet expressed is called centrality (*zhong* 中)."[55] Incipience is the first subtle [indication], the subtle beginning of activity. Right and wrong, good and evil, are perceivable in this. At the arising of a thought, if it is not good, then it is evil. As Mencius said, "The Way is twofold: either humane or not humane, that's all."[56] Virtue comprises nothing more than these five: humanity, rightness, propriety, wisdom, and honesty are the substance of virtue. Love, appropriateness, order, penetration, and protection are functions of virtue.[57]

---

53. *Xici* A.10.4; see chapter 3 above and section 4 below.

54. *Yulei* 94:3149. In other words, the good-evil distinction applies only to *intentional* activity. One could argue that this implies that the moral quality of an action is determined by its motivation or intentionality, which is the Mahayana Buddhist position (i.e., good intentional actions are those that are motivated by compassion; see Keown, *The Nature of Buddhist Ethics*, 178). But this is a direction not taken by Zhu Xi, who believes that a good act is one that is consistent with the objectively existing natural/moral order (*tianli* / *daoli*).

55. *Zhongyong* 1. What Zhu means here is that being authentic is simply the effortless expression of one's inborn nature, in harmony with the still center of one's being.

56. *Mencius* 4A.2.

57. *Yulei* 94:3149–50.

[4] As for Lianxi's statement, "In being authentic there is no acting; in incipience there is good and evil," once there is authenticity and then practice (*xing*), what was nothing happening (*wu shi* 無事) is now the incipient distinction between good and evil.[58] At that moment, one must exhaustively examine [oneself] to recognize right from wrong. At first there will be tiny, brief, subtle indications. When one has exhaustively examined oneself for a long time, one will gradually see their full extent. Naturally, there will be gaps in the moral order here. These determine the incipient, subtle indications and differentiate good and evil. If one can analyze it in this way, then things will be investigated and knowledge perfected. With knowledge perfected, intentions will be made sincere. With intentions sincere, the mind/heart will be rectified, the self will be cultivated, the family will be regulated, the state will be well governed, and all under Heaven will be at peace. It will be like a torrent of water, beyond one's own capacity, or like [General] Tian Dan's 田單 tactic of fastening torches to oxen to make them unstoppable.[59]

[5] *Daofu* 道夫[60] *said*: Being authentic is the actualized order of nature; it does not depend on effort. At the point of incipient activity, good and evil become manifest. What is authentic about goodness, then, is the Five Constant Virtues.[61] The Sage does not need to avail himself of cultivating activity; he quietly completes it. The worthy requires an effort to "overcome [the self] and return [to ritual propriety]."[62] Although the worthy must wait and the sage is simply born [with the capacity], nevertheless as far as their achievement goes they are the same. Therefore, it says, "One whose subtle signs of expression are imperceptible, and whose fullness is inexhaustible, is called spiritual."

---

58. Punctuating differently than the editors of the *Zhuzi quanshu* edition.

59. *Yulei* 94:3150. Referring to a general of the state of Qi during the Warring States period. In 285 BCE he saved the royal house of Qi by driving back an invasion by the state of Yan. See Sima Qian, *Shiji* (Historical Records), ch. 82.

60. Yang Daofu studied with Zhu Xi beginning around 1189. See Chan Wing-tsit, *Zhuzi menren*, 272–73.

61. In the *Yulei* this sentence begins, "What is achieved (*cheng*) by goodness. . . ."

62. Allusion to *Lunyu* 12:1 ("Yan Yuan [Hui] asked about humanity. The Master said, 'To overcome the self and return to ritual propriety is humanity'").

Reply: Certainly it is like this. But incipience is the subtle indication of activity. It is the interval between wanting to act and being about to act. Since there is good and evil [here], one must understand them at this point. If one waits until the expression is already manifest, then one will not be able to regulate one's undertakings; how can this produce understanding? This is why the sage and the worthy say, "[The noble person (*junzi*) is] cautious over what he does not see and apprehensive over what he does not hear."[63] The point of subtle incipience is extremely important.[64]

[6] *Question* on the section, "In being authentic there is no acting; in incipience there is good and evil." Can this be regarded as complementary to the Discussion of the Supreme Polarity Diagram? *Reply*: Yes. Master Zhou's writing all discusses this moral order (*daoli* 道理). [The questioner] then referred to the section "When pleasure, anger, pity, and joy are not yet expressed is called equilibrium" and the section "Mind/heart is unitary."[65] The Masters Cheng continued Master Zhou's school (*pai* 派); did they both clarify the centrality of the Supreme Polarity? *Reply*: Yes.[66] *Question*: They both discussed the moral order in this way. Is this how moral effort (*gongfu* 工夫) must nourish the unexpressed [mind/heart]? *Reply*: There is moral effort for the unexpressed (*weifa* 未發), and there is also moral effort to be applied to the already expressed (*yifa* 已發). If the already expressed is not looked after or not understood, one will be wrong. It is just that there should be priorities in time (*xian hou* 先後) and importance (*qing zhong* 輕重) between the efforts on the unexpressed and on the expressed.[67]

---

63. *Zhongyong* 1 (trans. Chan, *Source Book*, 98, slightly modified). The worthy is Zisi, Confucius's grandson, the reputed author of the text. The Sage is presumably Confucius, since Zhu Xi believed that the text contained Confucius's ideas and sayings as transmitted by Zisi.

64. *Yulei* 94:3150.

65. Cheng Yi uses the second phrase in his discussion of the first phrase (from *Zhongyong* 1) in *Cui yan* (Choice sayings) (*Er Cheng ji* ed.), 1:1183.

66. Zhu makes this claim despite the fact that *taiji* does not appear once in the writings or conversations of the Cheng brothers; see chapter 2 above.

67. *Yulei* 94:3150–51. *Jifa* 既發 (already expressed) is synonymous with *yifa*. Zhu probably means that one must first nourish the unexpressed mind, and should consider it more important (*zhong*), because it is the basis for its expressed phase.

[7] "In being authentic there is no acting" just means constantly preserving this actualized order right here [within oneself]. When one can first perceive incipient [activity], i.e., when one can first recognize good and evil, if this mind/heart is let go and not preserved then it has been turned upside down. How can it distinguish good and evil?

[8] *Someone mentioned* [Cai] Jitong's 蔡季通[68] statement: "The *Tongshu* says, 'In being authentic there is no acting; in incipience there is good and evil.' The [Discussion] of the Supreme Polarity [Diagram] says, 'Only human beings receive the finest and most numinous [*qi*]. With physical form they are born, and their spirit produces understanding. Their fivefold nature is stimulated to activity, and good and evil are distinguished.' These two statements are like the two sides [of a coin]. But since he says 'no acting,' how can there be good and evil incipiencies? I fear that this is a point that Master Zhou has failed to consider." What about this? *Reply*: At the time of "silent inactivity," of course, authenticity has no acting. When there is stimulation and activity, then there is good and evil. Incipience is the point of activity. In general, human nature cannot be inactive; you just need to leave it as it is [allow it to manifest itself authentically]. When the point of activity is left as it is, then the virtue of love is called humanity, and [the virtue] of rightness is called appropriateness. When it is not left as it is, then it is totally reversed. How can human nature be inactive? It is just that we must differentiate within it the natural [Heavenly] order and human desires.[69]

---

68. Cai Yuanding (1135–1198), Zhu's disciple and occasional collaborator (e.g., on the *Yixue qimeng* [Introduction to the Study of the *Yi*]).

69. *Yulei* 94:3151. Zhu's point here is that evil tendencies are not inherent in human nature (following Mencius), so that theoretically one could allow incipient action to express itself naturally. The statement that "human nature cannot be inactive" alludes to a complex discussion of good and evil in Zhu's "Treatise on Cheng Hao's Discourse on the Nature" (*Mingdao lun xing shuo*, in *Wenji* 67: 3275–76; or *Sibu beiyao* ed., 67:16b–18a; cf. Chan, *Source Book*, 597–600). Zhu agrees with Cheng Hao's claim that "Good and evil in the world are both the Principle of Nature [what I am translating here as "natural order"]. What is called evil is not original evil. It becomes evil only because of deviation from the mean" (Chan, 598). This is what Zhu means by action being "appropriate" to its circumstances. When action is appropriate, or accords with the moral nature, it is *ordered*, or consonant with the natural order.

[9] *Zhao Zhidao* 趙致道 *asked*: Master Zhou said, "In being authentic there is no acting; in incipience there is good and evil." This clarifies the unexpressed substance of the human mind/heart, and refers to the beginnings of its expressed phase. He probably wanted students to extend their [self-]examination to the subtle signs of germinal activity, to understand how to decide which to extirpate and which to adopt, so as not to lose [contact with] the original substance. Some think this is similar to Master Hu's [Hu Hong's] phrase, "same substance, different function."[70] So, in my confusion I attempted to plot this in the following diagrams:

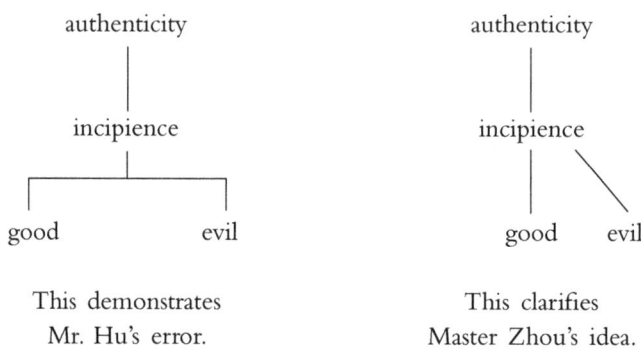

This demonstrates Mr. Hu's error.

This clarifies Master Zhou's idea.

Although good and evil are [equal and] opposite [in Hu's theory], they must be differentiated as servant and master. Although the natural order and human desire are different branches (*pai* 派), it is necessary to see them as legitimate (*zong* 宗) and illegitimat (*nie* 孽).[71] [However, as in Zhou's theory,] the movement from authentic activity to goodness is like a tree [growing] from root to trunk and from trunk to branch. The continuity from top to bottom is the manifestation of the moral mind/heart (*daoxin* 道心), or the outflowing of the natural order, which is the fundamental master of

---

70. Hu Hong (1100–1155), *Zhi yan* (On Understanding Words), in *Hu Hong ji,* 9; or *Sibu beiyao* ed., 1:5b.

71. "Branches" (*fenpai*), "legitimate" (*zong*), and "illegitimate" (*nie*) are family lineage terms.

this mind/heart and the legitimate descent-line (*zheng zong* 正宗) of authenticity. If it flowers off to the side like a parasitic growth, then although it may still be authentic activity, it is the manifestation of the human mind/heart (*renxin* 人心) and the outflowing of selfish desire, which is considered evil. It rejects what the mind/heart originally possesses in favor of a temporary lodger. It rejects the legitimate origin of authenticity in favor of the illegitimate. If you differentiate them late, then your selection will not be pure. Then the guest might take advantage of the host, and the illegitimate son might usurp the [legitimate] descent-line.

Students should be able to examine what accords with and what opposes [the natural order] between [the moments of] incipient subtlety and germinal activity. What comes out straight [i.e., as true, direct expression of authenticity and human nature] is the natural order; what comes out deviant is human desire. What comes out straight is good; what comes out deviant is evil. What comes out straight is one's original possession; what comes out deviant is not one's true offspring. What comes out straight is rooted [in one's nature]; what comes out deviant lacks a source. What comes out straight is compliant; what comes out deviant is contrary. What comes out straight is correct; what comes out deviant is perverse.

We should positively guide what comes out straight, and extinguish what comes out deviant. When this effort is perfected, then the expression of our mind/heart will spontaneously come out on course, and will ensure our possession of Heaven's decree. In this way we can see that before the unexpressed [phase of mind/heart] there is goodness but no evil. As the Masters Cheng said, "It is not the case that within human nature there originally are these two things [good and evil] in mutual opposition at birth." They also said, "Generally speaking, in every case of good and evil, first there is good and then there is evil."[72] I suppose this expresses it.

---

72. *Henan Chengshi yishu* 1 and 22A (*Er Cheng ji,* 10 and 292). In this text the first quote is not attributed to either brother specifically, but in the *Jinsilu* (*Reflections on Things at Hand,* trans. Chan, 19–20) Zhu Xi attributes it to Cheng Hao. The second quote is identified in the text as Cheng Yi's.

If we considered good and evil to be mutually opposed things, one vying with the other [as in the diagram of Hu's idea], then this would be the natural order and human desires appearing together from the same source (*tongchu yiyuan* 同出一源). The prior, unexpressed [phase of mind/heart] would already contain these two beginnings (*duan* 端), and "What Heaven endows is called human nature" [*Zhongyong* 1] would refer to something very dirty and impure. This is Mr. Hu's idea of "same substance, different function."

The Teacher replied: This explanation has got it.[73]

[. . . .]

[11] *Renjie* 人傑 *asked:*[74] [Cai] Jitong said: In the section, "In being authentic there is no acting; in incipience there is good and evil; among the virtues, loving is called humanity . . . ," Master Zhou failed to fully consider this: Since he says "In being authentic there is no acting," then how can he follow that with the words "good and evil"? *Reply:* Zhengchun 正淳, how do you see that? *Renjie said:* Since in being authentic there is no acting, I suspect that there is never any evil. How can the incipiencies of the learner's mind/heart be without evil? *Reply:* When it is not yet stimulated, the fivefold nature is completely contained [in the mind/heart]. How can there be anything but good? When it responds to events, then there is a point where attention doesn't reach, and this is evil. The sages and worthies of antiquity were constantly on guard lest before their lives were over their correctness would become like this. Master Yan was like this; he was "never unaware of what was not good [in himself]."[75]

[12] Some take good and evil as the distinction between male and female. Others take it as *yin* and *yang*. In general, any discussion of two mutually opposed things is about the principle of *yin* and *yang*. In terms of the distinction of *yin* and *yang*, we may speak of good

---

73. This rather lengthy "question," including the diagrams, is taken from a letter from Zhao Zhidao to Zhu Xi (*Wenji* 59:2863). For Zhao Zhidao see Chan Wing-tsit, *Zhuzi menren*, 293.

74. For Wan Renjie (Zhengchun) 萬人傑 (正淳) see Chan, *Zhuzi menren*, 248–49.

75. *Yulei* 94:3151, quoting Xu Gan 徐幹 (170–217), *Zhong Lun* 中論 (Balanced essays), 4:1.

and evil and we may speak of male and female; it depends on how one is using it. Therefore, good and evil can refer to *yin* and *yang* and can also refer to male and female.[76]

[13] [Concerning the passage:] "Of the virtues, loving is called humanity . . . preserving is called honesty." The virtues are what human beings obtain in their minds/hearts.[77] Loving (*ai* 愛), being right (*yi* 宜), being ordered (*li* 理), being penetrating (*tong* 通), and preserving (*shou* 守) are the functions of virtue. Humanity, rightness, propriety, wisdom, and honesty are the substances of virtue. Being ordered means having pattern (*you tiaoli* 有條理). Being penetrating means having full comprehension (*tongda* 通達). Preserving means being reliable (*queshi* 確實). These three sentences refer to to the human body/self (*shen* 身). Being authentic is the nature; incipience is feeling. The virtues refer to the combination of the nature and the feelings.[78]

[15] *Question* [about Zhu's comment on d above]: "The nature is what is obtained alone from Heaven." How can you say "obtained alone" (*du de* 獨得)?[79] *Reply*: This says that the sage completely embodies the clearest [*qi*], with no deficiency. This is what the sage alone obtains, as opposed to [the "worthy" who] "recovers" [it]. One who "recovers" has already lost it and returns to the beginning. This is not the same as the sage's obtaining it alone. [Similarly,] the word "at ease" (*an* 安) is opposed to the word "holds onto." To hold onto is to grasp; ease is spontaneous. In general Master Zhou's words are extremely well suited for designating what is important and unimportant. *Follow-up question:* Was Master Zhou's learning obtained by himself in his heart/mind? Or was there something transmitted [from a teacher]? *Reply*: There must have been something transmitted. He was Lu Shen's

---

76. *Yulei* 94:3152. There is of course a vast literature on Confucian conceptions of gender. For a brief account and further references see Adler, "Daughter/Wife/Mother."

77. *Yulei* has "body/self" (*shen* 身) instead of "mind/heart."

78. *Yulei* 94:3152. Incipient mental activity is feeling/disposition (*qing* 情) because it involves the psychophysical functioning of the mind.

79. The reason for the question is that, according to Mencian theory, human nature is possessed equally by all.

陸詵 son-in-law. Wengong's [Sima Guang's] "Record of the Sou River" contains Lu Shen's affairs. He was a sincere and generous man.[80]

[16] "One whose subtle signs of expression are imperceptible, and whose fullness is inexhaustible, is called spiritual." This says that his expression is subtle, mysterious, and imperceptible. His capacity is full to the brim and inexhaustible. "Expression" and "fullness" are what can be seen by others. For example, "one who is by nature like this, at ease like this," and "one who recovers it and holds onto it" both mean that the person is like this. "One whose subtle signs of expression are imperceptible and whose fullness is inexhaustible" means that in principle one is like this. "Spiritual" simply means the doings of a sage; it is not that there is a spirit apart from the sage, occupying another space.[81]

[18] *Question*: The *Tongshu* mentions "spiritual" five times.[82] Are the meanings the same? *Reply*: They must accord with what you see there.[83] *Question*: Does "spiritual" simply refer to the mysterious? *Reply*: Yes. There is also [the line in section 4] "That which is 'penetrating when stimulated'[84] is spiritual." Hengqu 橫渠 [Zhang Zai 張載] said, "The unity [of a thing] makes it spiritual; its duality makes it unfathomable."[85] Referring to creative transformation we say, "suddenly here, suddenly there; that is spirit." *Question*: How do you speak of it within human beings? *Reply*: Consciousness (*zhijue*) is certainly spiritual. If you cut your hand then your hand perceives

---

80. *Yulei* 94:3153. Cf. Zhu Xi's preface to this commentary, where he says, "No one knows where his teaching tradition came from," which refers to the heart of his teaching. Here he is saying that Zhou wasn't entirely without influences. Lu Shen (1012–1070) was a fairly prominent official from Hangzhou who opposed Wang Anshi. See Anon., *Zhejiang difang zhi* 浙江省地方志 (Zhejiang gazetteer), http://baike.baidu.com/view/2125021.htm.

81. *Yulei* 94:3153. In other words, Zhou Dunyi is speaking of spirituality as a human capacity, not "spirits" as independent entities. See Adler, "Varieties of Spiritual Experience."

82. [Zhang: In sections 3, 4, 9, 11, and 16.]

83. I.e., it depends on the context.

84. *Yijing*, *Xici* A.10.4 (*Zhouyi benyi*, 3:12b).

85. *Zheng meng* 正蒙 (Correcting youthful ignorance), in *Zhangzi quanshu*, 2:5b.

pain. If you cut your foot then your foot perceives pain. This is certainly spiritual. "Spirit is responsive, and therefore mysterious."[86]

[Zhou Dunyi's text and Zhu Xi's published commentary]

4. SAGEHOOD (Sheng 聖)[87]

[a] "Completely silent and inactive" (jiran budong 寂然不動)[88] means being authentic. "Penetrating when stimulated" (gan'er suitong 感而遂通)[89] means being spiritual. That which is active but not yet formed, between existing and not existing, is incipient.[90]

> That which is originally so and yet unmanifest is the substance of the actualized order.[91] That which is morally responsive (shan ying 善應) yet unfathomable is the functioning of the actualized order.[92] Between activity and stillness, substance and function, suddenly in the space of an instant there is the beginning (duan 端) of the appearance of the actualized order, and the auspicious and inauspicious omens of the multitudinous phenomena.

---

86. *Yulei* 94:3153–54. The last sentence is from section 4. Zhu's point is that "spirit" as a characteristic of people and things can refer to what we might call "action at a distance," or observed phenomena whose mechanisms are unknown.
87. [Zhang: This section discusses the mysterious functioning of authenticity, spirituality, and incipience. Only the sage, who is of this nature and equanimity, is able (to be like this).]
88. *Yijing*, *Xici* A.10.4 (*Zhouyi benyi*, 3:12b).
89. Ibid.
90. "Incipience" is the critical moment when activity begins to emerge from stillness. In the case of mental activity, it is at that moment when moral decisions (e.g., to nourish or to reject the incipient mental formation—*saṃskāra* in Buddhist thought) can be made. See chapter 3, "intellectual and spiritual cultivation."
91. The "original nature" (ben xing 本性).
92. "Moral responsiveness" is the authentic (cheng 誠) functioning of the "moral mind" (daoxin 道心).

[b] Authenticity is essential [*jing* 精, i.e., pure], and therefore clear. Spirit is responsive, and therefore mysterious. Incipience is subtle, and therefore obscure.

> To be clear and bright in body, with a will like that of a spirit, is to be "essential" and "clear." "To hurry without haste, to arrive without going"[93] is to be "responsive" and "mysterious." Although the order (*li*) has already sprouted, events are not yet apparent; they are "subtle" and "obscure."

[c] One who is authentic, spiritual, and incipient is called a sage.

> If one is "by nature like this, at ease like this" [section 3 above], then one is essential and clear, responsive and mysterious, and has the means to see into the obscure and subtle.
>
> [*Zhu Xi's additional comments*]
>
> [1] "'Completely silent and inactive' means being authentic" [4a]. Also, "'Great indeed is the originating power of Qian! The myriad things rely on it for their beginning.' It is the source of being authentic" [1b]. One must understand this "great originating power of Qian." Before "the myriad things rely on it for their beginnings," it is certainly "completely silent and inactive."[94]
>
> [2] "In incipience there is good and evil" [3b] refers to the masses of people. "Active but not yet formed, between existing and not existing" [4a] refers to the sage's tiniest active expression. This principle is wholly evident. As for "'completely silent and inactive' means being authentic" [4a]: when it reaches the point of being subtly active it is incipience. Incipience lies between authenticity and spirit.[95]

---

93. *Yijing*, *Xici* A.10.6 (*Zhouyi benyi*, 3:13a).

94. *Yulei* 94:3154. Zhu is stressing that the still phase of mind must be nourished as much as the active phase.

95. Ibid.

[3] *Lin* 林 *asked*: For entering into virtue there is nothing like using incipience. Is this the most important? *Reply*: Yes. *Question about* the *Tongshu*'s discussion of incipience: How is it between activity and stillness, substance and function? *Reply*: It is like when something is there and yet not there. [One can] see it in people.[96]

[4] Although incipience is already stimulated, it is at the point when stimulation has just occurred. When penetration is extended to the end, all is penetrated [comprehended]. If this is extended to its peak (*ji* 極), "harmonizing the myriad states and the common people even in unstable times,"[97] this is also penetration. But incipience is just the bit at the beginning.[98]

[5] [*Question*:] The *Tongshu* frequently discusses incipience. But this idea is not contained in the Supreme Polarity Diagram. *Reply*: [The "Discussion" says,] "The Five Phases are stimulated to activity." [Incipience] is when they are active but not yet differentiated [into good and evil] . . .[99]

[6] *Question about* "Authenticity is essential, and therefore clear" [4b]. The Teacher has explained it as "clear and bright in body, with a will like that of a spirit." But is this [what the *Zhongyong* means by] "When one is clear then one will be authentic"? *Reply*: Certainly we can see that [my] text here is rough. [But] Master Zhou's use of the word *essence* is the best. "Authenticity is essential" means it has nothing else mixed with it. For example, a lump of silver containing absolutely no copper or lead is thoroughly good silver. Therefore, here I used "clear and bright" to explain it. "A will like that of a spirit" is precisely the idea that "the Way of perfect authenticity is to be able to foreknow (*qianzhi* 前知)."[100] *Renjie followed up by saying*:

---

96. Ibid.
97. Quoting *Shujing, Yaodian* 1, referring to the sage-king Yao.
98. *Yulei* 94:3154.
99. Ibid.
100. *Yulei* 94:3155. Quoting *Zhongyong* 24, which discusses divination and concludes, "One with perfect authenticity is like a spirit." In his discussions of *Yijing* divination, Zhu Xi argues that a sage, characterized by perfect authenticity and "spiritual clarity" (*shenming* 神明), does not need to make use of divination to determine a course of action. See Smith, Bol, Adler, and Wyatt, *Sung Dynasty Uses of the I Ching,* 193–94.

In general when we read a text, because we have not yet thoroughly understood it, there are differences. When we approach it further we can see clearly. *Reply*: This is well said.

[7] *Anqing* 安卿 *asked*: How can a student become spiritual, authentic, and incipient? *Reply*: Follow it by exerting effort (*gongfu*).[101] Authenticity is where the "ruler" [the moral mind] resides. Where it emerges in functioning is spirit. Incipience is where one chooses.[102] But the critical point is incipience.[103]

[*Zhou Dunyi's text and Zhu Xi's published commentary*]

5. CAUTIOUS ACTIVITY (*Shen dong* 慎動)[104]

[a] To be active and correct is called the Way.

The means by which activity becomes correct is by according with the multitudinous Way that everything follows.

[b] To be functioning and harmonious is called virtue.

The means by which functioning becomes harmonious is by achieving the Way in oneself, without depending on anything external.

[c] To rebel against humanity, to rebel against rightness, to rebel against ritual propriety, to rebel against wisdom, and to rebel against honesty is to be completely depraved.

What is called the Way is nothing but the Five Constants. If not for these, then one's activity will be depraved.

---

101. [Original note in *Yulei*:] [Chen] Chun's record says, "It originates in authenticity; the strength comes forth in incipience."

102. [Chen] Chun's record adds: "between the two."

103. *Yulei* 94:3155.

104. [Zhang: This section says that when activity achieves its correctness, then functioning will achieve its harmony. If it does not achieve this harmony, then one is abused and injured. This is what is valuable about examining incipiencies.]

[d] To be depraved in one's activity is abuse. To do so to an extreme is injury.

Without achieving the Way, one's functioning is not harmonious.

[e] Therefore the noble person (*junzi* 君子) is cautious in activity.

Activity must be correct; then harmony will be found therein.

> [*Zhu Xi's additional comments*]
> [1] Concerning the *Tongshu*'s statement, "To be active and correct is called the Way. To be functioning and harmonious is called virtue," the Teacher said: Correctness is principle. If one achieves correctness even when active, the principle [of one's action] is certainly the Way. If one's activity is incorrect, then it is not the Way. Harmony is simply following principle. If one is accommodating in one's functioning, one certainly achieves this principle in oneself. If one is not accommodating in one's functioning, then one does not achieve this principle in oneself. Therefore, the following statement, "To rebel against humanity, to rebel against rightness, to rebel against propriety, to rebel against wisdom, and to rebel against honesty is to be completely depraved," is simply this principle. This is why it says, "The noble person is cautious in activity." *Zhiqing* [Huang Gan] *said*: In the *Taijitu* [*shuo*] it only says, "in activity it generates *yang*; in stillness it generates *yin*." The *Tongshu* also discusses incipience (*ji*), which is in the gap between activity and stillness. There is also this point.

[*Zhou Dunyi's text and Zhu Xi's published commentary*]

6. THE WAY (*Dao* 道)[105]

[a] The Way of the Sages is nothing more than humanity and rightness, centrality and correctness.

---

105. [Zhang: This section says that the Way lies in humanity and rightness, equilibrium and correctness. When one can preserve it, practice it, and enlarge it, then the Way is completed and virtue is provided for.]

"Centrality" is the same as ritual propriety. "Correctness" is the same as wisdom. The [Discussion of the] Diagram explains this fully.[106]

[b] Preserve it and it will be valuable.

How can anything be valued as much as the virtue of Heaven in oneself?

[c] Practice it and it will be beneficial.

How can according with lead to anything but benefit?

[d] Enlarge it and it will match Heaven-and-earth.

To fulfill and establish one's fundamental nature is simply [to actualize] one's complete substance.[107]

[e] How can it not be easy and simple? How can it be difficult to know?

The substance of the Way is one's fundamental nature; therefore, it is easy [to follow]. It is that which human beings certainly possess; therefore, it is easy to know.

[f] . . . By not preserving it, not practicing it, and not enlarging it.

Students who do this will, alas, miss their chance (ji).[108]

---

106. The same sentence is contained in the *Taijiitu shuo* (G), in a note added by Zhou.
107. I.e., to achieve the Way is to realize one's true nature, which is the nature of Heaven-and-earth.
108. Reading *ji* 幾 (incipience) as *ji* 機 (opportunity).

[*Zhou Dunyi's text and Zhu Xi's published commentary*]

7. THE TEACHER (*Shi* 師)[109]

[a] Someone asked: "Who makes all under Heaven good?" Reply: "The teacher." "What do you mean?" "[He is one whose] nature is simply centered between firm and yielding, good and evil."[110]

> The so-called nature here refers to the physical endowment [*qibing* 氣稟].[111]

[b] "I do not understand." Reply: "Firmness is good when it is right, direct, decided, dignified, capable, and certain. It is evil when it is violent, narrow, and limited. Yielding is good when it is compassionate, docile, and mild. It is evil when it is weak, indecisive, and treacherous."

> Firmness and yielding are just the major differentiation of *yin* and *yang*; within each of them is the further *yin-yang* differentiation into good and evil. Evil is just being wrong or incorrect, yet goodness too may not necessarily hit the mark in all cases.

[c] Only centrality (*zhong* 中) is "harmonious" (*he* 和) and "moderately regulated" (*zhong jie* 中節).[112] This is "the all-encompassing Way of the world."[113] It is the activity of the sage.

---

109. [Zhang: This section says that if one's physical constitution contains any imbalance, then one will miss the mark; thus the value of instruction in cultivating the Way.]

110. "Firm" (*gang* 剛) and "yielding" (*rou* 柔) refer to the solid (*yang*) and broken (*yin*) lines, respectively, of the *Yijing*.

111. Zhu Xi is referring to the physical nature (*qizhizhi xing* 氣質之性) as opposed to the original (moral) nature (*benxing* 本性). This is a distinction Zhu adopted from Zhang Zai and Cheng Yi, not Zhou Dunyi.

112. Quoting *Zhongyong* 1 (*Zhongyong zhangju*, 2a).

113. Ibid.

This refers to the correct way to achieve [fulfillment of] one's nature. However, in taking harmony to be centrality, [Zhou] is not in accord with the *Zhongyong*. What he refers to here is already-expressed (*yifa*) [activity] that neither goes too far nor not far enough. It is like what the *Shu*[*jing*] calls "holding fast to the Mean."[114]

[d] Therefore the sage establishes education, to enable common people to change their evil [tendencies], and on their own to reach equilibrium and stay there.

When one's evil [tendencies] are changed, then firmness and yielding are both good: one has the virtues of dignity and resoluteness, compassion and compliance, and lacks the afflictions of limitation and weakness. Reaching the Mean, one is sometimes dignified and resolute, sometimes compassionate and compliant, but always moderately regulated and lacking the imbalance of going too far or not far enough.

[e] Therefore, "those who first become aware (*jue* 覺) awaken those who become aware later,"[115] the unenlightened (*an* 闇) seek from the enlightened (*ming* 明), and the Way of instruction is established.

Instruction is simply the means by which to work on people's evil [tendencies] and correct people's uncenteredness.

[f] With the Way of instruction established, then good people will proliferate. When good people proliferate, then the Court will be correct and all under Heaven will be well governed.

---

114. Cf. *Shujing*, "Da Yu mo," trans. James Legge, *The Chinese Classics*, v. 3: 61–62. Zhu Xi is referring here to the all-important distinction in the *Zhongyong* between the unexpressed (*weifa* 未發) mind and the already-expressed (*yifa* 已發) mind, as discussed in chapter 3. *Zhong* 中 (centrality/equilibrium) is the condition before the expression of emotions, while *he* 和 (harmony) is their proper expression: going far enough and not too far. Zhou Dunyi seems to conflate the two phases of mind, and so "the Mean" is an apt translation here of *zhong*. However, see additional comment [5].

115. *Mencius* 5A.7 (*Sishu jizhu*, 5:9b), quoting Yi Yin; see section 10 below.

This is how to make all under Heaven good.

What this section refers to as firmness and yielding is the same as the Two Modes in the *Yi*.[116] Adding "good" and "evil" to each is the same as the Four Images in the *Yi*. The *Yi* goes on to add another level to make the Eight Trigrams, while this text and the Diagram stop at the Four Images. They can be considered water, fire, metal, and wood, and their point of equilibrium can be considered earth. The substance of the Way, then, is singular, while the details and outlines that people perceive are not the same. It is only in their fundamental substance that they do not differ, and so they proceed together and do not conflict.

[*Zhu Xi's additional comments*]

[1] *Question*: In the *Tongshu*, are the Four Images—firm and yielding, good and evil—all *yin* and *yang* ? *Reply*: Yes.[117]

[2] *Question* on "[The sage's] nature is simply in equilibrium between firm and yielding, good and evil." *Reply*: This "nature" refers to the physical nature (*qizhizhi xing*). Among the four, we reject both firm evil and yielding evil and emphasize either firm goodness or yielding goodness.[118]

[5] "*Zhong*" in the *Zhongyong* combines the meanings of "expressed and moderately regulated" and "going far enough and not too far." Therefore, Master Zhou says, "Only equilibrium is harmonious and 'moderately regulated.' This is 'the all-encompassing Way of the world.'" If we do not recognize this principle then we will certainly

---

116. "In Change there is the Supreme Polarity, which generates the Two Modes. The Two Modes generate the Four Images, and the Four Images generate the Eight Trigrams" (*Yijing*, *Xici* A.11.5 [*Zhouyi benyi*, 3:14b]). In identifying the firm and yielding as the Two Modes, Zhu is speaking in the mode of correlative cosmology, as in the rest of this paragraph. In his *Yixue qimeng* (Introduction to the study of the *Yi*) the Two Modes are *yin* and *yang* (see Li Guangdi, comp., *Zhouyi zhezhong* [The *Zhouyi* judged evenly], 1026, 1228); and in Shao Yong's *Jingshi yanyi tu* (Diagram Developing the *Yi* for Governing the World), reproduced in chapter 3, they are activity and stillness.

117. *Yulei* 94:3156. In Zhu Xi's *Yixue qimeng* and his *Zhouyi benyi*, the Four Images are mature *yin*, young *yin*, mature *yang*, and young *yang*. In Shao Yong's *Jingshi yanyi tu*, they are firmness, yielding, *yin*, and *yang*.

118. *Yulei* 94:3156.

not understand Master Zhou's words. This is why Master Cheng called *zhong* "the correct Way of the world"; the *Zhongyong zhangju* 中庸章句 [Zhu's commentary on the *Zhongyong*] takes *zhong* in the *Zhongyong* as combining the meanings of *zhong* and *he*; and the *Lunyu jizhu* 論語集註 [Zhu's commentary on the *Analects*] takes *zhong* to be impartial and going far enough but not too far. They are all this idea.[119]

[. . . .]

[*Zhou Dunyi's text and Zhu Xi's published commentary*]

8. GOOD FORTUNE (*Xing* 幸)[120]

[a] In human life, it is unfortunate not to hear about one's errors. To lack shame is a great misfortune.

If one does not hear about one's errors, a person is uninformed.

[b] Only with a sense of shame can one be taught. If one hears about one's errors, then one can become a worthy.

If one has shame, then one is able to put forth effort and receive instruction. If one hears about one's errors, then one can understand what to change to become worthy. But if one cannot be instructed, then, although one hears about one's errors one will not necessarily be able to change. From this we see that the misfortune of lacking shame is even greater.

---

119. Yulei 62: 2005. Cheng Yi's comment is quoted by Zhu Xi in *Sishu jizhu, Lunyu* 3:15a. The *Zhongyong zhangju* reference is to *Sishu jizhu, Zhongyong* 2a, although it is not explicit there. The *Lunyu jizhu* comment is in *Sishu jizhu, Lunyu* 3:15a. These interpretations of the term *zhong* in the *Zhongyong* seem to be contradicted by Zhu's published comment above, in 7 [c], where he explicitly says that Zhou Dunyi's conflation of *zhong* and *he* (as in the passages quoted here) is mistaken.

120. [Zhang: This section discusses the frequent shortcomings in the behavior of most people. If they value having a mind that understands shame, then they can be taught.]

[*Zhu Xi's additional comments*]

[1] "In human life, it is unfortunate not to hear about one's errors. To lack shame is a great misfortune." These two sentences are a single matter. Understanding shame arises from within one's heart/mind; hearing about one's errors comes from others. One must understand shame in order to reform one's errors. Therefore, shame is important.[121]

[*Zhou Dunyi's text and Zhu Xi's published commentary*]

9. THINKING (*Si* 思)[122]

[a] The *Hongfan* 洪範 says: "[The virtue of] thinking (*si* 思) is called perspicacity (*rui* 睿). . . . Perspicacity makes one a sage."[123] To be without thinking (*wusi* 無思) is the foundation (*ben* 本). When thinking is penetrating, this is its function. When there is incipient activity on the one hand, and authentic activity on the other, with no thinking and yet penetrating everything, one is a sage.[124]

> Perspicacity is penetration. To be without thinking is to be authentic. When thinking is penetrating, it is spiritual. This is what is meant by "One who is authentic, spiritual, and incipient is called a sage [4(c) above]."

[b] If one does not think, then one cannot penetrate subtleties (*wei* 微). If one is not perspicacious, then one cannot penetrate everything. Thus, [the

---

121. *Yulei* 94:3157.
122. [Zhang: This section discusses those who are not yet able to be like the sage, who is authentic without thinking.]
123. *Hongfan* chapter of the *Shujing*. See Legge, trans., *The Chinese Classics*, v. 3: 327.
124. "No thinking and yet penetrating everything" (*wusi er wu butong* 無思而無不通) is probably a pun on *Laozi* 37, "No doing and yet nothing undone" (*wuwei er wu buwei* 無為而無不為). "The foundation" (*ben* 本), is, in Zhu Xi's terminology, the "substance" (*ti* 體) of the mind in its "completely still and inactive" (*jiran budong* 寂然不動) phase (see chapter 3), or the centrality before the feelings are aroused.

ability] to penetrate everything arises from penetrating subtleties, and [the ability] to penetrate subtleties arises from thinking.

[The ability] to penetrate subtleties is perspicacity. [The ability] to penetrate everything is sageliness.

[c] Therefore, thinking is the foundation of the sage's achievement and the opportunity for good fortune or misfortune.

The ultimate (perfection) of thinking can make one a sage, who penetrates everything. It can also enable one to perceive incipience and penetrate subtlety, and to avoid misfortune and calamity.

[d] The *Yi* says, "The noble person perceives incipience and acts, without waiting all day."[125]

This is perspicacity.

[e] It also says, "Knowing incipience is his spirituality."[126]

This is the sage.

> [*Zhu Xi's additional comments*]
>
> [1] *Question* on "To be without thinking is the foundation. When thinking is penetrating, this is its function. . . . With no thinking and yet penetrating everything, one is a sage." I do not understand whether the sage does think or does not think. *Reply*: "With no thinking and yet penetrating everything" [characterizes] the sage. When it is necessary to think and then everything is penetrated, this is perspicacity. *Shiju* 時舉[127] said: The sage's "silent inactivity" is without thinking. Only with stimulation is there penetration, in a

---

125. *Xici* B.5.11 (*Zhouyi benyi*, 3:22b).
126. Ibid.
127. For Pan Shiju 潘時舉 see Chan, *Zhuzi menren*, 328.

particular response to it. *Reply*: The sage is not a dolt who only acts after being stirred by others, like Zhuangzi's "pushed to move, pulled to stop."[128] It is just that once he thinks, then he penetrates, without stopping to think.[129]

[2] Incipience is the hint of an event. When there is a hint, then one asks where it leads to. This method makes use of thinking.

[3] In reference to the *Tongshu*'s terms "penetrating subtleties" and "penetrating everything," [Zhu Xi] brought up what his teacher Li [Tong] had said: "When King Xuan of Qi spoke of being fond of sex, Mencius explained it thusly; when he spoke of being fond of wealth, he explained it thusly; when he spoke of being fond of courage, he explained it thusly.[130] In all [three] cases there was a moral principle that explained what to do. This is the moral principle of fully developing the mind/heart." At that time it was not understood. Now we know it is the moral principle of "penetrating everything."[131]

[*Zhou Dunyi's text and Zhu Xi's published commentary*]

10. BEING INTENT ON LEARNING (*Zhi xue* 志學)[132]

[a] The sage emulates Heaven. The worthy emulates the sage. The literatus emulates the worthy.

"Emulates" (*xi* 希) means to hope for (*wang* 望). The character was originally written 晞.

---

128. *Zhuangzi*, ch. 14 (Sibu beiyao ed.), 5:19a, although the second phrase is a rough paraphrase.

129. *Yulei* 94:3157.

130. *Mencius* 1B.3, 5. In all three passages Mencius uses historical examples to illustrate the principle that the ruler should allow his subjects to enjoy the same things he enjoys.

131. The point is that by "penetrating" specific historical examples Mencius induced a general principle connecting them all with King Xuan's moral dilemma. *Yulei* 94:3158.

132. [Zhang: This section says that for learning one must establish devotion/commitment (*zhi*). When one's commitment is great, then all things can be penetrated.]

[b] Yi Yin 伊尹 and Yan Yuan 顏淵 [Yan Hui 顏回] were great Worthies. Yi Yin was ashamed that his prince was not Yao or Shun. If one person did not attain his rightful place, it was like being whipped in the marketplace. Yan Yuan "did not transfer his anger and did not repeat an error,"[133] and "for three months did nothing contrary to humanity."[134]

> For this discussion, see the *Shu*[*jing*] and the *Analects*, which contain the affairs of both Worthies.[135]

[c] Be intent on having Yi Yin's intention. Learn what Yan Yuan learned.

This refers to the literatus emulating the worthy.

[d] If you exceed this you will be a sage. If you reach it you will be a worthy. Even if you do not reach it you will not miss out on an honorable reputation. The three go as far as they can according to the shallowness or depth of the effort they apply. One will not miss out on an honorable reputation because one possesses the reality of being good.

> Mister Hu [Hong] said:[136] Master Zhou worried about people who were concerned with having deliberate plans, healthy bodies and prosperous families, and enjoying worldly favors. Thus, he said, "Be intent on having Yi Yin's intention." He also worried about people who were concerned

---

133. *Analects* 6:2.

134. *Analects* 6:5.

135. Yi Yin was a minister to Tang, the founder of the Shang dynasty, and is honored in the Confucian tradition for having banished Tang's incompetent grandson, but when the grandson reformed and became virtuous, Yi Yin brought him back. See *Shujing*, Books of Shang: "Instructions of Yi," "Tai Jia" (1–3), and "Common Possession of Pure Virtue," in Legge, *The Chinese Classics*, vol. 3. Mencius says it is permissible for a minister to banish his superior only if his motive or intention (*zhi* 志) is good, as was Yi Yin's (*Mencius* 5A.6–7 and 7A.31; see also D. C. Lau, "Ancient History as Understood by Mencius," in Lau, trans., *Mencius*, appendix 4). Yan Yuan (Yan Hui) was Confucius's favorite disciple (see, e.g., *Analects* 6:3, 6:11, and section 23 below).

136. This is a section of Hu Hong's preface to the *Tongshu*, which is fully translated in chapter 1. The wording differs from that in the *Zhou Lianxi ji* (*juan* 7) and *Hu Hong ji* (161–62), but the meaning is the same.

with observing widely, laboring at their writing, respecting wisdom and ability, and admiring [Buddhist] silence and emptiness. Thus he says: Learn what Master Yan learned. People who are able to be intent on this intention and to learn this learning will understand the extreme greatness contained in this book and its limitless application.

> [*Zhu Xi's additional comments*]
>
> [1] *Dou* 竇 *asked*:[137] Does "Be intent on having Yi Yin's intention; learn what Yan Yuan learned" mean that intention is simply intention to practice the Way? *Reply*: "Be intent on having Yi Yin's intention" is not being intent for oneself. In general, the learning of the ancients was based on a desire to practice [the Way]. [Mencius said,] "Yi Yin worked in the fields in the outskirts of Youxin, and delighted in the Way of Yao and Shun."[138] If one's reason is to "order the state" and "pacify the world,"[139] everything will be understood . . .[140]
>
> [2] *Dou further asked*: Is "being intent on having Yi Yin's intention" being intent on practice? *Reply*: It is simply not being intent on oneself. People today serve as officials for the salary, but Yi Yin, "were he given the Empire he would have ignored it, were he given a thousand teams of horses he would not have looked at them."[141]
>
> [. . . .]

[*Zhou Dunyi's text and Zhu Xi's published commentary*]

11. COMPLIANCE AND TRANSFORMATION (*Shun hua* 順化)[142]

[a] Heaven generates the myriad things through *yang*, and fulfills the myriad things through *yin*. Generating (*sheng* 生) is humanity (*ren* 仁); fulfilling (*cheng* 成) is rightness (*yi* 義).

---

137. For Dou Congzhou 竇從周 see Chan, *Zhuzi menren,* 360–61.
138. *Mencius* 5A.7 (*Sishu jizhu* 5:9a), trans. D. C. Lau, slightly modified.
139. Two of the "eight items" of the *Daxue* (Great Learning).
140. *Yulei* 94:3158.
141. *Yulei* 94:3159, again quoting *Mencius* 5A.7 (*Sishu jizhu* 5:9a), trans. D. C. Lau.
142. [Zhang: This section discusses Heaven's generation and fulfillment of the myriad things through *yin* and *yang*. The sage, who educates and corrects the myriad people through humanity and rightness, is one with Heaven.]

Yin and *yang* refer to *qi*. Humanity and rightness refer to *dao*. The details are explained in the [Supreme Polarity] Diagram.[143]

[b] Therefore, when a sage is above [on the throne], he nourishes the myriad things with humanity and corrects the myriad people with rightness.

This is what is meant by determining them with humanity and rightness.

[c] The Way of Heaven proceeds and the myriad things comply [with it]. The virtue of the sage cultivates [others] and the myriad people are transformed. Great compliance and great transformation leave no visible trace. Since no one understands them, they are considered spiritual.

The Way of Heaven, Earth, and the sage are one.

[d] Therefore, everything under Heaven is originally contained in every person. How can the Way be distant? How can its methods be numerous?

The basis of all under Heaven is contained in the noble person. The Way of the noble person is contained in the mind/heart. The method of the mind/heart is contained in humanity and rightness.

> [*Zhu Xi's additional comments*]
>
> [2] *Question*: Spring's planting and summer's growth are humanity. Autumn's harvest and winter's storage are rightness. Is this also what is meant by establishing the Way of Heaven and the Human Way? *Reply*: In this book [the *Tongshu*] this is [parallel to] the discussion of the two *qi* and the Five Phases [in the *Taijitu shuo*].
>
> [. . . .]

---

143. This is a good example of how Zhu Xi integrates the *Taijitu shuo* and the *Tongshu*. While the *Taijitu shuo* clearly discusses the generation of the myriad things through the interaction of *yin* and *yang*, and it highlights humanity and rightness as two of four characteristics of the sage (the other two being centrality and correctness), it does not explicitly correlate these two pairs.

[*Zhou Dunyi's text and Zhu Xi's published commentary*]

12. GOVERNMENT (*Zhi* 治)[144]

[a] Teaching by speaking directly to everyone is not sufficient even in a village of ten households. How much more difficult in an extensive empire with millions of people! I say: Purify (*chun* 純) the mind/heart, that is all.

> "Pure" means unmixed. "Mind/heart" means the mind/heart of the people's ruler.

[b] "Purify" means to do nothing contrary to the four [virtues of] humanity, rightness, propriety, and wisdom, whether in activity or when still, in one's speech, appearance, seeing, and hearing.

> Humanity, rightness, propriety and wisdom are virtues of the Five Phases. Activity and stillness are the functioning of *yin* and *yang*. Speech, appearance, seeing, and hearing are the behaviors of the Five Phases. Of the virtues, honesty is not mentioned, and of the behaviors, thought is not mentioned. [As for the latter omission,] in desiring not to act contrary [to the four virtues] we can certainly consider thought to be the master, which must seek out the actuality [i.e., the concrete manifestations] of these four.

[c] When his mind/heart is pure, then worthy and talented men will assist him.

> The ruler selects people by himself. The Way of the minister is to agree and follow.

[d] When worthy and talented men assist him, the empire will be well governed.

---

144. [Zhang: This section discusses the sage as the foundation of government, taking his pure heart/mind as essential, and employing the worthy as urgent.]

When the various worthies each take responsibility for their office, then he [the ruler] need not depend on teaching by speaking directly to everyone.

[e] Purifying the heart/mind is indeed essential. Employing worthy men is urgent.

If the heart/mind is not purified, then one will be unable to employ worthy men. If one does not employ worthy men, then one will lack the means to widely transform.

[Zhou Dunyi's text and Zhu Xi's published commentary]

13. RITUAL AND MUSIC (Li yue 禮樂)[145]

[a] Ritual (li 禮) is order (li 理). Music is harmony.

Ritual is *yin*; music is *yang*.

[b] *Yin* and *yang* are harmonious only when ordered. Then the ruler is [truly] ruler, the minister is minister, father is father, son is son, elder brother is elder brother, younger brother is younger brother, husband is husband, and wife is wife. The myriad things are harmonious only when each achieves this order. Therefore, ritual is first and music follows.

This defines it with the concept of emphasizing stillness in centrality and correctness, humanity and rightness. Master Cheng's statement, "With reverent composure there is natural pleasure," is also [an example of] this principle. Students who do not know how to devote themselves to making harmonious music while holding onto reverent composure will seldom progress beyond the slow.

---

145. [Zhang: This section discusses the Way in which ritual and music are mutually necessary. It is the same as the meaning of *yin* and *yang* in the Diagram.]

[*Zhu Xi's additional comments*]

[1] Ritual and music are necessary for each other. But what is called music is only spontaneous harmony and pleasure in one's breast. It is not the type of pleasure that comes from expressing one's ideas and letting loose one's desires. But if one desires to have spontaneous pleasure in one's breast, without reverent composure one cannot. Therefore, Master Cheng said, "With reverent composure there is natural pleasure." And Master Zhou also placed ritual first and music after, as we can see.

[. . . .]

[*Zhou Dunyi's text and Zhu Xi's published commentary*]

14. STRIVING FOR ACTUALIZATION (*Wu shi* 務實)[146]

[a] For actualization to dominate [one's work] is good. For name [fame] to dominate is shameful. Therefore, the noble person advances his virtue and cultivates his work with unceasing diligence, striving for the dominance of actualization. If his virtue and affairs are not prominent, he apprehensively fears that others will know [about it]; he wants to distance himself from shame. The inferior person, on the other hand, is simply hypocritical. Therefore, the noble person is always at ease, while the inferior person is always anxious.

[One whose] actualization is cultivated and has no shame resulting from the dominance of name is therefore at ease. [One whose concern with]

---

146. [Zhang: This section says that learning must strive to actualize [one's moral potential]. This is what previous sections call being authentic. "Without authenticity there would be nothing (*Zhongyong* 25)"; there is nothing but hypocrisy in it.]

See above, Zhu's comment on section 2d. "Actualization" here, of course, means self-actualization. It should be noted that the words "actualization" (*shi* 實) and "fame/name" (*ming* 名) used throughout this section and the commentaries were prominent terms in the later Mohist canon and in the ancient "school of names" (*mingjia* 名家), where they referred to the relationship between things or reality and the words used to describe it. See Graham, *Disputers of the Tao,* and Graham, *Later Mohist Logic, Ethics and Science.* Here, of course, they have more distinctively Confucian meanings.

name dominates and has no goodness resulting from actualization being cultivated is therefore anxious.

[*Zhu Xi's additional comments*]

[1] Master Cheng [Yi] said: "The student should strive for actualization, without wanting current fame. If one has the intention of gaining current fame, then one is false, and the great foundation is already lost. How can learning take place? When it is for fame or profit, regardless of differences in clarity or turbidity, the [lack of] benefit to the mind will be the same."[147] And [Cheng Hao] said: "With actualization there is name; name and actualization are one thing. One who is fond of name will find that giving in to name is empty. For example, [Confucius said:] 'When a gentleman dies, his name is no longer spoken in the world,'[148] which means that when there is nothing good that can be said one should not give in to name."[149]

[*Zhou Dunyi's text and Zhu Xi's published commentary*]

15. LOVE AND REVERENT COMPOSURE (*Ai jing* 愛敬)[150]

[a] [What if I] do not measure up to a good person?

Someone asks, "Suppose there is a good person, and I cannot measure up. Then what?"

[b] If you do not measure up, then learn to do so.

The reply is that one must simply learn to be good.

---

147. Cheng Yi, in *Henan Chengshi yishu* 18 (*Er Cheng ji*, 219).
148. Attributed to Confucius in Sima Qian, *Shiji* (Historical records), 17:1943.
149. Cheng Hao, in *Henan Chengshi yishu* 11 (*Er Cheng ji*, 129).
150. [Zhang: This section uses good and evil as two clues to clarify the matters of self-cultivation and governing (correcting) others. This is known as reciprocity.]

[c] Question: [What if] there is a bad person?

He asks if someone is not good, then how does one handle it?

[d] If he is not good, then inform him that he is not good. Furthermore, exhort him, saying, "Suppose you change; you will then become a noble person."

> The reply is that if there is a person who is not good, then one informs him that he is not good, and exhorts him to change. One informs him lest he not know that this behavior is not good. One exhorts him lest he not know that what is not good can be changed into goodness.

[e] If one person is good and two are not good, then learn from the one and exhort the two.

> This is another reply. It says that if there is a mixture of good and evil people, then learn from the good and exhort the evil.

[f] If someone says, "This person has done something that is not good, but it is not a great evil," then say, "Who makes no errors? How do we know that he cannot change? If he changes, then he can become a noble person. Not changing results in evil. Evil is what Heaven hates. How can he not fear [Heaven]? How do we know that he cannot change?"

> This is another reply. If one hears about a person who has made an error, although one cannot inform and exhort him in person, still one must reply like this, hoping he might hear about it and change himself. When one intentionally [lit. mindfully] opposes order (*li*) it is called evil. When one unintentionally neglects order it is called an error.

[g] Therefore, the noble person possesses all goodness, and there is no one who does not love and revere him.

There is no goodness he has not learned, therefore "he possesses all goodness." There is no evil he has not exhorted, therefore he does not abandon anyone to evil. Since he does not abandon anyone to evil, there is no one who does not treat him with love and reverence.

[*Zhou Dunyi's text and Zhu Xi's published commentary*]

16. ACTIVITY AND STILLNESS (*Dong jing* 動靜)[151]

[a] That which has no stillness in activity and no activity in stillness is a thing.

Having physical form, it is limited to one aspect [i.e., to one mode or the other].

[b] That which has no activity in activity, and no stillness in stillness, is spirit.

Spirit is neither separate from physical form nor limited to physical form.

[c] It is not the case that having no activity in activity and having no stillness in stillness is neither activity nor stillness.

There is stillness within activity, and activity within stillness.

[d] Things, then, are not penetrating. Spirit renders the myriad things subtle.

The above sentence is connected with the meaning that comes out below.

---

151. [Zhang: This section brings to light the ultimate principle of activity and stillness. Penetrating throughout the creative process of transformation, there is nothing as exhaustive as this Way.]

This section is crucial to Zhu Xi's appropriation of Zhou Dunyi, as it clearly states the concept of the interpenetration of stillness and activity. As we saw in chapter 3, this was the cosmological verification of the solution Zhu found for his spiritual crisis regarding self-cultivation of the still mind or the active mind. Since this is fully discussed in chapter 3, my comments here will be limited.

[e] The *yin* of water is based in *yang*; the *yang* of fire is based in *yin*.

> Water is *yin*, yet it is generated from [the number] one, so it is based in *yang*.[152] Fire is *yang*, and yet it is generated from two, so it is based in *yin*. The statement "spirit renders the myriad things subtle" is like this.[153]

[f] The Five Phases are *yin* and *yang*. *Yin* and *yang* are the Supreme Polarity.

> This is the same as the statement [in the Discussion of the Diagram]: "The Five Phases are the unitary *yin* and *yang*; *yin* and *yang* are the unitary Supreme Polarity." [Here it is] discussed in reference to the substance (*ti* 體) of the "spirit which renders the myriad things subtle."

[g] The Four Seasons revolve; the myriad things end and begin [again].

> This is the same as the statement [in the Discussion of the Diagram]: "The five *qi* are harmoniously distributed, and the four seasons proceed. . . . The Nonpolar, the Two [modes], and the Five [Phases] subtly combine and congeal." [Here it is] discussed in reference to the function (*yong* 用) of the "spirit which renders the myriad things subtle."

[h] How undifferentiated! How extensive! And how inexhaustible!

> Substance is fundamental and unitary; hence, "undifferentiated." Function is dispersed and differentiated; hence, "extensive." The succession of activity and stillness is like an endless [inexhaustible] revolution. This refers to the connection of substance and function.[154] This section clarifies the ideas of the [Supreme Polarity] Diagram, which should be consulted.

---

152. This is based on the numerology of the *Hetu* (River Chart), as explained by Zhu in the *Yixue qimeng* (Introduction to the Study of the *Yi*). Specifically (with reference to the numbers of the Chart): "Heaven generates water from the one, and earth completes it with the six. Earth generates fire from the two, and Heaven completes it with the seven." [*Yixue qimeng*, section 1, in Li Guangdi, *Zhouyi zhezhong*, 1212.] Odd numbers are traditionally considered *yang*, and even numbers are *yin*.

153. I.e., spirit is the interpenetrating characteristic of the two bipolar modes of *qi*; *yin* and *yang* are not mutually exclusive opposites.

154. I.e., "function" is the functioning *of the substance*.

[*Zhu Xi's additional comments*]

[1] *Question* concerning "That which has no stillness in activity and no activity in stillness is a thing. That which has no activity in activity, and no stillness in stillness, is spirit." Does a so-called thing include human beings? *Master Zhu replied*: Human beings are included. *Question*: Is "spirit" the creative process of transformation in Heaven-and-earth? *Reply*: Spirit is precisely this principle (*li*). *Question*: Things are limited by having physical form. But since human beings have stillness in activity and activity in stillness, how can we say that they are like the myriad things? *Reply*: Human beings are certainly active within stillness and still within activity, yet still they are called things. In general, the term *thing* refers to formed *qi* having a fixed body. But since there is a certain flexibility within it, we must understand that implements are the Way, and the Way is implements.[155] There is nothing separate from the Way, including implements. All things have [are part of] this order (*li*). For example, this bamboo chair is certainly an implement. As for its suitability, it has the Way within it.[156]

[2] In this section, "That which has no stillness in activity and no activity in stillness is a thing" refers to physical implements. That which is physical cannot penetrate [other things]. Therefore, when it is active it has no stillness, and when it is still it has no activity. For example, water is only water, and fire is only fire. And so in reference to human beings, if they speak they are not silent, and if

---

155. Alluding to *Yijing, Xici* A.12.4: "What is above form (*xing'er shang* 形而上: metaphysical) is called the Way (*dao* 道); what is within form (*xing'er xia* 形而下) is called implements (*qi* 器)" (*Zhouyi benyi* 3:16a).

156. This is a good example of a student asking a penetrating question. Zhou Dunyi had defined "thing" (*wu* 物) and "spirit" (*shen* 神) as apparently mutually exclusive. But since humans (*renwu* 人物) are also things, this seems to preclude the possibility of humans being spiritual. Zhu Xi's response is rather vague; essentially, he is saying that the Way and implements have a nondual, interpenetrating relationship like that of activity and stillness. He could also have referred to Zhou's statement in the *Taijitu shuo* (G), "Only humans receive the finest and most spiritually efficacious [*qi*]. Once formed, they are born; when spirit (*shen*) is manifested, they have intelligence. . . ." to make the case on "quantitative" (i.e., in terms of degrees of purity) rather than qualitative grounds.

they are silent they are not speaking. Likewise in reference to things, if they fly they are not plants, and if they are plants they do not fly.

"It is not the case that having no activity in activity and having no stillness in stillness is neither activity nor stillness" refers to the metaphysical order (xing'er shangzhi li 形而上之理). Principle/order is spiritual and unfathomable. When it is active, it is simultaneously still. Therefore [Zhou] says "no activity." When it is still, it is simultaneously active. Therefore [Zhou] says "no stillness." Within stillness there is activity, and within activity there is stillness. When still it is capable of activity, and when active it is capable of stillness. Within *yang* there is *yin,* and within *yin* there is *yang.* The permutations are inexhaustible. And so he says, "The *yin* of water is based in *yang*; the *yang* of fire is based in *yin.*" The *yin* of water and the *yang* of fire are things; they are physical. That by which they are based in *yin* and based in *yang* is order; it is metaphysical.

Huang Gan said, "When we combine these two ideas they are complete. In terms of principle/order, activity and stillness are as follows: In stillness there is activity and in activity there is stillness; this is their substance. Being still yet capable of activity, and being active yet capable of stillness, is their function. In terms of things, activity and stillness are as follows: That which is active has no stillness, and that which is still has no activity; this is their substance. That which is active is incapable of being still, and that which is still is incapable of activity; this is their function."[157]

[4] What is called spirit is from the beginning not separate from things. For example, Heaven and earth are things. How can Heaven's [function of] gathering together be only activity? How can Earth's [function of] bringing to life be only stillness? These are spirit.[158]

[5] "The four seasons revolve, and the myriad things end and begin [again]." While the Way has things and seasons, it lacks form and body. If the Way lacked things and seasons, how could it generate [produce] as it does?[159]

---

157. *Yulei* 94:3160–61.

158. I.e., although Heaven is primarily associated with activity and Earth with stillness, they both also manifest the opposite function. This interpenetration is spirit.

159. *Yulei* 74:1528.

[6] "Undifferentiated" refers to the Supreme Polarity.[160] "Extensive" refers to what is after *yin-yang* and the Five Phases. Therefore, the last sentence says, "And how inexhaustible!" This refers to what is after "extensive": the inexhaustibility of the myriad things that come after *yin-yang* and the Five Phases.

[*Zhou Dunyi's text and Zhu Xi's published commentary*]

17. MUSIC (A) (*Yue shang* 樂上)[161]

[a] The ancient sages and kings systematized the ritual procedures and reformed education. The Three Bonds (*san gang* 三綱) were corrected, the Nine Divisions (*jiu chou* 九疇) were arranged, the hundred surnames [i.e., all people] were in great harmony, and the myriad things were all in accord.

"Bonds" are the main cords in a net. The Three Bonds are: the husband is the wife's bond, the father is the son's bond, and the ruler is the minister's bond.[162] "Division" means category. The Nine Divisions appear in the "Great Plan" [chapter of the *Shujing*].[163] "Accord" means obey. This is what is meant by "after order there is harmony."

[b] They created music to give expression to the airs (*qi* 氣) of the eight [directional] winds and to pacify the dispositions of all under Heaven.

---

160. The undifferentiated nature of Supreme Polarity is an important point for Zhu (see chapter 3).

161. [Zhang: This section discusses the different functions of ancient music and modern music, according to (the distinction between) order and disorder.]

162. The "Three Bonds," or "Three Mainstays," are a subset of Mencius's "Five Relations" (*wu lun* 五倫). The former imply hierarchical relationships, while the latter (which are several hundred years earlier) imply mutuality. See the brief discussion in de Bary and Bloom, eds., *Sources of Chinese Tradition*, 2nd ed., vol. 1, 344–45.

163. See Legge, trans., *The Chinese Classics*, v. 3: 320–44.

"The eight [kinds of musical] sounds that give expression to the winds of the eight directions" alludes to the *Guoyu* 國語 (Conversations of the States).[164] They "gave expression" and thereby made known the manifestations of order. They "pacified" and thereby regulated the harmonious flow.

[c] Therefore, the sounds of music are placid and not distressing, harmonious and not licentious. When they enter the ear they move the heart/mind; [yet] they are entirely placid and harmonious. Being placid, they calm the desirous heart/mind. Being harmonious, they ease the fierce heart/mind.

> Being "placid" is an expression of order. "Harmony" is a character of the placid. First placid, then harmonious is also [Zhou's] idea of "emphasizing stillness." However, the discussion of music by the ancient sages and worthies says "simply harmony." So what is here called "placid" is probably patterned after modern music; only later was its basis seen in the idea of being sedate and correct, respectful and grave.
> [Added by Zhang Boxing:] Master Zhu said: Following "the idea of 'being sedate and correct, respectful and grave,'" I wish I had added the six words, "therefore extremely simple and still."

[d] To be easygoing and evenly balanced is the height of virtue. In the transformation of all under Heaven, government is perfected. This is what is meant by the Way that matches Heaven-and-earth, the peak (*ji* 極) of antiquity.[165]

> The desirous heart/mind is calmed and therefore evenly balanced. The fierce heart/mind is eased and therefore easygoing. This refers to the greatness of the sages' transformative achievement in creating music. Some say that "in the transformation" (*hua zhong* 化中) should read "the transformation and fulfillment" (*hua cheng* 化成).

---

164. *Guo Yu*, Conversations of Zhou (C), 30 (http://ctext.org/guo-yu/zhou-yu-xia).
165. Paraphrasing *Laozi* 68

[e]¹⁶⁶ Later generations have neglected ritual. Their governmental measures and laws have been in disorder. Rulers have indulged their material desires without restraint, and consequently the people below them have suffered bitterly. Rulers have claimed that ancient music is not worth listening to and replaced it by or changed it into modern music, which is seductive, licentious, depressive, and complaining. It arouses desires and increases bitterness without end. Therefore, there have been cases of people destroying their rulers, casting away their fathers, taking life lightly, and ruining human relations, and it has been impossible to put an end to such atrocities.

> They have done away with ritual and lacked restraint; therefore their music has been agitated, seductive, and licentious. Government has been disordered and the people have suffered; therefore their music has been unharmonious, depressive, and complaining. Being seductive and licentious, it therefore arouses desires and leads to taking life lightly and ruining human relations. Being depressive and complaining, it therefore increases bitterness and leads to destroying rulers and casting away fathers.

[f] Alas! Ancient music appeased the heart but modern music enhances desires. Ancient music spread a civilizing influence, but modern music increases discontent.

> The difference between the ancient and the modern is simply that between the placid and the agitated, the harmonious and the unharmonious.

[g] To hope for perfect government without restoring ancient ritual and changing modern music is to be far off the mark.¹⁶⁷

> Only after restoring ancient ritual can one change modern music.

---

166. The remainder of this section (e-g) of Zhou's text is given in Wing-tsit Chan's translation (*Source Book,* 472–73), substituting "ritual" for "ceremonies."

167. In what is apparently an oversight, Chan here has omitted the word *ritual* [or *ceremonies*]. Zhu Xi's commentary, which Chan generally follows, makes no sense without it.

[*Zhou Dunyi's text and Zhu Xi's published commentary*]

18. MUSIC (B) (*Yue zhong* 樂中)[168]

Music is based in government. When government is good and the people are at ease, then the minds/hearts of all under Heaven are harmonious. Therefore, the sages created music to give expression to these harmonious hearts/minds. When it spreads throughout Heaven-and-earth, the *qi* of Heaven-and-earth is stimulated and there is great harmony throughout. When Heaven-and-earth are harmonious, then the myriad things are compliant. Therefore, the gods and spirits will approach [when sacrifices are offered], and birds and beasts will be tame.

> Since the music of the sages was not created by unreasonable force, the mystery of its creation enables it to really apprehend the origin of sound. Therefore, it results in the mutual emotional influence of Heaven and humanity.

> [*Zhu Xi's additional comments*]

> [1] *Question*: The Commentary on the *Tongshu* says, "the mystery of its creation really enables it to apprehend the origin of sound."[169] I do not understand how we can still determine this. *Reply*: Today the only dispute is with the first note of the yellow bell. When this is high, the rest are all high. When this is low, the rest are all low. Thus, it is difficult to attain the middle.[170] *Question*: What was Hu Anding's 胡安定[171] [theory of] music like? *Reply*: It was in the same family.[172]

---

168. [Zhang: This section discusses how the Way of music is connected with government. This is what is meant by "hearing its music, one knows its virtue."]

169. The wording of this quote differs slightly from that of the text, although the meaning is the same.

170. Just as the ruler's deviations from the Mean affect the rest of society.

171. Hu Yuan 胡瑗 (993–1059), Cheng Yi's teacher.

172. *Yulei* 94:3163.

[2] *Question* on "the origin of sound." *Master Zhu replied:* The calendar experts greatly emphasize this original sound. When this one is defined then what follows is defined; when the original sound is off then what follows is off. Only the system of the ancients, which today no longer exists, followed these principles [precisely]. [Such imprecision] will do for people, but laws cannot be imprecise. And in the case of music, today we can no longer verify them; today people can only discuss them. The production of all sounds comes from the human mind. When the human mind is active, things are caused to be so. When it comes to attaining the [ancient] system, this will not do.

[*Zhou Dunyi's text and Zhu Xi's published commentary*]

19. MUSIC (C) (*Yue xia* 樂下)[173]

When the sound of music is quiet then the listener's mind is pacified. When the music's lyrics are good then the singer is respectful. Thus, styles shift and customs change. The influence of weird sound and passionate lyrics is also like this.

[*Zhou Dunyi's text and Zhu Xi's published commentary*]

20. LEARNING TO BE A SAGE (*Sheng xue* 聖學)[174]

Can sagehood be learned?

Reply: It can.

Are there essentials?

Reply: There are.

I beg to hear them.

---

173. [Zhang: This section says that when the sound of music is quiet and the lyrics are good then there will be a corresponding effect on customs.]

174. [Zhang: This section says that what is essential in learning to be a sage lies in the unity of this mind.]

Reply: To be unified (*yi* 一) is essential. To be unified is to have no desire. Without desire one is vacuous (*xu* 虛) when still and direct (*zhi* 直) in activity.[175] Being vacuous when still, one will be clear (*ming* 明); being clear one will be penetrating (*tong* 通). Being direct in activity one will be impartial (*gong* 公); being impartial one will be all-embracing (*pu* 溥). Being clear and penetrating, impartial, and all-embracing, one is almost [a sage].[176]

> The point of this section is the most important. Although the meaning of the text is clear, it does no harm to explain it. If students are able to thoroughly contemplate it and energetically practice it, they will have the means to understand the "truth of nonpolarity" and the origin of the Two Modes and the Four Images. These are not external to this mind, and in the realm of daily functioning itself there is no separation from the power to use them.[177]

> [*Zhu Xi's additional comments*]
> [1] "Unity" is the Supreme Polarity. "Vacuous when still" is the stillness of *yin*. "Direct in activity" is the activity of *yang*. "Clear and penetrating, impartial and all-embracing" is the Five Phases. Basically, all of Master Zhou's discussions connect the Supreme Polarity and the various moral principles.

---

175. *Xici* A.6.2: "The stillness of Qian is focused; its activity is direct" (*Zhouyi benyi*, 3:6b).

176. This section uses terminology that was suspiciously close to Daoism and Buddhism for some Song Confucians. "Vacuous" is prominently used in the *Laozi*, and is similar to the central Mahayana term "emptiness" (*kong* 空) (although the latter, in Buddhist usage, does not mean nothingness or vacuity). The idea of being without desire is also found in the *Laozi*, and is of course part of the Four Noble Truths that are basic to all of Buddhism.

177. Zhu comes very close here to Lu Jiuyuan's position regarding the relationship of mind and principle/order (*li*): that principle can be directly apprehended in the ordinary functioning of the mind. Zhu's claim that the ultimate principle/order of Heaven-and-earth is not external to the mind depends on his other proposition that there are two aspects or dimensions of the unitary mind: the human mind (*renxin* 人心) and the moral mind (*daoxin* 道心). Thus, here he is referring to *daoxin*, which is the principle or substance of the mind, not its ordinary functioning. This is a distinction that Lu did not make. The comment demonstrates how central the methodology of self-cultivation was to Zhu Xi and his interpretation of Zhou Dunyi.

[2] Master Zhou only says "Unity is having no desire." This expression (*huatou* 話頭) is eloquent, but unexpectedly difficult to pin down. How can ordinary people be without desire? Therefore [Cheng] Yichuan only discussed the word "reverent composure" (*jing* 敬).[178]

[3] *Question*: Master Zhou said, "Unity is essential. Unity is having no desire." What does this mean? *Reply*: Concerning "unity is having no desire," of course unity is having no desire. When a person tries to have no desire, how can the mind not be unified? *Further question*: How does this compare with Master Cheng's statement, "Emphasizing unity (*zhu yi* 主一) means reverent composure"?[179] *Reply*: "Having no desire" and "reverent composure" are the same. This word "reverent composure" is especially clear. To seek to hold to reverent composure is somewhat like expending energy, which is not the same as being without desire altogether. People simply have desires, so this mind has a thousand starts and ten thousand connections. The words of this section are extremely important.

[4] *Question* on "Can sagehood be learned? . . . Unity is essential." *Reply*: This is a clearsighted unity, not a muddled unity. *Question*: What is a muddled unity? *Reply*: There must be a critical point where reverent composure is understandable. If it is a reverent composure resulting from lumping everything into one, then it is not reverent composure. This is only speaking in general terms. "Clear and penetrating" refers to the self; "impartial and all-embracing" means being receptive to external things. Being vacuous when still is the beginning of caring and nourishing [one's moral nature]. Only when there is clarity and penetration can one be impartial and all-embracing; if one strives to be impartial and all-embracing one definitely cannot understand it. "Vacuous when still; clear and penetrating" means "to purify one's thoughts and approach the spiritual."[180] "Direct in activity; impartial and all-embracing" means "to benefit one's functioning and ease the body."[181]

---

178. "*Huatou*" is the Chan Buddhist term for the key word or phrase of a *gong'an* 公案 (*kōan*), the use of which was emphasized by Dahui Zonggao, whom Zhu Xu visited in 1155 (see chapter 1). Zhu may therefore be alluding to the Buddhist resonances of Zhou Dunyi's "emphasis on stillness."

179. *Henan Chengshi yishu* 15 (*Er Cheng ji*, 169).

180. Quoting *Xici* B.5.3. Zhu defines "approaching the spiritual" as "the unknowability of the subtle, mysterious person" (*Yulei* 76:2586).

181. Quoting *Xici* B.5.3 (*Yulei* 94:3164).

• [Zhu Xi] also said: "Unity" is what is meant by Supreme Polarity. "Vacuous when still; clear and penetrating" is the same as the "stillness of *yin*" in the [Supreme Polarity] Diagram. "Direct in activity; impartial and all-embracing" is the same as the "activity of *yang*" in the Diagram.[182]

[5] *Question*: "Unity" is being purely undifferentiated and vacuous when still. It is when this mind is like a clear mirror or still water, without the slightest selfish desire added to it. Thus, its activity completely follows the outflowing of the natural order (*tianli*), without the slightest selfish desire disturbing it. "Vacuous when still" is its substance; "direct in activity" is its function. *Reply*: That's just how it is. "Vacuous when still" is easy to see; "direct in activity" is difficult to see. "Vacuous when still" is just as Yichuan [Cheng Yi] put it, "When there is mastery in [the mind's] centrality/equilibrium (*zhong*), then it is vacuous. When it is vacuous, then depravity cannot enter."[183] When things come and disturb it, then it becomes full [of nonessential considerations]. Being full, it is cloudy; being cloudy it is blocked. Being direct in activity is simply when the activity [of the mind] has not the slightest obstruction (*ai* 礙). If occasionally there is a selfish desire, then it will be obstructed and deflected. Whether or not you want it to happen like this, when there is a blockage [the mind's activity] will not be direct. Deflection leads to selfishness, and selfishness leads to narrowness.[184]

[6] *Question*: How does "clear and penetrating, impartial and all-embracing" correspond with the Four Images? *Reply*: Simply in the manner of spring, summer, fall, and winter. *Question*: Does clarity correspond with winter? *Reply*: It is said to be like the point of activity. *Question*: Is it like the origin [of activity]? *Reply*: Yes. But this is a metaphorical relationship; it is not exactly explained like this.[185]

[. . . .]

---

182. This passage follows the previous one in the *Yulei* (94:3164) but is not included in *Zhou Lianxi ji* by Zhang Boxing.

183. Cf. the nearly identical statement by one of the Chengs: "When there is mastery in [the mind's] equilibrium, then it is full (or real, *shi* 實). When it is full, then external worries cannot enter" (*Henan Chengshi yishu* 1 [*Er Cheng ji,* 8]).

184. *Yulei* 94:3163–64.

185. *Yulei* 94:3165.

• *Question*: Yichuan [Cheng Yi] said, "To be a *shi* (literatus) one must be intent on [becoming] a sage." Master Zhou said, "To be unified is essential. To be unified is to have no desire." How are these alike? *Reply*: In commenting on the writings of past sages and worthies, I'm afraid we find that sometimes their ideas are not very close, and sometimes there are errors. In this text that Master Zhou wrote himself there should not be errors.[186] As for "being unified is being without desire," if you are unified then you are without desire. If we look at times when we are without desires, how can the mind not be unified?[187]

PART TWO

[*Zhou Dunyi's text and Zhu Xi's published commentary*]

21. BEING IMPARTIAL AND CLEAR (*Gong ming* 公明)[188]

[a] One who is impartial toward oneself will be impartial toward others. There has never been one who was not impartial toward oneself and yet was able to be impartial toward others.

> This would be the sign of one who did not overcome his own selfishness, yet wanted official rules to regulate things.

[b] When one is not perfectly clear [*ming*] then doubts arise. Clarity is the absence of doubts. To say that being able to doubt is clarity is a thousand miles off the mark.

---

186. Implying that Cheng Yi's statement, which was recorded by someone else, might be in error.

187. *Yulei* 94:3163.

188. [Zhang: This section discusses the value of getting rid of selfishness in order to clarify order. It does not consist in using examination to raise doubts.]

This would be the sign of one who could not first perceive, yet wanted to be clear by deliberately deceiving and untrustingly calculating. Thus, clarity and doubt are actually polar opposites. "A thousand miles off the mark" does not even reach it!

[*Zhu Xi's additional comments*]

[1] Human mendacity (*zha*) is being dishonest. Our intelligence is sufficient for us to know [the truth]; this is called foresight. It is not necessary to lie or to be dishonest; reverting to lies and dishonesty and depending on them is unacceptable. Master Zhou says that with clarity there are no doubts. In most situations there are many doubts, which all arise from unclarity. If we examine [ourselves] we will be clear, and will master the darkness. . . .

[*Zhou Dunyi's text and Zhu Xi's published commentary*]

22. PRINCIPLE, HUMAN NATURE, AND ENDOWMENT (*Li xing ming* 理性命)[189]

[a] The manifest and the subtle: without intelligence one cannot perceive them.

> This discusses principle/order. *Yang* is bright, and *yin* is dark. Were it not for the most numinous [power] of the Supreme Polarity in the human mind, how would one be able to discern it?[190]

---

189. [Zhang: This section says that order (principle) is the Supreme Polarity of the mind, human nature is what is received unequally (*buqi* 不齊), and the endowment is the single foundation of multiplicity. It demonstrates to people the learning of reverting to the foundation.]

Zhang Boxing's characterizations of human nature and endowment here may be either a mistake on his part or a copyist's error, as they seem to be the reverse of what Zhu Xi would say.

190. An allusion to *Taijitu shuo* (F), "Only humans receive the finest and most spiritually efficacious (i.e., numinous) [*qi*]."

[b] There is firm good and firm evil, and the same for yielding. Rest in the mean (*zhong* 中) between them.

> This discusses human nature. The explanation refers to section 7b [The Teacher]; it is the ordering/principle of the Five Phases.

[c] The Two [Modes of] *qi* and the Five Phases transform and generate the myriad things. The five differentia are the two realities, and the two are fundamentally one. Thus, the many are one, and the one reality is divided into the many. Each one of the many is correct; the small and the large are distinct.[191]

> This discusses the endowment. "The Two [Modes of] *qi* and the Five Phases" are that by which Heaven bestows the myriad things and generates them. From the product (*mo* 末) we can deduce the origin (*ben* 本); thus, the differentiation of the Five Phases is the reality of the Two *qi*, and the actuality of the Two *qi* in turn is based on the polarity of the unitary order/principle (*yi lizhi ji* 一理之極). Speaking of this in conjunction with the myriad things, it is simply the unitary Supreme Polarity. Going from the origin to the product, there is the reality of the unitary order, and the myriad things dividing it take it as their substance. Therefore, among the myriad things each possesses the unitary Supreme Polarity; all things small and large have their own distinct portion.
>
> This section has the same meaning as section 16 [Activity and Stillness].
>
> [*Zhu Xi's additional comments*]
> [1] [This section title is] like the *Xici* 繫辭 and *Wenyan* 文言 [appendices to the *Yi*]; if they were Confucius's writing, why

---

191. This clarifies the notion of "nonduality" by clearly distinguishing it from "monism." Differences are real yet are united in a more fundamental unity, such as the relationship of *yin* and *yang* to *taiji*.

192. Since they do contain those words, Zhu means that the texts have been corrupted by later disciples (he believes that the appendices were written by Confucius).

would they contain the words, "The Master said"?[192] I have always questioned such instances, just like Wufeng 五峯 [Hu Hong] in his edition of the *Tongshu*. He discarded the original section headings, and above each section he added the words "Master Zhou said." Once the section headings of the *Tongshu* were discarded, the fact that within this section there originally were no such words as "order, nature, and endowment" made it impossible to understand. I think "The manifest and the subtle: without intelligence one cannot perceive them" discusses principle/order. "There is firm good and firm evil, and the same for yielding. Rest in the mean between them" discusses human nature. From here on discusses endowment. But the section did not contain these three words, until we added the three words that Master Zhou [originally] had used. Without these, this book would have followed the *Xici* and *Wenyan* of the *Yi* in the damage done by disciples. *Question*: In his [edition of the] *Tongshu*, why does [Hu] Wufeng often substitute his own ideas? *Reply*: His problems are many.

[2] In this section, Master Zhou's first two sentences [a] refer to principle; the next three sentences [b] refer to human nature, and the next eight sentences [c] refer to endowment. The section does not contain these three words, yet it is only by means of these three headings that [the meaning of] the section can be revealed. The words in the section themselves certainly contain these categories. "Intelligence" and "the one" are the Supreme Polarity, and "the mean" is the mean attained by the endowment of *qi*. "Firm good and firm evil" and "yielding good and yielding evil" are the fivefold human nature, which corresponds to the Five Phases. Beginners never realize that this is the Supreme Polarity.

[4] "The manifest and the subtle" simply means the various details of principle, such as the difficulty of understanding moral principle in human affairs on one's own. For example, the humanity of the ruler, the loyalty of the subject, the compassion of the father and the filiality of the son: these principles are extremely clear, but how intricate are *yin* and *yang*, nature and endowment, and the comings and goings of ghosts and spirits!

[. . . .]

[*Zhou Dunyi's text and Zhu Xi's published commentary*]

23. MASTER YAN (*Yanzi* 顏子)[193]

[a] Master Yan "had only one dish [of rice] to eat, only one gourdful [of water] to drink, and he lived in a squalid lane. Others could not have endured such distress, yet it did not alter his happiness."

For this discussion, see the *Analects* [6:9].

[b] Now, wealth and honor are what people love. Yet Master Yan, neither loving nor seeking them, took pleasure in being humble. What was in his mind?

This poses the question by bringing out the core [of the idea].

[c] In the world there is extreme honor and extreme wealth, which can be loved and sought after. Yet he [Master Yan] was one who differed from others in seeing what was great and ignoring what was petty.

> The meaning of "extreme honor and extreme wealth that can be loved and sought after" is precisely what Master Zhou taught the Masters Cheng [quoting the Chengs]: "He always instructed us to look for the things that Zhongni 仲尼 [Confucius] and Master Yan enjoyed. What activities did they enjoy?"[194] But students must think deeply and concretely embody them; one cannot merely explain them in words.

[d] Seeing what was great, his mind was at peace. With his mind at peace, nothing was insufficient. With nothing insufficient, then wealth and honor,

---

193. [Zhang: This section refers to Master Yan to show the greatness of the Way. When one takes pleasure in oneself, then whether one is rich or poor cannot express it.]

194. Quoted by Zhu Xi in his commentary on *Analects* 6:9, in *Sishu jizhu, Lunyu* 3:11b. The passage is from *Henan Chengshi yishu* 2A (*Er Cheng ji*, 6).

poverty and humble station were all the same [to him]. Being all the same, then he was able to transform and equalize [others, i.e., regard others as equal].[195] Thus, Master Yan was second only to the Sage [Confucius].

The meaning of the word *equalize* (*qi* 齊) is complex. I fear it may be an error. It may mean either "transform" (*hua* 化), as in "being great and transforming,"[196] or it may mean "equal to," as in "being equal to the sage." "Second only" means he is almost equal, but not quite.

[*Zhu Xi's additional comments*]

[1] *Question* on Master Yan's "not altering his happiness" [a]. This is when selfish desires are eliminated. The natural order flows through (*tianli liuxing* 天裡流行) the one mind, stopping nowhere. This is the principle of the highest wealth and honor. Among all things in the world there is nothing more valuable. How can there be anything more pleasurable? *Master Zhu replied*: What Master Zhou means by highest honor and highest wealth is in contrast to being poor and humble. Now we use this expression to mean fear of shallowness. But selfish desires are still not eliminated, such as the mouth's [fondness] for tastes and ear's for sounds; these too are desires. When we get what is desired this further binds us to selfish desire. How can we be happy enough? If we don't get what is desired, we just seek it further, and the mind is still not satisfied. The only thing to do is to eliminate selfish desire. The natural order flows though activity and stillness, speech and silence throughout our daily functioning; there is nothing that is not the natural order. When it fills the heart, how can it not be pleasurable? This has nothing to do with being poor, thus it doesn't diminish one's happiness.

---

195. According to Mencius (7B.25), the capacity to "transform" (*hua* 化) others is the hallmark of the sage (actually the *junzi* 君子, but the same applies). "Equalizing" (*qi* 齊) others, or seeing all things as equal, is a characteristic of a Daoist sage in the tradition of Zhuangzi (see *Zhuangzi,* ch. 2). Given Zhou Dunyi's Daoist connections, this is not an implausible thing for him to say, although it seems to trouble Zhu Xi in his commentary. Zhu also addresses it in additional comment 15 (not included here).

196. *Mencius* 7B.25.

[11] Master Cheng said that the minds of the sages and worthies were one with the Way, and so anywhere they went they were happy. If we take the Way as a [separate] thing and take pleasure in it, then the mind and the Way are two. This is not what Master Yan did.

[. . . .]

[*Zhou Dunyi's text and Zhu Xi's published commentary*]

24. TEACHERS AND FRIENDS (A) (*Shi you shang* 師友上)[197]

[a] The most revered thing in the world is the Way; the most honored is virtue; the most rare [difficult to attain] is the human being. What is rare about the human being is having the Way and virtue in one's own body.

> This summarizes the meaning of the section above. Although order (*li*) is clear, nevertheless the human mind is darkened by material desire, and few are able to understand it. Thus, every word is carefully weighed.

[b] Without teachers and friends, it is impossible to seek out and obtain in one's own body that which makes the human being the most rare.

> This is why the noble person must exalt his teachers and feel affection for his friends.

[*Zhou Dunyi's text and Zhu Xi's published commentary*]

25. TEACHERS AND FRIENDS (B) (*Shi you xia* 師友下)[198]

[a] Morality (*daoyi* 道義) is valued and honored only when it is possessed by a person.

---

197. [Zhang: This section speaks of the Way and virtue. The highest honor can only be attained by exalting one's teachers and being affectionate with one's friends.]
198. [Zhang: This section says that morality depends on having teachers and friends. A person without teachers and friends misses the importance of their meaning and the pleasure of associating with them.]

Master Zhou frequently stated this idea. It is not [mere] reiteration; it is the urgent meaning of a repeated injunction.

[b] People at birth are ignorant. As they grow, if they have no teachers and friends they become stupid. This is why morality acquires honor and reverence when it is possessed by a person in reliance on teachers and friends.

I think this passage connects with the following sentence.[199]

[c] Is the meaning [of teachers and friends] not important? Is it not a pleasure to associate with them?

Few people understand this importance and this pleasure.

[*Zhou Dunyi's text (no comment by Zhu Xi)*]

26. TRANSGRESSIONS (*Guo* 過)[200]

Zhong You 仲由 [Zilu 子路] was happy to hear about his transgressions, and his good name [reputation] was inexhaustible. Today, when people transgress, they are not happy for others to correct them. It is like concealing one's illness and avoiding a doctor, preferring to harm oneself without being aware of it. Alas!

---

199. I.e., the passage ends in the middle of a sentence. The translation here includes part of the next passage, following Zhu Xi's suggestion.

200. [Zhang: This section speaks of [Confucius's disciple] Zhong You [Zilu], who was happy to hear about his transgressions and had the courage to improve himself. People today are unable to reform, even though they harm themselves.]

[*Zhou Dunyi's text and Zhu Xi's published commentary*]

27. POWER (*Shi* 勢)[201]

[a] The empire is simply power. Power is either weak or strong.

> In the alternation of weak and strong, power necessarily goes to the strong. The weak get weaker and the strong get stronger.

[b] Extreme strength cannot be overcome. If one recognizes its strength and promptly opposes it, one can [succeed].

> If one recognizes it before its strength peaks, then one might be able to overcome it.

[c] As for the effort of overcoming [strength], if one does not recognize it early the effort will not be easy.

> Overcoming it lies within human effort. Whether the effort is difficult or easy depends on whether it is recognized early or late.

[d] When effort is exerted without success, it is due to Heaven. When it is not recognized or no effort is made, it is due to the person.[202]

> If one does not recognize it, one will not know to apply effort. Without effort, then there is no remedy regardless of recognition.

[e] Is it due to Heaven? Then how can a person find fault?

---

201. [Zhang: This section discusses the motive forces (*ji*) in the world. Power is what creates conflict. When strong, it is difficult to overcome.]

202. This is an example of Heaven being interpreted as the cause of things that occur by chance or for unknowable yet natural reasons; cf. p. 43.

We might ask about power that cannot be overcome. Does it result from the actions of Heaven? If it is not Heaven, and comes from what the person does, then there is nothing that can exonerate the fault.

[*Zhu Xi's additional comments*]

[1] *Question* on "Extreme strength cannot be overcome. If one recognizes its strength and promptly opposes it . . ." *Master Zhu replied:* This discusses power in the world, such as the First Emperor of Qin. His strength was so great that the six states could not resist. At the end of Eastern Han, the eunuchs' authority was so strong that they could not be eliminated. At the beginning of the Shaoxing [period] they beheaded Chen Shaoyang just to consolidate power south of the lower Yangze valley, but this extreme strength was overcome.[203] It is difficult to recognize the motive force of strength, yet overcoming it is easy.[204]

[*Zhou Dunyi's text and Zhu Xi's published commentary*]

28. LITERARY EXPRESSION (*Wen ci* 文辭)[205]

[a] Writing (*wen* 文) is the vehicle of the Way. When the wheels and shafts of a carriage are ornamented but cannot be used, the ornamentation is in vain. How much more so an empty carriage!

"Writing is the vehicle of the Way," just as a carriage is the vehicle of things. In making a carriage it is necessary to ornament the wheels and shafts; in writing it is necessary to improve upon one's words and explanations. In both cases one desires others to love and use it. But when I ornament something and others cannot use it, it is empty ornamentation with no concrete use. How much more so a carriage that does not carry

---

203. This refers to Chen Dong (1086–1127), who was executed by the first emperor of the Southern Song, Gaozong.

204. *Yulei* 94:3168.

205. [Zhang: This refers to writing as a vehicle for the Way. People who write without using the Way are like an empty carriage that is not capable of being used.]

things, or writing that is not a vehicle for the Way! Although beautifully ornamented, what good is it?

[b] Literary expression is an art. The Way and virtue are real. If one is devoted to what is real and expresses it artistically in writing, its beauty will be loved. Being loved, it will be transmitted, and Worthies will be able to learn it and achieve its object. This is education. Thus, it is said, "When one's words are not written, they will not go far."[206]

> This is like a carriage carrying things with wheels and shafts that are ornamented.

[c] But the unworthy will not learn it even if father and elder brother are nearby, or teachers and tutors exhort them. Even if forced, they will not comply.

> This is like an already ornamented carriage that someone will not use.

[d] They do not know how to devote themselves to the Way and virtue; they lower themselves to being experts in literary expression. This is nothing more than art [i.e., it does not express concrete reality]. Alas! This is a long-standing defect.

> This is like a carriage that does not carry things but is just beautifully ornamented. Some question whether those who have virtue necessarily have words; [if not,] they would not necessarily depend on artistic expression to transmit [their ideas]. Master Zhou, in this section, seems to distinguish [between morality and literary expression], taking literary expression as an activity that requires effort. What about this?
>
> I say, the human capacity for virtue can be possessed partially; it can be long or short. For some, their ideas are brilliant and words are insufficient

---

206. *Zuozhuan*, Duke Xiang, 25th year; Legge, trans., *The Chinese Classics*, vol. 5: 512, 517.

to express them. These will not be transmitted far. Thus, Confucius said, "Language should be far-reaching" (*Analects* 15:40). And Master Cheng said, "We get the ideas of the 'Western Inscription' [by Zhang Zai], but had it not been for the power of Zihou's 子厚 [Zhang's] brush, he could not have done it [i.e., transmitted his ideas]."[207] This is correctly put. But words sometimes can be few and yet not lacking virtue. There are usually many who have virtue and can express it in words. There are usually few who have virtue and yet are unable to express it in words. Students must first devote themselves energetically to virtue.

[*Zhou Dunyi's text and Zhu Xi's published commentary*]

29. THE COMPREHENSIVENESS OF THE SAGE (*Sheng yun* 聖蘊)[208]

[a] [Confucius said:] "To those who are not eager to learn I do not explain anything, and to those who are not bursting to speak I do not reveal anything. If I raise one angle and they do not come back with the other three angles, I will not repeat myself."[209]

> For this discussion see the *Analects*. It refers to the Sage's teaching. He required [his students to have] ability, and did not underemphasize their active participation.

[b] The Master said, "I wish to do without speech.... What ever does Heaven say? Yet the four seasons run their course through it and all things are produced by it."[210]

---

207. Cf. the nearly identical statement by a Cheng disciple, Bochun, in *Er Cheng yishu* 2A (*Er Cheng ji*, 39).

208. [Zhang: This section speaks of the greatness of the Way of the Sage [Confucius], whose comprehensiveness is not easy to understand. Only Master Yan's profound depth and essential purity began to be able to apprehend it. To seek hurriedly to understand it will result in extreme shallowness.]

209. *Analects* 7:8, trans. Dawson, *The Analects*, 24.

210. *Analects* 17:17, trans. Dawson, 71–72. In Zhu Xi's edition this passage is 17:19.

For this discussion also, see the *Analects*. It speaks of the Way of the Sage not being dependent upon words for its brilliance. Therefore, he says this.

[c] So then, were it not for Master Yan, the Sage's comprehensiveness might not have been seen. Master Yan was the one who brought out the Sage's comprehensiveness and taught ten thousand generations without limit. Was he not equally profound?

> "Comprehensiveness" is the term for what is contained within. Zhongni [Confucius] left no traces, but Master Yan subtly left traces [in the form of his personal example]. Confucius's teaching was important to express, and he never expressed the comprehensiveness of his Way in his own words. Among his students, only Master Yan grasped its entirety. Therefore, because of the traces of his progress and cultivation, Confucius's comprehensiveness could later be seen. It is like the fact that Heaven does not speak, yet the four seasons run their course and all things are produced.

[d] The ordinary person, having heard or understood one thing, is anxious that others will not quickly know he has it. To be in haste to be known by others by reputation is very superficial.

> Sages in general are of different kinds; the higher and lower are very far apart. There are those whose clarity (*ming* 明) does not depend upon teaching. Their words are, accordingly, correct, profound, and extremely substantial. They warn against the dangers of shallowness and superficiality. Compared to the profundity of the Sage's words, the ordinary person's words are superficial. The one is profound and substantial, the other is shallow and superficial. The former speaks of the head, the latter speaks of the tail. These reciprocal phrases clarify it.
>
> > [*Zhu Xi's additional comments*]
> > [2] Students often rely on language to observe the sages and do not examine the reality of the flow of the natural order, which does not depend on words to manifest itself. In this way, by following the words one will not get what they are saying. Therefore, the Master

(Fuzi 夫子) issued this warning. He also said, "the four seasons run their course and all things are produced"; there is nothing that is not the natural order displaying the reality of its flow. It does not depend on words to be seen. In the Sage's alternation of activity and stillness, there is nothing that is not the expression of the essential meaning of the wondrous Way. It is simply Heaven. How can it depend on words for its manifestation? As Master Cheng said, "The Way of Confucius is like the clarity of the sun and stars, but it suffers from disciples who cannot fully understand it." Therefore, he says, "I wish to do without speech." Master Yan silently understood, but the others could not help asking questions. Therefore, [Zigong 子貢] said, "What will be handed on by your disciples?"[211] He [Confucius] also said, "What ever does Heaven say? Yet the four seasons run their course through it and all things are produced by it." So we can say that this is extremely clear.

[. . . .]

[*Zhou Dunyi's text and Zhu Xi's published commentary*]

30. ESSENCE AND COMPREHENSIVENESS (*Jing yun* 精蘊)[212]

[a] The essence of the Sage [Fuxi 伏羲] was displayed in his drawing of the hexagrams [of the *Yi*].[213] The comprehensiveness of the Sage is expressed by means of the hexagrams. Were the hexagrams not drawn, the essence of the Sage could not have been seen. Were it not for the hexagrams, it would almost be impossible to know about the comprehensiveness of the Sage.

"Essence" means subtlety, like the *Yi* before [the hexagrams] were drawn, or the most rudimentary order. When Fuxi drew the hexagrams, he

---

211. Ibid.

212. [Zhang: This section speaks of the Sage's essence and comprehensiveness in terms of the *Yi*, which is the ancestor of writing and the progenitor of meaning and principle. The comprehensiveness of Heaven and Earth, ghosts and spirits, is all contained in this.]

213. While the "comprehensiveness of the Sage" in the previous section refers to Confucius, here the Sage is Fuxi, who first drew the hexagrams of the *Yi*.

concentrated simply on clarifying this [order]. "Comprehensiveness" means the general content of the hexagrams, such as the principle of auspicious or inauspicious growth or decline, or the Way of progress and retreat, preserving or losing—the broadest matters. Given the hexagrams, their forms can be followed.

[b] How can the *Yi* merely be the source [first] of the Five Scriptures? It is the mystery of Heaven and Earth, ghosts and spirits!

Yin and *yang* have their natural fluctuations; hexagram figures have their natural structures (*ti* 體). This is how the *Yi* as a book is the ancestor of writing and the progenitor of meaning and principle. But not only that. Although the general regulation of *yin* and *yang* [pervades] the great extent of Heaven and Earth and the obscurity of ghosts and spirits, its principle was fully contained in the drawing of the hexagrams. This is how the essence and comprehensiveness of the Sage are necessarily contained therein.

> [*Zhu Xi's additional comments*]
>
> [1] In "the essence of the Sage was displayed in his drawing of the hexagrams; the comprehensiveness of the Sage is expressed by means of the hexagrams," Lianxi looks at the *Yi,* but is also able to look at life.[214]
>
> [3] "Essence" and "comprehensiveness" are not the same. "Essence" means the finest essence. "Comprehensiveness" means including all moral principles. *Question*: When Fuxi first drew [the hexagrams], was his comprehensiveness already manifest (*fajian* 發見) therein? *Reply*: We can say that it was already contained therein, but we cannot say that was already manifested therein. When he first drew them, there was not yet the idea of the four virtues of Qian.[215] And when King Wen first extended [their meanings], although he and Confucius were able to extend the ideas [by writing the texts], their moral principles did not go beyond those contained in Fuxi's original

---

214. *Yulei* 94:3169.

215. These are *yuan* 元 (originating), *heng* 亨 (penetrating), *li* 利 (carrying out), and *zhen* 貞 (being correct) in the hexagram text of Qian.

drawings. This is what is meant by [Fuxi's] comprehensiveness. It is like the comprehensiveness of wearing a worn-out robe, which can contain [all] inside [but does not do justice to the wearer].[216]

[. . . .]

[*Zhou Dunyi's text and Zhu Xi's published commentary*]

31. QIAN [Heaven, hexagram 1], SUN [Decrease, hexagram 41], YI [Increase, hexagram 42], AND ACTIVITY (乾損益動)

[a] "The noble person is creatively active and unceasing in being authentic."[217] But he must "control his anger and repress his desires,"[218] and move toward the good and correct his transgressions[219] before he can reach his goal. Among the functions of Qian this is the best. Of the greatness of Sun and Yi, nothing surpasses this. The Sage's meaning is profound indeed!

> This uses the line text of Qian and the Greater Image Commentary on Sun and Yi to explain how to think about being authentic. "Creatively active and unceasing" is the substance. Eliminating evil and advancing the good is the function. Without substance, the function would have nothing to enact. Without function, the substance would have no means [to be enacted]. Thus, [Zhou] discusses them in terms of these three hexagrams combined.
> Some say that [in the third sentence] the word *qi* 其 ("this") could also be *mo* 莫 ("nothing").[220]

---

216. *Yulei* 94:3170.

217. This sentence is composed of three fragments from the texts of Qian 乾 (Heaven): *Yao* 爻 (Line text), 3rd line; *Daxiang zhuan* 大象傳 (Greater Image Commentary); and *Wenyan* 文言 (Words on the Text), 2nd line. *Zhouyi benyi* 1:2a, 1:4a, 1:5b.

218. From *Daxiang* commentary to Sun 損 (Decrease), (*Zhouyi benyi*, 2:17a).

219. Paraphrase of *Daxiang* commentary to Yi 益 (Increase) (*Zhouyi benyi* 2:18b).

220. This would change the reading only slightly, and not the meaning ("nothing is better" instead of "this is the best"). There is probably some corruption in this and the following sentence.

[b] "The auspicious, the inauspicious, repentance and regret arise from activity."[221] Alas! The auspicious is only one [of the four]. Can we not be careful about activity?

> Of the four, there is one good and three bad. Thus, people commonly meet with blessings infrequently and with calamities often. One cannot be too careful.
>
> This section discusses what the *Yi* says about the comprehensiveness of the Sage.
>
> [*Zhu Xi's additional comments*]
>
> [6] *Question*: The beginning of this section, "control his anger and repress his desires, and move toward the good and correct his transgressions," is all about the process of self-cultivation. Then it abruptly speaks about activity. Why is that? *Master Zhu replied*: What is meant by "control his anger and repress his desires, and move toward the good and correct his transgressions," is that in activity there are various kinds of transgressions and failings, so before acting one must examine them. The absence of inauspiciousness, repentance, and regret is why [Zhou] mentions activity the second time.[222]

[*Zhou Dunyi's text and Zhu Xi's published commentary*]

32. JIAREN (Family Members, hexagram 37), KUI (Opposition, hexagram 38), FU (Return, hexagram 24), AND WUWANG (No Error, hexagram 25) (家人睽復無妄)

[a] There is a foundation for ruling the world; it is called the [individual] person.[223] There is a model (*ze* 則) for ordering the world; it is called the family.

---

221. *Xici* B.1 (*Zhouyi benyi* 3:17a). These are four of the basic oracular pronouncements that form the core of the original text of the *Yi*.

222. *Yulei* 94:3171.

223. Cf. the *Daxue* (Great Learning): "From the Son of Heaven to the common person, in each case self-cultivation is the foundation." The core text of the *Daxue*, particularly the "eight items," is alluded to throughout this section, including the commentary.

"Model" means a thing that can be observed and taken as a rule (*fa* 法). In vernacular speech it would be *zeli* 則例 (law) or *zeyang* 則樣 (style, type).

[b] The foundation must be proper (*duan* 端); the proper foundation is nothing but the authentic (*cheng* 誠) mind. The model must be good; the good model is nothing but harmonious relations.

If the mind is not authentic, the person cannot be correct. If relations are not harmonious, the family cannot be regulated.

[c] The family is difficult [to regulate], while the empire is easy. For the family is close, but the state is distant.

What is close is difficult; what is distant is easy. But if one does not do the difficult first, one will never be able to do the easy.

[d] If family members are separated, it is surely caused by the wife. Thus, Kui (Opposition) comes after Jiaren (Family Members). "When two women live together, their wills do not cooperate."[224]

Kui follows Jiaren in the hexagram sequence of the *Yi*. "When two women . . ." comes from the text of the *Tuan* commentary on Kui. [The image of] two women is [based on] the Kui hexagram's [two component trigrams,] Dui below and Li above. Dui is the youngest daughter, and Li is the middle daughter.[225] The nature of the yielding *yin* is outwardly harmonious and pleasant, and inwardly suspicious and jealous. Thus, living together, their wills are different.

---

224. *Tuan* commentary to Kui (Opposition) (*Zhouyi benyi* 2:12a).

225. The Eight Trigrams symbolize a family: father, mother, three sons, and three daughters. Zhu Xi's exegesis here is a good example of his theory that the interpretation of the texts of the *Yi* must be based first on the structure of the hexagrams, i.e., taking into account Fuxi's original creation of the *Yi*. See Smith, Bol, Adler, and Wyatt, *Sung Dynasty Uses of the* I Ching, ch. 6.

[e] This is why Yao "sent down (*lijiang* 釐降) his two daughters to Guirui" [to marry] Shun, to determine whether to abdicate to him, saying "I will test him."[226]

> *Li* means "order," and *jiang* means "down." *Gui* is the name of a river, and *rui* is the north side of the river, where Shun lived. Yao ordered his two daughters to marry Shun, intending to test Shun and [eventually] give him the empire.

[f] Thus, to see how one rules the empire, observe his family. To see how he rules his family, observe his personal life. When his personal life is proper, we say his mind is authentic. An authentic mind is simply one that turns away (*fu* 復) from activity that is not good.

> When activity that is not good ceases externally, then a good mind is born within and there is nothing [internally or externally] that is not actualized (*shi* 實).

[g] Activity that is not good is error. When error is turned around (*fu* 復), there is no error. With no error, one is authentic.

> Master Cheng said, "'No error' means being authentic."[227]

[h] Thus, Wuwang (No Error) follows Fu (Return) and says, "The former kings vigorously nourished the myriad things according to the season."[228] How profound!

---

226. *Shujing* (Book of Documents), "Yaodian" 堯典 (Canon of Yao). See Legge, trans., *The Chinese Classics*, vol. 3, 26–27.

227. *Yichuan Yizhuan* 伊川易傳 (Cheng Yi's commentary on the *Yi*) (*Er Cheng ji* ed.), 822. The line is actually "'No error' is being perfectly authentic." This may be a point that Cheng Yi picked up from Zhou.

228. *Daxiang* commentary to Wuwang (No Error) (*Zhouyi benyi* 1:50a).

Wuwang follows Fu in the sequence of hexagrams. "The former kings . . ." refers to the *Daxiang* commentary on Wuwang in order to clarify nourishing things according to the season. Only one who is perfectly authentic can do this, and so [Zhou] praises the profundity of the intention.

This section brings to light what four hexagrams say about the comprehensiveness of the sage.

> [*Zhu Xi's additional comments*]
>
> [1] An authentic mind simply turns away from action that is not good. When activity that is not good is simply eliminated externally, then the good mind is actualized internally. Simply holding onto this mind is to preserve it.

[*Zhou Dunyi's text and Zhu Xi's published commentary*]

33. WEALTH AND HONOR (*Fu gui* 富貴)[229]

The noble person takes agreement with the Way as honor, and personal peace as wealth. Therefore, he is always at peace, with nothing lacking. He regards ceremonial carriages and caps as small change; he regards gold and jade as dust. The weight [of his riches] cannot be exceeded.

> The principle here is easy to clarify, yet it bears repeating. It seeks for people to have the means to truly understand the importance of morality, and not be influenced by external things.

> [*Zhu Xi's additional comments*]
>
> [1] Teacher Zhou says that the Way is the highest honor. There is not one thing that comes up to it. We see our foolish contemporaries losing control to external things, like falling into a pit of fire. I cannot bear to see them. It is for this reason that I say "not one thing." Most people's minds are an empty shell, so they appear like madmen. They are simply unaware of themselves.

---

229. [Zhang: This section speaks of the Way of the noble person. What is inside is important; what is outside is taken lightly.]

[*Zhou Dunyi's text and Zhu Xi's published commentary*]

34. BEING SUPERFICIAL (*Lou* 陋)[230]

The Way of the Sages enters through the ear, is preserved in the mind/heart, is comprehended in one's moral behavior, and is enacted in one's affairs and undertakings. Those who engage merely in literary expression are superficial.

> The idea is the same as in the section above. It seeks for people to truly understand the importance of morality, and not to fall into the superficiality of literary expression.

>> [*Zhu Xi's additional comments*]
>> [2] The literature (*wen*) of the ancient sages and worthies can be called magnificent. But at first, how did they have the ideas and learning to create this kind of literature? They had this reality [*shi* 實] within, so they necessarily had this literary [expression] without. It is like Heaven having *qi*, so there must be the light of sun, moon, and stars; or earth having form, so there must be the array of mountains, rivers, plants, and trees. Since the minds of sages and worthies had this brilliant and pure reality fully replete within, its display without was clearly in order. Its glory overspread and could not be concealed. So they did not have to rely on spoken language; they wrote books, which we call literature. But they embodied the myriad affairs themselves, whether in speech or in silence. What people can see is only the literature. Now to name the greatest of their words, they are the hexagram drawings of the *Yi*, the recorded words of the *Shu*, the songs sung in the *Shi*, the affairs recorded in the *Chunqiu*, the decorum of the *Li*, and the rhythm of the *Yue*. These were all arranged as the Six Scriptures and passed down through the myriad generations. This literature is magnificent; later generations have definitely not been able to come up to it. But as

---

230. [Zhang: This section speaks of studying the sages, which requires one to seek out the Way and virtue. One cannot fall into mere literary expression.]

for what makes it magnificent and unsurpassable, how can it not come from the self (*zi* 自)? Yet the world doesn't recognize this.

[. . . .]

[*Zhou Dunyi's text and Zhu Xi's published commentary*]

35. DELIBERATION AND DISCUSSION (*Ni yi* 擬議)[231]

Being perfectly authentic, one acts. Acting, one changes. Changing, one transforms. Thus, it is said, "Deliberate before speaking; discuss before acting. By such deliberation and discussion one can complete one's transformation."[232]

> What the *Zhongyong* and the *Great Commentary* of the *Yi* mean is not the same.[233] But here we are speaking of them together, not distinguishing their meanings. Someone says, "'Being perfectly authentic' is the self-nature of the actualized order. Deliberation and discussion are the process by which one authenticates it."

[*Zhu Xi's additional comments*]

[1] "Acting" is acting toward another when stimulated. "Changing" is altering one's old customs. But if there is a flaw remaining, one's transformation will melt away without a trace.

[. . . .]

---

231. [Zhang: This section speaks of the actualized order and the Way of nature. One who has not yet achieved authenticity should value deliberation and discussion to complete the transformation.]

232. *Zhouyi, Xici* A.8 (*Zhouyi benyi* 3:7b).

233. It is unclear whether Zhu is referring to the term "being perfectly authentic" or to the title of the section. "Being perfectly authentic" (*zhi cheng* 至誠) occurs six times in the *Zhongyong* (chs. 22, 23, 24 twice, 26, and 32), but not all in the *Xici*. In fact the word *cheng* by itself only occurs twice in the *Yi*, both times in the *Wenyan*. And the term *deliberation and discussion* (*ni yi*) occurs once in the *Xici* (quoted here), but not all in the *Zhongyong* (nor does *ni* by itself).

[Zhou Dunyi's text and Zhu Xi's published commentary]

36. PUNISHMENT (Xing 刑)[234]

[a] Heaven gives birth to the myriad things in the spring and ceases in the autumn. Not to cease after things have come alive and been completed would be going too far. Therefore comes the autumn for completion. The sage models Heaven in governing and nourishing the myriad people. He regulates them with punishment. As the people flourish, their desires become active and their feelings overwhelming, and benefit and harm come into conflict. If not stopped, there would be injury and destruction and no more human relations. Therefore, they receive punishment to regulate [their behavior].

This idea is roughly the same as in the eleventh section.

[b] Feelings are unreliable [false] and obscure; they change in a thousand ways. They can only be regulated with centrality and correctness, clarity and intelligence, firmness and decisiveness. Song [Conflict, hexagram 6] says, "It is beneficial to see the great man,"[235] for "the firm [line] has gained the central position."[236] Shihe [Biting Through, hexagram 21] says, "It is beneficial to use litigation"[237] to "clarify through activity."[238]

> Centrality and correctness are the foundation; clarity and decisiveness are the function. But without clarity, decisiveness has no way of working; without decisiveness, clarity has no place to work. The two also have a temporal relationship. "Centrality" in Song is related to "correctness";

---

234. [Zhang: This section says that the Way of being a ruler lies in being centered and correct, clear and intelligent, firm and decisive. Of these three, not one can be lacking.]

235. Yijing, hexagram text of Song 訟 (Zhouyi benyi 1:19b).

236. Yijing, Tuan commentary to Song (Zhouyi benyi 1:20a).

237. Yijing, hexagram text of Shihe 噬嗑 (Zhouyi benyi 1:43b).

238. Yijing, Tuan commentary on Shihe (Zhouyi benyi 1:44a).

"clarify" in Shihe is related to intelligence. "Firm" in Song and "active" in Shihe mean "firmness and decisiveness."

[c] Ah! Throughout the empire, those who control punishment direct the lives of the people. In appointing them to their position, can one not be careful?

> [*Zhu Xi's additional comments*]
>
> [1] The mind of the sage nourishes and brings [things] to life. In reality, it has the same virtue as Heaven-and-earth. Some things are contrary to principle and offensive to heaven, so in judging their importance one must decisively [apply] unchanging principle. It is like the revolution of the four seasons in heaven and earth: bitter cold for half [the year], yet the mind that nourishes and gives life is always flowing through it.

[*Zhou Dunyi's text (no comment by Zhu Xi)*]

37. BEING IMPARTIAL (*Gong* 公)[239]

The Way of the Sage is perfectly impartial. Someone said, "What does that mean?" I replied, "Heaven-and-earth are perfectly impartial."

[*Zhou Dunyi's text (no comment by Zhu Xi)*]

38. CONFUCIUS (A) (*Kongzi shang* 孔子上)

The *Spring and Autumn* [*Annals*] rectifies the Kingly Way and clarifies the great models [of the past]. Confucius compiled it for the kings of later generations. The rebellious ministers and wicked sons who were put to death in the past are a means of arousing fear in those to come. It is fitting that for ten thousand generations without end, kings have sacrificed to Confucius to repay his inexhaustible virtue and achievement.

---

239. Sections 37–39 lack notes by Zhang Boxing.

[*Zhou Dunyi's text and Zhu Xi's published commentary*]

39. CONFUCIUS (B) (*Kongzi xia* 孔子下)

Confucius was the only one whose Way and virtue were lofty and abundant, whose educational influence was unlimited, and who could truly form a triad with Heaven and Earth and be equal to the Four Seasons.[240]

> That which has a Way as lofty as Heaven is *yang*. That which has virtue as abundant as Earth is *yin*. That which has educational influence as unlimited as the Four Seasons is the Five Phases. Confucius [embodied] the Supreme Polarity!

[*Zhou Dunyi's text and Zhu Xi's published commentary*]

40. MENG [Ignorance, hexagram 4] AND GEN [Keeping Still, hexagram 52] (蒙艮)[241]

[a] "The ignorant youth (*tongmeng* 童蒙) seeks me out,"[242] and I "correct"[243] him and "determine his course of actions,"[244] as in divination. Divination is inquiring of the spirits. [To ask] a second or third time is a violation. In that case, I make no pronouncement.

> This connects with the following three sections, which variously refer to the hexagram text, the *Tuan* commentary, and the Greater Image commentary on Meng to elucidate the meaning. *Tong* is a youth; *meng* is ignorant. "I" means the teacher. "Divination" is casting yarrow stalks

---

240. "Form a triad with Heaven and Earth" is an allusion to the "perfectly authentic" person of *Zhongyong* 22.
241. [Zhang: This section refers to two hexagrams to clarify the idea of emphasizing stillness. This is also the comprehensiveness of the sage.]
242. Hexagram text of Meng (*Zhouyi benyi* 1:15b).
243. *Tuan* commentary on Meng (*Zhouyi benyi* 1:16a).
244. *Daxiang* commentary on Meng (*Zhouyi benyi* 1:16b).

to determine the auspicious and inauspicious. It says that the youthful and ignorant person comes seeking me to alleviate his ignorance, and I use the correct Way to determine his course of action. It is like divination, "inquiring of the spirits" to resolve one's doubts; the spirits pronounce "auspicious" or "inauspicious" to determine one's course of action. Whether inquiring of spirits or seeking a teacher, only once yields clarification. If the first divination yields a pronouncement, then a second or third is wrong. In that case the spirits will not pronounce "auspicious" or "inauspicious." Likewise, a teacher will not necessarily determine one's course of action.[245]

[b] "Below the mountain issues forth a spring";[246] still [mountain] and clear [water]. When disturbed, [the water] is mixed up; when mixed up, it is not clear.

"Beneath the mountain issues forth a spring" is from the Greater Image commentary. The mountain is still and the spring is clear; they [both] have the means to complete their unexpressed goodness, and so the course of action can reach fruition. "Disturbed" [corresponds] to the "second and third" [divinations]. "Mixed up" [corresponds to] the "violation." "Not clear" [corresponds to] "no pronouncement." Thus, "disturbed," it is not still; "mixed up," it is not clear. When you are unable to preserve your unexpressed goodness, then announcing it will not be enough to complete your course of action; on the contrary you will produce confusion. It is better not to announce one's stupidity.

[c] Be cautious! This means [to follow] the "timely mean"![247]

"Timely mean" is from the *Tuan* commentary text; it teaches hitting the right point. The first time there is a pronouncement. When violated, there

---

245. "Inquiring of spirits" can be taken in two ways. It can be simply a metaphor for divination, using the language of more "popular" forms, such as a spirit-medium diviner. Or "spirits" can refer to the yarrow stalks, which in the *Xici* (A.11.3, A.11.8) are called "spiritual things" (*shen wu* 神物). What is certain is that Zhu Xi, and most probably Zhou Dunyi, did not believe that personalized gods or spirits had anything to do with *Yijing* divination.

246. *Daxiang* commentary on Meng (*Zhouyi benyi* 1:16b).

247. *Tuan* commentary on Meng (*Zhouyi benyi* 1:16a).

is no pronouncement. When still and clear there is a decision. When disturbed and mixed up there is no decision. These both [illustrate] the timely mean.

[d] "Keep the back still (*gen* 艮),"[248] for the back is not seen. When still (*jing* 靜), one can stop [at the right point]. To stop is not to act [deliberately]. To act [deliberately] is not to stop [at the right point]. This Way is profound!

> This section refers to the Image commentary of the Gen hexagram and elucidates it. *Gen* is to stop. "The back" is the place that is not seen. "Keep the back still" is to stop in the place that is not seen. When one stops in the place that is not seen, then one is still (*jing*). When still, one stops and has no acting. Once there is a mind to act, then it is not the Way of stopping.
>
> This section brings to light two hexagrams. Both discuss "the comprehensiveness of the sage" and the idea of emphasizing stillness.

---

248. Hexagram text of Gen (*Zhouyi benyi* 2:34b).

Chapter Eight

Zhu Xi's Postfaces and Notes

I. Postface to master zhou's *taiji* and *tongshu* [1169]
(*zhouzi taiji tongshu houxu* 周子太極通書後序)[1]

Above are Master Zhou's writings compiled together. Today there are editions from Chongling, Lingling, and Jiujiang, which all have similarities and differences. The Changsha edition was the last to appear, so that is the one I have compiled.[2] I have examined the other editions in the most careful detail, but they seem to be incomplete.

The profundity of the Teacher's learning is embodied in the *Taiji* Diagram, and the words of the *Tongshu* manifest the comprehensiveness of this Diagram. The sayings of the Cheng brothers on the nature and endowment all follow his theories. We can see this by observing the [*Tongshu*] chapters on authenticity [1–2], activity and stillness [16], and order, nature, and endowment [22] and comparing them with such examples of the Chengs' writings as [Cheng Hao's] epitaph for [his friend] Li Zhongtong 李仲通,[3] his epitaph for [his

---

1. This is the postface to the Jian'an edition of Zhou's works, the second published by Zhu Xi (without commentary). It is not included in Zhang Boxing's *Zhou Lianxi ji*, but is found in *Wenji* 75 (*Zhuzi quanshu*, vol. 24:3628–30).
2. The Changsha edition was published by Zhu Xi himself in 1166 (Shu, *Nianpu*, 348).
3. "*Li Sicheng muzhi ming*" 李寺承墓志銘, in *Er Cheng ji*, 497–99.

son] Cheng Shaogong 程邵公,[4] and [Cheng Yi's] "Essay on What Master Yan Loved to Learn."[5]

Therefore, when Pan Qingyi 潘清逸 [Pan Xingsi 潘興嗣] wrote the Teacher's epitaph,[6] in listing the books he wrote he specifically put the *Taiji Diagram* first, so I do not doubt that the Diagram belongs at the head of the Discussion. But when the Master personally transmitted the books to the two Chengs, [the Diagram] followed the Discussion, according to Qi Kuan/Juzhi 祁寬居之.[7] Those who transmitted it saw it like this, with the Diagram wrongly placed after the Discussion, and did not correct it. This caused the subtle meaning of the Master's symbolism and deep ideas [in the Diagram] to be obscure and unclear, and readers of the *Tongshu* in turn were unaware of its meaning, so some editions were lacking. But the Changsha edition of the *Tongshu* that the Hu family transmitted was not [wrongly] reordered. It is missing the section titles, with "The Master said" added instead of them. Although this does not harm the general meaning of the book, it is not the Master's original, and without the titles it is difficult to understand: for example, the "Order, nature, and endowment" section [22]. Several editions include inscriptions, poems, and events, many of them repeated. Some [of these] do not succeed in bringing to light the Master's Way for the benefit of students.

Therefore, I have relied especially on Pan's epitaph, which places the Diagram at the beginning, taking it as the Master's essential idea so as to comprehend the discussion of the [*Tong*]*shu*. As for the [*Tong*]*shu*'s correct sequence of sections, I have also returned to the original order, and have

---

4. "*Cheng Shaogong muzhi*" 程邵公墓志, in *Er Cheng ji*, 494–95. The conclusions of both epitaphs speculate as to the reasons for these deaths in terms of the cosmology of *qi* and its mixed endowment in the human constitution. For example, the conclusion of the epitaph for his son begins as follows: "Activity and stillness are the foundation of *yin* and *yang*. The interactions of the five *qi* are mixed and uneven. . . ." (continuing with what became the standard Cheng-Zhu theory of the mixed endowment of pure and impure *qi*); the parallels with chapters 1, 2, 16, and 22 of the *Tongshu* are clear.

5. "*Yanzi suo hao he xue*" 顏子所好何學 in *Er Cheng ji*, 577. This obviously resonates with *Tongshu* sections 10, 23 and 29, all of which mention Master Yan (Yan Yuan or Yan Hui).

6. "*Lianxi xiansheng muzhi ming*" 濂溪先生墓志銘, in *Zhou Lianxi* 10:19a–20b.

7. However, in the 1144 postface to the *Tongshu* by Qi Kuan that we have (*Zhou Lianxi* 7:3b), he says that what he found in Zhou's house contained no diagram. See Zheng Jixiong, "*Cong jingdian quanshi de jiaodu lun rudao Yi tu de leixing yu bianyi*," 112; and A. C. Graham, *Two Chinese Philosophers*, 166–67, 174 n.60.

selected the real events from the Master's life from the records of Pu Zuocheng, Kong Sifeng, and Huang Taishi, eliminating duplications and combining them into one chapter for contemplation.[8] Of what has been transmitted in the Master's writings, his words and deeds are contained herein.

What Mr. Pan calls the *Yitong* 易通 I suspect is *Tongshu* 通書, and the *Yishuo* 易說 alone [among the works mentioned by Pan][9] has been lost. Regarding the many different writings gathered by my friends, each called a traditional text, even the briefest look makes me smile at their superficiality. They are all by scholar-officials from the period of the "[three] hall system,"[10] who [simply] pieced together vestigial residues. They are completely unlike the *Tushuo* and *Tongshu*; we can know they are false without inquiring. But we don't know whether or not the world has the ability to get the truth. By extending the Diagram and Discussion we know what they express: the very essence of polarity. Fine words disappear; what a pity.

---

8. "*Lianxi xiansheng shizhuang,*" in *Zhou Lianxi* 10:20b–22b.

9. "He delved deeply into the study of the *Yi*. He wrote the *Taiji* Diagram, the *Yishuo* (Discussion of the *Yi*), the *Yitong* (Penetrating the *Yi*) in several tens of sections, and ten scrolls of poems; these today are stored in his house" (*Zhou Lianxi ji* 10:20b).

10. The "three-hall system" (*sanshe fa* 三舍法), which Zhu Xi opposed, organized the Imperial University (*Taixue* 太學) into three classes through which students could pass in order to qualify for official positions without taking the standard civil service examinations. It was established by the Northern Song prime minister Wang Anshi (1021–1086) during the reform period of 1069–1085, overturned (1085–1093) by the anti-reformers led by Sima Guang (1019–1086), and then revived (1093–1125) under prime minister Cai Jing 蔡京 (1047–1126). See Levine, *Divided by a Common Language,* 158, and Lee, *Government Education and Examinations in Sung China,* 64–65, 77–80, 231–33. On Wang Anshi see Liu, *Reform in Sung China*; on Zhu Xi's (and his predecessors' in the Cheng school) opposition to Wang Anshi's reforms see de Bary and Bloom, *Sources of Chinese Tradition,* 609–28.

Zhu's disparaging reference to the "period of the [three-] hall system" is probably directed at the Cai Jing era, when the writings of Cheng Yi, among many others, were declared heterodox (Wilson, *Genealogy of the Way,* 37 and Levine, *Divided by a Common Language,* 150–57). Cai Jing and Wang Anshi before him were attempting to impose a narrow conformity on the thinking of Confucian officials (see Liu, *Reform in Sung China,* 88; and Lee, *Government Education and Examinations in Sung China,* 240). The irony, of course, is that the eventual dominance of Zhu Xi's own system over other varieties of Confucian thinking in the Southern Song, and its becoming the official standard for the civil service examinations during the succeeding Yuan dynasty, resulted in the same kind of stifling orthodoxy (see Tillman, *Confucian Discourse and Chu Hsi's Ascendancy*). For some of Zhu Xi's criticism of the three-hall system see his unsubmitted 1187 memorial on education (*Wenji* 69, in *Zhuzi quanshu,* vol. 23: 3355–64), partially translated in Lee, *Government Education and Examinations in Sung China,* 232–33.

I have read Zhu Neihan/Zhen's 朱內翰震 *Jin Yi shuobiao* 進易說表 (Memorial Presenting the *Yi*), which says that this Diagram was transmitted from Chen Tuan 陳摶 to Chong Fang 种放 to Mu Xiu 穆修 and on [to Zhou Dunyi].[11] Hu Wufeng/Renzhong 胡五峯仁仲 [Hu Hong] wrote the "Preface to the *Tongshu*" in which he says that the Master went beyond the learning of Zhong and Mu, and especially their teacher [Chen Tuan], who was not at this level.[12] The subtlety of the Master's learning is completely contained in this Diagram. If he got it from someone else, it certainly was not Zhong and Mou. That being the case, then how could they have added this diagram to the Master's learning? I have questioned this. After examining [Pan's] eulogy I have come to the conclusion that the Master composed it himself; he did not receive it from anyone.[13] Mr. [Hu] never saw what this eulogy said. Still, Mr. Hu writes of the *Tongshu*'s meaning:

> People see the brevity of this book but do not understand the greatness of his Way. They see the quality of his writing but do not understand the essence of his ideas. They see the surface of his words but do not understand the extent of their flavor. . . . People who are truly able to establish Yi Yin's intention and to cultivate Master Yan's learning will then understand the extreme greatness contained in the words of the *Tongshu,* and the inexhaustibility of the sagely enterprise.[14]

This is a statement that cannot easily be matched, but those who read this book should understand it. Accordingly, I have selected it to connect with posterity.

Respectfully written by Zhu Xi of Xin'an 新安 on the *wu-shen* 戊申 day in the sixth month of the *ji-chou* 己丑 year of Qiandao 乾道 [1169]

---

11. Zhu Zhen (or Zhu Hanshang [1072–1138]) was a student of Xie Liangzuo (1050–1121), who had been a student of the Cheng brothers. See Zhu Zhen's account in Smith, *Fathoming the Cosmos and Ordering the World,* 115.

12. See Hu Hong, *Tongshu xulüe* (Outline preface to the *Tongshu*), in *Zhou Lianxi* 7:1b, translated above in chapter 1.

13. Because Pan doesn't mention the Daoist connection.

14. Hu Hong, *loc. cit.* For Yi Yin and Master Yan, see *Tongshu,* section 10b.

II. Revised Postface to Master Zhou's *Taiji* and *Tongshu* [1179]
(*Zaiding Zhouzi Taiji Tongshu houxu* 再定周子太極通書後序)[15]

Above is Master Zhou's Supreme Polarity Diagram with its Discussion in one chapter (*pian* 篇) and the *Tongshu* in forty sections (*zhang* 章). The old edition of surviving writings, in nine chapters, included "Surviving Affairs" (*Yishi* 遺事) in fifteen passages (*tiao* 條) and a "Biography" (*Shizhuang* 事狀) in one chapter. What I have put in order has been corrected and rewritten. Years have passed since I commented on the Master's writings. What has been handed down is extensive, but there are inevitable errors. Only the Changsha and Jian'an editions are adequate, yet they are still incomplete.

The profundity of the Master's learning, to the extent that it can be symbolized, is complete in the Taiji Diagram. The words of the *Tongshu* are the means of expressing the entirety [of his learning], especially the chapters on authenticity [1–3], activity and stillness [16], and order, human nature, and endowment [22]. The writings of the Chengs also follow his ideas: [Cheng Hao's] epitaph for [his friend] Li Zhongtong, his epitaph for [his son] Cheng Shaogong, and [Cheng Yi's] "Essay on What Master Yan Loved to Learn,"[16] together with their sayings, express [Zhou's ideas]. Pan Qingyi [Pan Xingsi] knew this [the centrality of the Diagram], for when he wrote the Master's epitaph,[17] in listing his books he specifically put the Taiji Diagram first, followed by the *Yishuo* and *Yitong*.

[Note by Zhang Boxing:]

Zhu Zhen/Hanshang/Zifa 漢上朱震子發 says that Chen Tuan transmitted the *Taiji* Diagram to Chong Fang, Fang transmitted it to Mu Xiu, and Xiu transmitted it to the Master. Hu Hong/Renzhong of Hengshan [in Hunan] says that the tradition of Chong and Mu, and

---

15. This is the postface to the Nankang edition, which Zhu published one month after receiving the old Zhou family edition of Zhou's writings from Yang Fang (*Nianpu* 628). It follows the *Tongshu* in *Zhou Lianxi ji* (6:23b–26a) and *Zhuzi quanshu* (vol. 13:130–33), and is also found in *Wenji* 76:3652–54.

16. See notes to 1169 postface.

17. *Zhou Lianxi ji* 10:19a–20b.

especially their teacher [Chen Tuan], was not at [Zhou's] level.[18] Qi Kuan/Juzhi of Wudang says that the images of the Diagram were orally described to the Cheng brothers but never written down.[19] They [Hu and Qi] probably never saw Pan's eulogy. According to Mr. Hu, who did not examine the depths of the Master's learning, it is completely contained, from beginning to end, in the Diagram. The Master's *Yishuo* (Discussion of the *Yi*) has long been lost. Two [similar] books are not it: the *Guashuo* 掛說 (Discussion of the Trigrams/Hexagrams) was written by Chen Zhongsu 陳忠肅, and the *Xicishuo* 繫辭說 (Discussion of the Appended Phrases) is full of decadent Buddhist and Daoist [or Laoist] sayings; its superficiality is laughable. For example, it says, "The flourishing of the *Yi* is the Way of the world; it is like the monkey-keeper deceiving the monkeys."[20] One look at this and we can know that it was definitely not written by the Master. The *Yitong* is, I suspect, the *Tongshu,* and the *Yishuo* was probably an explanation of the Scripture [*Yi*], a comprehensive discussion of its general meaning, not attached to the scripture itself [like a commentary]. We don't specifically know when the word *Yi* was dropped [from the *Yitong*] and the present title was first used.

However [unlike Pan's description], the various editions all added [the Diagram] after the *Tongshu,* so readers mistakenly took it as the *Tongshu*'s conclusion. This caused the subtle meaning of the Master's symbolism and deep ideas to be dark and unclear, and those who discussed the *Tongshu* in turn did not understand that its general meaning was here [in the Diagram]. The Changsha edition [1166] did not correct this, and its *Tongshu* follows Mr. Hu's emendation, with the sequence of sections often changed. It also lacks the section titles, replacing them with "Master Zhou says," all of which is not the Master's original. For example, the "Principle, nature, and endowment" section cannot be understood without the title. Its supplementary inscriptions and poems make this [Changsha] edition quite thorough. But in some places it fails to make clear the Master's Way, and [Hu's] followers have

---

18. See Hu Hong's preface to the *Tongshu,* translated in chapter 1.

19. Qi Kuan, *Tongshu houba* 通書後跋 (Postface to the *Tongshu*), in *Zhou Lianxi ji* 7:2b–3b.

20. A reference to the "three in the morning" story in *Zhuangzi,* ch. 2.

repeated [these shortcomings]. Therefore the Jian'an [1169] edition relied mainly on Pan's eulogy, placing the Diagram section before the [*Tong*]*shu,* putting the titles before each section, and returning to the original. I have also combined into a single biography the real events of the Master's life as recorded by Pu Zuocheng 蒲左承 [Pu Zongmeng 蒲宗孟], Kong Sifeng 孔司封 [Kong Yanzhi 孔延之], and Huang Taishi 黃太史 [Huang Tingjian 黃庭堅], eliminating duplications and critically examining them.[21] [A note in the text at this point gives some examples of the differences among these records.] As for the subtlety of *daoxue,* there are various gentlemen who have not been able to understand it, and others who consider the statements of the Chengs and their disciples to be correct. This can be seen by considering the writings, words, and deeds of the Master into account.

Only after consulting the edition of Yang Fang 楊方 from Linting 臨汀 did I understand that the common editions were not completely correct.[22] [Here Zhu inserts a note giving examples of textual errors that he corrected.] I also obtained He Jun's 何君 "Preface to poetry from Yingdao" and the statements of those who had traveled to Chongling 舂陵 [village],[23] and understood that the theories expressed in the "Biography" about Lianxi's chosen name missed the basic idea.[24] [Another note giving details, omitted here.] After proofreading the old texts I understood the extent of the writing mistakes and the faulty transmission of the records of that time. [Another note with examples.] I also read the honorable Zhang Zhongding's 張忠定 statements and understood that the discussions about the transmission [of the *Taijitu*] from Xiyi 希夷 [Chen Tuan] to Chong [Fang] to Mu [Xiu] had not completely unraveled its complications.[25]

---

21. Pu Zongmeng (1022–1088) was a good friend of Zhou's and married his younger sister. Kong Yanzhi (1013–1074), a direct descendant of Confucius, was an official and poet. Huang Tingjian (1045–1105) was a famous calligrapher.

22. Yang Fang is the person who brought the Zhou family edition of Zhou's works to Zhu Xi, just a month before this postface was written (*Nianpu* 626, 628).

23. Zhou was born in Chongling village, Yingdao 營道 county, Hunan province.

24. Referring to the name Lianxi, which he gave to the stream near where he retired and which became the most common name for him used by his later followers.

25. Zhang Zhongding (Zhang Yong 張詠 [946–1015]) was an official of the Northern Song. Chen Xiyi is Chen Tuan.

[Note by Zhang Boxing:]

Zhang Zhongding followed the learning of [Chen] Xiyi and says that the variations of *yin* and *yang* agreed with the ideas of the Discussion of the Diagram. But I question the theory of transmission. The main point is certainly that only after the Master realized it his own mind did he connect everything—the principle of Heaven-and-earth, hard and soft, dark and light, high and low, fine and coarse—and first make this Diagram in order to express these mysteries.

I have long wanted to make these corrections and fill in the deficiencies, yet I worried that I was unable. Since I have been appointed Prefect of Nankang, I have connected with the Master's teachings after more than a hundred years. Although my virtue is not in his category, and my shame and awe are profound, I look up to the high mountain and sigh deeply. I have accordingly picked up the old books, made more corrections, appended this discussion, and had woodblocks carved in order to share with like-minded literati.

Respectfully written by Zhu Xi of Xin'an on the *wu-wu* 戊午 day in the fifth month, summer, of the *ji-hai* 己亥 year of Chunxi 淳熙 [1179][26]

III. Postface to Commentaries on the Supreme Polarity and the Western Inscription
(*Ti taiji ximing jie hou* 題太極西銘解後)[27]

When I first wrote the commentaries on the *Taiji* [*tu shuo*] and the *Ximing*, I did not dare to send them out to people. Recently I have seen scholars (*ru* 儒) frequently discussing what is lacking in the two texts. Some of them have never penetrated their meanings, and wrongly slander them. This is something I lament. I therefore send out these commentaries to students and

---

26. Zhang Boxing's edition lacks the date.

27. *Wenji* 82:3880. The "Western Inscription" is Zhang Zai's most famous piece of writing; a section of his *Zheng meng* (Correcting youthful ignorance) that he supposedly wrote on the wall of his house.

followers so that they will spread these traditions, and so that those readers who are good enough will get the ideas from these texts and understand that they cannot be discussed frivolously.

Submitted by Huiweng 晦翁[28] on the *ji-si* 己巳 day in the second month of the *wu-shen* 戊申 year of Chunxi 淳熙 [1188]

---

28. Toward the end of his life Zhu Xi sometimes referred to himself as Huiweng, or Old Man Hui (based on his style name Hui'an 晦庵).

Bibliography

Abramson, Marc S. *Ethnic Identity in Tang China*. Philadelphia: University of Pennsylvania Press, 2008.

Adler, Joseph A. "Confucianism as Religion / Religious Tradition / Neither: Still Hazy after All These Years." Minzu University of China, 2010 (unpublished).

———. "Daughter/Wife/Mother or Sage/Immortal/Bodhisattva? Women in the Teaching of Chinese Religions." *AsiaNetwork Exchange* XIV, no. 2 (Winter 2006): 11–16.

———. "Divination and Sacrifice in Song Neo-Confucianism." In *Teaching Confucianism*, edited by Jeffrey L. Richey, 55–82. New York: Oxford University Press, 2008.

———. "The Great Virtue of Heaven and Earth: Deep Ecology in the *Yijing*." In *Religious Diversity and Ecological Sustainability in China*, edited by James Miller. London: Routledge, forthcoming.

———. "Response and Responsibility: Chou Tun-i and Neo-Confucian Resources for Environmental Ethics." In *Confucianism and Ecology: The Interrelation of Heaven, Earth, and Humans*, edited by Mary Evelyn Tucker and John Berthrong, 123–49. Cambridge: Harvard University Center for the Study of World Religions, 1998.

———. "Varieties of Spiritual Experience: *Shen* in Neo-Confucian Discourse." In *Confucian Spirituality*, vol. 2, edited by Tu Weiming and Mary Evelyn Tucker. New York: Crossroad, 2004.

———. "Zhou Dunyi: The Metaphysics and Practice of Sagehood." In *Sources of Chinese Tradition*, 2nd ed., vol. 1, edited by Wm. Theodore de Bary and Irene Bloom, 669–78. New York: Columbia University Press, 1999.

———. "Zhu Xi's Spiritual Practice as the Basis of his Central Philosophical Concepts." *Dao: A Journal of Comparative Philosophy* 7, no. 1 (March 2008): 57–79.

Alston, George Cyprian. "Rule of St. Benedict." In *The Catholic Encyclopedia,* vol. 2. New York: Robert Appleton Company, 1907. http://www.newadvent.org/cathen/02436a.htm; accessed Feb. 19, 2012.
Ames, Roger T. "Translating Chinese Philosophy." In *An Encyclopedia of Translation: Chinese-English, English-Chinese,* edited by Chan Sin-wai and David E. Pollard, 731–46. Hong Kong: The Chinese University Press, 1995.
Anonymous. *Zhejiang difang zhi* 浙江通志 (Zhejiang gazetteer). http://baike.baidu.com/view/2125021.htm.
Anonymous.[1] *Zhuru mingdao* 諸儒鳴道 (Various Confucians propagating the Way).
Berkowitz, Alan. "On Shao Yong's Dates (21 January 1012–27 July 1077)." *Chinese Literature: Essays, Articles, Reviews (CLEAR)* 5, no. 1/2 (July 1983): 91–94.
Berling, Judith A. "Paths of Convergence: Interactions of Inner Alchemy, Taoism and Neo-confucianism." *Journal of Chinese Philosophy* 6 (1979): 128–48.
Birdwhistell, Anne D. *Transition to Neo-Confucianism: Shao Yong on Knowledge and Symbols of Reality.* Stanford: Stanford University Press, 1989.
Bol, Peter K. "Cheng Yi and the Cultural Tradition." In *The Power of Culture: Studies in Chinese Cultural History,* edited by Willard J. Peterson, Andrew H. Plaks, and Ying-shih Yü. Hong Kong: University of Hong Kong Press, 1994.
Bray, Francesca. "Introduction." In *Graphics and Text in the Production of Technical Knowledge in China: The Warp and the Weft,* edited by Francesca Bray, Vera Dorofeeva-Lichtmann, and Georges Métailié, 1–78. Leiden: Brill, 2007.
Brooks, E. Bruce, and A. Taeko Brooks. *The Original Analects: Sayings of Confucius and His Successors.* New York: Columbia University Press, 1998.
Bruce, J. Percy. *Chu Hsi and His Masters.* London: Probsthain, 1923.
Callicott, J. Baird, and Roger T. Ames, eds. *Nature in Asian Traditions of Thought: Essays in Environmental Philosophy.* Albany: State University of New York Press, 1989.
Chaffee, John. "The Historian as Critic: Li Hsin-ch'uan and the Dilemmas of Statecraft in Southern Sung China." In *Ordering the World: Approaches to State and Society in Sung Dynasty China,* edited by Robert P. Hymes and Conrad Schirokauer. Berkeley: University of California Press, 1993.
———. "Sung Biographies: Supplementary Biography No. 2" (Li Hsin-ch'uan). *Journal of Sung-Yuan Studies* 24 (1994): 205–15.
Chan Sin Yee. "The Confucian Conception of Gender in the Twenty-First Century." In *Confucianism for the Modern World,* edited by Daniel A. Bell and Haem Cabbing, 312–33. Cambridge: Cambridge University Press, 2003.
Chan Sin-wai and David E. Pollard, eds. *An Encyclopedia of Translation: Chinese-English, English-Chinese.* Hong Kong: The Chinese University Press, 1995.

---

1. According to Hoyt Cleveland Tillman (*Confucian Discourse,* 29), relying in part on Chen Lai, this was probably written by students of Zhang Jiucheng in the 1160s.

Chan, Wing-tsit. "Chu Hsi and Yüan Neo-Confucianism." In *Yüan Thought: Chinese Thought and Religion Under the Mongols,* edited by Hok-lam Chan and Wm Theodore de Bary, 197–231. New York: Columbia University Press, 1982.
———. *Chu Hsi: Life and Thought.* Hong Kong: Chinese University Press, 1987.
———. *Chu Hsi: New Studies.* Honolulu: University of Hawaii Press, 1989.
———. "Chu Hsi's Completion of Neo-Confucianism" (1973). Rpt. in his *Chu Hsi: Life and Thought,* 103–38. Hong Kong: Chinese University Press, 1987.
———. 陳榮捷. *Zhuzi menren* 朱子門人 (Zhu Xi's disciples). Taibei: Xuesheng shuju, 1982.
———, ed. *Chu Hsi and Neo-Confucianism.* Honolulu: University of Hawaii Press, 1986.
———, trans. *A Source Book in Chinese Philosophy.* Princeton: Princeton University Press, 1963.
Chang Chung-yüan. *Creativity and Daoism: A Study of Chinese Philosophy, Art, and Poetry.* 1963; Rpt. New York: Harper and Row, 1970.
Chang, Carsun. *The Development of Neo-Confucian Thought,* vol. 1. New York: Bookman, 1957.
Chang, Garma C. C. *The Buddhist Teaching of Totality: The Philosophy of Hwa Yen Buddhism.* University Park: Pennsylvania State University Press, 1971.
Chen Chun 陳淳 (1159–1223). *Neo-Confucian Terms Explained (The Pei-hsi tzu-i).* Translated by Wing-tsit Chan. New York: Columbia University Press, 1986.
Chen Chun 陳春. *Liezi Zhang zhu* 列子張注 (Zhang Zhan's commentary on the *Liezi*). 1813; *Huhai lou congshu* 湖海樓叢書 ed.
Chen Lai 陈来. *Zhuzi shuxin biannian kaozheng* 朱子书信编年考证 (Critical examination of the dating of Zhu Xi's letters). Shanghai: Renmin chuban she, 1989.
———. *Zhu Xi zhexue yanjiu* 朱熹哲学研究 (Research on Zhu Xi's Thought). Taibei: Wenlin, 1990.
———, ed. *Zaoqi daoxue huayu de xingcheng yu yanbian* 早期道学话语的形成与演变 (The Formation and Evolution of the Early Period of *Daoxue* Discourse). Hefei: Anhui jiaoyu chubanshe, 2007.
Chen Yong. *Confucianism as Religion: Controversies and Consequences.* Leiden: Brill, 2013.
Chen Yufu 陳郁夫. *Zhou Dunyi* 周敦頤. Taibei: Dongda, 1990.
Ch'en, Kenneth K. S. *Buddhism in China: A Historical Survey.* Princeton: Princeton University Press, 1964.
Cheng, Chung-ying. "Categories of Creativity in Whitehead and Neo-Confucianism." *Journal of Chinese Philosophy* 6 (Sept. 1979): 251–74. Rpt. in Cheng, *New Dimensions of Confucian and Neo-Confucian Philosophy,* 537–57. Albany: State University of New York Press, 1991.
Cheng Hao 程顥 and Cheng Yi 程頤. *Er Cheng ji* 二程集 (Collection of the two Chengs). 4 vols. Beijing: Zhonghua shuju, 1981.
Ching, Julia. "The Goose Lake Monastery Debate (1175)." *Journal of Chinese Philosophy* 1 (1974): 161–78.
———. *The Religious Thought of Chu Hsi.* Oxford: Oxford University Press, 2000.

Chow, Kai-wing, On-cho Ng, and John B. Henderson, eds. *Imagining Boundaries: Changing Confucian Doctrines, Texts, and Hermeneutics.* Albany: State University of New York Press, 1999.

Chow Yih-ching. *La Philosophie Morale dans le Néo-Confucianisme (Tcheou Touen-yi).* Paris: Presses Universitaires de France, 1954.

Chu Ping-tzu 祝平次. "Ping Yu Yingshi xiansheng de Zhu Xi de lishi shijie: Songdai shidafu zhengzhi wenhua de yanjiu" 評余英時先生的《朱熹的歷史世界：宋代士大夫政治文化的研究》(On Yu Yingshi's *Zhu Xi's Historical World: A Study of the Political Culture of the Song Dynasty Scholar-Officials*). *Chengda zhongwen xuebao* 成大中文學報 19 (2007): 249–97.

Craig, Edward, ed. *Routledge Encyclopedia of Philosophy.* London: Routledge, 1998.

Davis, Edward L. *Society and the Supernatural in Song China.* Honolulu: University of Hawaii Press, 2001.

Dawson, Raymond, trans. *The Analects.* Oxford: Oxford University Press, 1993.

de Bary, Wm. Theodore. *Neo-Confucian Orthodoxy and the Learning of the Mind-and-Heart.* New York: Columbia University Press, 1981.

———. *The Trouble with Confucianism.* Cambridge: Harvard University Press, 1991.

———, and Irene Bloom, eds. *Sources of Chinese Tradition*, 2nd ed., vol. 1. New York: Columbia University Press, 1999.

Du Zheng 度正. *Zhouzi nianpu* 周子年普. In Yu Hao 于浩, comp. *Song Ming lixuejia nianpu* 宋明理學家年普, 2 vols. Beijing: Beijing Tushuguan, 2005.

Ebrey, Patricia Buckley. *Chu Hsi's Family Rituals: A Twelfth-Century Chinese Manual for the Performance of Cappings, Weddings, Funerals, and Ancestral Rites.* Princeton: Princeton University Press, 1991.

———. *Confucianism and Family Rituals in Imperial China: A Social History of Writing about Rites.* Princeton: Princeton University Press, 1991.

Erikson, Erik H. *Young Man Luther: A Study in Psychoanalysis and History.* New York: Norton, 1958.

Feng Youlan 馮友蘭. *Zhongguo zhexue shi* 中國哲學史 (History of Chinese Philosophy), 2 vols. Shanghai: Shangwu, 1934.

Fingarette, Herbert. *Confucius: The Secular as Sacred.* San Francisco: Harper and Row, 1972.

Forke, Alfred. *Geschichte der Neueren Chinesischen Philosophie.* Hamburg: Cram, de Gruyter, 1938.

Foulk, T. Griffith. "Myth, Ritual, and Monastic Practice in Sung Ch'an Buddhism." In *Religion and Society in T'ang and Sung China,* edited by Patricia Buckley Ebrey and Peter N. Gregory, 147–208. Honolulu: University of Hawaii Press, 1993.

Franke, Herbert, ed. *Sung Biographies.* 2 vols. Wiesbaden: Franz Steiner, 1976.

Fung Yu-lan [Feng Youlan]. *History of Chinese Philosophy,* 2 vols. Translated by Derk Bodde. Princeton: Princeton University Press, 1952–53.

Gabelentz, Georg von der. *Thai-kih-thu, des Tscheu-Tsï: Tafel des urprinzipes, mit Tschu-Hi's commentare nach dem Hoh-pih-sing-li.* Dresden: Im commissions-verlag bei R. v. Zahn, 1876.

Gardner, Daniel K. *Chu Hsi and the Ta-hsueh: Neo-Confucian Reflection on the Confucian Canon*. Cambridge: Harvard University Council on East Asian Studies, 1986.

———, trans. *The Four Books: The Basic Teachings of the Later Confucian Tradition*. Indianapolis: Hackett, 2007.

———, trans. *Learning to Be a Sage: Selections from the Conversations of Master Chu, Arranged Topically*. Berkeley: University of California Press, 1990.

Gimello, Robert M. *Chih-yen (602–668) and the Foundations of Hua-yen Buddhism*. PhD dissertation, Columbia University, 1976.

———. "Learning, Letters, and Liberation in Sung Ch'an." In *Paths to Liberation: The Marga and its Transformations in Buddhist Thought*, edited by Robert E. Buswell and Robert M. Gimello. Honolulu: University of Hawaii Press, 1992.

———. "Wu-t'ai Shan 五臺山 During the Early Chin Dynasty 金朝：The Testimony of Chu Pien 朱弁." *Chung-Hwa Buddhist Journal*, No. 07 (1994): 501–612.

Graham, A. C. *Disputers of the Tao: Philosophical Argument in Ancient China*. LaSalle: Open Court, 1989.

———. *Later Mohist Logic, Ethics and Science*. Hong Kong: Chinese University Press, 1978.

———. *Two Chinese Philosophers: Ch'eng Ming-tao and Ch'eng Yi-ch'uan*. London: Lund Humphries, 1958.

———. *Yin-Yang and the Nature of Correlative Thinking*. Singapore: Institute of East Asian Philosophies, 1986.

Gregory, Peter N. "Sudden Enlightenment Followed by Gradual Cultivation: Tsung-mi's Analysis of Mind." In *Sudden and Gradual: Approaches to Enlightenment in Chinese Thought*, edited by Peter N. Gregory, 279–320. Honolulu: University of Hawaii Press, 1987.

———. *Tsung-mi and the Sinification of Buddhism*. Princeton: Princeton University Press, 1991.

———, and Daniel A. Getz Jr., eds. *Buddhism in the Sung*. Honolulu: University of Hawai'i Press, 1999.

Hall, David L., and Roger T. Ames. *Thinking Through Confucius*. Albany: State University of New York Press, 1987.

Han Yu 韩愈. *Han Yu wen* (Writings of Han Yu). Taibei: Shangwu, 1969.

Hartman, Charles. "Bibliographic Notes on Sung Historial Works: The Original *Record of the Way and its Destiny (Taoming lu)* by Li Hsin-ch'uan." *Journal of Sung-Yuan Studies* 30 (2000): 1–61.

———. *Han Yü and the T'ang Search for Unity*. Princeton: Princeton University Press, 1986.

Henderson, John B. "Chinese Cosmographical Thought: The High Intellectual Tradition." In *The History of Cartography*, Vol. 2, Book 2: *Cartography in the Traditional East and Southeast Asian Societies*, edited by J. B. Harley and David Woodward, 203–27. Chicago: University of Chicago Press, 1994.

———. *The Development and Decline of Chinese Cosmology*. New York: Columbia University Press, 1984.

———. *Scripture, Canon, and Commentary*. Princeton: Princeton University Press, 1991.

Hershock, Peter D. *Chan Buddhism*. Honolulu: University of Hawaii Press, 2005.

Hervouet, Yves, ed. *A Sung Bibliography (Bibliographie des Sung)*. Hong Kong: Chinese University Press, 1978.

Hu Guang 胡廣, comp. *Xingli daquan shu* 性理大全書 (Great Compendium on Human Nature and Principle; 1415). Siku quanshu ed. Taibei: Commercial Press, 1986.

Hu Hong 胡宏. 胡宏集 (Hu Hong Collection). Beijing: Zhonghua shuju, 1987.

Hu Wei 胡渭, *Yitu mingbian* 易圖明辨 (Clarification of the diagrams of the *Yi*). Beijing: Zhonghua shuju, 2008.

Huang Zongxi 黃宗羲 and Quan Zuwang 全祖望, comps. *Song-Yuan xue'an* 宋元學案 (Scholarly record of the Song and Yuan dynasties), 2 vols. Taibei: Guangwen shuju, 1971.

Huang Zongyan 黃宗炎, *Tuxue bianhuo* 圖學辯惑. In Huang Zongxi 黃宗羲, *Yixue xiangshu lun* 易學象數論 (Essays on the Image-Number Study of the *Yi*), 454–73. Beijing: Zhonghua shuju, 2010.

———. *Zhouyi xunmen yulun* 周易尋門餘論 (Supplementary essays on schools of inquiry on the *Yijing*). In Huang Zongxi 黃宗羲, *Yixue xiangshu lun* 易學象數論 (Essays on the Image-Number Study of the *Yi*), 335–427. Beijing: Zhonghua shuju, 2010.

Huang, Siu-chi. "Chu Hsi's Ethical Rationalism." *Journal of Chinese Philosophy* 5 (1978): 175–93.

———. "The Concept of *T'ai-chi* (Supreme Ultimate) in Sung Neo-Confucian Philosophy." *Journal of Chinese Philosophy* 1 (1974): 275–94.

Hymes, Robert P. *Statesmen and Gentlemen: The Elite of Fu-chou, Chiang-hsi, in Northern and Southern Sung*. Cambridge: Cambridge University Press, 1986.

———. *Way and Byway: Taoism, Local Religion, and Models of Divinity in Sung and Modern China*. Berkeley: University of California Press, 2002.

Jameson, Melanie Alison Cohn. *South-Returning Wings: Yang Shih and the New Sung Metaphysics*. PhD dissertation, University of Arizona, 1990.

Jones, David, and He Jinli, eds. *Rethinking Zhu Xi: Emerging Patterns within the Supreme Polarity*. Albany: State University of New York Press, forthcoming.

Jorgensen, John. *Inventing Hui-neng, the Sixth Patriarch: Hagiography and Biography in Early Ch'an*. Leiden: Brill, 2005.

Josephson, Jason Ananda. *The Invention of Religion in Japan*. Chicago: University of Chicago Press, 2012.

Kasoff, Ira. *The Thought of Chang Tsai*. Cambridge: Cambridge University Press, 1984.

Keown, Damien. *The Nature of Buddhist Ethics*. New York: St. Martin's, 1992.

Kim Bounghown. *A Study of Chou Tun-i's (1017–1073) Thought*. PhD dissertation, Univ. of Arizona, 1996.

Kim, Yung Sik. *The Natural Philosophy of Chu Hsi: 1130–1200*. Philadelphia: American Philosophical Society, 2000.

Kohn, Livia, ed. *Chen Tuan: Discussions and Translations*. Cambridge: Three Pines Press, 2001.

———. *Daoism and Chinese Culture*, 2nd ed. Cambridge: Three Pines Press, 2004.

———. *Daoism Handbook*. Leiden: Brill, 2000.

Lackner, Michael. "Diagrams as an Architecture by Means of Words: The *Yanji tu*." In *Graphics and Text in the Production of Technical Knowledge in China: The Warp and the Weft,* edited by Francesca Bray, Vera Dorofeeva-Lichtmann, and Georges Métailié, 341–77. Leiden: Brill, 2007.

Lau, D. C. *Tao Te Ching: A Bilingual Edition*. Hong Kong: Chinese University Press, 1982.

———, trans. *Mencius,* rev. ed. Harmondsworth: Penguin, 2003.

Lee, Thomas H. C. *Government Education and Examinations in Sung China*. Hong Kong: The Chinese University Press, 1985.

Legge, James, trans. *The Chinese Classics,* 2nd ed., 4 vols. 1893; rpt. Hong Kong: Hong Kong University Press, 1960.

———. *The I Ching: The Book of Changes,* 2nd ed. 1899; rpt. New York: Dover, 1963.

Levey, Matthew. *Chu Hsi as a "Neo-Confucian": Chu Hsi's Critique of Heterodoxy, Heresy, and the "Confucian" Tradition*. PhD dissertation, University of Chicago, 1991.

———. "Chu Hsi Reading the Classics: Reading to Taste the Tao—'This is . . . A Pipe,' After All." In *Classics and Interpretations: The Hermeneutic Traditions in Chinese Culture,* edited by Ching-i Tu, 245–71. New Brunswick: Transaction Publishers, 2000.

Levine, Ari Daniel. *Divided by a Common Language: Factional Conflict in Late Northern Song China*. Honolulu: University of Hawai'i Press, 2008.

Li Guangdi 李光地, ed. *Xingli jingyi* 性理精義 (Essential Meanings of Nature and Principle [1717]). Sibu beiyao 四部備要 ed.

———, ed. *Zhouyi zhezhong* 周易折中 (The *Yijing* Judged Evenly), 2 vols. 1716; rpt. Taibei: Zhen Shan Mei, 1971.

———, ed. *Zhuzi quanshu* 朱子全書 (Zhu Xi's "Complete Works"), 2 vols. 1714; rpt. Taibei: Guangxue, 1977.

Li Xinchuan 李心傳 (1166–1243). *Daoming lu* 道命路 (Record of the fate of the Way). Baibu congshu jicheng ed.

———. *Jianyan yilai chaoye zaji jiaji* 建炎以來朝野雜記 (Miscellaneous records of court and country since the Jianyan period [1127], first collection [1202]). 2 vols. Beijing: Zhonghua shuju, 2000.

Li Yuangang 李元綱. *Shengmen shiye tu* 聖門事業圖 (Diagrams of the Accomplishments of the Sages [1170]). In *Baichuan xuehai* 百川學海, compiled by Zuo Gui 左圭. Shanghai: Bogu zhai, 1921.

Liang Shaohui 梁紹輝. *Zhou Dunyi pingzhuan* 周敦頤評傳 (Critical Biography of Zhou Dunyi). Nanjing: Nanjing daxue chubanshe, 1994.

Liu Shu-hsien. "The Confucian Approach to the Problem of Transcendence and Immanence." *Philosophy East & West* 22, no. 1 (1972): 45–52.

———. "A Philosophical Analysis of the Confucian Approach to Ethics." *Philosophy East & West* 22, no. 4 (1972): 417–25.

Liu, James T. C. *China Turning Inward: Intellectual-Political Changes in the Early Twelfth Century*. Cambridge: Harvard University Council on East Asian Studies, 1988.

———. *Reform in Sung China: Wang An-shih (1021–1086) and His New Policies.* Cambridge: Harvard University Press, 1959.

Liu, Kwang-Ching, ed. *Orthodoxy in Late Imperial China.* Berkeley: University of California Press, 1990.

Louis, François. "The Genesis of an Icon: The *Taiji* Diagram's Early History." *Harvard Journal of Asiatic Studies* 63, no. 1 (2003): 145–96.

Lynn, Richard John, trans. *The Classic of Changes: A New Translation of the* I Ching *as Interpreted by Wang Bi.* New York: Columbia University Press, 1994.

Makeham, John, ed. *Dao Companion to Neo-Confucian Philosophy.* Dordrecht: Springer, 2010.

McClatchie, Rev. Canon [Thomas]. *A Translation of the Confucian* Yijing *or the "Classic of Change."* 1876; rpt. Taibei: Cheng Wen, 1973.

McRae, John R. *Seeing Through Zen: Encounter, Transformation, and Genealogy in Chinese Chan Buddhism.* Berkeley: University of California Press, 2003.

Metzger, Thomas A. *Escape from Predicament: Neo-Confucianism and China's Evolving Political Culture.* New York: Columbia University Press, 1977.

Moore, Cornellia N., and Lucy Lower, *Translation East and West: A Cross-Cultural Approach.* Honolulu: University of Hawaii College of Languages, Linguistics and Literature and the East-West Center, 1992.

Mou Zongsan 牟宗三. *Xinti yu Xingti* 心體與性體 (The substance of mind and the substance of human nature). Vol. 1. Taibei: Zheng zhong, 1968.

Needham, Joseph. *Science and Civilisation in China,* vol. 2: *History of Scientific Thought.* Cambridge: Cambridge University Press, 1956.

———, and Lu Gwei-djen. *Science and Civilisation in China,* vol. 6, part 6: *Medicine.* Cambridge: Cambridge University Press, 2000.

Neskar, Ellen G. *The Cult of Worthies: A Study of Shrines Honoring Local Confucian Worthies in the Sung Dynasty (960–1279).* PhD dissertation, Columbia University, 1992.

Neville, Robert C. "Units of Change—Units of Value." In *Nature in Asian Traditions of Thought,* edited by J. Baird Callicott and Roger T. Ames, 145–49. Albany: State University of New York Press.

Nielsen, Bent. *A Companion to* Yi Jing *Numerology and Cosmology.* London: RoutledgeCurzon, 2003.

Nylan, Michael. *The Shifting Center: The Original "Great Plan" and Later Readings.* Sankt Augustin: Institut Monumenta Serica, 1992.

Okada Takehiko 岡田武彦. *Zazen to seiza* 坐禅と靜坐. Tokyo: Ofusha, 1966.

Paper, Jordan D. *The Fu-Tzu: A Post-Han Confucian Text.* Leiden: E. J. Brill, 1987.

Peterson, Willard. "Making Connections: 'Commentary on the Attached Verbalizations' of the Book of Change." *Harvard Journal of Asiatic Studies* 42 (1982): 67–116.

Plaks, Andrew. *Ta Hsueh and Chung Yung (The Highest Order of Cultivation and On the Practice of the Mean).* London: Penguin, 2003.

Pregadio, Fabrizio. *Great Clarity: Daoism and Alchemy in Early Medieval China.* Stanford: Stanford University Press, 2006.

———, ed. *The Encyclopedia of Taoism,* 2 vols. London: Routledge, 2008.
Qian Mu 錢穆. *Zhuzi xin xue'an* 朱子新學案, 4 vols. Taibei: San Min, 1971.
Radhakrishnan, Sarvepalli, and Charles A. Moore, eds. *A Sourcebook in Indian Philosophy.* Princeton: Princeton University Press, 1957.
Reader, Ian. *Religion in Contemporary Japan.* Honolulu: University of Hawaii Press, 1991.
Regis, P. [Jean Baptiste de], trans. *Y-King: Antiquissimus Sinarum Liber Quem ex Latina Interpretatione.* Edited by Julius [von] Mohl. 2 vols. Stuttgartiae et Tubingae: Sumptibus J. G. Cottae, 1834.
Robinet, Isabelle. "The Place and Meaning of the Notion of *Taiji* in Taoist Sources Prior to the Ming Dynasty." *History of Religions* 29, no. 4 (1990): 373–411.
———. *Taoist Meditation: The Mao-shan Tradition of Great Purity.* Albany: State University of New York Press, 1993.
———. "*Taiji tu.*" In *The Encyclopedia of Taoism,* 2 vols., edited by Fabrizio Pregadio, Vol. 2, 934–36. London: Routledge, 2008.
Roth, Harold D. *Original Tao: Inward Training (Nei-yeh) and the Foundations of Taoist Mysticism.* New York: Columbia University Press, 1999.
Ruan Yuan 阮元, ed., *Shisan jing zhushu* 十三經注疏 (Commentaries on the Thirteen Classics), 2 vols. Yangzhou: Jiangsu Guangling, 1995.
Rutt, Richard, trans. *The Book of Changes (Zhouyi): A Bronze Age Document.* Richmond: Curzon Press, 1996.
Schafer, Edward H. *Pacing the Void: T'ang Approaches to the Stars.* Berkeley: University of California Press, 1977.
Schipper, Kristofer and Franciscus Verellen. *The Taoist Canon: A Historical Companion to the Daozang.* Chicago: University of Chicago Press, 2004.
Schirokauer, Conrad. "Chu Hsi and Hu Hung." In *Chu Hsi and Neo-Confucianism,* edited by Wing-tsit Chan, 480–502. Honolulu: University of Hawaii Press, 1986.
———. "Chu Hsi's Sense of History." In *Ordering the World: Approaches to State and Society in Sung Dynasty China,* edited by Robert P. Hymes and Conrad Schirokauer, 193–220. Berkeley: University of California Press, 1993.
———. "Neo-Confucians Under Attack: The Condemnation of *Wei-hsüeh.*" In *Crisis and Prosperity in Sung China,* edited by John Haeger, 163–198. Tucson: University of Arizona Press, 1975.
Schlütter, Morten. *How Zen Became Zen: The Dispute over Enlightenment and the Formation of Chan Buddhism in Song-dynasty China.* Honolulu: University of Hawai'i Press, 2008.
Shao Yong 邵雍. *Huangji jingshi shu* 皇極經世 (Governing the World by the Royal Ultimate). Sibu beiyao 四部備要 ed.
Shaughnessy, Edward L., trans. *I Ching: The Classic of Changes.* New York: Ballantine, 1996.
Shu Jingnan 束景南. *Zhu Xi nianpu changbian* 朱熹年普長編 (Zhu Xi's Chronological Record, Extended Edition), 2 vols. Shanghai: Donghua shifan daxue chuban she, 2001. Cited as *Nianpu.*

———. *Zhuzi dazhuan* 朱子大传 (Biography of Master Zhu), 2 vols. Beijing: Shangwu, 2003.
Sima Qian司馬遷. *Shiji* 史記 (Historical records). Rpt. Beijing: Zhonghua shuju, 1996.
Slingerland, Edward. *Confucius: Analects, with Selections from Traditional Commentaries.* Indianapolis: Hackett, 2003.
Smart, Ninian. *Dimensions of the Sacred: An Anatomy of the World's Beliefs.* Berkeley: University of California Press, 1996.
Smith, Jonathan Z. *Imagining Religion: From Babylon to Jonestown.* Chicago: University of Chicago Press, 1982.
Smith, Kidder Jr., Peter K. Bol, Joseph A. Adler, and Don J. Wyatt. *Sung Dynasty Uses of the I Ching.* Princeton: Princeton University Press, 1990.
Smith, Richard J. *Fathoming the Cosmos and Ordering the World: The* Yijing *(I-Ching, or Classic of Changes) and its Evolution in China.* Charlottesville: University of Virginia Press, 2008.
Smith, Wilfrid Cantwell. *The Meaning and End of Religion.* 1963; rpt. Minneapolis: Fortress Press, 1991.
Song Daofa 宋道发. "Zhou Dunyi de fojiao yinyuan" 周敦頤的佛教因緣 (Zhou Dunyi's Buddhist influences), 2008. http://www.foyuan.net/article-196969-1.html; accessed Aug. 4, 2010.
Spence, Jonathan. "Chang Po-hsing and the K'ang-hsi Emperor." *Ching-shi wen-t'i*, 1, no. 8 (1968): 3–9. Reprinted in Jonathan Spence, *Chinese Roundabout: Essays in History and Culture.* New York: W. W. Norton, 1992.
Standaert, Nicolas. *The Interweaving of Rituals: Funerals in the Cultural Exchange Between China and Europe.* Seattle: University of Washington Press, 2008.
Streng, Frederick. *Understanding Religious Life*, 3rd ed. Belmont: Wadsworth, 1985.
Sun, Anna. *Confucianism as a World Religion: Contested Histories and Contemporary Realities.* Princeton: Princeton University Press, 2012.
Swanson, Gerald. "The Concept of Change in the Great Treatise." In *Explorations in Early Chinese Cosmology,* edited by Henry Rosemont Jr., 67–93. Chico: Scholars Press, 1984.
Tang Junyi 唐君毅. *Zhongguo zhexue yuanlun: Daolun pian* 中國哲學原論:導論篇 (The Foundations of Chinese Philosophy: Introduction). Taibei: Xuesheng shuju, 1986.
———. *Zhongguo zhexue yuanlun: Yuanxing pian* 中國哲學原論:原性篇(The Foundations of Chinese Philosophy: Inquiry into Human Nature). Taibei: Xuesheng shuju, 1989.
Taylor, Rodney L. "Chu Hsi and Meditation." In *Meeting of Minds: Intellectual and Religious Interaction in East Asian Traditions of Thought,* edited by Irene Bloom and Joshua A. Fogel, 43–74. New York: Columbia University Press, 1997.
———. *The Confucian Way of Contemplation: Okada Takehiko and the Tradition of Quiet-sitting.* Columbia: University of South Carolina Press, 1988.

——. *The Cultivation of Sagehood as a Religious Goal in Neo-Confucianism: A Study of Selected Writings of Kao P'an-lung (1562–1626)*. Missoula: Scholars Press, 1978.

——. *The Religious Dimensions of Confucianism*. Albany: State University of New York Press, 1990.

Teng Aimin. "On Chu Hsi's Theory of the Great Ultimate." In *Chu Hsi and Neo-Confucianism*, edited by Wing-tsit Chan, 93–115. Honolulu: University of Hawaii Press, 1986.

Thompson, Kirill Ole. "Hierarchy of Immanence: Chu Hsi's Pattern of Thought." *Wen shi zhe xuebao* 文史哲學報 (Bulletin of the College of Liberal Arts, National Taiwan University) 44 (1996): 151–80.

——. *An Inquiry into the Formation of Chu Hsi's Moral Philosophy*. PhD dissertation, University of Hawaii, 1985.

Tillman, Hoyt Cleveland. *Confucian Discourse and Chu Hsi's Ascendancy*. Honolulu: University of Hawaii Press, 1992.

——. "Proto-Nationalism in Twelfth-Century China? The Case of Ch'en Liang." *Harvard Journal of Asiatic Studies* 39 (1979): 417–21.

——. *Utilitarian Confucianism: Ch'en Liang's Challenge to Chu Hsi*. Cambridge: Harvard University Council on East Asian Studies, 1982.

——. "Zhu Xi's Prayers to the Spirit of Confucius and Claim to the Transmission of the Way." *Philosophy East & West* 54, no.4 (October 2004): 489–513.

——, and Christian Soffel. "Zhang Shi's Philosophical Perspectives on Human Nature, Heart/Mind, Humanness, and the Supreme Ultimate." In *Dao Companion to Neo-Confucian Philosophy*, edited by John Makeham, 125–51. Dordrecht: Springer, 2010.

Tomoeda Ryūtarō. *Shushi no shisō keisei* 朱子の思想形成 (The Formation of Zhu Xi's Thought). Tōkyō: Shunjūsha, 1969.

Tu Weiming. *Neo-Confucian Thought in Action: Wang Yang-ming's Youth (1472–1509)*. Berkeley: University of California Press, 1976.

——, ed. *Confucian Traditions in East Asian Modernity: Moral Education and Economic Culture in Japan and the Four Mini-Dragons*. Cambridge: Harvard University Press, 1996.

Tu, Ching-i, ed. *Classics and Interpretations: The Hermeneutic Traditions in Chinese Culture*. New Brunswick: Transaction Publishers, 2000.

Tuo Tuo 脫脫, ed. *Song shi* 宋史 (History of the Song). Beijing: Zhonghua shuju, 1959.

Van Ess, Hans. "The Compilation of the Works of the Ch'eng Brothers and its Significance for the Learning of the Right Way of the Southern Sung Period." *T'oung Pao*, 90 (2004): 264–98.

Waddell, Norman, trans. "*Wild Ivy:* The Spiritual Autobiography of Hakuin Ekaku," Part I. *The Eastern Buddhist* 15, no. 2 (1982): 71–109.

Wang Bi 王弼 and Han Kangbo 韓康伯. *Zhouyi Wang-Han zhu* 周易王韓注 (Commentary on the *Yijing* by Wang and Han). Sibu beiyao 四部備要 ed.

Wang Bo 王柏 (1197–1274). *Yanji tu* 研幾圖 (Diagrams on the Fathoming of Incipience). Congshu jicheng chubian ed. Taibei: Shangwu, 1939.

Wang Deyi and Julia Ching. "Li Hsin-ch'uan." In *Sung Biographies,* 2 vols., edited by Herbert Franke, Vol. 1:562–64. Wiesbaden: Franz Steiner, 1976.

Wang, Robin R. *Yinyang: The Way of Heaven and Earth in Chinese Thought and Culture.* New York: Cambridge University Press, 2012.

Wang Xianqian 王先謙. *Zhuangzi jijie* 莊子集解 (Collected Explanations of the *Zhuangzi*). Taibei: Taiwan Commercial Press, 1980.

Watson, Burton, trans. *The Complete Works of Chuang Tzu.* New York: Columbia University Press, 1968.

———, trans. *Hsün Tzu: Basic Writings.* New York: Columbia University Press, 1963.

Wickes, Dean R. "Chang Po-hsing" [Zhang Boxing]. In *Eminent Chinese of the Ch'ing Period,* edited by Arthur W. Hummel, 51–52. 1943: rpt. Taibei: Ch'eng Wen, 1975.

———, trans. *I Ging: Das Buch der Wandlungen* (1924). Rpt. Düsseldorf: Eugen Diederichs, 1970.

Wilhelm, Richard, trans. *The I Ching or Book of Changes,* 3rd ed. Translated by Cary F. Baynes. Princeton: Princeton University Press, 1967.

Williams, C. A. S. *Chinese Symbolism and Art Motifs: A Comprehensive Handbook on Symbolism in Chinese Art Through the Ages,* 4th ed. North Clarendon, VT: Tuttle, 2006.

Wilson, Thomas A. *Genealogy of the Way: The Construction and Uses of the Confucian Tradition in Late Imperial China.* Stanford: Stanford University Press, 1995.

Wu Jing-Nuan, trans. *Yi Jing.* Washington, DC: The Taoist Center, 1991.

Wu Kang 吳康. *Shaozi Yixue* 邵子易學 (Master Shao's Study of the *Yi*). Taibei: Shangwu, 1969.

Wu Renhua 吳仁華, ed. *Hu Hong ji* 胡宏集 (Hu Hong collection). Beijing: Zhonghua shuju, 1987.

Wu, John C. H. *The Golden Age of Zen,* 2nd ed. Introduction by Thomas Merton. New York: Doubleday, 1996.

Yampolsky, Philip B., trans. *The Platform Sutra of the Sixth Patriarch.* New York: Columbia University Press, 1967.

Yang, C. K. *Religion in Chinese Society: A Study of Contemporary Social Functions of Religion and Some of their Historical Factors.* Berkeley: University of California Press, 1961.

Yang Shi 楊時. *Yang Guishan xiansheng quanji* 楊龜山先生全集 (Complete writings of Yang Shi). Taibei: Xuesheng shuju, 1974.

Yao, Xinzhong, ed. *RoutledgeCurzon Encyclopedia of Confucianism.* 2 vols. London: RutledgeCurzon, 2003.

Yijing 易經 (Scripture of Change). In Zhu *Zhouyi.*

Yoshikawa Kojiro 吉川幸次郎 and Miura Kunio 三浦国雄. *Shushi shu* 朱子集. Tokyo: Asahi Shinbunsha, 1972.

Yu, Anthony C. *State and Religion in China: Historical and Textual Perspectives.* Chicago: Open Court, 2005.

Yu Yamanoi. "The Great Ultimate and Heaven in Chu Hsi's Philosophy." In *Chu Hsi and Neo-Confucianism,* edited by Wing-tsit Chan, 79–92. Honolulu: University of Hawaii Press, 1986.

Yu Yingshi 余英時.*Zhu Xi de lishi shijie: Songdai shidafu zhengzhi wenhua de yanjiu* 朱熹的歷史世界：宋代士大夫政治文化的研究 (Zhu Xi's Historical World: A Study of the Political Culture of the Song Dynasty Scholar-Officials). Taibei: Yunchen, 2003.

Zhang Dainian. *Key Concepts in Chinese Philosophy.* Translated by Edmund Ryden. New Haven: Yale University Press, 2002.

Zhang Delin 張德麟. *Zhou Lianxi yanjiu* 周濂溪研究 (Research on Zhou Dunyi). Taibei: Jia Xin Foundation, 1979.

Zhang Shi 張栻. *Zhang Shi quanji* 張栻全集 (Complete collection of Zhang Shi), 2 vols. Edited by Yang Shiwen 楊世文and Wang Ronggui 王蓉貴. Changchun: Changchun chubanshe, 1999.

Zhang Zai 張載. *Zhangzi quanshu* 張子全書 (Complete works of Master Zhang). Sibu beiyao ed.

Zheng Jixiong 鄭吉雄. "*Cong jingdian quanshi de jiaodu lun rudao Yi tu de leixing yu bianyi*" 從經典詮釋的角度論儒道《易》圖的類型與變異 (On the Genre and Changes of the Confucian and Taoist I-Ching Figures and Images—a Perspective of Classical Interpretation). *Renwen xuebao* 人文學報, no. 24 (2001): 93–184. (Taiwan: National Central University).

Zhengtong Daozang 正統道藏 (Daoist Canon of the Zhengtong period). Taibei: Yiwen yinshuguan, 1962.

Zhou Dunyi 周敦頤. *Taijitu xiangjie* 太極圖詳解 (Detailed explanation of the Supreme Polarity Diagram). Compiled by Zhang Boxing 張伯行. Beijing: Xuefan chuban she, 1990.

———. *Zhou Dunyi ji* 周敦頤集 (Collection of Zhou Dunyi). Edited by Chen Keming 陳克明. Beijing: Zhonghua Shuju, 1990.

———. *Zhou Lianxi xiansheng quanji* 周濂溪先生全集 (Complete collection of Zhou Dunyi's works). Compiled by Zhang Boxing [same text as above]. In *Zhengyi tang quanshu* 正誼堂全書 (Library of Zhengyi Hall [1708]). Baibu congshu jicheng 百部叢書集成 edition (vols. 218–219). Cited as *Zhou Lianxi ji.*

———. *Zhouzi quanshu* 周子全書 (Master Zhou's Complete Works [1756]). Compiled by Dong Rong 董榕 (1711–1760). Edited by Hu Baoquan 胡寶瑔 (1694–1763). Taibei: Wuling, 1990.

Zhu Jieren 朱傑人, Yan Zuozhi 嚴佐之, Liu Yongxiang 劉永翔, eds. *Zhuzi quanshu* 朱子全書 (Zhu Xi's Complete Works), 27 vols. Shanghai: Shanghai guji chuban she; Anhui jiaoyu chuban she, 2002.

Zhu Xi 朱熹. *Bachao mingchen yanxing lu* 八朝名臣言行路 (Record of the words and deeds of famous officials from eight dynasties). In *Zhuzi quanshu,* edited by Zhu Jieren, Yan Zuozhi, Liu Yongxiang. Vol. 12.

———. *Daxue huowen* 大學或問 (Some questions on the *Daxue*). In *Zhuzi quanshu*, edited by Zhu Jieren, Yan Zuozhi, Liu Yongxiang. Vol. 6:505–47.

———. *Hui'an xiansheng Zhu wengong wenji* 晦庵先生朱文公文集 (Zhu Xi's collected papers [1532]). In *Zhuzi quanshu*, edited by Zhu Jieren, Yan Zuozhi, Liu Yongxiang. Vols. 20–25. Cited as *Wenji*.

———. *Introduction to the Study of the Classic of Change* (*I-hsüeh ch'i-meng*). Translated by Joseph A. Adler. Provo: Global Scholarly Publications, 2002.

———. *Sishu zhangju jizhu* 四書章句集注 (Collected comments on the Four Books in chapters and sentences). In *Zhuzi quanshu*, edited by Zhu Jieren, Yan Zuozhi, Liu Yongxiang. Vol. 6. Cited as *Sishu jizhu*.

———. *Yi-Luo yuan-yuan lu* 伊洛淵源錄 (Record of the sources of the Cheng school). Siku shanben ed. Cited as Zhu *Yi-Luo*.

———. *Yixue qimeng* 易學啟蒙 (Introduction to the study of the *Yi* [1186]). In *Zhouyi zhezhong* (The *Zhou Yi* judged evenly, 1715), edited by Li Guangdi 李光地. Rpt. Taibei: Zhen Shan Mei, 1971.

———. *Zhouyi benyi* 周易本易 (Original meaning of the Zhou Changes). 1188. Rpt. Taibei: Hualian, 1978.[2]

———. *Zhuzi yulei* 朱子語類 (Zhu Xi's classified conversations). Compiled by Li Jingde 黎靖德, 1270. In *Zhuzi quanshu*, edited by Zhu Jieren, Yan Zuozhi, Liu Yongxiang. Vols. 14–18. Cited as *Yulei*.

———, and Lü Zuqian 呂祖謙, comps. 1175. *Reflections on Things at Hand: The Neo-Confucian Anthology*. Translated by Wing-tsit Chan. New York: Columbia University Press, 1967.

Zhu Zhen 朱震. *Jin Zhouyi biao* 進周易表 (Memorial presenting the *Zhouyi*). In *Hanshang yizhuan* 漢上易傳 (Zhu Zhen's commentary on the *Yi*). Tongzhitang jingjie ed. 1680; rpt. Taibei: Taiwan Datong shuju, 1969. Vol. 1.

Zhuangzi 莊子. *Sibu beiyao* 四部備要 edition.

Zottoli, P. Angelo, S.J. *Cursus Litteraturae Sinicae*, vol. 3: *Studium Canonicorum*. Shanghai: Ex Typographia Missionis Catholicae, 1880.

---

2. The traditional dating of the *Zhouyi benyi* is 1177, and I have given it as such in previous publications. However, Shu Jingnan, in *Zhuzi nianpu changbian*, says that the commentary Zhu Xi wrote in 1177, which was called the *Yizhuan* 易傳 (Commentary on the *Yi*), was an earlier version based on the Wang Bi ordering of the text (with the *Tuan*, *Xiang*, and *Wenyan* commentaries collated with the hexagrams to which they applied) and is not extant. The *Zhouyi benyi* is based on Lü Zuqian's ordering (in his *Gu Zhouyi* 古周易), with those commentaries given separately. For Zhu Xi's colophon to Lü's commentary (which is no longer extant) see *Wenji* 82:3889–90.

Index

Activity (*dong*) and stillness (*jing*), 58–59, 70, 115, 122, 126–28, 130–31, 134–35, 143, 160, 164, 168, 173–81, 185–86, 188–92, 199, 204, 207, 210, 213, 226, 230, 239, 241, 243, 247, 255, 260–61, 269–71, 274, 277, 285, 299–300, 303; interpenetration of, 6, 8, 73, 75, 77–109, 111, 113, 132, 138, 142, 206, 211, 262–63
aesthetic order, 10, 43, 67, 105
Ai lian shuo (On loving the lotus), 31), 51
Ames, Roger T., 10, 43, 67, 105, 123
Analects (*Lunyu*), 13, 16, 18, 21–22, 33–34, 61, 68, 215, 248, 252, 276, 283–84
"Appended arguments," 50, 198–200
Aquinas, Thomas, 138

Benedit of Nursia (St.), 138
Bodde, Derk, 119–20, 126
Bruce, J. Percy, 119–20
Buddha-nature (*foxing*), 17, 19, 88, 195
Buddhism, 3–4, 7, 9, 13, 17–28, 31, 35–36, 42, 46–48, 54, 59, 63–66, 70, 84–90, 101, 104–109, 127, 139, 144, 148, 152, 155–57, 177, 182, 185, 188, 192, 195–97, 230, 239, 253, 269–70, 304; *see also* Chan Buddhism; Huayan Buddhism

Cai Jing, 16, 301
Cai Yuanding, 87, 89, 92, 233
Cantongqi, 155
centrality (*zhong*), 88–89, 94, 100, 164, 230, 271; and harmony (*he*), 59, 82–83, 85, 93, 95, 97, 99, 106, 165, 185, 188–89, 191, 208, 245–46, 249; and correctness (*zheng*), 165, 168, 188, 190–91, 198–201, 208, 217, 243–44, 254, 256, 294; and Supreme Polarity, 119, 124, 132, 134, 232
Chan Buddhism, 17, 20–22, 24, 26–27, 35, 42, 46, 59, 84–85, 88, 104, 108, 156, 195, 270
Chan, Wing-tsit, 53, 73, 114, 119, 121–22, 130, 140, 228, 266
Chang, Carsun, 119, 121
Changsha (Tanzhou), 89, 116
Changsha edition, 112, 220, 299–300, 303–304

323

Chao Yuezhi, 155
Chen Chun, 47, 49, 60, 134–36, 242
Chen Lai, 8, 13, 88, 91, 184, 310
Chen Liang, 5, 16, 48
Chen Tuan (Xiyi), 33, 35, 71–72, 155, 157, 302–306
Chen Zhongsu, 304
cheng (being authentic), 30, 52, 56–58, 60, 62, 66, 73, 80–82, 87, 98, 100–101, 142, 171, 174, 177, 189, 200, 203–204, 206–209, 215–16, 221–37, 239–42, 249, 257, 287, 289–91, 293, 296, 299, 303
Cheng Chung-ying, 106, 178
Cheng Hao, 4–6, 14, 17, 19, 21, 27–34; 36–38, 41, 45–46, 48–50, 53–56, 58–63, 65–66, 68–73, 81, 88–89, 92–93, 96–98, 111, 127–28, 133, 137–38, 148, 167, 189, 194–96, 219–20, 224, 232–33, 235, 245, 258, 271, 276, 299–300, 302–305; as first sage since Mencius, 27–28, 32
Cheng school, 4, 16–17, 48, 51, 72, 301
Cheng Shaogong, 300, 303
Cheng Yi, 4–6, 9, 14, 17–19, 21, 27–34, 36–38, 41, 43, 45–46, 48–50, 53–56, 58–63, 65–66, 68–73, 79, 81, 84, 88, 93–94, 99–101, 108–109, 118, 124, 126–28, 130, 133–34, 137–38, 142, 148, 163, 172, 175–76, 182, 194–201, 206, 219–21, 224, 232, 235, 245, 248, 258, 267, 271–72, 276, 278, 283, 285, 290, 299–305; Commentary on the *Yi*, 74; on *jing* (reverent composure), 70, 84, 89, 92, 96, 98, 106–107, 192, 197, 256, 257, 270
Cheng-Zhu school, 4, 6–7, 12, 14, 19, 59, 62, 79, 82, 135–39, 143, 167, 177, 300
Chong Fang, 33, 35, 71, 154–55, 302–303
Chongling, 30, 33, 41, 299, 305

Chou, Yih-ching, 120–21
Chunqiu (Spring and Autumn Annals), 23, 34, 161, 217, 292, 295
Chunqiu fanlu (Luxuriant Gems of the Spring and Autumn Annals), 17, 161
Commentary on the *Tongshu*, 206, 218–98
Confucianism, 3, 7, 11–13, 17–18, 21–22, 36, 48, 101, 135, 151–52; religious dimension, 8–10, 67, 139–42
Confucius (Kongzi), 6, 11–13, 16, 18, 20–27, 33–34, 40–41, 46, 48–49, 60–64, 74, 77, 82, 129, 143, 172–73, 195, 197, 206–207, 213, 217, 219, 225, 227, 232, 252, 258, 274, 276–77, 279, 283–86, 295–96, 305
Confucius2000.com, 141

Dahui Zonggao, 35, 88, 104, 195, 270
Daoism, 3–6, 13, 20–22, 25–28, 35–38, 42, 47–48, 63–72, 75, 84–88, 101, 107–109, 117–18, 127, 135, 138, 140, 144, 148, 152–58, 167, 188, 192, 196, 228, 269, 277, 302, 304
Daonan school, 29, 36, 88
Daoqian, 35, 104, 195
daotong (succession of the Way), 14, 37–75, 143, 157, 167, 190, 203
daoxin ("mind of dao," moral mind) and/or *renxin* (human mind), 11, 45, 64–65, 83, 102, 116, 234–35, 239, 269
daoxue (Learning of the Way), 4, 12, 19, 31–33, 38, 44, 49–50, 53, 56–57, 59, 62, 64–65, 67, 73, 305
Daozhou Prefecture, 30, 53, 58–59, 159
Daxue (Great Learning), 48, 62–67, 81–82, 92, 108, 195, 224, 253, 288
de Bary, Wm. Theodore, 24, 27, 42, 44, 61, 142
Diagram Developing the *Yi* for Governing the World (*Jingshi yanyi tu*), 86, 247

Diagram of the Legitimate Succession of the Transmission of the Way (*Daozhuan zhengtong tu*), 32
Discussion of the Supreme Polarity Diagram; see *Taijitu shuo*
divination, 11, 26, 40, 43, 60, 116, 140, 143, 218, 241, 296–97
Dong Zhongshu, 61, 161, 163

emphasizing stillness, 36, 70, 84, 98–99, 109, 165, 167–68, 188–92, 256, 265, 296, 298
"Essay commemorating the shrine to the Three Masters at the Yuanzhou prefectural school," 51, 54

"Final Notes to Commentary on the *Taijitu shuo*," 50, 196–97
Five (Six) Scriptures (Classics), 6, 19, 45, 63, 74, 195, 215, 286, 292
Five Phases (*wuxing*), 39, 57, 103, 113, 115, 126–30, 132–33, 152, 161–64, 168, 172–73, 179–87, 189, 195, 211, 213, 219, 223–24, 226, 229, 241, 254–55, 261, 264, 269, 274–75, 296
Fu (hexagram), 9, 43, 216, 288, 291
Fung Yu-lan (Feng Youlan), 119, 125–26, 140
Fuxi, 25–26, 40, 43–48, 60–61, 64, 75, 143, 155, 157, 193, 285–87, 289

Gen (hexagram), 218, 296, 298
ghosts (*gui*) and spirits (*shen*), 41, 44, 165–66, 169, 188–89, 215, 275, 285–86
gods, 11, 40, 42, 44, 78–79, 129, 141, 267, 297
gong'an (*kōan*), 21, 88, 270
gongfu (moral effort/cultivation), 92–94, 192, 232, 242
Goose Lake Monastery, 68
Graham, A.C., 31, 69–70, 127

Guashuo (Discussion of Trigrams/Hexagrams), 304
Guifeng Zongmi, 156–57
Guoyu (Conversations of the States), 265

Hall, David L., 10, 43, 67, 105
Han dynasty, 12, 25, 40, 116–17
Han Yu, 24–26, 61, 155, 197
Henan (province), 4, 27, 29–30, 54–56, 59–60, 63, 66, 219
Hetu (River Chart), 39, 152, 180, 261
hexagrams, 26, 40, 43, 45–46, 48, 57, 60, 100, 116, 143, 148, 152, 155, 157, 165–66, 169–70, 174, 179, 188, 192, 206, 215–18, 221, 223, 285–89, 291–92, 294, 296, 298, 304
honesty, faithfulness (*xin*), 207–208, 226, 229–30, 237, 242–43, 255, 273
Hongfan (Great Plan), 119, 131, 182, 209, 249, 264
Hongzhi Zhengjue, 88, 108
Hu Anguo, 29, 32, 53–54, 72
Hu Hong (Wufeng), 29–30, 32, 35–36, 53, 71–72, 83, 89–90, 112, 148, 184, 206, 209, 220, 234, 252, 275, 302–303; "Preface to Master Zhou's *Tongshu*," 32
Hu Xian, 29
Hu Yuan (Anding), 71, 267
Huang Gan, 59–60, 135, 151, 157, 172, 225, 243, 263
Huang Tingjian (Taishi), 30, 301, 305
Huangdi, 26, 45, 48, 64
huangji (royal ultimate), 87, 119, 131–32, 134–35, 186
Huayan Buddhism, 104, 109, 127, 156, 185
Hui'an xiansheng Zhu wengong wenji (Zhu Xi's Collected Papers), 149
Huineng, 20, 42
Huiweng, 307

humanity/humaneness (*ren*), 18–19, 70, 125, 152, 164–65, 168–69, 182, 185–86, 188, 190–94, 198–201, 207–10, 226–31, 233, 236–37, 242–43, 252–56, 275

Hunan (province), 29–30, 35, 41, 53, 59, 93, 95–96, 106, 111, 116, 143, 303, 305

Hunan school, 29, 36, 56, 59, 83, 88–89, 92, 109

Hu-Xiang school, 29

incipience (*ji*), 58–59, 83, 91, 94, 151, 186, 204, 206–209, 224, 228–44, 249–51

Jian'an edition, 111–12, 143, 148, 220, 299, 303, 305

Jiangzhou, 38–39, 51, 72, 74, 80, 152–53

Jiaren (hexagram), 216, 288–89

Jinsilu (Reflecting on Things at Hand), 53, 68, 134, 143, 235

jiran budong, gan er sui tong (silent and inactive, when stimulated it penetrates), 86, 91, 94, 100, 164, 230, 239, 249

Kong Sifeng (Yanzhi), 301, 305
Kong Yingda, 131
Kui (hexagram), 216, 288–89
Kun (hexagram), 97, 114, 116–17, 162, 168, 183, 189

Laozi / *Laozi* (*Daodejing*), 13, 20, 22, 36, 54, 68, 84, 107, 118, 140, 144, 152, 155, 199, 228, 249, 265, 269

li (principle, order), 4, 6, 14, 18–19, 22, 27, 39, 41, 44–45, 55, 62, 69, 71, 78, 83, 100, 116, 126, 134, 167, 181, 190–91, 183, 198, 200–201, 204, 213, 221–24, 227–28, 236–37, 240, 256, 259, 262, 269, 273–78, 286, 295, 306; flowing out/ordering, 39, 57, 79, 88, 105, 108–109, 122, 126, 130, 174, 177, 179, 222–24, 271, 277, 284–85; metaphysical, 104, 128, 133, 173, 179, 263; and *cheng* (being authentic), 80, 100–101, 171, 177, 204, 222, 225–28, 230, 233, 239, 293; and *qi*, 79, 115, 182; as moral order (*daoli*), 45, 82, 100, 125, 142–43, 159, 166, 170–71, 188, 195–96, 207, 230–32, 243, 251, 286; as natural order (*tianli*), 45, 74, 82, 100, 105, 109, 116, 122, 125, 129, 135, 142–43, 164, 166, 187, 190, 195, 228, 230, 234–36, 271, 277; as nature (*xing*), 80, 83, 87, 101; as specific principles, 171, 173, 180, 182, 262, 286; as *taiji*, 114–15, 117, 121, 123–27, 129, 133–34, 170, 172, 180; as unitary, 105–106, 126, 129, 133, 163, 171, 178, 199, 219, 238; of creativity, 88, 100–101, 114, 129, 172, 177; of mind/heart (*xin*), 125, 133, 138, 269; of *zhong* (centrality/equilibrium), 87; in Huayan Buddhism, 104; see also *taiji*

Li Tong, 29, 36, 73, 83–84, 88–90, 93, 109, 111, 114, 148, 220
Li Xinchuan, 31–32, 59
Li Yuangang, 32
Li Zhongtong, 299, 303
Lian Stream (Lianxi), 41, 159
Liji (Record of Ritual), 63, 197, 292
ling (numinous, spiritually efficacious), 163, 168, 186, 195, 233, 262, 273
Lizong, Emperor, 62
Louis, François, 158
love (*ai*), 23, 31, 51, 70, 207, 211, 228, 230, 233, 236–37, 258–60
Lü Dalin, 224
Lu Jiushao, 5, 67–68, 149, 157, 167, 173
Lu Jiuyuan (Lu Xiangshan), 5, 35, 38, 47–48, 67–68, 72, 81, 149, 157, 167, 173, 179, 269

Lü Zuqian, 5, 38, 53, 68, 112
Luo Congyan, 29, 84
Luo school, 4, 29, 38
Luoshu (Luo Writing), 39, 152
Luoyang, 4, 27, 29, 159

Mandate of Heaven (*tianming*), 25, 39–40, 42–45, 73, 143, 219, 235
Maspero, Henri, 120–21
Master Zhu's Commentary on the Discussion of the Supreme Polarity Diagram, 170–201
Master Zhu's Explanation of the Diagram, 160–66
Mencius (Mengzi), 5, 11–12, 14, 19–20, 23–28, 32–35, 39–42, 45–46, 49, 54–56, 60–63, 65–66, 68, 72–73, 78, 80–81, 89, 97–98, 112, 137–38, 143, 185–87, 190, 194, 219, 226, 230, 233, 251–53, 264, 277
Meng (hexagram), 218, 296
Ming dynasty, 5, 62, 153, 158
Mo Di (Mozi), 23, 25, 33
Mou Zongsan, 8
Mount Lu, 38, 41, 47
Mu Xiu, 33, 35, 71, 154–55, 302–303

Nankang edition, 112, 148, 220, 303, 306
nature (*xing*), 9, 11, 18–19, 30, 39, 44–45, 70–71, 73, 78, 81, 83, 87, 91, 93–95, 100, 102–103, 113, 116, 122–23, 127, 138, 161–65, 168, 174, 180–87, 189, 194, 197–98, 204, 206–208, 213, 221–26, 229–30, 233, 235–40, 244–47, 270, 273–75, 299–301, 304; and endowment (*ming*), 37, 57, 80, 99, 101, 174, 182, 190, 199, 206, 207, 221–23, 225, 245, 275, 299; see also *li* as nature
Needham, Joseph, 121
Neo-Confucianism, 3–6, 11–12, 20

Neskar, Ellen G., 47
night *qi*, 97–98
Nine Regions/Divisions (*jiu chou*), 40, 211, 264
nonduality, 86, 101, 128, 175, 179, 184, 262, 274
non-obstruction (*wu-ai*), 104–106, 109, 164, 171, 185, 271
North Pole, 122, 134

original (fundamental) nature (*ben xing*), 80–81, 93, 136, 180, 182, 185, 204, 222–24, 239

Pan Xingsi (Qingyi), 147, 300, 303–305
Penetrating the Scripture of Change; see *Tongshu*
physical nature (*qizhizhi xing*), 43, 45, 80, 87, 102, 181–82, 185, 190, 195, 245, 247
pivot/axis (*shuniu*), 118, 121, 128–29, 134–36, 170, 172
Platform Sutra, 13, 20, 22–23, 84, 95, 107
pole star, 117, 121–22, 129
"Postface to Commentaries on the Supreme Polarity and the Western Inscription," 306–307
"Postface to Master Zhou's *Taiji* and *Tongshu*," 50, 299–302
"Principle, Nature, and Endowment" (section of *Tongshu*), 206, 213, 273–75, 300, 303–304
Prior Heaven Diagram (*Xiantian tu*), 157
Pu Zuocheng (Zongmeng), 301, 305

qi (psycho-physical-spiritual stuff), 4, 6, 10, 16, 22, 39–41, 43–45, 60, 69–70, 73–74, 79–81, 87, 93, 97–98, 101–102, 113–16, 118, 120, 127, 129, 133–34, 137, 160–64, 166–68,

qi (psycho-physical-spiritual stuff) (*continued*)
172–73, 175–77, 179–87, 189–90, 193, 195, 199, 212–13, 219, 222–23, 233, 237, 245, 247, 254, 261–62, 264, 267, 273–75, 292, 300; see also *li* and *qi*; physical nature
Qi Kuan, 148, 220, 300, 304
Qian (hexagram), 56–57, 98–100, 114, 116–17, 162, 168, 170, 183, 189, 207, 215, 221–25, 240, 269, 286–87
Qian Mu, 8
Qin dynasty, 61
Qing dynasty, 72, 142, 149, 152–53
Qing, Julia, 8, 71–72
quietism, 63, 70, 84–85, 109, 188
quiet-sitting (*jingzuo*), 36, 67, 84–85, 88, 90, 97–98, 101, 142

Rao Lu (Shuangfeng), 135, 172
"Record of the Reconstruction of Zhou Dunyi's Study in Jiangzhou," 38–41, 51, 72, 74, 80
Reader, Ian, 141
Ren Jiyu, 141
revelation, 24, 44, 153
reverent composure / reverence (*jing*), 58, 70, 84, 89, 92, 96–98, 106–108, 125, 191–92, 197, 211, 256–58, 260, 270, 279
"Revised Postface to Master Zhou's *Taiji* and *Tongshu*," 303–306
rightness (*yi*), 39, 68, 165–66, 168–69, 182, 185–86, 188, 190–94, 198–201, 207–208, 210, 226, 228, 230, 233, 237, 242–43, 253–56
ritual (*li*), 16, 63, 81–82, 141–42, 187, 197, 210–12, 256–57, 264, 266
ritual propriety (*li*), 39, 164, 185–86, 190, 194, 207–208, 210, 226–27, 229–31, 237, 242–44, 255, 292
Rongdao County, 159

sagehood (*sheng*) / sage (*shengren*), 5, 8–11, 13–14, 19–20, 23–28, 30, 32–34, 38, 40, 42–68, 72–73, 75, 77–82, 84, 86–87, 90, 93, 100, 106–107, 112, 114, 129, 138, 143, 157, 164–66, 168–69, 172, 174, 177, 187–93, 196, 198, 203–13, 215–17, 219, 221, 224–32, 236–55, 264–72, 277–78, 283–88, 291–98, 302
self-cultivation, 6, 17, 20–22, 47, 60, 65, 77–98, 101–102, 106–109, 111, 138, 142, 190–91, 260, 269, 284, 288
Shao Yong, 5, 29, 32, 38, 46–47, 69, 86–87, 116, 128, 155, 157, 177, 247
sheng-sheng (birth and growth), 100, 172, 177, 183–84, 225
Shennong, 26, 45, 48, 64
Shi Jie, 25–26, 45–46
Shihe (hexagram), 217, 294–95
Shijing (Scripture of Odes), 34, 45, 73, 128, 292
Shou Ya, 31, 155
Shu Jingnan, 13, 74, 88, 91, 111, 198
Shujing (Scripture of Documents), 23, 34, 45, 64, 73, 119, 131, 182, 241, 246, 249, 252, 264, 290, 292
Shun, 23–26, 45, 48, 55, 64, 66, 197, 209, 216, 252–53, 290
Sima Guang, 16–17, 31, 38, 224, 238, 301
sitting meditation (*zuochan*), 84–85
Song (hexagram), 217, 294–95
Song dynasty, 3–44, 48–50, 55, 59–68, 72, 80–81, 84–88, 112, 116, 123, 127, 132–38, 142–44, 150–57, 167, 172, 281, 301
Spring and Autumn Annals; see *Chunqiu*
substance (*ti*) and function (*yong*), 61, 70, 94–95, 103, 109, 160, 164–66, 189, 193, 198, 200, 230, 234, 236, 239, 241, 261, 263, 269, 271, 287
Summa Daologica, 66, 138, 142

Sun (hexagram), 215, 287

taiji (Supreme Polarity), 5–8, 14, 38, 53, 57–58, 68–70, 74, 87, 89, 98, 100–103, 105–106, 108–109, 111–38, 143, 148, 156, 158, 160, 162–68, 169–200, 203, 211, 221, 224–28, 232, 247, 261, 264, 269, 271, 273–75, 296; as center, 132, 134–36, 186, 232; as creativity, 158, 170, 178; as extreme, ultimate, 123, 131, 136; as principle of bipolarity, 100, 105, 117, 122, 126, 130–31, 134, 143, 172, 175–76; as "Supreme/Great Ultimate," 6, 14, 69, 119, 121, 123, 125, 128, 132

Taiji Preceding Heaven Diagram (*Taiji xiantian tu*), 153–54

Taiji shuo (Discussion of Supreme Polarity), 98–100, 143

Taijitu (Supreme Polarity Diagram), 3, 5, 30, 33, 35–37, 47, 50, 54, 56, 58–59, 61, 68–73, 103, 112, 117–18, 143, 147–48, 151–59, 181, 194–96, 219, 222, 299–301, 303, 305–306

Taijitu shuo (Discussion of the Supreme Polarity Diagram), 3, 5, 8, 30, 35–37, 50–53, 55–57, 68–69, 71, 73, 75, 78, 84, 86, 99–100, 102–103, 106, 111–15, 119–20, 122, 124–25, 127–31, 137, 143, 147–49, 153, 157, 161–62, 165–201, 203, 204, 219, 221, 225–26, 229, 233, 241, 243–44, 254, 262, 273, 306

Taiyi, 117

Tang dynasty, 20–21, 24, 40, 61, 131

Tang Junyi, 8

Tang, King, 24–26, 48, 252

Three Bonds (*san gang*), 211, 264

Three-hall system, 301

Tillman, Hoyt Cleveland, 7, 12, 67

Tongshu (Penetrating the *Scripture of Change*), 3, 6, 8, 30, 32, 34–38, 50–52, 54, 56–59, 61, 66, 68, 70–71, 73, 80, 84, 89, 95, 100, 102–106, 108, 111–14, 127–28, 132–33, 143, 147–48, 155, 159, 171, 174, 177, 188, 192, 203–304

trigrams, 39, 46, 74–75, 87, 116–17, 134, 152, 155, 157–58, 165, 174, 178–79, 188, 247, 289, 304

tu (diagrams), 46, 151–52

Tu Weiming, 140

Tuan (appendix to the *Yijing*), 289, 296–97

Two Modes, 4, 73–74, 87, 102, 108, 113, 115–17, 126, 130, 134, 168, 174–75, 178–79, 219, 247, 269

Wan Renjie, 236, 241
Wang Anshi, 4, 16, 238, 301
Wang Bo, 151–52
Wang Mouhong, 13
Wang Tong, 25–26
Wang Yangming, 5
Wei Boyang, 155

weifa / yifa (unexpressed/expressed) problem, 7, 59, 82–83, 90–101, 111, 127, 131, 142–43, 165, 173, 188–89, 232, 246

Wen, King, 23–25, 40, 48, 286

Wenyan (appendix to the *Yijing*), 274–75, 293, 322

Western Inscription (*Ximing*), 31, 38, 196–97, 283, 306

Wilson, Thomas A., 66

Wisdom (*zhi*), 39, 54, 75, 185–86, 190, 194, 207–208, 210, 226, 229–30, 237, 242–44, 253, 255

Wu Wang (hexagram), 184, 216, 221, 288, 291

Wu, King, 23, 25, 48

wuji (Non-polarity), 5, 36, 53, 68–69, 71, 75, 84, 103, 106, 108, 113–14, 117–22, 127–29, 131, 135, 160, 162,

wuji (Non-polarity) *(continued)*
164–67, 170–73, 181, 183, 195, 261, 269
Wuji Diagram (*Wujitu*), 153–55
wuji er taiji (nonpolar and yet Supreme Polarity), 57, 68, 102, 105, 113, 122, 129, 131, 168–73, 186

Xian (hexagram), 114, 183
Xici (appendix to *Yijing*), 59, 74, 86–87, 116, 119, 122, 124, 126, 132, 138, 225, 274–75, 304
Xici shuo, 304
Xin tong xing qing (mind/heart connects nature and feelings), 95, 101–102
Xin'an, 302, 306
xing'er shang (metaphysical), 69, 79, 104, 115, 160, 175, 179, 262–63
xing'er xia (physical), 69, 79, 115, 160, 173, 175, 179, 262
Xuan, King of Qi, 89–90, 251

Yan Yuan (Yan Hui, Master Yan), 33–34, 46, 48, 60, 195, 206, 209, 213, 215, 219–20, 231, 236, 252–53, 276–78, 283–85, 300, 302–303
Yang Fang, 303, 305
Yang Shi, 19, 21, 29, 32, 35, 84, 88, 124, 132
Yang Xiong, 25–26, 193
Yang Zhu, 23, 25, 33
Yao, 23–26, 45, 48, 55, 64, 66, 197, 209, 216, 241, 252–53, 290
Yi (hexagram), 215, 287
Yi Yin, 24, 34, 209, 246, 252–53, 302
Yijing (Scripture of Change), 3, 6, 9, 11, 26, 31, 34, 40, 43, 45, 48, 56–57, 59, 69, 71, 74–75, 86, 97–98, 100, 114, 116–17, 119–20, 124–27, 129–30, 134, 138, 143, 152, 155, 157, 160, 162–66, 170, 172–75, 177–80, 183–84, 188–89, 192–93, 198, 204, 206, 221–23, 238–41, 245, 247, 250, 262, 292, 294, 297
Yi-Luo yuan-yuan lu (Sources of the Yi-Luo school), 32, 38, 51
Yingdao County, 30, 59, 305
Yishuo (Discussion of the *Yi*), 147, 206, 301, 303–304
Yitong (Penetrating the *Yi*), 114, 147, 159, 219, 301, 303–304
Yixue qimeng (Introduction to the Study of the *Yi*), 43, 47, 87, 180, 233, 247, 261
Yu, 24–26, 34, 40, 45, 48, 64, 197, 246
Yu Fan, 117
Yuan dynasty, 62, 152, 301
yuan, heng, li, zhen (four virtues of Qian), 98–99, 200, 207, 221, 223, 286

Zengzi (Zeng Shen/Can), 48–49, 60–61, 63–65, 195, 230
Zhang Boxing, 59, 149–50, 158–66, 168–70, 176–77, 206, 218, 220–21, 265, 271, 273, 295, 299, 303, 306
Zhang Jiucheng, 21, 35, 56
Zhang Shi, 5, 30, 36–38, 54, 56–59, 65, 71, 83, 88–92, 111–12, 132, 148, 196–97, 220; "Preface to Master Zhou's Explanation of the *Taiji* Diagram," 56–57
Zhang Zai, 5, 19, 29, 31–32, 38, 52–53, 62, 70, 79–81, 95, 99, 101–102, 109, 167, 196–97, 224, 238, 245, 283, 306
Zhang Zhongding (Yong), 305
Zhao Huiqian, 158
Zhao Zhidao, 234–36
Zhen Dexiu, 49, 60–62
Zheng Qiao, 151–52
Zheng Xuan, 69, 117, 126

Zhongyong (Centrality and Commonality), 18, 39, 49, 57–58, 62–67, 73, 80–83, 87, 92, 99–100, 112, 131, 162, 166, 177, 184–85, 189, 204, 224, 227, 232, 236, 241, 246–48, 293, 296
Zhou dynasty, 13, 23–25, 48
Zhou, Duke of, 23, 25–27, 41, 45, 48–49
Zhouyi benyi (Original Meaning of the *Zhou Yi*), 74–75, 126, 143, 322
Zhu Song, 15, 29
Zhu Zhen, 35–36, 71, 117, 148, 153–55, 157, 302–303
Zhuangzi, 13, 85, 117–18, 129, 140, 144, 251, 277, 304
Zhuzi quanshu (Zhu Xi's Complete Works), 149, 205, 218–19
Zhuzi yulei (Zhu Xi's Classified Conversations), 149
Zilu, 214, 279
Zisi, 49, 60–61, 64–66, 82–83, 184, 232
zongjiao (religion), 139

www.ingramcontent.com/pod-product-compliance
Ingram Content Group UK Ltd.
Pitfield, Milton Keynes, MK11 3LW, UK
UKHW041922140426
5217IPUK00014B/281